W9-CCX-706

ALSO BY DAN BOUK

How Our Days Became Numbered: Risk and the Rise of the Statistical Individual

Democracy's Data

Democracy's Data

The Hidden Stories in the U.S. Census and How to Read Them

Dan Bouk

MCD FARRAR, STRAUS AND GIROUX NEW YORK

MCD
Farrar, Straus and Giroux
120 Broadway, New York 10271

Copyright © 2022 by Dan Bouk
All rights reserved
Printed in the United States of America
First edition, 2022

Grateful acknowledgment is made for permission to reprint lines from
"Madam and the Census Man" from *The Collected Poems of Langston Hughes* by
Langston Hughes, edited by Arnold Rampersad with David Roessel, Associate Editor,
copyright © 1994 by the Estate of Langston Hughes. Used by permission of
Alfred A. Knopf, an imprint of the Knopf Doubleday Publishing Group,
a division of Penguin Random House LLC. All rights reserved.

Illustration credits can be found on pages 359–362.

Library of Congress Control Number: 2022019954
ISBN: 978-0-374-60254-3

Designed by Abby Kagan

Our books may be purchased in bulk for promotional, educational, or business use. Please
contact your local bookseller or the Macmillan Corporate and Premium Sales Department at
1-800-221-7945, extension 5442, or by email at MacmillanSpecialMarkets@macmillan.com.

www.mcdbooks.com • www.fsgbooks.com
Follow us on Twitter, Facebook, and Instagram at @mcdbooks

1 3 5 7 9 10 8 6 4 2

In memory of David T. Bailey,

who told stories well

Contents

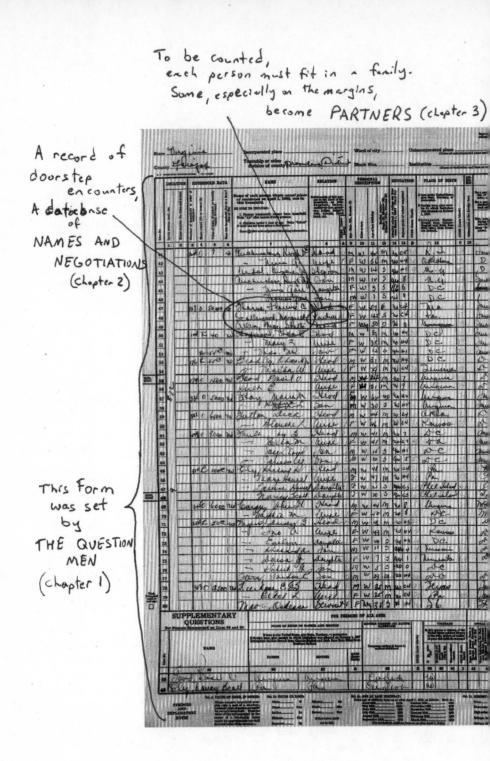

To be counted,
each person must fit in a family.
Some, especially on the margins,
become PARTNERS (chapter 3)

A record of
doorstep
encounters,
A database
of
NAMES AND
NEGOTIATIONS
(chapter 2)

This Form
was set
by
THE QUESTION
MEN
(chapter 1)

Data has many authors.
Some even sign their names.
Politics put them in place.
They were COUNTING WITH FRIENDS (chapter 4)

Data can be designed to speak, and designed not to; designed so some people count & others do not.
Behind those designs we find SILENCES AND WHITE SUPREMACY (chapter 5)

A census sheet could be a battleground for fighting over national policy.
Should the U.S. government be responsible for Americans' economic lives?
That question pitched UNCLE SAM v. SENATOR TOBEY (chapter 6)

and then war came, and the census became a weapon.
THE INVENTORY AND THE ARSENAL

A Note on Method

In early 1940, about 120,000 people marched across the United States, through its densest cities, to its farthest reaches. They carried with them large sheets of paper, on which they wrote down, by hand, the details they gleaned or the judgments they rendered about more than 131 million U.S. residents. It was an audacious, astounding effort. (Every decennial population census is.) Its aim was to count and record significant data about each person in the country. (Census takers also gathered data that year about the nation's businesses, factories, mines, farms, and homes—but those efforts are not our primary concern in this book. Any mention simply of "the census" should be understood to mean the every-ten-years census of population.) In 2012, seventy-two years after those sheets of confidential information were first filled in, they became publicly available, as dictated by federal law. (The Census Bureau is barred from releasing any individually identifiable information it collects to anyone, even to other agencies of the government, for a period of seventy-two years from the moment of collection. It can and does publish statistical tabulations right away.) The 1940 census sheets are now accessible on microfilm and in digitized formats, and they are the key source that made this book possible. I have read thousands of these sheets both on my own and working with student researchers employed in my history lab at Colgate University. They offer glimpses into the lives of individuals who might otherwise be lost to history. The sheets also afford a peek into the mundane functioning of a modern democracy, revealing what a government values and how it regards the people it governs.

To fully understand the data inscribed on those sheets required me to investigate the records of the U.S. Census Bureau (what the National Archives calls Record Group 29) as well as the preserved papers of key political officials. It required consulting various government documents as well as databases constructed in later years from census records. In the course of writing this book, I also examined census-related drawings and paintings; I even read a surprising amount of census-inspired poetry. I relied, through it all, on the publications of the census historian Margo Anderson, supplemented by excellent books on the history of racial and ethnic classifications in the United States' and other nations' censuses.[1] And, of course, I examined the published results and official population statistics released by the Census Bureau. Those results and statistics, published in the 1940s across a series of thick volumes, were the reason that the census was taken—they delivered state population totals that governed the distribution of seats in the U.S. House of Representatives, informed government decisions on how to best allocate resources, and inspired discussion and debate about the nation's accomplishments, failures, and prospects.

Through it all, I sought to treat those whose lives had been captured in the data with the dignity that each deserved, while I asked the question: what is our democracy, if this is its data?

Democracy's Data

0

Stories in the Data

There are stories in the data. You just have to know how to read them.

Imagine a table of numbers, column after column of digits and decimals gleaming with precision, ornamented only by an aura of objectivity. This is data, to be sure.

Now loosen the hold that image of data has on us. Let in some other visions of how data might be manifested.

Think of a form to be filled in, on paper or a screen, intended to gather information that can later be quantified. That form is like a street corner, a conference room, a transit hub. People and institutions meet on that form. Someone, somewhere designed that form, deciding on the set of questions to be asked or the spaces to be left blank. Maybe they also listed some possible answers or limited the acceptable responses. You then encounter this designed environment as you hunch over the form. Or maybe, instead, a questioner brings the form to the threshold of your home, to your doorstep. That questioner then tackles the difficult task of fitting the unruly reality of your life within the form's straight-ruled lines. The final resulting form and all that is written upon it as well as all the negotiations that shaped it, whether backstage or offscreen, so to speak—all of this is data too. The data behind the numbers.

To find the stories in the data, we must widen our lens to take in not only the numbers but also the processes that generated those numbers. When we read these stories in the data, it helps us see the journey that any set of numbers has taken, and it helps us realize that numbers are just one crystallization of a much deeper, richer data set—they are one product of some instrument for making sense of our world, our lives, our societies.[1] Exploring beyond and before important numbers (in our case, the census's numbers), we see how reading data can reveal deeper truths about our nation's systems, our institutions, and ourselves.

I decided to write this book after I started thinking in a new way about an enormous and essential data set that would allow me to read deeply, beyond the numbers. As a historian, I had relied on the U.S. census for years, taking it as a source of facts, and usually taking it for granted. Like most people, I turned to the census more often for numbers than for stories.

Then, one day in 2017, while I was looking for something else in some historical government records, I had an epiphany. I realized that the right sort of investigation could reveal how the U.S. government in the course of a census translates people into data; it could also help us all understand better how individual people, families, communities, and the nation are transformed by counting.

I believe in the census, the way I believe in democracy—in part because in the United States the census and democracy are intimately intertwined. The numbers the census churns out represent "the people" to the government, and they shape the political representation those people enjoy. As long as the people to be counted have a significant say in what matters and how the numbers will be used, then the census overflows with democratic potential. As long as the people control their own enumeration, then the quest to count each person is one of the purest expressions of democratic values.

As my epiphany unfurled, I saw how the census stood waiting to help us understand the democratic potential of data.

Actually, the *historical* censuses stood waiting to help. You see, the census holds its cards close to the vest, protecting fiercely for seventy-two years everything apart from its published results. (Those results range from reports of each state's population to more specific tables showing local totals within a state or numbers arranged by age or by income levels or by a whole host of possible categories. All those tables fill thousands of printed pages or electronic spreadsheets, and yet they still tell only a tiny fraction of the whole story.) If I wanted to read deeply, beyond the numbers, I would need to look to the past, to an already-unlocked census. In such a census I could read not only the published statistical tables but also the manuscript materials recording millions of interactions and the asking and answering of billions of questions. In such a census I could peer into the deliberations of its designers, dig into records of the debates of politicians and the machinations of elites, and investigate the uses and abuses of the data at every stage of its creation.

Since I wanted to study a census that could speak to our concerns today—about the promise and perils of Big Data, about the ways data can or should drive governance, and about the continued role of the census in making American democracy possible—I landed on 1940, an open census and also a modern data-making enterprise. I chose 1940 for the same reason that Americans tracing their roots often start their genealogical investigations with the 1940 census: as the most recently available in manuscript form—that is, as the handwritten, raw records behind the statistics—it offered the best opportunity to bridge the past and the present. (By the time you are reading this, the vaults of the 1950 census will have been thrown open, exposing a new trove of stories waiting to be unearthed, and you will know how to search for them.)

For anyone who has filled out a census form in recent decades, the 1940 version might come as a shock. The present form is short, asking for only a few pieces of information: the name and birth date of all individuals at a particular address, along with their ethnic origin and race (you can check more than one), their sex (you cannot check more than one, and you must choose male or female), and their relationships within the household. The 1940 form, by contrast, had over thirty questions: about where people had come from, the education they had received, the families they lived in, and even the money they earned. The Census Bureau calculated that it recorded more than four billion answers to all those questions.[2]

So this was Big Data—old-fashioned Big Data, perhaps, but Big Data nonetheless—and, looking at it closely, we can spot the seeds of today's information-infused institutions.[3] The 1940 census paved the way for the use of modern statistical sampling methods and advanced computing machinery in government. It fostered a new generation of social scientists who were lured into service by Franklin Roosevelt's New Deal, bringing about a professionalization of the Census Bureau itself. It generated data that allowed politicians and bureaucrats to manage the nation's economy and ensure the financial security of many Americans.

Like Big Data today, 1940's data also had its darker side. It was soiled by backroom deals and extreme politicization. Officeholders accrued power by handing out census jobs. Partisans attacked the census to gain attention on the eve of a presidential election. The 1940 census took for granted that men should rule households and white people should run the government. (This was mostly true of every census until the Civil Rights movement in the 1960s began using the census to expressly challenge patriarchy and white supremacy.) The 1940 census asked questions that many people deemed too personal and excessively intrusive. It imposed categories and labels on individuals that often fit them poorly. Finally, with a world war raging across the Atlantic and the Pacific, the census resulted in reprehensible decisions to use Americans' data against them.

Using the 1940 census as my text, my data, I set out to read what stories I could find. And there were plenty—far more than one book could ever encompass. As I scoured the manuscript census records alongside the statistics of the Census Bureau, the papers of influential politicians, and the creative treasures of Depression-era American culture, the stories in the data bubbled to the surface. I found sad and troubling stories, touching and tender stories, stories of deception and stories of revelation, and stories of power used and power abused. The 1940 census proved a seemingly unending wellspring of stories about the awe-inspiring effort of a people to know their nation and a nation to know its people.

Let's begin our inquiry by examining the data generated at a single doorstep.

On April 16, 1940, a census taker named Selena Catalano in the city of Rochester, New York, interviewed Nellie Oakden about her family: about her husband, Howard, age forty-five, born in Pennsylvania, who had left school after the eighth grade; about Nellie herself, who had finished high school; about their children, beginning with the oldest, nineteen-year-old Joseph, followed by Hope, Howard Jr., Emily, and little eleven-year-old Nellie. Selena Catalano documented this encounter on a sheet of white paper about the size of the front page of a newspaper. Eighty-plus years later, all the data she recorded still exists.[4] That is remarkable. Even more remarkable is the thought that it will likely continue to exist as long as there is a United States of America, maybe even longer.

The census began as a relatively simple tool to tether political clout to each state's head count. The framers of the Constitution and their Enlightenment-era values linked data to democracy and democracy to data. Each state's say in governing the country would henceforth be proportional to its official population.

By 1940, the census had developed into an extensive stocktaking of the American people, a picture of who they were, where they came from, what they did, and how they lived. It also evolved into a guarantor of each individual's place in history. As a Census Bureau statistician explained it in 1934, "Nobody need feel that he merely lives and dies without having the facts about his existence permanently recorded."[5] The census promised representation in this respect too: not merely representation by an elected official, but also representation in the nation's statistics and records.

Looking at only the census's published results, I would not be able to distinguish the Oakdens from any other family, nor see any hint of Selena Catalano's labors. In the official tables, the Oakdens donned statistical disguises, dissolving into larger aggregates. A reader would see them (and yet not see any one of them clearly) within the figure 13,479,142 transmitted to Congress in 1941 to serve as the official population of New York State, or within the total U.S. population of 131,669,275.[6] Looking at only those published results, I could easily overlook the work the Catalanos and the Oakdens of the country did to fit their lives into forms. And that labor has for too long been overlooked in writings about the census and about data generally. These days, sooner or later, we are all counted, and we all become enumerators. (Every time you fill out a form online, you enumerate yourself on behalf of one entity or another.) For that reason alone, we should see what we can learn from the careful study of the ordinary work done by those who counted (and so represented) their fellow Americans and by those Americans who did—or sometimes didn't—cooperate with their enumerators.[7]

I found Selena Catalano because Selena Catalano found my family eighty years ago over a Rochester doorstep. Fifteen-year-old Howard Oakden, Jr., would one day become my grandfather. I never realized he was a "junior" until I found his name listed on Catalano's census sheet. I've seen old photographs of young Howard, and each time I have been struck both by how much that young person resembled the older man I'd seen playing cribbage or filling out crosswords. I have been struck, too, by the realization that I carry my grandfather with me, in my very bones. In photos he stands long, lean, and sinewy; his limbs, like mine, hide their strength, calling to mind tentpoles and toothpicks. Despite his last name, he is not grand like an oak but tangled and roped like an ironwood. None of that shows up in the census, of course. The census is designed to tell us some things and not others.

I went looking for my grandpa because what brings most people into contact with these handwritten census records is the search for their families. Wherever I went in my research to write this book (to the National Archives in D.C., to many public libraries offering access to census records), I found myself surrounded by people devoted to genealogical inquiries. They were already reading data, and there are, as we shall see, ways to read even more and more deeply into that data.

Selena Catalano discovered the entire clan of seven Oakdens living in half of a duplex at 39 Locust Street, paying $25 a month in rent. The family had moved to the city within the last five years, which, I realized, made them a lot like many other rural-to-urban migrants during the Great Depression. In their case, they had left behind the small town of Lindley on New York's Southern Tier (not far from Pennsylvania) to try their luck in the city. They were all American citizens, each born in the United States, who had landed in an Italian neighborhood; Catalano registered an Italian-born naturalized citizen in about a third of the homes she surveyed. (This is not so surprising: then, as now, a substantial proportion of the U.S. population had migrated from somewhere else.) My great-grandfather (Howard Sr.) appears to have scraped by in 1939, able to find work for only twenty-two weeks that year, earning $338, little more than the family's annual $300 rent. His oldest child (Joseph) seems to have just begun an apprenticeship doing advertising for a distribution firm, but he had not been able to contribute any wages to the family the year before. My grandpa, Howard Jr., was still in high school and earned no wages—or none the family admitted to. Times were tough, which my grandpa had never let on—at least not to me.

My grandparents had told me different sorts of things. I interviewed them once, right as I was beginning college, wanting to capture stories that otherwise might slip away. I sat down with them in their kitchen and pulled out a tiny handheld tape recorder. I still have my handwritten notes too. Thanks to that interview, I know a story about how my grandparents met. "Uh-oh, your seams are crooked," Howard had said to my grandmother, Lorraine, one day when he saw her walking home from Jefferson High School. "All girls worried about their [stocking] seams being straight," my grandmother explained to me during that interview. Howard added slyly that from then on Lorraine dropped into the "girls' room" every day before she left school and intentionally skewed her stockings before walking home in front of him.

Did that part really happen? Maybe. Maybe not. Grandma kept mum.

My grandparents told me stories—"seamy" stories of love!—that I couldn't hear anywhere else. They had other stories, maybe more private or less savory, that they kept entirely to themselves. Many people turn to the census to find details in which they might root such stories. And the census sheets have other sorts of stories to tell as well. While many may come to the census looking for their families, they can come away learning something about the United States of America itself.

Reading the rows and columns of the census sheet and sussing out their logic, I catch glimpses of Nellie and Howard Oakden's America, of the population that Selena Catalano labored to count. I find unmistakable signs of a nation that was reeling. Economic, social, and environmental disasters had made migrants of millions: from those whom folk singer Woody Guthrie immortalized as "Dust Bowl refugees" to the six million African Americans fleeing Jim Crow persecution, following family and friends on the Great Migration north. Depression-era hardships had set the nation in motion, and those unsettled times were reflected on every census sheet. In order to better measure just how unsettled the nation had become, the 1940 census not only recorded each person's current residence but also asked where each had lived five years earlier. The heading "Residence, April 1, 1935" signals the government's intense interest in migration. In a similar way, the following seven columns read like a response to the Great Depression: they counted the employed, the unemployed, and those dependent on emergency government work. In contrast, only a single column addressed the question of citizenship. Its thin stripe of ink testifies to waning concerns about immigration sixteen years after Congress had virtually halted all entry into the United States from outside the Western Hemisphere.

Census forms are filled with a dense matrix of straight lines. But all those lines disguise the messiness of the count, the messiness of being human. Why didn't the census survey ask if a person was sinewy like ironwood or thick in the trunk like an oak, or about how straight each girl's stocking seams were, or about the various paths people took to love? If those questions sound ridiculous, that is evidence that we have come to believe that some ways that governments think about people are natural and others are not. We could count otherwise, the biologist Robin Wall Kimmerer reminds us: "If you took a biologically inclusive census of the people in this town, the maples would outnumber humans a hundred to one," she writes. "In our Anishinaabe way, we count trees as people, 'the standing people.'" If the government counted trees as people, as in Kimmerer's Indigenous tradition, her (and my) corner of the United States would be revealed to be a "nation of maples."[8]

We too easily forget that counting "the people" required first defining who "the people" were and what mattered about each person. We have forgotten the history that birthed "appropriate" census questions. We forget that those questions and the categories created to generate data might even inspire new ways of thinking about ourselves and our neighbors. In every boring bureaucratic form, there lurks drama, conflict, and the quintessentially modern struggle to fit messy lives into standardized categories.

It appears that my grandpa and his parents cooperated with Selena Catalano, as did most Americans with their enumerators, but I cannot tell if Nellie smiled while she answered. The encounter with a census taker, after all, was often fraught, unpleasant, or downright combative. The census taker ("enumerator" was the official term) determined a person's one true, official name—even though names and identities are frequently fluid, shifting from context to context, like when a person migrates or marries and changes their name. Tensions may arise when the person writing down the official name has insufficient sympathy for the desired self-expression of the person being counted. A census taker in 1940 also recorded a person's race, choosing from a fixed menu of limited options, often with little or no input from the person so identified. The census also required that each individual be registered as belonging to a family or "household," which worked for many in the white middle class but proved more complicated for workers on plantations, noncitizens, queer people, even (it turns out) young office workers, and many, many more folks who, for whatever reason, lived on the statistical margins of society. Fitting into a form can be uncomfortable when the form has not been designed with you in mind.

A new question made the census feel particularly uncomfortable for some in 1940. For the first time in its history, this census gathered income data for each person—at the behest of big business, big labor, and big government, and much to the chagrin of conservative politicians who resisted the idea that government should be responsible for individual economic outcomes and quite a few (mostly white) Americans around the country who worried about new invasions of their privacy. Some individuals ultimately revolted against this new question—some openly, some more surreptitiously. Some even imagined turning to violent resistance. Whether motivated by a sense of patriotism, duty, or obligation, or the idea that their cooperation could lead to better days, my grandfather's family answered the question and so revealed its striking poverty.

The person most immediately responsible for fitting my grandpa into a form was Selena Catalano. But even her part in this databasing drama is about as straightforward as my grandmother's stocking seams. As I examined the other census sheets from Grandpa Oakden's district, I realized that Catalano wasn't even intended to be the one interviewing Great-Grandma Nellie. Another enumerator, Faith M. Van Deusen, was supposed to count them. Van Deusen had been assigned to cover the blocks of Rochester's tenth ward surrounding Edgerton Park and Jefferson High School. She had begun the count there. She worked six days, through April 10. Then something happened. A local census official (a so-called squad captain) sent in Catalano to finish the count. It's possible Van Deusen had shown herself to be bad at her work, but there's nothing in her completed forms to suggest that. It's more likely that she got sick or got a better job—the sort of thing you couldn't turn down in the middle of one of the country's most severe economic depressions ever. Catalano filled her shoes, finished the enumeration, and ensured that my family was counted.

Catalano's brief accounting of the Oakden family would eventually travel in a leather portfolio to Washington, D.C., where it would be sorted and vetted (through a process called "editing") to make sure everyone in the family had been described or categorized in an acceptable fashion. With the data suitably tamed (or "cleaned," as today's data workers might say), the descriptions of Nellie, Howard, Joseph, Hope, Howard Jr., Emily, and little Nellie would all be represented as holes punched through stiff paper cards (each about the size of a business envelope) and then fed into specially designed machines for sorting and counting.

Being counted meant that my great-grandparents would be represented in Congress; it meant that they would be represented in official reports used to plan for America's future. And those reports mattered ever more too, with the advent of a new, more interventionist federal government—one offering a safety net for the aged, disabled, or poor through Social Security; one seeking to house millions in new homes and, increasingly, in new suburbs; one guaranteeing more rights to workers to organize and unionize; a government working more closely with both business and consumers to ensure a high basic standard of living for ever more people. World War II made such representation even more significant. Being counted meant the Oakdens had an official record they themselves could draw on if they needed proof of age or citizenship to work in a defense industry. Their census status as native-born white Americans opened the door to the welfare state, to better jobs, to better homes, and it would protect them when census data were weaponized against so-called "enemy aliens": Germans, Italians, and, with tragic consequences, Japanese and Japanese Americans.

I've told the story about my Oakden forebears because it illustrates what reading data can look like. I examined multiple manifestations of the data. I read the questions that were asked. I read the information entered in response to those questions and even figured out who gathered the data in the first place. But I did not stop with the form itself. I looked at the later transformations of the data, as it mutated and proliferated in reports and official statistics. And I dug into my personal archives for old photographs and notes from interviewing my grandparents. I interpreted what I discovered using what I knew about American history and what I learned from the official archives of the Census Bureau. I have an undergraduate degree in computational mathematics, but reading data doesn't require special expertise in computing or math. Instead, it requires careful observation; thoughtful, curious questioning; and creative but also cautious interpretation—in short, it requires the modes of inquiry that lie at the heart of the humanities and social sciences. Data are not exclusively the province of computer coders, hackers, and quants. Data belong to a particular time and place, and they carry the imprint of that time and place. What my family's story helps make clear is that to read census data, or any similar data, is to encounter a complicated, multilayered cultural object, a deep, often tangled text.

When I say that a data set is a text, I am not speaking metaphorically. Data are textual, just as books are textual. A data set is a text in the same way that a photograph, a painting, or a film can be considered a text.

Like other texts, data sets usually have authors, and they have subjects.

Some data may emerge from a single author and have a single subject, as with, say, an athlete who measures out grams of protein consumed at each meal, tracks times registered in sprints, or records body weight as read from a scale each day. More often, data sets have multiple authors: there are people who come up with questions to ask or characteristics to measure; there are those who design the forms or instruments to gather the data; there are those charged with interviewing or observing others and recording what they discover. Even the subjects of large studies (such as a census) act as co-authors, insofar as they are asked to explain themselves to an interviewer or on a form. As an apparatus for generating a data set grows more complicated and involves more people as authors, differences in power and status among those authors leave marks on the data. Sometimes every aspect of the data turns out to be a product of debate and negotiation.

Like other texts, data sets belong to old, though not necessarily exalted, traditions and genres. The forms we now fill out daily to make a doctor's appointment or to order dinner online belong, for instance, to a tradition of "blank" forms that reaches back at least to Johannes Gutenberg, who used his printing press to produce big batches of indulgences for the Catholic Church, each leaving a space for a name to be written identifying the sinner seeking absolution.[9]

Like other texts, data sets take up space as some manner of object. Interviewers might write down initial responses on a sheet of paper, for instance. Then a clerk might transfer those responses onto a more compact, mobile tool, like an index card. Such cards may seem to have been around forever, but they had to be invented: first to aid libraries in keeping track of their collections and later to help banks and insurance companies keep track of their customers. Eventually scientists, too, realized that this technology would allow them to organize information about their subjects.[10] Another clerk might have, in past decades, translated the index card's information into punched holes in a different paper card as part of a system for counting and sorting mechanically that was invented in the 1880s expressly for the U.S. census. These days, that clerk would probably key the information into an electronic database. From those cards or that database, a researcher might prepare printed tables of numbers, and these, too, would take some physical form. Statistical tables themselves are a technology for data visualization, though we seldom think of them that way. They make it possible to see large sets of numbers, compare them, and reference them all at once.[11] They can also inspire emotions in their readers: the sense that everything is accounted for, a feeling of order and certainty, even when that which is being measured (like the spread of a pandemic) is chaotic and out of control. (One of the early, influential uses of statistical tables was to track deaths from plague.)[12] Today, data often comes to us via a series of electrical signals streaming on a phone or computer screen, which reveals an evolution in materials and style rather than a revolution of kind. Even in the cloud, data sets remain materially instantiated texts.

Like any other texts, data sets will bear the imprint of their times, revealing the values of their authors and perhaps of the wider society, with its patterns of power and wealth and domination, with its ideals of truth and beauty and justice. Data makers decide what counts and who counts. The questions they ask, the categories they attend to, and the labels they apply all hail from their way of seeing the world and judging what matters. When those being represented in the data are people who have different ideas or values, they might protest or shrink away, they might insist on alternate labels or write outside the lines, they might fib to fit or, instead, decide to make a fuss. Thus, the project of making accurate personal data might require collaboration and contestation, both of which help make it possible to "see," understand, aid, or even govern people.

Like other texts, data sets can live multiple lives after they are released. Perhaps published as a graph or a chart or a map or a spreadsheet, data can move from place to place, lent out by a library or uploaded to a clearinghouse or simply passed from hand to hand. They may be used to explore possibilities, prove points, administer programs, or (too frequently) target the vulnerable. In the abundant literature on Big Data, the enthusiasts and the skeptics agree on a set of verbs elaborating the manifold fates of a data set: it can be mined, stripped, organized, hoarded, analyzed, encrypted, or visualized. Of even greater interest or concern is that data are priced, brokered, and sold, funneling billions of dollars into the coffers of the world's most valuable companies.[13]

Few talk about "reading" data, apart from innovative scholars like Lindsay Poirier and Caitlin Rosenthal.[14] But everyone should approach data as a thing to be read. To talk of reading data is to acknowledge that data are more than a series of facts and figures. Data sets are texts. Data sets are a way of seeing the world. We cannot really figure out what to do about our data-driven reality if we do not understand that way of seeing.

When I was a student, I read books that opened my eyes to beauty and complexity in the world that I had never seen before. I recall a volume by Robert Pinsky called *The Sounds of Poetry*, which taught me how to see and hear the craft and structure that undergird a poem.[15] I recall Michael Baxandall's art-history classic *Painting and Experience in Fifteenth-Century Italy*, which revealed to me the ways that art could speak not just of beauty but of a specific confluence of politics, economics, and culture in a particular time and place.[16] I recall Carol Willis's *Form Follows Finance*, which explained why the skylines of Chicago and New York differed—how law and money helped define distinct architectural styles.[17] I remember few of the specific examples presented in those books, but poems, paintings, and skyscrapers all now speak to me in ways I would not have imagined possible.

I hope that this book will help people hear data speak in new ways. I hope readers will develop an admiration for data's depths, for the ways that sweat and blood suffuse a data set. Some people fall in love with the appearance of data as a thing more or less certain, simple, and precise. I think there is more beauty and also more truth in acknowledging and even appreciating the roots of data in the uncertain, complicated, and often hazy spaces of life.

Looking squarely at the processes that make the data can also be disturbing, though. Reading the data is often unsettling. The word "data" derives from the Latin for "things given," and, indeed, data is often something given, something imbued with the legitimacy and prestige of the giver, something to be accepted, used, and taken for granted.[18]

Reading the data calls into question the given-ness of the givens, the data-ness of the data. And it exposes the mess ordinarily hidden by the neat grid of a table or spreadsheet: the assumptions made, the values expressed, the politics negotiated, the interests coordinated, the people helped, and the people hurt in the process of putting together a data set.

Readers accustomed to taking data for granted and to assuming that data can at least approximate a universal ideal of objectivity may find what follows particularly troubling. But the point of this book is not to reject objectivity—or data. I follow feminist scientists who insist that the best way to save objectivity as an ideal is to admit the context of every investigation. They teach us that we can have truth and facts when we specify for what conditions the truth and the facts obtain. When we admit the contingencies that shape our data and the distinct position and point of view that defines our data, then we have a better shot at learning true things.[19]

Looking closely at the census, in particular, may prove disturbing for another reason: our data reflect back to us many of the deficits of our democracy. Those deficits, those failures, stand out in stark contrast to the ideals of order, completeness, fairness, and control so deeply woven into the conventions of data.

Looking closely at the census, we're invited to ask: what is our democracy, if this is its data? The answers we arrive at will be revealing and important, though not always comforting.

The enumerator approaches a porch. In his hand he carries a leather portfolio filled with census sheets, each a physical instantiation of one vision of the United States and what matters in those United States—it is, in 1940, the vision of those I'll call "the Question Men," the white elites representing government, big business, big labor, and philanthropy who wrote their priorities into the census, as chapter 1 will explain.

The Census Bureau at that time staged a series of photographs of doorstep encounters, featuring starlets and heartthrobs borrowed from Twentieth Century Fox's movie sets. A man with slicked-back hair sporting a striped tie and a dark suit and holding large sheets of paper sits on a sofa next to a woman who looks to the ceiling, evidently counting on her fingers—the picture of exaggerated perplexity in a polka-dot dress. In another photo, a woman in striped skirt and blazer, two feathers bursting from her floppy-brimmed hat, smiles across a threshold into the eyes of a petite, curly-haired young starlet in a dark dress with a white collar. The enumerator's arms are filled by the large census-issued portfolio, along with her purse. The starlet's hand rests on the front doorknob, a reminder that this little chat will soon be over. In my favorite photo, a male enumerator sits on the edge of a porch, perched at the feet of film star Tyrone Power, who leans forward from what appears to be a deck chair, gazing into the distance: this just-beyond-the-doorstep encounter looks relaxed, even glamorous.

Of course, the participants in these photos were actors paid to make the meetings look appealing. Everyone photographed was well-off, well-dressed, and white. In actual practice, the meeting of two minds over a census sheet required more collaboration and conversation, as people tried to describe their circumstances in a way that Washington, D.C., would understand. In real life, the encounters involved interpersonal negotiations across lines of difference and inequities in power, sometimes even simply to decide what name to put down on the census sheet, as chapter 2 explains. In communities living on the margins of society, enumerators and the enumerated had to come up with language that would make space for the queer, the colonized, or the poor in a system not designed with them in mind. Chapter 3 explains how such collaborations created a rash of individuals labeled, in tantalizing and fleeting fashion, simply as "partners."

Real enumerators were not actors cast by a talent agency. They were ordinary Americans, nearly half of whom were women, of whom most were classified as "housewives."[20] They were selected through a patronage process, then tested and trained to make them proper sensors for the state, as chapter 4 explains. The enumerator arrived at each door trailing a web of intersecting commitments to science and politics, the two impossible to untangle. And as chapter 5 reveals, politics—and in particular the politics of white supremacy—ran deeply through the entire census, exposed by who or what was counted and who or what was not.

In a presidential election year, as 1940 was, partisan politics posed a particular challenge, and chapter 6 reveals the marks those politics left within the data following an epic fight over the new question about individual income. As the United States geared up for World War II, first in its factories and then fighting on foreign shores, national security policies turned doorstep data into a weapon that could be leveled against Americans themselves—a cautionary tale told in chapter 7 that reminds us of the damage made possible by confidential data unwisely unleashed in a flawed and frightened democracy.

The story of a census might seem to end when the numbers are published, but that, too, is an illusion. Once the numbers are out in the world, they are subject to being reinterpreted, reimagined, or rejected. The Census Bureau can tabulate tables of facts, but it has little control over what others in government, in the media, or in ordinary living rooms will do with those facts. As chapter 8 makes clear, new negotiations, new political machinations, and new visions for the United States reframed and reconstituted data even after it was supposedly finished. The nation's facts appeared to be knitted together, but not even leather bindings could fix them in place.

If, when all is said and done, we study only the numbers that a census produces, we will come away with an incomplete, possibly distorted picture of the nation. We will miss the way that uncertainties roil beneath the measurements. More important, we'll overlook sources that stand ready to tell us even more than the numbers about the government and society those numbers represent. That's because the process of taking the census requires first positing a vision for the United States and its people. Then, each step of the way, that vision runs smack into the beliefs, circumstances, and material constraints of the country's actual population. Census architects or census takers see the world in one way and yet must find a way to enumerate and classify people who may see the world quite differently or behave in unexpected ways. The clash of preconceived, orderly ideas with the disorder of daily life can tell us quite a lot about the possibilities and realities of the moment that brought forth the data.

Focusing on the published numbers and calling solely them the "data" misleads us. We fall for an illusion of completeness, a fantasy of order, and a framing of the world as Washington, D.C., wishes to present it. The numbers are not necessarily wrong, and I am not saying we are wrong to rely on them for administration and investigation. The numbers may well be accurate, even as they tell only a fraction of the story. That is why I am drawn, over and over in this book, to the doorstep encounter.[21]

The doorstep is the nexus where the best-laid plans for an orderly census process encounter a profoundly complicated reality. Focusing on the doorstep, and the data produced there, rather than on the data in its tabulated, numerical form quickly disabuses us of any notion that the making of data can be segregated from social dynamics or political forces. At the doorstep, negotiations are had and tweaks are made as reality becomes data on its way toward becoming numbers and facts. Those negotiations and tweaks aren't beside the point; they should not be forgotten. They have much to tell us about our nation too. They're part of the data. That's why we should bother to read for stories in the data. That's why I wrote this book.

When we settle for studying only the official numbers released in the immediate wake of a census, we also settle for the democracy that such a count can sustain. Our democracy is only as good as our data, and our data is only as good as our democracy. Readers will, by the time they have turned the final page of this book, see census data differently and realize that one path to achieving a more equitable and inclusive country involves thinking deliberately and strategically about the census questions we campaign for, the answers we give, the uses of the census we allow, and the values we inscribe in the entire process of manufacturing the nation's data.

The census concerns us all. What does it say about us, that these are our data, that this is what we seek to know?

To learn how to ask and answer that query, we will begin in Washington, D.C., and pay a visit to the Question Men.

TABLE 1.—*Populations of the States, 1940, and apportionment of Representatives in Congress, 1940 and 1930*

State	Population, Apr. 1, 1940	Present number of Representatives[1]	Apportionment of 435 Representatives, 1940					
			Method of major fractions			Method of equal proportions		
			Number of Representatives	Change from 1930		Number of Representatives	Change from 1930	
				Gain	Loss		Gain	Loss
	(1)	(2)	(3)	(4)	(5)	(6)	(7)	(8)
United States	131,669,275	435	435	10	−10	435	9	−9
Alabama	2,832,961	9	9			9		
Arizona	499,261	1	2	1		2	1	
Arkansas	1,949,387	7	6		−1	7		
California	6,907,387	20	23	3		23	3	
Colorado	1,123,296	4	4			4		
Connecticut	1,709,242	6	6			6		
Delaware	266,505	1	1			1		
District of Columbia	663,091							
Florida	1,897,414	5	6	1		6	1	
Georgia	3,123,723	10	10			10		
Idaho	524,873	2	2			2		
Illinois	7,897,241	27	26		−1	26		
Indiana	3,427,796	12	11		−1	11		−1
Iowa	2,538,268	9	8		−1	8		−1
Kansas	1,801,028	7	6		−1	6		−1
Kentucky	2,845,627	9	9			9		
Louisiana	2,363,880	8	8			8		
Maine	847,226	3	3			3		
Maryland	1,821,244	6	6			6		
Massachusetts	4,316,721	15	14		−1	14		−1
Michigan	5,256,106	17	18	1		17		
Minnesota	2,792,300	9	9			9		
Mississippi	2,183,796	7	7			7		
Missouri	3,784,664	13	13			13		
Montana	559,456	2	2			2		
Nebraska	1,315,834	5	4		−1	4		−1
Nevada	110,247	1	1			1		
New Hampshire	491,524	2	2			2		
New Jersey	4,160,165	14	14			14		
New Mexico	531,818	1	2	1		2	1	
New York	13,479,142	45	45			45		
North Carolina	3,571,623	11	12	1		12	1	
North Dakota	641,935	2	2			2		
Ohio	6,907,612	24	23		−1	23		
Oklahoma	2,336,434	9	8		−1	8		−1
Oregon	1,089,684	3	4	1		4	1	
Pennsylvania	9,900,180	34	33		−1	33		−1
Rhode Island	713,346	2	2			2		
South Carolina	1,899,804	6	6			6		
South Dakota	642,961	2	2			2		
Tennessee	2,915,841	9	10	1		10	1	
Texas	6,414,824	21	21			21		
Utah	550,310	2	2			2		
Vermont	359,231	1	1			1		
Virginia	2,677,773	9	9			9		
Washington	1,736,191	6	6			6		
West Virginia	1,901,974	6	6			6		
Wisconsin	3,137,587	10	10			10		
Wyoming	250,742	1	1			1		

[1] The present apportionment of Representatives is based on the 1930 census. The method followed in 1930 was the method of major fractions. In that instance the use of the method of equal proportions would have resulted in the same apportionment.

The Oakdens made their first *public* appearance in the 1940 census data in this table, prepared to apportion seats in the House of Representatives among the states. The Oakdens are not labeled or publicly identified. They are included in New York's 13,479,142 persons and represented by one of the state's 45 members in the U.S. House of Representatives.

Before they appeared as numbers, the Oakdens were made into data on a confidential census sheet—what is often called the "manuscript census," because it was written by hand. The manuscript census remains confidential for seventy-two years. These sheets were released in 2012. In these excerpts (taken from the middle of a sheet [rows 22–28] with the column headings pasted in above), the family members are (in the leftmost sections of the sheet) parsed according to characteristics that the census used to define a person. Moving left to right across the sheet, the enumerator must first name the house, using an address, and then name the people (last name first, with a line to indicate a repeated last name in subsequent lines). Next the enumerator must place each person in a household, indicating their relationship to the first person listed (the "head"). Next the enumerator ascribes to each person a set of state-sanctioned identity labels.

Note the mark next to "Nellie" in row 23. That indicates that she was the person spoken to at that doorstep, answering for all the others.

Note the cross-outs in column 13. These were errors, corrected in the field or possibly later by a census data editor in D.C.

Row 26 features a data depiction of my grandfather, Howard Oakden, Jr.

CITIZENSHIP	RESIDENCE, APRIL 1, 1935										
Citizenship of the foreign born	City, town, or village having 2,500 or more inhabitants. Enter "R" for all other places.	COUNTY	STATE (or Territory or foreign country)	On a farm (Yes or No)	CODE (Leave blank)						CODE
16	17	18	19	20	D	21	22	23	24	25	26
	Lindley	Steuben	New York	yes	5642	no	no	yes	—	—	3
	Lindley	Steuben	New York	yes	5642	no	no	no	no	H	
	Lindley	Steuben	New York	yes	5642	yes	—	—	—	—	1
	Lindley	Steuben	New York	yes	5642	no	no	no	no	S	
	Lindley	Steuben	New York	yes	5642	no	no	no	no	S	
	Lindley	Steuben	New York	yes	5642	no	no	no	no	S	
	Lindley	Steuben	New York	yes	5642						

Reading farther right toward the center of the sheet, we find the Oakdens probed for evidence of the Great Depression's effects.

Note the blank spaces in column 16 on the left: those blanks mean that the Oakdens were all U.S. citizens by birth.

The answers in columns 17–20 indicate the family had moved from a farm. Had the Oakdens stayed put, these columns would have been blank.

Note the answers in column 21 and column 23: they indicate that my great-grandfather (in the top row) was not working during the census's reference week (March 24–30, 1940) but that he was seeking work.

The "H" in column 25 marks Great-Grandmother Nellie as one who did the housework, while the three "Ss" indicate students—anyone with such marks would not be counted as unemployed.

PERSONS 14 YEARS OLD AND OVER—EMPLOYMENT STATUS											
26	27	28	29	30	F	31	32	33	34		
	26	Gardner	Farm	Pu	866	VV	1	22	338	no	22
								d	d	no	23
30		Apprentice Advertising	Distributors	Pu	412	60	1	J	O	no	24
								d	J	no	25
								0	J	no	26
								J	J	no	27
											28

The rightmost third of the census sheet evidenced new interest in Americans' economic lives.

Column 26 reveals that my great-grandfather had been unemployed for 26 weeks in 1939 and earned only (according to column 32) $338 in wages, which was all the family reported having to live on. The "nos" in column 34 mean none of the household had any other non-wage source of income. This is a portrait of hard times, depicted in handwritten data.

Selena Catalano patrolled Enumeration District (E.D.) 65–112. That faint "112" floating over the section marked "Edgerton Park" was written on the map that Catalano would have been given to guide her investigations. Catalano's E.D. is superimposed here on a section of another map, one created around this same time by the Home Owners' Loan Corporation.

Scans and reprints of the census sheets do not give a proper sense of their scale. Look at them here in the hands of actual people (well, actors posing as if they're enjoying an intimate statistical conversation).

1

The Question Men

A conference convened at 10:00 a.m. sharp on March 3, 1939, in Washington, D.C., to design a frame for a democracy's data.

Before any count could be made, before any households could be visited, the framework and values that would guide that count and those visits had to be hashed out. There is a story behind the census questionnaire itself, a story of the people whose worldviews determined what personal details would be recorded and which would be ignored. To really understand a data set we need to learn as much as we can about its designers: Where did they come from? What did they dream and desire? And who *wasn't* invited to help frame the data? Whose experiences and values were simply brushed aside?

To comprehend the official intentions that structured the 1940 census, we have to learn more about the men who gathered in that conference room on the morning of March 3, 1939.

The 10:00 a.m. start made it possible for the New Yorkers attending the conference to sleep in their own beds the night before and still arrive on time. One of those New Yorkers was conference chairman Dr. Louis I. Dublin, who worked for the Metropolitan Life Insurance Company with the title "Third Vice-President and Statistician." Dublin would have taken a train that morning, probably riding in a comfortable Pullman car. Then he would have hailed a taxi to take him to the Census Bureau's office in the Department of Commerce.[1]

Did Dublin think about how much Washington, D.C., had changed since the last census conference ten years earlier? He had chaired that conference too. At that time, in Dublin's New York City, the construction craze had peaked. Dublin's office hovered high above Madison Square Park in the Metropolitan Life Tower—at seven hundred feet, once (briefly) the tallest building in the world—which paled in comparison to the skyscrapers that followed it in the twenties, each taller than the last, driven heavenward by the ambitions of investors and speculators.[2] A handful of the country's richest men put together $50 million and incorporated Empire State to build a 1,250-foot marvel of an office building. The punishment for such dreams of Icarus came swiftly. They signed on the dotted line in 1929, just in time to witness the stock market's collapse. It would be decades before the Empire State Building turned a profit.[3] No one was in a hurry to build any more towers in New York.

Plans for a growing Washington, D.C., had also been hatched in the heady twenties but only became a reality in the early thirties. No one built skyscrapers in D.C., as they had in New York. Instead, the federal government made space for itself in long, grand buildings of monumental white stone. Dublin would have seen the most change along Pennsylvania Avenue, the broad thoroughfare that links the White House to the Capitol. The Post Office department suddenly had neighbors in magnificent classical structures. Rolling up Pennsylvania Avenue, Dublin would have seen the National Archives looming like a Greek temple to American history, then the Department of Justice, the Internal Revenue Service, and the Department of Labor, all new. His taxi would have pulled over to let him out a little before the avenue dead-ended at the Treasury Department. There, stretching three massive city blocks, stood the new Department of Commerce building. It was hewn from sixty thousand tons of Indiana limestone and Connecticut granite and roofed by six acres of terra-cotta tiles. When it first opened its doors, a headline in *The Washington Post* read: "Size of Building Baffles Writers."[4]

A little before ten, Dublin entered the Commerce building, passing a row of Greek columns, only to be greeted inside by more Greek columns. Someone had probably met him at the door, maybe even the director of the census, William Lane Austin. The men then proceeded to the building's auditorium so that the two-day conference could begin.

Looking around the room, Dublin encountered more evidence of the growth of the federal government.[5] He saw representatives from old and established institutions such as the War and Navy departments (founded in 1789 and 1798) and the Departments of Agriculture (founded in 1862), Interior (founded in 1849), and Labor (1913). Beside them, surrounding them, stood representatives of a new kind of government institution, men from the Works Progress Administration (WPA, 1935), the Federal Power Commission (1920), the Federal Home Loan Bank Board (1932), the Federal Housing Administration (1934), the Social Security Board (1935), the Veterans Administration (1930), and the Central Statistical Board (1933). Commentators remarked on the alphabet soup created by Herbert Hoover's New Era and Franklin Delano Roosevelt's New Deal, a soup of new institutions known by their acronyms. To understand how government was growing and changing, one had only to study one's ABCs—that is, the lists of new administrations, boards, and commissions.

Even with representatives of all those different government agencies in attendance, the Census Bureau's contingent was bigger.

Everyone else in the room was there at the invitation of the secretary of commerce himself: Harry Hopkins, one of Roosevelt's longtime aides, had signed each letter inviting its recipient to the two-day conference in Washington, D.C. "This census involves the vital interests of business, Government, and the general public alike," wrote Hopkins. Accepting this invitation meant the recipient would "share with us [the Department of Commerce] this joint responsibility to assure the maximum of value and usefulness to all interests concerned."[6]

The census director, separately, insisted that the event was not "under any circumstances" supposed to be a "field day" for the federal employees. He had selected Dublin to lift up the voices of the rest of the people in the room—those representing what the director called "the public interests."[7]

Who, after all, was the census for, if not the public?

According to a 1940 filmstrip called *Know Your U.S.A.*, the census provided "unbiased facts to measure markets for business and the farmer, the plans of school and health officials, the needs of local governments;

facts to guide the lawmakers; facts from which a free people can count its gains and chart its future." It closed with the census slogan that year: "You cannot know your country, unless your country knows you."[8]

This was a charming slogan. It's even Socratic, if we twist it a bit: The unexamined country is not worth living in. But to live in an examined country means that everyone in the nation must answer the knock on the door, invite an interviewer inside, and tell the truth.

Today, the census sells itself with less romance, appealing instead to the immediate material consequences of the count. The census, we hear, decides who has power in Congress, who gets a say in the Electoral College, and how trillions of dollars in federal funds are allocated. Answer the census, we're told, or else. Or else, our votes won't matter as much as they should. Or else, fire stations will go unbuilt. Or else, the shelves of libraries will stand empty. Or else, the poor will go hungry and won't be able to see a doctor. "You cannot know your country, unless your country knows you" and "Get counted or your community suffers" differ less than they might seem to at first, because even in 1940 it was clear that the "self-knowledge" the census offered had significant political and economic value.

The public interests represented in the Commerce auditorium included General R. E. Wood, who was listed in the census as an executive of a "Mail Order House," which was a little like listing Jeff Bezos as the manager of a delivery company.[9] Wood chaired the board of the biggest, most popular, and most important mail-order firm: Sears, Roebuck and Co. Americans of all walks of life could peruse the Sears catalog, find an appealing flannel shirt or a dress made from new fabric fibers (like rayon!), maybe a rifle or a radio, an eighty-rod roll of barbed wire, or even a windmill, and have it delivered anywhere in the nation.[10] The revolutionary egalitarianism of the U.S. Postal Service, which by virtue of its low-cost service bound the backwoods and delta plains to industrial centers and big cities, made Sears possible. (The postal service also depended on the census, to decide where to open branches and how to allocate resources.) Now Wood as its chief was engineering the addition to its mail-order business of a brick-and-mortar empire. As he steered Sears, Wood studied the census.[11] He and Sears couldn't know its markets unless the census knew each American.

Wood was a natural choice for this meeting. Roosevelt's New Deal policies had come under significant fire from some big business groups, and those policies had no greater enemy than the du Ponts and the groups, like the National Association of Manufacturers, buoyed by their chemicals, plastics, and explosives fortune.[12] But that didn't mean everyone in the corporate world hated Roosevelt. Wood had been an early and enthusiastic supporter and had taken it upon himself to build relationships between the new administration and big business, beginning by recruiting his friends and colleagues to serve on a Committee to Rebuild Price and Purchasing Power in 1933. Money men had disliked or distrusted Roosevelt's early decision to leave the gold standard, because they disliked inflation and the way it devalued the interest they earned. But Wood joined Roosevelt's side—he believed inflation, and greater purchasing power, were necessary to revive the depressed nation's economy. He (and Sears) also needed the rural customers they relied on to have enough money to order more goods.[13]

Alongside Wood in that auditorium, Dublin would have seen other business leaders whom the director of the census and the secretary of commerce had seen fit to invite. There was the president of the American Retail Federation, Dr. David R. Craig. Even the National Association of Manufacturers sent a representative, the organization's secretary, Noel Sargent. Whether they liked the administration or not, these men wanted a say in the census. They must have agreed with the sentiment spoken by a Census Bureau official a few months later: "We cannot escape the fact that markets are people."[14] To know America as a market, the census had to interview every American and ask the right questions.

Dublin, a vice president for the nation's largest life insurer, could hold his own among the business elite, and he probably realized that he'd been selected because he could talk more or less comfortably with the other people in that auditorium too. Dublin had crafted a career by building bridges among business, progressive reform, and academic science. He'd earned a Ph.D.—in biology—from Columbia and was lured to Metropolitan by a visionary executive committed to building a "New

Socialism." Instead of a socialism dependent on government action and state control, this socialism entrusted the fate of the masses to enlightened corporations. The title of the history of Metropolitan Life that Dublin would soon publish was "A Family of Thirty Million," where thirty million referred to the number of Americans insured by the company. But Metropolitan did not merely insure a fifth of the country's entire population against an untimely death, offering a form of savings and security to people who seldom had access to a bank. It also offered free visits to doctors and nurses, introduced and made normal (even obligatory) the yearly physical exam, campaigned for improved sanitary conditions, and distributed millions of pamphlets filled with health advice or explaining important medical concepts like the germ theory of disease. Dublin's corporate ascent began with the job of justifying the expense of all that "socialistic" activity. It had been his job to prove that health care was a good investment.[15]

Dublin began building an economic case for health interventions, and yet that case was soon deemed superfluous by his superiors. Even before he could finish gathering his evidence, Metropolitan Life's "welfare work" had already proved its value to the company through the goodwill it garnered and the publicity it accrued. The age of "corporate responsibility" as advertising was dawning. The warm glow of good works raised Dublin's profile too, both inside and outside the company. He grew to the status of public intellectual, building for the nation an economic justification for all health work. Under his hand, the Metropolitan Statistical Bureau blossomed into one of the most trusted sources for American statistics, second only to the Census Bureau. Reformers looked in vain in the census to discover how many people died in car crashes or lost limbs to industrial accidents. But Dublin had access to reliable figures in his employer's private statistical stash, and through the Metropolitan Life's *Statistical Bulletin* he made them widely available.

Margaret Scattergood probably read the *Statistical Bulletin*. She was in that auditorium with Louis Dublin because William Green, the president of the American Federation of Labor (AFL), had sent her as his representative. Scattergood was an AFL researcher, which meant she did for the nation's unions what the CIA did for the national government—

that was how she would describe her work a decade later to CIA officials. Scattergood's analogy was apt.[16] She worked for the AFL gathering intelligence about employers that might give an edge to its members—mostly men in skilled trades, who enjoyed a higher status than other workers—as they fought for a living wage, for reasonable hours, for safer working conditions. But the AFL also kept a wary distance from state power—it offered workers an alternative to the government, or at least it had done so until the Great Depression made grudging cooperation with the New Deal necessary.

By contrast, Scattergood's colleagues at the meeting, Ralph Hetzel and Sidney B. Katz of the Congress of Industrial Organizations, sat in the auditorium as representatives of a group firmly allied with the president and his agenda. Progressive leaders in the union movement had left the AFL in 1935 to form the Congress of Industrial Organizations (CIO) for all workers, independent of old hierarchies of craft and skill. Roosevelt signed the Wagner Act in 1935, putting the power of the federal government behind the rights of workers to band together and bargain collectively. It was a decisive move and one that further empowered the CIO in its campaigns to sign up steelworkers, autoworkers, garment workers, and the rest of America's growing industrial army—even government workers, including those in the Census Bureau. In 1936, the previously nonpartisan trade unions came out strong for Roosevelt, linking his administration to the cause of unionism through unprecedented slogans like "The President Wants You to Organize."[17] The unions had earned a place in the Department of Commerce auditorium, a place to campaign for data about the masses, for the masses. Your country can't be organized, unless your country knows you.

As Dublin surveyed the rest of the faces before him, he saw the newest breed of political actor in the room: the academics and professional statisticians or, in a label sometimes used for them, the "brains." From the beginning of his presidency, Roosevelt had relied on professors to give him advice and shape his policy. A reporter for *The New York Times* dubbed a group of those close advisors, all from Columbia University, the "Brains Trust" (shortened to "Brain Trust" later).[18]

Franklin Roosevelt's administration did not invent the idea that university scientists should guide the apparatus of state. The notion dates back at least to Abraham Lincoln, to the founding of the land-grant colleges and universities. Those institutions—now often marked by an "A&M" or "State" in their names, like Texas A&M and Michigan State—focused on agricultural and mechanical (that is, engineering) sciences, funded by endowments of federal land, land often recently taken from Native Americans.[19] In the late nineteenth century the federal government established special "experiment stations" within these universities to support and encourage original research that would be of use to the nation, its business, its people, and its government.

But the idea of a university that served the state was not originally American; it was German. All the great research universities of the nineteenth century grew up in German-speaking lands. Wilhelm von Humboldt, a great philologist in his own right and brother to a famous world explorer (Alexander), founded the University of Berlin (now Humboldt University) on the model of the University of Göttingen, where he had studied. Humboldt thus sowed in Prussia the seeds of an intellectual revolution. These new universities still had lecture halls where charismatic professors could profess their beliefs or just read aloud from rare books, but they also offered new kinds of spaces, like seminar rooms filled with maps or codices for the close and collaborative study of documents; museums and libraries, where whole universes of experience were to be collected; and, of course, laboratories filled with Bunsen burners (named for the German chemist Robert Bunsen) and glass beakers. New academic celebrities arose too, stars who would be recruited and poached by the Göttingens and Berlins, stars who published widely, stars who attracted (and sometimes trained) streams of eager graduate students.[20]

Americans joined those streams of graduate students entering German universities, or, it would be more accurate to say, they flooded Germany's universities. American students—and their money—buoyed the German university system further. What American universities are today, German universities were then. American students lit their Bunsen burners in German laboratories, learning how to make chemical fertilizers and artificial dyes. They learned, too, how the same nitrogen that made plants grow faster could create devastating explosives. They sat in German seminar rooms around massive wooden tables, working out the origins of words and meanings, studying the past as stored in official documents. Germany was actually a much newer nation-state than was the United States—it was united only in 1873 at the end of the Franco-Prussian war. From the fervor of the new-kindled nationalism grew a new kind of social science, fact-filled and ethically rich, devoted to the study of nations and states. One of those American students who made the Atlantic crossing was W.E.B. Du Bois, whose 1899 social survey *The Philadelphia Negro* introduced the German style of social science to the study of race in the United States and whose masterpiece *The Souls of Black Folk* was cousin to the sort of fieldwork done by the Brothers Grimm to capture the spirit/soul (*Geist*) of many European nations (*Volk*).[21] The data-driven methods of German social science entered the Census Bureau at the turn of the century too, borne by the first genera-tion of professional scientists to run the newly permanent Census office—men like Walter F. Willcox, who studied in Berlin, and Joseph A. Hill, who earned a Ph.D. from the University of Halle (located near Leipzig).[22]

The biggest "brain" in the Commerce Department auditorium hailed from Princeton University. Frank W. Notestein had earned a Ph.D. un-der Walter Willcox before getting the nod to head the Office of Popula-tion Research, a research center housed at Princeton but funded entirely by external foundation grants. It was a think tank that used the money of America's robber barons to develop new theories about how popula-tions change and to train—one postdoctoral researcher at a time—a generation of mathematically sophisticated, data-driven demographers. Many of Notestein's chief patrons joined him in the auditorium, the first and foremost being Frederick Osborn. Officially, Osborn represented the Eugenics Research Association at the meeting. Behind the scenes, Osborn rubbed elbows with the Roosevelts, sat on elite boards, and arranged for the funding that ran the Office of Population Research. Osborn championed eugenics, and he believed demography would pro-vide the tools to make eugenic policies succeed.

Eugenics has become a dirty word these days (and with good reason), but in the early twentieth century the term commanded the respect of towering figures in science.[23] It was the study of selective human breeding bent on "improving" the population. It was thought, for instance, that such people would not have "defects" that would lead to poverty (as if being poor were an inborn biological trait). It was likewise believed that a better person would be white. Such beliefs were treated as serious science, and they became deadly serious. Across the Atlantic, Hitler's Nazi regime made eugenics central to its policies, often borrowing American laws and practices in doing so. Still, Osborn worked to show that his eugenics was different; it depended less on forced sterilization or government edicts saying who could or couldn't have children and instead sought to engineer society so that only the already well-off, who he believed were necessarily superior, would reproduce. As the historian Emily Klancher Merchant has explained, he reasoned that "manipulating the social and economic contexts in which childbearing decisions were made in order to encourage some people to have more children and other people to have fewer children was perfectly fine."[24] Osborn believed demography (and data) could make possible this kind of eugenic nudging—for example, distributing contraception at no cost to the poor while doling out college scholarships to the children of college graduates.

Dublin had published his own eugenic research. "If we can be careful to control, or better yet entirely check, the reproduction of the obviously unfit, we are in no danger of racial deterioration," he told his fellow statisticians in 1925.[25] But Dublin unsettled some usual eugenic racial hierarchies. He pointed out that if one looked at the longevity of groups in the United States, the much-favored Anglo-Saxon stock—the English and the Germans—who were thought to be superior were actually outperformed, outlived, by Russian immigrants, who were predominantly Jews. This inconvenient fact cast doubt on the racial hierarchies that eugenics was busy building to differentiate between "lower" and "higher" races of white people.[26] Though he rarely (if ever) said as much publicly, the question was personal for Dublin.

There was a reason he and his Ph.D. had ended up in the business world and not among the academics. That reason was Dublin's Jewish heritage. He was born in Lithuania in 1882. According to 1930 census records, his parents were both born in "Russia," and Dublin's "mother tongue" was "Yiddish."[27] Dublin grew up in New York City and attended the City University of New York, which was at that time teeming with smart, ambitious, socially minded Jews. Dublin seldom spoke of his background, but his mentors and his peers did. His advisor at Columbia declined to recommend him for any academic positions. An eminent Johns Hopkins biologist disliked Dublin for his resistance to birth control but also because he deemed Dublin "the vilest product of low Jew germ-plasm it has been my fortune to meet"—this from a 1921 letter to a colleague.[28] Whether or not Dublin identified with his religious or ethnic background—indeed, in years spent studying his life, I never found him to refer to himself as Jewish—antisemitism had profoundly shaped and limited his career. Perhaps that made it all a bit sweeter as he walked through the colonnaded halls and into the Commerce Department auditorium. He had ended up on top, at least for that day.

In his triumph, did Dublin reflect on who was missing from that room? For one, he would have spotted only two women in that auditorium. That was not because women didn't do statistics or deal with data. As Dublin well knew, many women excelled in statistical work. Dublin co-authored a number of studies with his assistant, Bessie Bunzel, and Metropolitan Life employed many highly skilled women computers and clerks.[29] Dublin also corresponded with the Census Bureau's most skilled mathematician, a woman named Elbertie Foudray. His daughter, Mary, showed up in the 1940 census listed as an "economist" working for a "social agency"—she was, in fact, directing the National Consumers League.[30] Women often excelled in statistical work, but only a few (like Mary Dublin) were promoted to positions of power. Then as now, they did not get equal representation in the rooms where the big decisions were made.

Nor, for that matter, did anyone who wasn't white. That only white people were represented in the Commerce auditorium was no mere accident. In December 1938, the census director, William Lane Austin, had written to the secretary of commerce. He had raised "a suggestion" he had received that "there should be a Negro member" on the census committee on population, probably "the head of Tuskegee Institute" Dr. Frederick Douglass Patterson, a veterinary scientist. Austin opined that bringing in a Black representative was "not essential at this time."[31] His bosses at Commerce appear to have agreed.

For his part, Louis Dublin was a prominent racial liberal. Metropolitan Life, his employer, dominated the market for insuring African Americans—it held two-thirds of all policies on Black lives in the United States in the 1920s.[32] As a result, Dublin had millions of Black policyholders' data to use to prove the vitality of Black America. In the face of prominent voices predicting that Black people outside of enslavement were destined for extinction, Dublin insisted that African Americans were merely lagging behind whites in terms of life expectancy and were bound to catch up in a matter of decades. Dublin's optimism didn't stop Metropolitan Life from treating African Americans as their de facto subprime risks, though—it probably even encouraged the practice. Black policyholders paid more for less coverage than their white counterparts of similar age, health, and circumstances. The data that Dublin used to predict a better future for African Americans emerged from a segregated insurance system designed to extract value from an oppressed, poor population.[33] So, again, it probably did not surprise Dublin that he had been invited to convene a whites-only gathering to decide how the American population should be measured. In the world where he operated, this was how decisions got made.

I had read about this conference and seen it mentioned in many places as I began studying the 1940 census. In the context of later controversies, particularly over a question about income, this conference was frequently invoked to justify the census's decisions, to show that they had been made by expert, responsible men. Yet for the first couple of years of my research, I found no detailed records from the conference. I dug through file after file, box after box in the National Archives, to no avail. I did not think I would ever discover what actually happened in that room. Then, in what would be my final trip to the archives in the summer of 2019, I was working my way through Director Austin's papers, and there it was: the summary minutes of the meeting, one that (although not a complete transcript) would allow me to reconstruct, more or less, how the Question Men built the data's frame.

Dublin called the meeting to order. The Census Bureau had provided a draft of the "schedule" of questions to be asked in 1940. "Let us satisfy ourselves," said Dublin, "that the proper items have been included; that the items which have been deleted are those which can best be spared"; and that, on the whole, the census questions reflected "the best judgment of this Conference."[34] Dublin turned the room's attention away from the columns in the hallways to the columns that would organize each census sheet. The conference's attendees controlled the allocation of space on a 23¾" x 12½" sheet of paper, a valuable, limited resource. Census officials thought 32 numbered columns, the count in 1930, was the most that could be squeezed into that space. Asking a new question meant adding a new column, which meant that some other question, some other column, had to go. Each new question had the potential to reveal something about the country and its inhabitants, but it would also necessarily obscure some other aspect of the American experience.

The choices that Dublin and his peers were making would have consequences.

The census "made" the facts that its columns defined. It hid the facts that its columns denied.

Two decades earlier, in 1920, those consequences had been startlingly clear. That year, almost half the space on the form was devoted to questions about the citizenship status of Americans, about where each was born and their "mother tongue" and the place of birth and mother tongue of each person's parents. In the ensuing decade, nativist voices in Congress used that data to draw attention to the growing population of foreign-born Americans who hailed from "undesirable races"—especially Italians, Eastern Europeans, and Russian Jews—and to frame that population as a problem. The solution was immigration restriction: make entry to the country illegal for all but a few, and rig the immigration quotas to fence out undesirables as much as possible. (The United States pretended to be against discrimination among white races and wanted to avoid any international embarrassment that might arise from insulting European nations; the country had given up any pretense of nondiscrimination against Asians much earlier with the 1882 Chinese Exclusion Act.) So Congress turned again to census data. Congress used 1920 census figures and earlier census data on nativity to construct a measure of the percentage of the population that traced some part of its origins to each nation of the world and it set immigration quotas to match. By design, the system amplified the Englishness of the American population, and so Great Britain enjoyed the highest quota. In describing the national-origins principle, Congress excluded freedpeople and Native Americans from the analysis. That legislative trick denied Africa the quota space that would otherwise have been due it in recognition of the millions of Americans descended from Africans who had been kidnapped and shipped across the Atlantic and into slavery.[35]

The census in 1920 showcased immigration and foreignness but kept a stony silence about another issue facing the country. Southern states, aided and abetted by Northern indifference, had suppressed the vote of their African American citizens in the closing decades of the nineteenth century. So Black activists from organizations like the NAACP began to press their cases. They demanded that Congress penalize states for disfranchisement, as the Fourteenth Amendment to the U.S. Constitution dictated: offending states should have representation decreased in Congress in proportion to the percentage of their population prevented from voting. To this demand that the Constitution be obeyed, members of both parties, from North and South, were able to reply: alas, there is no data on the numbers of those so disfranchised.[36] "Are you allowed to vote?" had not been a question on the census, and its absence conveniently allowed the persistence of white supremacy and gross racial injustice.

The choices made in setting the questions for a census thus shaped the policies that could be dreamed up, argued for, and executed. That was why Dublin's committee had convened, to provide guidance and justification for deceptively prosaic decisions (that is, which questions would be typed on a paper form) that might turn out to change the course of the country.

In every suggestion to add a new question or to take one away, we must look for a set of deeper values and concerns and even a distinct way of thinking about what it means to be a person. Two weeks before the conference convened, the chairman of the House of Representatives' Committee on the Census telephoned Director Austin to request the addition of a question concerning "incapacitation" or, as we might say today, "disability."[37] Chairman Matthew Dunn, who had lost sight in both eyes by the age of twenty,[38] sought a return to an earlier census tradition (ended in 1930) that concerned itself with the capacities of Americans' bodies.[39] When conference attendees from the Association of Statisticians of American Religious Bodies petitioned for two questions "on religious affiliation," they sought to bind religion to governance in a new (constitutionally questionable) way. As the historian and legal scholar Barbara Welke has noted, "The U.S. Census, which from the beginning marked the population by sex and race, and, beginning in the 1830s by disability, never inquired as to religious identity."[40] These religious statisticians hoped for the first time to cast every American counted by the census as an actual or potential church member, as souls that were saved or were not. One request sought to restore disability as a central federal concern, while the other intended to draw religious practice to the fore for the first time. Both would fail.

Representatives from the expanding federal government, from the Veterans Administration and the Social Security Board, made their own requests, casting every American as a potential bearer of an entitlement. They sought to join the census to their administrative system for ensuring Americans got what their government promised them. The War and Navy departments asked that "usual occupation" be added alongside present occupation, a recognition of the damage done by the Great Depression. The military anticipated war—indeed, war had already come to most of the world—and so military leaders looked to the census for a catalog not only of the nation's present productive capacities but also of its productive potential. What work a person could do mattered to military planners as much as the realities forced upon workers by the ongoing economic disaster.

These, though, were not the issues that most concerned the assembled conferees. They cared much more about the future of America's breeding stock, the condition of America's housing, the fate of its cities and countryside, and, most of all, about Americans' incomes, about their purchasing power and their standards of living.

First up was sex. It was Frank Notestein who explained that studying reproductive potential was even more important than the study of industrial or agricultural production. According to Notestein, "The population of the United States is barely fertile enough to maintain itself." This was a situation the country shared with "much of the western world," he argued. "When this fact is revealed to the general public through the publication of the results of the 1940 census of population, some definite plan will be called for."[41] Census data would inform pronatalist policies. Notestein believed census data could reveal which groups were not bearing their fair share of offspring and which were bearing too many, and it could help explain *why* Americans now had fewer children. The problem was not only that reproduction had slackened but that those families Notestein most wanted to have more children—generally well-off, white, native-born families—were having fewer. Notestein never mentioned "race suicide," and yet behind his warnings loomed the fear of the white race losing out in some imagined battle of births.

Dublin assigned Notestein to a committee to thrash out the merits of his idea, and it did not take it long to reach a consensus: figuring out just how quickly the white American race was falling behind was indeed important. It was not, however, so important that it deserved one of the census sheet's precious thirty-two columns. It was, instead, just important enough to warrant cheating the limits of the census. It was just important enough to justify radically reimagining the census.

The census had always been, as required by the Constitution, an "actual enumeration" of the population.[42] The census counted the people, as governments had done since antiquity, since (we can say with little exaggeration) people figured out how to write down numbers.[43] But new

possibilities for counting people and for learning about them arose in
the nineteenth century, when a branch of mathematics most famous for
how useful it was in settling debts incurred by gentlemen playing dice
met up with the vast troves of data generated by a new kind of bureaucratic nation-state.[44] Probability met statistics.

The tools of probability, apart from pencil and paper, were dice to be
rolled (like at a craps table), spinners to be spun (like roulette wheels),
and urns filled with balls (as in a lottery drawing). Did I mention that
probability was famous for its utility to gamblers? A wanderer who
stumbled into a probability laboratory might be forgiven for thinking it
a casino. Inside the Census Bureau, researchers had been working for
some time to bring that casino into the census.[45] If it was possible to
draw a few balls of different colors from an urn and from those draws
make a precise prediction of how many balls of each color were in that
urn, why couldn't the census draw a few people from the population, ask
how many children they'd had, and then make a precise prediction
about the entire nation's fertility? When the urn was the entire United
States of America, its people became the balls. Here was the democratic
"experiment," cast in a radical, mathematical light.

As it happened, the Census Bureau's scientists had invented just such
a technique, a method called "sampling." The census count in 1940
amounted to a count of all the balls in the urn. But it was also something
like the urn itself—the census count was a container for all Americans,
from which a "sample" could be plucked out at random and examined
more carefully. Since that sample had to be drawn from all across the
country, and since bureau researchers hoped to spare themselves the expense of sending out enumerators again after the first census, the census
sheet would be designed so that the sampling happened in real time
alongside the full count. Two lines on each enumeration sheet would be
pre-marked, and whichever person happened to land in that predetermined line during the count would be subject to further scrutiny. They'd
be asked a host of supplemental questions, and chief among those were
to be questions of fertility.

While a subcommittee discussed the potential uses of sampling in
the census, another worked under an order to consider how the census

should handle housing issues. It was customary to ask if a particular home or apartment was rented or owned and how much the home was worth or how high the rent. In 1930, the census schedule added a question to the housing section asking if each household possessed a radio set—it was a reasonable question and one that could help gauge the reach of a crucial new form of mass media. The reach of radio mattered to government (after all, a few years later Franklin Roosevelt would use the radio to invite himself into Americans' homes for a series of "fireside chats" explaining his fight against the Great Depression), and certainly it mattered to advertisers and to those to whom they sold their advertisements. Not everyone thought the question was reasonable, though—one Manhattanite wrote a satirical poem and sent it to the president to complain that of all her "secrets for Uncle Sam," she was being asked about her radio. It seemed to her "a business plot," as indeed it probably was.[46]

The radio question was set to be axed to make room for more pressing inquiries. But questions concerning housing had only grown more pressing in the last ten years. The U.S. government now had a direct hand in the housing markets, ensuring mortgages and regulating loans. President Roosevelt and his entire administration wanted Americans to live in good homes, but did they? How far had the nation's standards fallen? For those in the housing business, the questions were: What potential markets lay untapped? What neighborhoods needed new homes now or would need them soon? (Not for nothing, but the Sears catalog sold homes too.) The housing subcommittee couldn't finish its work in a day, not when tackling so large a topic. In the end, the Census Bureau found a way to cheat the limits of the questionnaire again. This time it convinced Congress to authorize an entire Census of Housing to run alongside the population and agriculture censuses. The same enumerators would fill out all the forms: one for people, one for farms, and now one for homes. The housing schedule had thirty-one columns all to itself. How old was the family's dwelling? Did they have running water? Indoor toilets? What sort of lighting? With all that added space, the radio question remained intact.

The biggest shift on the census sheet came through adding columns for the place (such as a town or city), county, and state where each person enumerated had lived five years earlier. These questions displaced those about the place of birth of parents and mother tongues, as fit the changing times. International migration no longer worried the men in this room, now that immigration had been so strictly limited by law. Migration within the United States, on the other hand, concerned them a great deal. Everything had come crashing down over the last decade, an economic catastrophe followed closely by ecological disaster, leaving Americans across the country in ruins. Farmers who had somehow managed to hold on when prices collapsed and stayed collapsed for years, farmers who had avoided foreclosure (frequently by a major life insurer, like Dublin's Metropolitan), who had held on to their land—they had been both lucky and resourceful and were rewarded for that luck and resourcefulness with the privilege of waking up with dust in their teeth.[47] They became the migrants Woody Guthrie called "Dust Bowl refugees" heading west seeking opportunity and following the crops. Once in California, more often than not they were cursed as "Okies," regardless of where they came from. They scraped by in the tent camps captured by the photographer Dorothea Lange, who worked for the government's Farm Security Administration, charged with documenting the plight of the luckless toilers.[48] The census in 1940 would continue that work, serving as a tool for tracing the movement of the Dust Bowl refugees.

Then there was the movement of Southern tenant farmers and freedpeople and their children who were leaving the cotton fields to try out new lives in cities in the North. As the cultural historian Saidiya Hartman has put it, "*The Negro was on strike.* By 1920, it was undeniable. The small movement of black folks from the south, which began as early as the 1880s, had become a mass movement. It was nothing short of a refusal of the plantation regime."[49] Sharecroppers and tenants, shorn of political influence, subject to campaigns of terror and violence, walked away. The census in 1940 would keep accounts of that "general strike" of Black farm workers, of their ongoing "Great Migration."

The most significant change to the entire census sheet was actually simply the addition of a thin column reserved for marking down income from wages. Those who crafted "the income question," as it came to be called, recognized that it might be controversial. Ironically, that potential for controversy convinced them that the income question should be asked of *everyone*. If income were only sampled, they reasoned, neighbors might talk and wonder why one person was so singled out while others were not. Such conversations might lead to worry and embarrassment that was better avoided. The Census Bureau hoped that income would not turn out to be controversial and consoled itself that Canada had been successfully asking such a question for decades.

Asking the income question signaled a new turn in the American economic and political order. In a land of farms and cottage industry, few had worked for wages. Asking the income question signaled that the United States was no longer a land dominated by propertied wealth, feudal relations, family enterprise, or mass enslavement—it had become a land of wage workers. Such was the path forecast for all modern societies by Marx and Engels in the *Communist Manifesto* in 1848. Wage labor took root in the earliest years of the independent American republic, particularly in New England, with its rivers jammed with mills and factories. The spread of wage labor enabled the rise of life insurance corporations, like Dublin's Metropolitan—because life insurance served as a modern substitute for land and wealth. It protected families against the pains and insecurity that came with the loss of a wage earner.[50] The eventual dominance of the wage called into being the new welfare state. Roosevelt's Social Security system, after all, offered the promise of a secure retirement funded by money automatically drawn from the wages of workers.

The income question united the conference's disparate coalitions. Income information, set to be tabulated at as fine a resolution as possible, promised a map of purchasing power to be exploited by big business. That same income information, alongside occupation categories and unemployment data, promised labor unions, the Department of Labor, and the Public Works Administration the information they needed to fight for higher wages or better housing or jobs programs. Notestein and the academic eugenicists sought correlations between income levels and the number of children that couples had. They wanted to know if wealth encouraged people—especially white people—to have children, or if (as they feared) high wages somehow led to barren wombs. Business, labor, the New Deal, and science came together to seek a new vision of the nation—whether as markets, workers, or populations—predicated on the paycheck.

The Question Men conferred for two days before they got to go home. They left behind a brief transcript of their debates and discussions. More important, they left behind the 1940 census schedule—a document they framed to be itself a frame, a frame for the nation's data, a frame for every individual and the aspects of them that mattered to the nation. "You cannot know your country, unless your country knows you." Of course, what the country could "know" about you was limited to what these men in a D.C. auditorium deemed worth knowing.

The historian of quantification Caitlin Rosenthal teaches students to read the "frame" of the data—the column headings and row names, whatever organizes and constrains the data. One looks through the frame to see what the numbers say, as is only natural. But the frame has its own story to tell, a story about those who decided what mattered and what didn't, a story about the values and worldviews of the data's architects. And one cannot fully understand any data unless one knows what it includes, what it privileges, what it deprecates, and what it overlooks. Reading the frame of the census helps us see and understand what the men in that auditorium cared about and to appreciate how the census was shaped by their concerns.

A short film would play at theaters across the country calling the 1940 census "the greatest inventory of the world's greatest democracy."[51] The Question Men opened the door to that language, not necessarily the superlatives ("greatest"!), but certainly the logistical lingo: their census *was* an *inventory* of democracy. Their census took stock of the nation's economic capacity, its labor reserve, its standards of living, its living spaces, its reproductive potential. Their census inventoried markets, workers, and populations; it imagined democracy as the efficient management of whatever it counted.

I suspect Louis Dublin felt good as he boarded his train home for New York. Framing data can be deeply satisfying work. Set the questions, label the columns, and let the neat grid of straight lines do its thing:

establish order in a world where order is far too rare. That order would remain when the final data was translated into *facts*, each accorded a proper place on a statistical table.

The job of making a messy reality fit into the Question Men's frame, the job of finding the right place in the grid for every person—that job fell to those who would meet at the nation's doorsteps. In the meantime, Dublin headed back to the skyscrapers of Manhattan.

WHO DUBLIN SAW, AS DEPICTED IN THE DATA
THAT THEY, THE QUESTION MEN, DESIGNED

This is a census-data roll call for the 1939 Washington, D.C., conference that determined the questions for the 1940 census. In the following tables, the census records for as many conference attendees as possible have been snipped and pasted together. It wasn't possible to track down each attendee's 1940 census record, so these tables are not complete, but in them we can see many of the attendees through the framework that they themselves designed. The first entries display (most of) the government's presence.

THE GOVERNMENT'S ATTENDEES

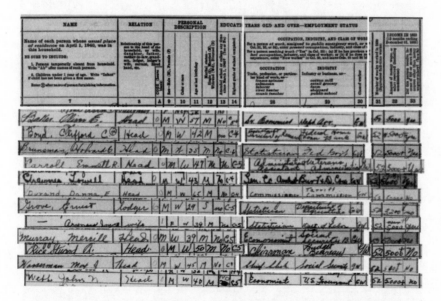

Note there are only two people not labeled "head" in column 8. One is also the only person with an "F" in the next column, indicating she was female. Her name entry reads "— Aryness Joy" with the line before Aryness standing in for the last name of her husband (not pictured). Joy, an economist and statistician, went by Aryness Joy in her Labor Department office, though, so her professional name is printed here.

Note, too, the wages earned. Nearly every person here is listed as receiving $5,000+ annually, placing them all in the census' highest income bracket. The sole exception among the government workers at the conference was a Department of Agriculture statistician named Ernest Grove ($3,200), the other person not labeled "head."

Finally, note that most of these attendees either finished college (indicated by a "C-4" in column 14) or went on to graduate school (indicated by "C-5," regardless of how many years of graduate education an individual completed).

THE CENSUS BUREAU CONTINGENT

Note the occupations listed in column 28. Here we find a surfeit of statisticians, alongside geographers, a publicist, a clerk, and an economist. The one blank occupation slot belongs to William Mott Steuart, who also reported earning no wages in 1939: that's because he was retired, having been the census director during the 1930 count.

THE BUSINESS LEADERS

Note new entries now in column 30, where the "GWs" of prior tables (which indicated "government workers") are now replaced by "PW" for "private worker" or "E" for "employer."

Noel Sargent in the second line has his occupation listed as "economist," which doesn't quite capture his role as a leader of a powerful industry lobby, the National Association of Manufacturers.

Note the crossed-out lines in column 28 indicating Robert Elkington Wood's occupation. "Retired Army officer" has been written in and then struck through. Who knows for certain what happened here, but it seems likely that Wood (who liked to be called General Wood) insisted it be written there, and a census data editor later removed it. "Executive" is written underneath and remains there for the Sears, Roebuck and Company president.

WORKERS FOR SOCIAL WELFARE

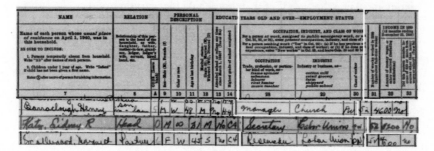

Note that these individuals work in heretofore unlisted industries: "church" or "labor union." They also make less money. Note that Margaret Scattergood is listed in column 8 as a "partner." What that means is discussed further in chapter 3.

THE PROFESSIONAL BRAINS

NAME	RELATION	PERSONAL DESCRIPTION				EDUCATION		YEARS OLD AND OVER—EMPLOYMENT STATUS		OCCUPATION, INDUSTRY, AND CLASS OF WORKER			INCOME IN 1939		
Name of each person whose usual place of residence on April 1, 1940, was in this household.	Relationship of this person to the head of the household									OCCUPATION	INDUSTRY				
										Trade, profession, or particular kind of work	Industry or business				
7	8	9	10	11	12	13	14			28	29	30	31	32	33
Ribault, Sarah	Head		M	W	60	M	W0			Trader	Insurance			52	5000
Fontaine, Frank	Head		M	W	45	M		C5		Teacher	College	Pd		52	4900
May, Stanley	Head		M	W	44	M		C4		Asst. forester	Rockfeller Lumber	GM		52	2000
Robertson, Frank	Head		M	W	37	M		C5		Research worker	University	Pd		52	5000
OSBORN, FREDERICK ⊗	head		M	W	50	M		C5		capitalist scientist	banking publishing	OA		52	0
Schneider, Laurence 2	Head		M	W	63	M		C5		animal worker	animal research	Pd		52	5000
Stephan, Frederick	Head		M	W	36	M		C		Sr. statistician	Scientific Assoc	Pd			
Horton, Pascal	Head		M	W	47	M		C4		Consultant	Population Budget				

The occupations in column 28 for this group vary from "teacher" to "research worker" and even include a "capitalist scientist"—that last designation having been given to Frederick Osborn, the wealthy champion of eugenics. Osborn's industries are listed as both "banking" and "publishing," and he did not have to give up any information about his wages because he claimed to be operating on his "own account" as indicated by the "OA" in column 30.

Note that here, as in all the preceding tables, the entry for column 10 is "W," indicating "white" for the individual's race. Almost every entry throughout has been C-4 or C-5 in column 14, indicating college or graduate training. All save a few show "M" for "male" in column 9, and nearly all indicate that the person enumerated was the "head" of their household for census purposes.

2

Names and Negotiations

No person's name would appear in the published tables of numbers put out by the 1940 census. In those statistics, individuals were supposed to dissolve. Names abound, however, deeper in the data, in the manuscript census records. To know America, America had to know "you"; and America, in the guise of the Census Bureau, came to know "you" by a name written on a census sheet.

What's in a name? Now, that is a very old question, familiar to many a teenager today tasked by a teacher with reading *Romeo and Juliet*.[1] It turns out to be a fruitful question for thinking about what happened at each doorstep, where census enumerator and enumerated stood face-to-face, filling in the Question Men's form. "Name" was one of the first questions to be answered, one of the first tests of whether what followed would be a cooperative exchange or would instead culminate in conflict.

What's in a name? That turns out to be the perfect question to show-case how power relations shape every census record and every bit of data, often in ways we can never fully account for.

What's in a name? A negotiation, perhaps? And so much more.

In 1944, one of the great poets of the era, Langston Hughes, published a poem about issues of identity and the negotiations involved in writing a name in the census,[2] about the names we choose and those that are imposed on us. It began like this:

The census man,
The day he came round,
Wanted my name
To put it down.

Hughes's protagonist refused to let the enumerator put her name down just any old way. When that census taker told Alberta K. Johnson that he needed to write out her full middle name, she insisted he could not, that he must not. He wanted it to be "K-A-Y," but she said it was simply K. The poem is lively and beautiful, a wicked takedown of "the man" or, more precisely, the "census man."

Reading Hughes's poem forced me, for the first time, to think carefully about the "Name" column in the manuscript census sheets, a column that had previously seemed to me the most simple and straightforward.

Hughes's poem inspired this chapter and fundamentally reshaped the way I think about census data, even though the conflict at the heart of his poem is silly, absurd, and just plain wrong. Here's the thing: There would have been no reason to fight about a middle initial, since no census enumerator would have insisted on writing a middle name out fully. Middle names were not required and seldom recorded on census sheets. Langston Hughes—who did not himself answer the questions of the enumerator nine years earlier—appears in the 1940 schedules as just plain Langston Hughes (with the job title "writer" in the industry "literature"). His roommates, similarly: Kit Clark, Dell Ingram, and William Artis (who answered the questions for the others, as indicated by a circled "X" next to his name). Hughes's neighbor (an inspiration?) appears as Alberta Maynard.[3] Not a middle name among them. Some people did have middle initials—such as the man taking the census that day, Thomas *W.* Moseley.

The instructions to enumerators in 1940 read: "Enter the last name or surname, then the given name in full, and the initial of the middle name, if any . . ."[4] They even allow for a first initial followed by a full middle name, according to the preference of the person being interviewed. There was no reason a census taker would object to Alberta K. Johnson's name.

Yet the poem is not wrong that encounters with census takers could place in peril a person's dignity or self-sovereignty. That is one of its deeper truths. The literary scholar Kasia Boddy highlights the poem's concern with "who controls identity"[5]—Alberta K. Johnson wrestles her enumerator for the right to be known as she wishes to be, as her mother named her. The scholar Dellita L. Martin has written, in this vein: "The census taker's ignorance of the black naming tradition and his arrogance combine to ignite Madam's temper. He does not know, or even care, that many black people choose to use initials in place of a full name because it signifies distinction, because it marks a privilege to name oneself or one's own . . ."[6] Martin assumes the enumerator is white in this reading, which seems reasonable; however, that wasn't the case for Langston Hughes, whose household had been enumerated in 1940 by a Black man. But if the census taker is imagined as white, then the fight over identity takes on additional significance.

The race critical code studies scholar Ruha Benjamin has written, "I will admit, something that irks me about conversations regarding naming trends is how distinctly African American names are set apart as comically 'made up' . . . Blackness is routinely conflated with cultural deficiency, poverty, and pathology . . . it harbors a willful disregard for the fact that everyone's names were at one point made up!"[7] Benjamin wasn't writing about Hughes's poem, but she can still help us understand what was happening in that poetic encounter—the census taker's disdain for "K." perhaps emerged from his assumption that Black names were, on their faces, more "made up" than everyone else's names.

"Madam" Alberta K. Johnson fights for her name. That name was a gift from her mother. By changing it, by writing it differently, the census man would dishonor both mother and daughter. The poem reminds us that more is happening in this encounter than a simple act of counting. Respect and honor were also up for grabs.

Johnson didn't set out to fight, though. In fact, she couldn't have played her role more by the book. When asked her name, she gives it in the most proper of forms: last name, then first name, then middle initial—just as the enumerator should write it down. Johnson has sized up the situation properly: a bureaucracy has come calling, and bureaucracies like their names directory style.

In the other poems Hughes wrote about his fictional "Madam," Alberta K. Johnson carves out a living in a world quite like our own: one dominated by bureaucratic institutions whose offices might well send unwelcome visitors to her home. She's turned down when seeking a job from the federal work program, the WPA. She turns out a rent collector after showing him the leaking roof, cracked windows, and scurrying rats. She ducks the phone company when it wants her to pay for a call from a no-good lover. She refuses to file a report with a Juvenile Court official inquiring after an adopted child. Johnson well knows how offices like to see a person's name—directory style—but that's about the only accommodation she'll make to any institutional desire.

The lives of the people Langston Hughes wrote about were being increasingly hemmed in by bureaucratic rules. Legal papers mattered more and more, and, thus, so did stable, official names (which, if they did not exist in a stable, official fashion, would have to be made stable and official). This is another truth the poem offers: that names don't just belong to their bearers but also play a powerful role in the world. All births had to be documented after 1933, when all the U.S. states adopted new laws and practices. Each birth certificate held a blank for a name—a stable, official name. Migrants entering the United States needed papers now too—visas or permits or health certificates with their names on them—and those without papers became a new class of people: the "undocumented," the "illegal aliens." (It hadn't been possible for a person to be "illegal" or "undocumented" throughout most of the nineteenth century, before the United States instituted immigration restrictions.)[8] Workers now needed paperwork too, just to get and keep a job. To satisfy the child-labor provisions of the Fair Labor Standards Act of 1938, workers might need a document proving their age. The rollout of the Social Security insurance program in 1937 also required paper proofs of identity and age, and in many fields it became impossible to get a job without a stable, official Social Security number tied to a stable, official name.[9]

As paper records waxed in power, the Census Bureau got to work, digging into its manuscript census sheets to create official documents based on prior enumerations showing a person's name and age. In the late 1930s, a Works Progress Administration project aided the census in this arduous task by building a new kind of name index, called Soundex.[10] The bureau knew as well as anybody that its records didn't always spell names properly and that spellings shifted over time, and so it built an alphabetized index based on phonetics that allowed bureau officials to find any record based on the sound of a name and so provide people with the evidence they needed to get along in a document-hungry world.

Reading the data in the light of Langston Hughes's poem, I realized that thinking about "names" could help us realize and appreciate the growing importance of bureaucracy in the lives of ordinary people, an importance not fully captured in the 1940 numbers alone. By lingering on "Madam's" middle initial, we can appreciate how bureaucratic empowerment made the data recorded about each person more consequential and, thus, made encounters at the doorstep all the more fraught.

Johnson didn't try to pick a fight about her name. The enumerator did. He exerted his power, the power that came with holding the pen. He took a tongue-lashing for it, but who knows what he wrote down? Johnson could make her stand, but the enumerator could write down what he wanted to.

Every name we read today on a census sheet was the result of just such an encounter. A person asserted their identity, said their name. An enumerator might accept only some part of that identity, some version of that name, and record that. All we can read is the enumerator's scrawl—any negotiations or fights are lost to us. The doorstep encounter where the data get made almost always remains a mystery.

The census taker negotiated the "names" of doorsteps themselves even before it negotiated the names of the people standing on them.

In 1940, enumerators began each census entry by writing down an address. Column 1 asks for a street name, and column 2 for a house number. The form presumed a single-family home as the norm. There was no space for apartment numbers. Enumerators had to be particularly creative in some circumstances, finding a way to address a home with nothing remotely like a conventional address. In rural California, enumerators often left blank the spot for a street name and house number and wrote in things like "1 mi. S. of Rosedale Hy + 1 mi. E. of Junetta Ave"[11]—this to indicate a camp for refugees from the Dust Bowl of Oklahoma, a tent town located about a mile south and east of two roadways. The job got a bit easier in more organized camps, like those constructed to house National Park Service laborers near Yosemite, where "Cabin 12" precedes "Tent 46."[12] Then there were the boat people. Hazel F. Knight, making the rounds in Seattle at Fisherman's Wharf, solved the problem by writing "Boat" in the space for the house number, followed sometimes by the boat's proper name, a *Rover* or a *Rudolf* or an *Azalea*.[13]

Numerical addresses owed their very existence to censuses. House numbers are essentially names state offices assigned to lodgings. According to one historian, the idea of marking houses with consecutive numbers dates to the desire of Enlightenment monarchs—like the Austrian Maria Theresa—to make a better count of men who could be conscripted into the military. Houses were also sometimes numbered to count minority groups, like the Jews of Prague in one of the earliest cases, in 1727, or to make it easier for rulers to find places where soldiers could be billeted.[14] (This practice of quartering soldiers in private homes was common enough, and widely enough disliked, to be proscribed during peacetime in the U.S. Bill of Rights, in the Third Amendment.) Odd-numbered houses on one side of the street, even-numbered houses on the other, had to be invented too. Philadelphia, the nation's temporary capital at the time, alternated odds and evens in order to make it easier to conduct the federal census in 1790.[15] New York City copied its neighbor in 1793, as did Paris in 1805.[16] Though people quickly came to rely on numerical addresses to find one another, send letters, or navigate strange and growing cities, those uses were accidental benefits of an apparatus meant to serve the data makers in imperial or national bureaucracies.

While every stoop was to be thus "named" in the earliest censuses, very few of the nation's people were afforded the same honor. Census takers recorded only the names of heads of households, disproportionately adult white men. For instance, an enumerator near Philadelphia's wharf in 1790 wrote down a name, like that of the carpenter Robert Storey, followed by a number indicating that his household held three white men over fifteen years old, five white males fifteen or under, and seven white women (for whom ages were unspecified). Note that the census, from the start, concerned itself with marking people as either "white" or not, and as either men or women. These were distinctions the census gave added significance. Storey's household—which may have included journeymen or apprentice woodworkers, as well as his own children—included no enslaved persons and no "other free persons," a category obliquely encompassing free people of color. Native Americans were explicitly excluded from the count.

This system of counting and naming derived from—and reinforced—the practices of early American democracy. All inhabitants—be they citizens or not, whether grown or infants, male or female—were to be counted and represented in Congress (apart from excluded Native Americans and enslaved people who were each counted as three-fifths of a person). Only a select group in each state possessed the power to choose those representatives in Congress, and only a select group—usually just white men possessing property—could actually vote. Storey's Pennsylvania was one of the most democratic states, insofar as its constitution had opened up the franchise to all tax-paying freedmen, which meant that nearly every person listed in the census as a head of household would have had the right to vote.[17] The census represented everyone, but it dignified only free heads of each "family" with an individual name, a distinct identity.

Then, in 1840, this way of structuring the data failed in a spectacular fashion, resulting in a long and bitter controversy. That controversy concerned slavery and freedom, as did so many other controversies in the decade preceding the eruption into civil war.[18] A doctor who specialized in mental illness—and who knew intimately the statistics kept by insane asylums, which were surprisingly statistical institutions[19]—noticed irregularities in the published returns in 1842. One of those irregularities concerned the extraordinarily high rate of insanity among free Blacks in the North. At first the doctor attributed this to a supposed racial inferiority: he assumed that Black bodies and minds could not bear the burdens of modern freedom. In the ensuing years, prominent voices among the slaveholding elite picked up and amplified this argument since it justified the persistence of slavery. But the doctor recanted it after further study, deciding, on closer inspection, that the numbers had to be false: in some extreme cases, towns in the North that had no Black residents nevertheless were listed as harboring multiple insane Black people. Southern elites persisted in believing that the statistics portrayed something true about Blackness, while their opponents insisted that the statistics had been intentionally perverted by the proslavery officials responsible for the census, chiefly that great apologist for slavery, John C. Calhoun.

More recently, the historian Patricia Cline Cohen explained that a technical flaw in data management was responsible for the illusion of mass insanity among free Blacks. The forms for the 1840 census had become impracticably elaborate. For each household, the enumerators had to wend their way through more than seventy columns of blanks, finding the right one to fill in for each case. They had to tally all the white males in each household between the ages of zero and five, five and ten, or thirty and forty, and so on, and then do the same for women. Then they had to tally the male free people of color under ten, from ten to twenty-four, twenty-four to thirty-six, and so on, and then do the same for women, and then do the same for enslaved men and women. Only then did the enumerator get to columns asking for tallies of household members engaged in various classes of labor, and then for whites who were deaf (in three more age groups), then white and blind, then the white "insane and idiots," and then all those same categories for "colored persons," all followed by tallies of people being educated (in primary schools, in grammar schools, in colleges, etc.). On close examination of the actual forms filled out by enumerators, Cohen discovered that in the quest to fit all the categories on the same page, census printers had made a "blind and insane" grouping in the "white" section, yet in the "colored" section, they created an "insane and idiots" grouping. Oddly, it was in these "colored" columns that Cohen found tallies for many all-white households with older inhabitants, some of whom were presumably senile and likely (in 1840) to be labeled "idiots" as a result. Evidently some enumerators, looking for a place to tally such individuals, simply used the column where the word "idiot" appeared. They placed anyone they labeled an "idiot" in the same column, which was supposed to be a column only for African Americans. They created, in the process, the illusion of excess idiocy and insanity affecting African Americans. A missing word within an overly elaborate form appears to have been at the root of the misleading evidence pointing to an epidemic of idiocy and insanity in free Black communities, an epidemic that never existed. The fight over slavery fueled the controversy, but it likely began with a failure in the data management system.

In 1850, the census began enumerating each free individual by name. The great American philosopher Ralph Waldo Emerson called this time the "age of the first person singular."[20] It stemmed from and contributed to a great expansion of American democracy, a period during which free men, regardless of how little property they owned, asserted and frequently achieved a universal right to the franchise.[21] That was a significant extension of democracy, which the census took even further by naming every free individual, not just those who could vote. The motivation for that extra step was as much bureaucratic as it was any abstract democratic principle, though. It enabled a more accurate tally of a growing population that the government wanted to parse into ever finer slices.

The decision to name each free person in the census count in 1850 had less to do with acknowledging the dignity of individuals than with preventing an 1840-style failure in the data system. If each person in a household was named and afforded a line on a form, that meant many more rows for the enumerator to fill in but—more important—far fewer columns. The enumerator would no longer have to place each person's age within the proper range in the proper part of the form or check a box for the right combination of race and insanity. The enumerator would simply fill in the answers for exactly the same characteristics for each person: an age for each, a race for each, marital status, etc. This simplification shifted some of the work of ordering, grouping, and adding away from the enumerator. All such processing would instead be done centrally, in offices with specially trained staff and eventually with machines.[22] The democratization of names in the census form came as part of the separation of census taking from data processing.

The painter Francis William Edmonds captured the census's transition to individual data in an 1854 canvas, *Taking the Census*. At the center of the image stands an amply fleshed patriarch, his feet planted on his own hearth. In earlier censuses, only this man's name would have been recorded by the white-bearded, gold-vested census taker, an "assistant marshal" hired for this purpose and apparently a man of some wealth and status himself. The census taker, tended by a boy who carries his inkwell, would have listed the patriarch in 1840 and then left tally marks or a number for the other members of the household. Five such members are visible in the painting: three smirking children peek out from behind the skirts of a woman, probably their mother, who holds an infant. But in 1850, the census taker's task has changed, and so has the patriarch's. As he counts on his fingers, he appears to be grappling with some great intellectual challenge, while his family looks on in mirth and anticipation: will Father accomplish the task of naming all his children?

The painting reminds us that the individualization of the data did not bring with it social or political revolution. The subject of the painting, its central focus, remains a property-holding white man—even if the artist is having fun with him. The joke, after all, is the possibility that the father doesn't even know his own children's names or ages, but it does not cut deep. In fact, the effect of the joke is to justify that paternal ignorance while reaffirming the right of the patriarch to bloviate. Meanwhile, George Washington, the great patriarch of the American nation, looks on from a portrait over the fireplace, silently blessing the encounter.

Politics assured that the revolutionary potential of individualized data was minimized. The initial plan put forward by the statisticians called for the data of enslaved people to be gathered in individualized form too. Slaves would be enumerated by name, their family relations recorded, their ages and birthplaces collected. But proslavery politicians had no desire to generate new public knowledge about the people they forced into service. They did not want to generate fodder for abolitionist tracts, nor could they accept the possibility that by recording the names of the enslaved, the census would dignify each as a member of the nation. The Three-Fifths Compromise, made during the Constitutional Convention of 1787, meant that enslaved people counted only as partial people for the purposes of apportioning representation. The plan for the census of 1850 threatened to treat the enslaved as whole, entire persons— as persons with names. Congress, controlled by proslavery forces and their appeasers, put an end to that threat. The census act for 1850 insisted that the only names written on "slave schedules" were the names of slave owners.[23]

Power resides in the act of naming, in the receipt of a name, and in a name acknowledged. The refusal to acknowledge the names of enslaved persons had been an insult widely shared up through 1840, when most free people weren't named either, but that changed with the data revolution of 1850. Many a genealogical researcher has felt the injustice of a documentary snub that allows their free ancestors to be found, while those once enslaved lie buried in obscurity.[24]

The census used names to order its data. People, too, used their names, sometimes strategically, to make their way in the world. The utility of names, and the importance of asserting control over them, stands out in the story of a great American: an elegant writer, a fiery orator, an influential abolitionist whose reinterpretation of the Declaration of Independence made possible what Abraham Lincoln called a "new birth of freedom"—Frederick Douglass.

Douglass was probably counted in the 1830 census, but he would have appeared as a number, not as a name. A lonely "1" jotted down on a particular wide paper form, indicating a solitary male slave between the ages of ten and twenty-four in the household of Hugh Auld in Baltimore, might well stand for Douglass. We cannot say for sure that was he, because the census afforded him no name.[25] Nor did it name Auld's wife, who, Douglass tells us in his famous *Narrative of the Life of Frederick Douglass,* was named Sophia—the person who taught him to read. Nor did that census sheet name the other enslaved person in that household, a young woman who is not mentioned in Douglass's narrative either. Nor did it name the other eight free white people who lived in the house, one of whom must have been the child Thomas Auld, whom the young Douglass spent his own childhood caring for.

Frederick Douglass appeared in the census for the first time as a named person in 1840.[26] He had by that point run away from his enslavers and was living with his small family in their own home in New Bedford, Massachusetts, an abolitionist center that was home to many who were formerly enslaved.[27] If the enumerator knew Douglass's status as a fugitive, he made no note of it. Rather, Douglass appeared, by name, as head of his household and as a number "1" tallied under "Free Colored Persons" for males between ages twenty-four and thirty-six. An entry for a female between those same ages and one for a female under ten (both also under "Free Colored Persons") would have represented Anna Douglass and their baby daughter, Rosetta—neither of them appeared by name.

The enumerator probably did not know that Douglass's last name was just barely older than his daughter. Frederick had become "Frederick Douglass" in the New Bedford household of abolitionist Nathan Johnson, who sheltered fugitive enslaved persons, a couple of years before the census taker arrived to count him. It was to be the last of many names that he had used. His mother had given him the name Frederick Augustus Washington Bailey at his birth. In slavery, he trimmed the imperial glory and nationalist pride, leaving simply Frederick Bailey. When he fled Baltimore, he disguised himself as a sailor and disguised his name too, becoming Frederick Stanley for a little while. In New York, he stepped into another name, Frederick Johnson, and as Frederick Johnson he married Anna Murray—Johnson was the name on the couple's marriage certificate. Frederick found there to be an overabundance of Johnsons in New Bedford, though—"so many Johnsons," he complained—and so he sought yet another name. "I gave Mr. [Nathan] Johnson the privilege of choosing me a name," he later wrote. With Johnson's choice, Frederick Douglass was born, or reborn, in 1838.[28]

The rest of Frederick Douglass's growing household stopped being merely numbers in 1850—as did all other free people. His wife never appeared in the census as Anna Murray (her maiden name) or Anna Johnson (her first married name). She debuted in the records as Anna Douglass.

By the time of the 1850 enumeration, Frederick Douglass had moved to Rochester, New York, and had published the narrative of his escape from slavery. He was well on his way to becoming a celebrity. His book also told the story of his name. What, I wonder, did that enumerator in Rochester's seventh ward—a Mr. Warner—think when he wrote down Douglass's name in the census ledger? He must have known of the famous abolitionist and his newspaper, *The North Star*. Warner may have even read Douglass's celebrated narrative of his life as a slave and his escape to freedom. If he had, then Warner might have had reason to pause at the "Name" column.

Who stood before him? Was he enumerating Frederick Bailey or Frederick Stanley or Frederick Johnson or Frederick Douglass? Was that man's spouse Anna Murray or Anna Johnson or Anna Douglass? Census takers didn't ask for official papers, but had he insisted, he would have discovered on the marriage certificate that these were, in fact, Johnsons in the household.

That wasn't, and isn't, how names actually work, though. Warner could have been intimately familiar with the details of Douglass's narrative and might well have known all the complications of his identity, and he still would have written down "Frederick Douglass" without giving it a second thought. Douglass himself explained why: "I am more widely known by that name than by any of the others," and that fact was reason enough for Douglass to say, "I shall continue to use it as my own."[29] Douglass's story reminds us that names are things we *use*, as well as things that others *use* to grasp and hold on to a sense of us. Names don't spring fully formed from the platonic ideal of our identities. Names are social technologies, built and negotiated through extensive social systems. From 1850 on, one of the most important social systems to deal with names would be the census—and yet, when it comes to questions of identity, the census can tell us only so much.

A census record will tell us the name an enumerator wrote down, but it may not tell us the entire story. Even in the middle of the twentieth century, when names were supposed to be becoming a more regular, reliable social technology, there were still complications. Even as a phalanx of bureaucrats fought to assign each person a stable, official name, and even as those stable, official names became keys to accessing a new array of opportunities and entitlements, many individuals resisted (and resist still today). Names, as a result, can be surprisingly slippery.

This could be true even for the names of those appointed to manage the census, as is evidenced by the story of a midlevel census official whose ambiguous, overlapping identities cost him his job.

That official worked for the 1940 census's massive field operation as an assistant supervisor. The Census Bureau divided the country into more than one hundred areas, each with its own area office, presided over by an area manager. Each area office oversaw about a half dozen supervisor districts (sometimes more, sometimes less), headed up by a supervisor and usually an assistant supervisor. Those supervisors were charged with hiring and managing the teams of enumerators who conducted the counts within their enumeration districts. One of the assistant supervisors in a Los Angeles, California, district was named— well, actually, I won't give him a name just yet. Because his name, or more precisely his names, became a question of some importance in the context of a larger political controversy—and the story of his name or names speaks to the nature of names as they get recorded as data.

The roots of the controversy that swept up this mysterious official began in January 1939 when a newly elected Democrat took a seat in the seventy-sixth United States Congress representing Los Angeles County. As a member of the party in power, he enjoyed the privilege of picking a supervisor and an assistant supervisor for his district. The *Los Angeles Times* announced his selections: Cornelius Kelly and Wesley L. Pawl.[30] Their district sat in Area 5, subject to area manager Elijah B. Lewis's oversight.[31]

A "leader of the political faction" opposed to the new congressman informed the U.S. district attorney that he believed the new census appointees were Communists. The district attorney informed the Federal Bureau of Investigation (FBI), which in turn informed an investigator for the Department of Commerce named Carl Rogers. By the time Rogers made it to Los Angeles, the area manager, Lewis, had already started sniffing for any covert Communists who might be conducting the census under his watch.[32] Rogers and Lewis did not find a vast Communist conspiracy, but (as we'll see) they did discover a strange case involving a changing name.

Rogers advised his superiors in Washington, D.C., to let the matter of supposed Communists drop without a formal hearing. Rogers had met with the accusers, who were affiliated with the Los Angeles American Legion—the city's branch of a national organization for U.S. veterans. They did not present convincing evidence, and Rogers decided the whole thing boiled down to an effort to embarrass and discredit a political rival. (The accusers' reasoning came across as troublingly circular: one man insisted he knew "[district supervisor] Kelly was a Communist or otherwise he could not have been recommended and appointed to this job."[33] By that logic, any person appointed would have been deemed a Communist, possibly even this accuser.) Rogers did not think the bureau should credit such red-baiting with any more public attention. He thought the Legion men were just looking for an excuse to unfairly smear their congressman by attacking his appointees. Rogers's superiors seem to have agreed. (Rogers did, however, suggest a quieter FBI investigation, just to be sure no one had released any confidential census information improperly. It's not clear if such an investigation took place.)

Had Rogers found evidence of Communists working for the census, then he would have faced a tricky situation. The Communist Party was a perfectly legal party in California. To be a Communist was not in itself a crime. But the 1940 census began with a census of business and manufacturers that depended on the honest answers of business owners who were often not particularly keen about opening their books to strangers sent by the government. Census Bureau officials worried, with reason, that placing known Communists in charge of the business census—and then the population census—would have just made everything harder.

So area manager Lewis had started the search for Communists even before Rogers arrived on April 11. Lewis went to the L.A. County Registrar of Voters to see if any of his area's officials were registered as Communists—which, again, was perfectly legal, though not very popular. California had only about eighteen hundred registered Communist voters in 1934, and the Soviet nonaggression pact with Hitler had driven that number down to a mere eight hundred in 1940.[34] Lewis looked into the records of all the district employees and didn't find any who had been registered Communists within the last eight years—until he got to the record for Wesley L. Pawl, assistant supervisor.

The problems began with Pawl's voter registration, which wasn't even Pawl's registration to begin with. Instead, Lewis discovered a voter registered by the name Wesley L. Pawloski, who had been a registered Communist from 1932 to 1935, at which point he registered as a Democrat. This voter, Pawloski, signed his name very much like Pawl had on his application for a census job. If this Pawloski was also Pawl, then that still didn't mean the census was employing a Communist, but it did mean it employed a past party member. So, Lewis next sent an aide to the address on file for Pawl. The aide knocked on the door. A woman answered.

"Hello, Mrs. Pawloski?" the aide asked.

"That's me," answered the woman, snared in the trap.

Pawl was Pawloski.

Lewis, with Rogers's blessing after the latter's arrival on the eleventh, went to talk to Pawl who was also Pawloski. Pawl had been off on Catalina Island training extra enumerators that day. The population census had already begun a little more than a week earlier, but it wouldn't count permanent residents of the tourist-trap island for a few more weeks. By the time Pawl got to Lewis's office as summoned, it was 8:00 p.m., and he promptly confessed that he had (in Rogers's paraphrase) "misrepresented his name in his application for employment by the Bureau of the Census." Rogers and Lewis agreed that Pawl had "withheld material evidence in making his application for employment with a Federal Bureau"[35]—his name—and for that he lost his job.

Had Pawl or Pawloski—perhaps we should call him Wesley—actually "misrepresented" his name? It is not clear to me that he had.

But Rogers and Lewis thought so. Wesley had been asked about his relevant work experience on his application to be an assistant district supervisor.[36] He'd been asked about his drinking and drug use. He'd been asked whether or not he'd worked for the census before, whether he currently held political office, whether he was a veteran, whether he'd ever been arrested. He was never asked about his political affiliation. Had he been, he would likely have answered, "Democrat," for that was the truth in 1940. So Wesley couldn't be fired for lying about being a Communist (and it wasn't even clear if that was really a fireable offense). He could be fired for lying about his name. And so he was.

I wonder if Wesley hesitated at all when he filled in the "name" blank on his application form. Could he have known his choice would come back to haunt him? That it would cost him a job that he, an unemployed man, desperately needed?[37] What had he felt, looking at that application? Why had he written Pawl instead of Pawloski? Was it a misrepresentation, or evidence instead of the instability of identity?

A blank for "name" appears at the top of nearly every form an ordinary person is asked to fill out. But names, like identities, can bend with context and change with time. If you fill out the form yourself, you have to decide which sort of context this is and how formal the version of your name is required. You may even have to decide who you are in this particular context, since the names we use can change along with changes in religion, gender, marital status, or residence. (Frederick Douglass faced such decisions repeatedly throughout his life.) And if another person holds the pen, you may have to convince them to record you with the name you think is best. For all those reasons, the name on the form can be the result of a negotiation. A name is an identifier that an individual accepts (more or less grudgingly) and that some office or company or government accepts too (also sometimes grudgingly). Of course, occasionally, that name might also be a deliberate deception.

The reader of historical data, looking back nearly a century, must accept some ambiguity when it comes to names. We'll never know what was said at those millions of doorsteps, what names were proffered, what names rejected, what names misspelled, what names intentionally altered. We'll never know, in most cases, who each person really believed themselves to be. We'll simply know individuals by the names scrawled on a sheet of paper, often by a stranger.

A decade earlier, exactly, on April 11, 1930, an enumerator named

May A. Coates captured for the census a Wesley L. Pawloski: a forty-year-old white man living in rented rooms, employed as the foreman of a hardwood company. (Maybe he discovered the Communist Party through a trade union.) He is shown married to Helen Pawloski, also forty, an assistant manager of a bakery. Their daughter, Ruth, sixteen, lived with them.

Wesley's story seems like it might follow the white immigrant name-change narrative: an arrival at Ellis Island after a voyage in the crowded steerage compartment of an oceanic steamer; a careless or domineering immigration officer trimming an ending "ski" or "opoulos"; a name forever altered. Wesley's story doesn't follow that narrative, though—almost no one's story followed it exactly like that. Immigration officers didn't change names—they mostly copied them from passenger manifests. If an immigrant's name changed, he usually changed it before embarking, or a ship's agent changed it (whether out of carelessness or malice or prejudice, who knows?). Or, as in Wesley's case, the name changed after immigration.

Some genealogical researchers are driven to distraction by frequent claims—usually handed down from generation to generation—that Ellis Island officials Americanized or otherwise bastardized a family's name. They write articles like "Why Your Family Name Was Not Changed at Ellis Island" or "No, Your Ancestors' Names Were Not Changed at Ellis Island."[38] One of my favorites is by a journalist named Jennifer Mendelsohn, who has set out to reveal the immigrant ancestries of those who espouse rabid anti-immigrant sentiments, a work she calls #resistancegenealogy. Mendelsohn's Twitter page features this other, much longer hashtag too: #nameswerentchangedatEllisIsland.[39]

Census takers *did* change some names—not always on purpose and not always at the behest of the person enumerated. The writer Jen Deerinwater lamented in a recent essay that "racist enumerators and agents also forced Indigenous people to assume Christian names, or inaccurately spelled Native names." That was often true of the decennial census taker and, even more important, of the takers of special Indian censuses that still serve today as crucial evidence used by individuals asserting their citizenship in a Native American nation and by those nations themselves in affirming their status as sovereign tribes. "I've been left to wonder," wrote Deerinwater, "what my ancestor's name originally was before U.S. government officials got their hands on it."[40]

It is difficult to say what happened in Wesley's case.

Wesley kept Pawloski for a long time, using it (apparently) into his forties. And Wesley was not himself an immigrant. He was born in Michigan. But both his parents, and both Helen's parents, were immigrants—the census taker put them all down as born in Poland.

We don't know how or why Wesley adopted Pawl instead. Was he shedding his Communist past? Or seeking work in the Depression and looking for a way around xenophobic discrimination?

At any rate, he did not go back to Pawloski after he lost his job as a census supervisor.

On April 18, 1940 (a week after Wesley's firing), Mary E. Murrell interviewed the head of household living in Los Angeles in a rented house on a street named (appropriately) "Defiance." We'll never know for certain what happened in their interview, but we do know what Murrell wrote down.

"Paul, Wesley L."

It's the same person. That's for sure. This Wesley lived with Helen and a now-married Ruth with her eleven-month-old child. Murrell recorded his occupation as census supervisor. Had he possibly once even hired or trained her? Was she the one who picked the name to write down?

Pawloski was Pawl was Paul.

We're left with mostly unanswerable questions. Had Wesley, having already lopped off the Eastern European "oski," decided to try to pass as a nondescript white American by becoming "Paul"? Or had Murrell erred, hearing Pawl as Paul, exposing her own biases and preconceptions? Was the census taker the real-life, honest-to-god corrupter of names that immigration officers are so often said to have been? Based on what I have seen, the answer could be yes—census takers were far from perfect when it came to transcribing names.

One thing that seems clear is that even after Wesley had been fired for "misrepresenting" his name, he refused to just go back to being solely Pawloski.

Paul. Pawl. Pawloski. Who's to say which was the real Wesley? Perhaps they all were, at some point, in the proper context.

What's in a name? Sometimes it's an organizer of data, a social technology, an assertion of dignity, or the product of negotiation. Sometimes it might even be a mistake.

Who was Wesley, really? It depended on who asked and who wrote it down. It isn't the sort of question that the census can answer.

REPRESENTING DOUGLASS IN THE DATA

The representations of Frederick Douglass in the census from decade to decade illustrate how hierarchy and status determined—prior to 1850—whose names would be recorded and preserved in the nation's records.

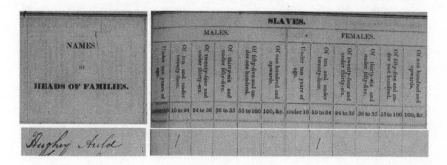

In 1830, Douglass—an enslaved African American man—would have appeared in the census as a "1" only. The sole "1" under the "Males" and "Slaves" headings in this census clipping *might* be Douglass.

A decade later, Douglass had asserted his freedom and asserted his right, as a man, to be a head of household. In this census sheet clipping he appears by name (under the abbreviation Fred[K]) in 1840 and also as a number (the sole "1" under the "Males" and "Free Colored Persons" headings), while his wife, Anna, and daughter, Rosetta, were represented only by numbers under the "Females" heading.

The Name of every Person whose usual place of abode on the first day of June, 1850, was in this family.	Age.	Sex.	White, black, or mulatto.	Profession, Occupation, or Trade of each Male Person over 15 years of age.	Value of Real Estate owned.	PLACE OF BIRTH. Naming the State, Territory, or Country.	
			DESCRIPTION.				
3	4	5	6	7	8	9	
Frederick Douglass	33	m	m	Editor	6000	Maryland	✓
Anna	35	f	b			"	
Rosetta	11	f	b			Mass	✓
Lewis H.	10	m	b			"	✓

In 1850, all free persons were named in the census, so Douglass appeared by name along with all his family members in this clipping from a census sheet. Note that the shift to naming all free people also came with an expansion of the details collected about each. The data had expanded well beyond the categories of age, sex, and color.

3

Partners

How does a data set deal with people who defy its expectations? How can a data set encompass those its designers never imagined? These questions can't be answered with the published numbers, the final facts. They can be answered only by seeking out stories deep within the data, stories like this one:

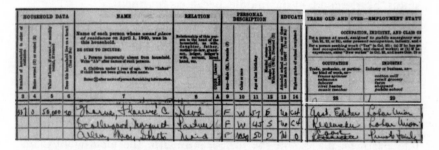

Margaret Scattergood had been one of the few women in the room when the Question Men decided on their census questions. A year and two months later, Scattergood faced those questions herself. She had to fit herself into the frame her colleagues had constructed, but that would not be easy. Scattergood had been an outlier in the Commerce Department auditorium; she would be an outlier on the census sheets too.

The manuscript census schedules tell us that an enumerator named Richard Gray visited Scattergood's house in Fairfax County, Virginia, on May 25. He was late, reaching this country home nearly a month after rural spaces were supposed to be enumerated—it seems likely that he had attempted to enumerate the household earlier but could not find the residents at home. On this visit, he appraised the house's value at an impressive $50,000—it was (and is), by all accounts, beautiful, bucolic, and grand.

Gray then listed three residents: fifty-seven-year-old Florence Thorne, white, single, with four years of college education, the "assistant editor" for a "labor union"; forty-five-year-old Margaret Scattergood, white, single, college educated, and a "researcher" for a "labor union"; and fifty-year-old May Stotts Allen, divorced and (apparently) entirely unschooled—she was listed as "W" for white, which was then scratched over with a darker "Ng" for "Negro." Gray was supposed to mark which of the people in the household he spoke to directly, but he did not in this case and so it's impossible to say if Scattergood encountered the questions herself.

We do know how Gray made sense (in census terms) of these three middle-age women living together. Gray made the eldest, Florence Thorne, the "head" of the household in the "Relation" column, writing her name first. Allen he listed last, as the "maid," related by her servile status. Scattergood, in the middle, became a "partner."

"Partner" is a curious label, a term that can have a jumble of meanings. Partners might run businesses or law firms. Some of us have partners in crime. These days, "partner" mostly means lover or companion. Used by queer and straight alike, married or not, "partner" now often indicates a long-term intimate connection. That usage isn't even new; in his 1667 masterpiece *Paradise Lost*, John Milton made the parents of humanity into partners, placing in the ur-lover's mouth, the mouth of Adam, speaking of Eve, this lament: "I stand Before my Judge . . . to accuse My other self, the partner of my life."[1]

Is that what census takers had in mind when they labeled Margaret Scattergood—along with just under two hundred thousand other people in the continental United States—partners?

For most of the U.S. census's first century, it wasn't possible to be labeled a partner, as Scattergood was in 1940. The "Relation" column, which asked all individuals in a household to explain their position vis-à-vis the family's "head," didn't even come into being until 1880.

This column reminds us of the census's hidden-in-plain-sight secret: the survey may list individuals to make the data easier to manage, but individuals are not its fundamental unit. The census is and was a census of *households*. To be counted by the census, a person must be placed within something resembling a family. To count a person in 1940, the Census Bureau demanded that there be a "head" of that person's household. It struggled to make sense of people who lived in arrangements that defied the bureau's expectations.

Before the 1850 census, only heads of household (male by default) were named in the survey, and the rest of the household became simply a set of tally marks or numbers attached to that name. The 1850 shift to naming each individual looked revolutionary, but it was (as we've seen) mostly a data-management strategy, and it left the essential nature of the census unchanged—the basic organizing unit of the count was what its architects originally called the "family." The statisticians devising the census instructed enumerators to name male heads of household first and then list the wife, children, and then servants or lodgers or other members of the "family" who were not related by blood (such as an apprentice). In coming decades, families were rebranded as "households," but the logic remained unchanged. Even in 2020, any American who filled out a census form had to place themselves within a household (though without any explicit "head"), even if just in a household of one.

So why did it become necessary to put labels on household "relations"? Why make that shift in 1880? It might have had something to do with another big change that happened at the same time: the statisticians were also given the authority, for the first time, to organize the enumeration and oversee the recruitment of enumerators (with the approval of each ruling-party congressman).[2] As Washington, D.C., won more control over the question-askers in the field, it simultaneously might have worried about the agents it couldn't control. The "Relation" column might have been a tool for keeping an eye on the people asking the questions as much as on those who were answering them.

If that sounds strange or like wild speculation, it isn't. In fact, it's the precise justification given by key Census Bureau professionals for keeping the "Relation" column in later years.

On the one hand, Census Bureau officials faced the enduring problem of trying to squeeze too many questions into too little space. That consideration led to a vote in 1917 to get rid of the "Relation" question, freeing up a column for other inquiries. On the other hand, officials faced an enduring problem that would ultimately rescue the column from removal: enumerators sometimes made up people, a fraudulent practice common enough to have its own census-specific name: "padding." (There was actually a whole census-specific vocabulary for making up people, including the lovely verb "curbstoning" that alluded to the enumerator who filled out the census sheet with imagined data while sitting at the curb, unencumbered by actual knowledge of actual people in actual homes.)

The 1910 census had been plagued by padding fiascos—most spectacularly in Tacoma, Washington. Boosters intent on inflating their city's status and influence conspired with local enumerators to make up more than thirty thousand people.[3] The enumerators themselves, who were paid for each head they "counted," proved perfectly happy to help. They invented about a quarter of the city's reported population!

Census Bureau officials wondered what they could do to prevent another epidemic of fraudulent entries. Unsurprisingly, they decided to ask Congress to change the census law to make it easier to prosecute rogue enumerators. Their other big move was more surprising, and also quite telling. They decided to overturn their earlier space-saving decision: the "Relation" column had to stay.

Relation data served as a valuable tool for sniffing out padded entries. The bureau's chief statistician for population called the column a "deterrent": "if fictitious entries shall have been made by an enumerator," he explained, they would likely show up as unattached individuals or as "boarders" or "lodgers" added to existing (real) households. Census supervisors on the lookout for an "undue number of such entries" or noticing "the excessive size of families due to such cause, in an ordinary residential district," could trigger a closer investigation to catch the fraudsters.[4] The officials doubted that enumerators would be clever enough to invent normal-looking families at scale, so the "Relation" category survived as a tool for rooting out fraud.

Maybe concerns about padding were even responsible for the column's creation in the first place. There had, after all, been earlier padding scandals, as when Minneapolis invented a tenth of its population in 1890.[5] But did padding fears play a role in the 1880 decision? Ultimately, we don't know.

What we do know is that the relationship category—as a category, as part of the frame of the data—tells us something about the nation and the institutions that required it. It gives evidence that the data's designers believed that there was such a thing as a normal family and that they (the designers) would know it when they saw it. And it points to a bureaucratic system concerned about disciplining possibly corrupt workers.

The idea of using relationship data as a deterrent to fraud rested on statisticians' faith that they could distinguish normal from abnormal households and that real people would belong to normal households. But partners—by definition—didn't belong.

"The fiction of the census is that everyone is in it," wrote the theorist of nationalism, Benedict Anderson, "and that everyone has one—and only one—extremely clear place."[6] But governments exert power by deciding what each possible "clear place" is, and people with power have an easier time getting themselves placed as they'd like to be placed. "Partners" became "partners" because no "extremely clear place" for them could be found. They defied norms.

Census enumerators resorted to the "partner" label just over 50,000 times in their very first effort to label every American's spot in a "family" in 1880. That translated to about 0.1 percent of everyone enumerated, 0.1 percent of the population with no other "clear place."[7]

Some of those partners look like holdovers from the earlier era of family-centered enterprises. The dry goods merchants Henry and George Combs might have been brothers, but an enumerator in 1880 labeled George a "partner" to Henry. There are, in fact, quite a few dry goods merchants or dealers who show up in that census as partners. The term proved useful for fitting merchant capitalism into the form.

It also made it possible to aggregate unattached, usually male workers who were at that moment driving the development of American industry in the West. In Nevada an enumerator might (and did) fill a sheet with partners, all Italian immigrants working as "coalburners."[8] In California, enumerators used the "partner" label to describe large groups of Chinese immigrant men living together, at a moment when a quarter of the California workforce was Chinese.[9] The Chinese, like the Italian miners, were busy building the West. The census translated their impromptu labor camps into households of partners.

Such partnerships scared many white Americans, who cast them as direct competitors to the nuclear family. Sinophobes, especially in California, did not see laborers powering industrial development. They saw an unassimilable people whose failure to live in traditional family arrangements and whose willingness to work for lower wages threatened the ability of white working men to act as proper heads of their households.[10]

One enumerator in San Francisco came upon a household of Chinese workers living together, working in a laundry. He didn't bother to classify them as partners. Instead, he turned their occupation into a familial relation. They became laundrymen in both the "Relation" and "Occupation" columns, creating another category for those who didn't fit the census's expectations. "Laundryman" wasn't an official label in 1880, but neither (as far as I can tell) was "partner."

In the instructions to enumerators that year, the Census Bureau felt the need to define a family but not to specify all the acceptable family relation labels. The bureau cautioned enumerators that families for statistical purposes might not look like, well, families. "The word family, for the purposes of the census, includes persons living alone," read the instructions, "equally with families in the ordinary sense of that term, and also all larger aggregations of people having only the tie of a common roof and table." Note that "table" mention. Tables mattered. Tables defined families—urban families, at least: "In the case . . . of tenement houses and of the so-called 'flats' of the great cities, as many families are to be recorded as there are separate tables."[11]

Over the next sixty years, through six censuses, "partner" slid into an officially sanctioned status. It became a clear place for placing the otherwise unplaceable.

The 1940 instructions told enumerators: "If two or more persons who are not related by blood or marriage share a common dwelling unit as partners, write *head* for one and *partner* for the other or others."[12] It was the very last line in the section on relations, almost an afterthought, a literal last resort.

Over those same sixty years, the furniture that defined a family changed, as did the language describing families. A "household" was now defined by its sinks and stoves: "If a married son or daughter or any other person lives in a separate portion of the house that has its own cooking or housekeeping facilities, such persons constitute a household separate."[13] Families were distinguished by their tables, households by their pots and pans. All of these definitions studiously avoided beds. No beds. Enumerators were definitely not instructed to determine who was sleeping with whom.

To prepare enumerators to properly place each person into their one and only slot, Census Bureau officials contrived a narrative describing a hypothetical enumerator (a Harold W. Thompson) visiting a town in Middle America (Royce, Iowa, to be precise). In that town there lived a Miss Maude Riggs and Miss Grace T. Sanders—they were single, white, college-educated, working women living together. Maude taught piano lessons (eighteen a week); Grace was a librarian. Their housekeeper and her daughter lived with them as well. Enumerators in training in the continental United States (in the forty-eight states that then accounted for all of the states) learned to identify partners by seeing how the hypothetical Harold filled in the census blanks for Maude, Grace, and their servant's family.[14] The least believable part of the entire scenario was that Harold's entries weren't written by hand; they were typed. (Imagine if an enumerator had really lugged around a typewriter from house to house. What a workout!)

At any rate, the invention of Maude and Grace was the attempt of the Census Bureau to craft an officially abnormal household (one that, it must be said, bore a passing resemblance to Margaret Scattergood's actual living arrangements). Why did they settle on Maude and Grace? Were a pair of rooming women the archetypical partners? Certainly they fit a trope that would have been familiar to the Question Men and the statisticians, many of whom had grown up in New England, who would have known of so-called Boston or Wellesley marriages. Both terms applied to pairs of women who, independent of financial support from a man, shared a home, often for a very long time, who tended to be highly educated and who were engaged in an intimate relationship that may or may not have been sexual. Accepting the concept of the Boston marriage spared some possibly embarrassing questions or inconvenient answers.

Maybe that explains Maude and Grace too. Their invention presented an abnormality that did not threaten, one that did not trespass against the most serious of mid-century taboos—the pairing did not suggest any illicit mixing of genders or races. Maude and Grace, woman and woman, well educated and well educated, white and white—that would do for a partnership in the United States.

In America's colonial hinterlands, the Census Bureau persisted in avoiding any taboos and hewed close (again) to common tropes. The training narrative for Hawaii—which was still a territorial possession and so subject to a distinct census—didn't mention any partners, which was (as we'll see) an odd omission.[15] But a different test for Hawaiian enumerators asked this question: "Suppose a group of men not related by blood or marriage have a common dwelling unit, each paying a share of the rent, what entries are made in the relations column?"[16] This anonymous gaggle of men were partners in Hawaii.

In Alaska, meanwhile, the special census training narrative imagined another pair, this time of men: dry goods merchants in a manner of speaking, one the proprietor, the other a clerk, living together—they sold cigars. Again, the example segregates the sexes and races. John Harris and Edward Brown were imagined as members of a prominent Indigenous group, "Haidan Indians."[17] (The Central Council of the Tinglit and Haida Indian Tribes of Alaska had been founded a few years earlier in 1935 and is, according to the group, "only one of two federally recognized tribes in Alaska" today.)[18] Maybe the Census Bureau authors' imaginations had failed them in their efforts to invent Native respondents, and they landed on a tired trope—or on a crude advertising gimmick. Since the mid-nineteenth century, non-Native cigar shop operators in the United States marked their doorsteps with large wooden figures meant to be Indians to attract customers.[19] Whoever wrote this sample narrative represented Native Alaskans as a pair of fictional cigar store Indians who also happened to be partners—a feeble effort to illustrate how enumerators should place the unplaceable.

When the 1940 census actually took to the field, though, the reality of relationships that would eventually be corralled as "partners" refused to be limited to tropes and taboos.

The "partner" puzzle first presented itself to me as I began researching this book. I had been reading through 1940 census sheets for over a year and had never noticed a "partner" label. Then I received a message from a colleague at Columbia University's Teachers College, Ansley Erickson, asking what it meant when two women were living together and one was marked "partner" to the other. Erickson had found such a record. I did not have an answer for her then, but I knew I needed to find one.

I also had a personal reason for wanting to learn more. "Partner" was a descriptor we had started to use more often in our family, a term that fit better as our marriage got queerer and queerer. But I had no idea where the term in the census had really come from, so I began looking around.

Beyond my personal reason, I was drawn to studying the "partner" label by a hunch. I believed that chasing after "partners" would help me think about how census data dealt with queer and other marginalized people generally. I believed that chasing after "partners" might also provide an opportunity to offer some token of historical recognition to people who lived on the margins of their society, the sort of people who always have less of a shot at making it into the history books. Chasing after "partners" did not disappoint on either count. Indeed, it led me to a series of doorstep encounters I could never have imagined from examining the final census numbers alone.

The first question was how to find "partners" in the census. When I had started my work, the term wasn't searchable on most databases. (That has since changed, opening up new opportunities for you, my fellow data readers, to explore.) The academic data center IPUMS did have a tally of the number of times "partners" had been enumerated on census sheets within the forty-eight states in 1940: 190,836 times, which is actually quite a high number. It's several orders of magnitude greater than "concubine/mistress and children" (110) and about on par with "cousins" (151,892) or "visitors" (184,707). Still, it was less than 5 percent (approximately 4.4 percent) of the number of "lodgers" and less than 1 percent (approximately 0.7 percent) of the number of "spouses" (effectively "wives").[20] "Partners" were still rare, and tracking them down might not be easy.

Those 190,836 partners represented about 0.15 percent of the total population enumerated. Each enumerator carried a leather, government-issued portfolio holding something in the neighborhood of 20 enumeration sheets to be completed. Since each two-sided sheet fit 80 names, on average, enumerators counted about 1,600 people apiece. Taking 0.15 percent to be the overall likelihood of an entry being a "partner" and multiplying it by those 1,600 enumerated by the average census taker, we get 2.4. That's the number of "partners" we'd expect to find somewhere in every enumerator's portfolio of sheets, if partners were evenly distributed across the United States.

But it turned out that partners were not evenly distributed. That quickly became clear.

If, as I suspected, the "partner" label marked people whose lives didn't fit comfortably within the bounds of "normal" mid-century American life, my search for partners should start in those places, those communities, that took in misfits, bohemians, and the queer—I needed to start at the margins.

The margins of this book are blank, empty. The margins of society teem. The margins of this book might invite all manner of readers' transgressions: comments, disagreements, expletives, even fancy little "manicules" pointing a finger to a line of text. The margins of society are similar in that regard—full of transgressions, comments, disagreements, expletives, and plenty of pointing fingers too.

But how does one find the margins of society? They are not, as the margins of this book are, simply at the extreme edges.

As it happens, in the decade preceding the 1940 census, the U.S. government began a project that mapped the margins of American society.

Roosevelt's New Deal had aimed to save people's homes from foreclosure in the depths of the Great Depression, and to do that it created the Home Owners' Loan Corporation (HOLC). HOLC rescued a million homes and the families inside them over three years, from 1933 to 1936. Toward the end of its run, HOLC staff cooperated with local real estate powerhouses in 239 cities to get a sense of which neighborhoods were good investments and which were judged to be poor risks. As historian Amy Hillier put it, the "City Survey Program produced detailed reports for each city along with a series of now infamous security maps that assigned residential areas a grade from one to four. Areas with African Americans, as well as those with older housing and poorer households, were consistently given a fourth grade, or 'hazardous,' rating and colored red."[21] These maps now serve as totemic reminders of the power of "redlining," a practice that made it difficult or impossible for people in disfavored regions to secure mortgages or insurance to buy or build homes. As Hillier's research has shown, these maps did not so much cause redlining as they made visible the already existing discrimination built into the housing market. When the New Deal created the Federal Housing Administration (FHA) to make it easier for more Americans to get access to a good mortgage, FHA officials relied on the advice of the sort of folks who informed these maps, and so doomed the sort of places graded poorly to a future of decay and blight. As the scholars who put these maps online have explained: "More than a half-century of research has shown housing to be for the twentieth century what slavery was to the antebellum period, namely the broad foundation of both American prosperity and racial inequality."[22]

These maps show us these two-hundred-plus cities through the eyes of each city's elites in the mid-to-late 1930s—a city as it looked to bankers, real estate agents, appraisers, and government officials. The maps show us what places looked good and respectable to the powerful, and which did not. So while these maps had been devised for risk assessment, to guide and inform government mortgage relief, they work well as a guide to each city's margins. The margins were the places colored yellow or red, the blocks spurned by scores of three or four, the places respectable folks avoided.

On April 2, 1940, Lillian Rita Davis knocked on her very first door, an apartment in a small building on New York City's West Eleventh Street.[23] It was a marginal neighborhood—or maybe better to call it edgy—at the edge of respectability, the edge of wealth and legitimacy. New York's powerful labeled the area a three or C, colored yellow for Caution. It was "a very old district" made up mostly of "tenements" according to the accompanying report. About 20 percent of the buildings were "Rooming houses, etc. Miscellaneous."[24] Any reference to rooming houses augured a poor grade, because rooming houses filled up with people unbound from conventional nuclear families. (The exceptions were a couple of the poshest neighborhoods, near Central Park, where the rooming houses were luxury residential hotels.)

Emily H. Brand answered the door. She told Davis she worked as a secretary for a theater, getting by with not much money. She was college educated, twenty-nine, white, and single. She told Davis that she lived with Katrina S. Grant, who was also college educated, twenty-seven years old, white, and single. Grant earned quite a bit more money, as a social worker. We don't know if Brand called Grant her partner, or her roommate, or her friend, or her companion, or her lover. All we know is that Davis saw the pair—a pair seemingly plucked from the training materials—as a head (Brand) and a partner (Grant).

Davis went on to record twelve more "partners" in her district, many more than the three that pure chance would predict. Partners had a way of coming in clumps, clumps clustered at the margins, in places like Greenwich Village.

Davis's partners usually paired to people designated with the same sex. (The census, then and now, reduces the actual variety of the world to only two options for sex or gender: man or woman, excluding or misgendering nonbinary and transgender people in the process.) Among those partnerships, five partners were women living with another woman, the pairs always within a few years in age. They included a pair of doctors, two travel agents (who may have been business partners too), an editor and a secretary, and a secretary and a stenographer who both worked for the YMCA. Another stenographer was aptly named Tessie Finger and partnered to a secretary whose name was the delightfully alliterative, pleasure-proclaiming Lee Lustgarden. (At least those were the names the enumerator wrote down.) Two of the partners were male-male, including a police detective who lived with a patrolman.

There is no way of knowing if these living arrangements enabled intimate relationships, if they were romantic or sexual, or if they were simply the result of people finding roommates to help pay the rent. Whatever the reasons for the pairings, these partnerships troubled the premise that every household had to have a head, and for that reason, we can count them queer. They pushed the boundaries of the data's assumptions and transgressed the Question Men's ideas about what a normal household looked like.

At 280 West Fourth Street, Davis spoke to Justine Polier, a family court judge, living in a rented house with an unusual household. Polier's husband, marked as "head," was Shad Polier, a lawyer for the National Labor Relations Board. Next Davis listed two children, a "son" (with a different last name) and an "adopted daughter" (from Frankfurt, Germany). Next came Viola Bernard, marked as "partner"—but whose partner was she? Was Bernard (a white, college-educated, divorced woman) partnered to Justine, or to Shad, or to both? Davis listed Bernard as a doctor in a psychiatric institution, which undersells her significance. Her papers are preserved at Columbia University, recognizing Bernard's significance as a founder of community psychiatry and her work as an activist.[25] Maybe she and Justine met as part of the Non-Sectarian Committee for German Refugee Children (and maybe that's how the Poliers' daughter came to be adopted). Maybe they met professionally, the social psychiatrist and the family court judge working for child welfare. Last, as was usual in the order of census enumerations, came the family's Irish maid, Henrietta Doyle, who was in this odd family, but in the eyes of the census a peripheral part of it. This fascinating family found a way to be counted, with the help of the partner label, while keeping whatever secrets they had to keep.

Davis found and labeled twelve partnerships even though she only completed seven census sheets (containing about 280 people). Her days of wrestling murky reality into state-approved statistical buckets came to a sudden end when she got a new job ("found employment in private industry" according to a note on one of the sheets) and left the census.[26]

Uptown, in Harlem, Vera Maude Smith knocked on her first door in Enumeration District (E.D.) 31–1723B on April 16, 1940.[27] The neighborhood Smith enumerated had been shaded red, scored with a D or 4. The accompanying description explained: "Formerly a good residential area largely one-family dwellings. Now almost entirely negro–tenements and converted dwellings into rooming houses. Rentals are fair due to crowding."[28] It's worth pausing on that last line to let it sink in. In the eyes of the banker or real estate man, the crowding of Harlem driven by the strict racial segregation enforced by the realtors drove up rental rates and so made rentals the one thing that were worth investing in. The rest of the neighborhood suffered from both withheld credit and artificially cramped quarters.

If the Greenwich Village partners looked as though they had walked right out of the sample sheets used to train enumerators, the Harlem partners reveal the limits to such illustrations. Looking to Harlem, we see evidence that what "partner" meant and how it manifested varied from place to place, from community to community. Partners came in clumps, and each clump had a distinct character, variations that we can read and recognize in the manuscript data.

The first time the enumerator Vera Maude Smith applied the "partner" label was for a household that was at once typical of the other fourteen partner pairs in Smith's district and in some respects a significant outlier. What made it typical was what made it most different from the partner households in Greenwich Village: it was a partnership featuring at least one married person—this was the norm for partnerships in Smith's Harlem. Smith's first partner was forty-two-year-old Elizabeth Hickson, who was listed as divorced. Smith marked Hickson's race as

"Ind" for Indian—as in Native or Indigenous—but that appears to have been an error on Smith's part, because in a supplementary question, Hickson revealed that her mother was born in India (and her father in Indiana), which would have made Hickson's race "Hindu" according to the census. Hickson became "partner" to the head of her household, William Roth, a forty-five-year-old handyman by trade and one of the few white men living in Smith's district.

Smith marked Roth with an "M" for married. But he was not married to Hickson. The census was silent on the identity of his spouse. The census was not finished in its marking of the Roth record, though—just as it would not be finished with others who were separated from spouses. Some weeks or months later, after the enumerator Smith's portfolio of sheets had traveled to Washington, a Census Bureau editor would take a pen to Smith's sheets (and every other census sheet), preparing the entries Smith made so that they could be punched into paper cards and eventually tabulated. Whenever that editor found a married person living apart from their spouse, that editor placed a line through the letter "M" and replaced it with a number: "7." Ordinarily, every "M" on a sheet was supposed to be translated onto a punch card as a "2" in the second row. (Row "1" was for "S," or single people.) But married people living apart from their spouses did not get to be ordinary M2s; they instead were reclassified as a distinct group, M7s, at the bottom of the punch card—an explicitly marginal category, at the very edge of the card. The Census Bureau treated married people living apart from their spouses as anomalous and also as a group subject to statistical scrutiny.

As Smith made her rounds enumerating, she ran into more pairs that she judged to include a partner, and at least one person in most of those pairs was married, just not married to the person they lived with. So Smith kept writing down an "M" that an editor in Washington would change to a "7," rendering the record remarkable or possibly suspect. There was Olivia Parker, a thirty-one-year-old Black woman, an M7 pastry chef with two children, whom Smith listed as a partner to Ollie Simmons, a twenty-five-year-old single Black man, a dancer. There was Herbert Hill, a twenty-five-year-old Black man, a porter, partnered to James Parker, a twenty-two-year-old Black man who worked in a garage as an auto mechanic. There was Inez Reid, a single twenty-five-year-old Black woman with two years of college education, working as a servant, partnered to Frannie Dozier, a twenty-seven-year-old Black woman, an M7 from South Carolina who also worked as a servant. A couple of doors down from them lived Arline Brooks and Marie Wescott, both M7s, both in their twenties and from South Carolina, working in a dress factory; and so Smith made Wescott partner to Brooks. The Great Migration of African Americans from the rural South to cities like New York and neighborhoods like Harlem enabled or caused or forced many spouses to separate, for a short while or for good. Hearts were broken; others were freed.[29] The census sheets cannot tell us which were which.

Back downtown on New York's Upper East Side, in E.D. 31–1272, Patrena Greco counted at a crease in the social fabric where the posh met the poor, a margin of the margins.[30] One half of Greco's district belonged to an area ranked A or 1 by the moneymen—that was the half near Fifth Avenue, with all its glitz, glamor, and gold. "One of the choicest residential sections," read the evaluator's text, even though there were some rooming houses. The other, more easterly half of Greco's district ranked at the bottom, colored in red, for D or 4. "An old and poor district with substantial tendency for improvement from the worst thru modern apartment at fair to high rentals," read the description, which also noted a large population of foreign-born residents, especially Italians.[31]

Greco counted fourteen partnerships in all, seven woman-to-woman, seven man-to-man. All involved whites only, but with a difference from those over in Greenwich Village: these partners came from abroad. Greco listed as "partners" a pair of Polish waiters in their thirties—they lived near the forty-year-old waitresses also deemed partners. There were Norwegian partners and Irish partners (two sets) and French partners (a dressmaker partnered to a milliner). There were multiple nurses and hospital workers in the partnerships. The partner couples included lawyers, clerks, and supervisors. A Danish antique shop decorator partnered to a bank clerk. An English woman—twenty-seven years old, possibly independently wealthy—partnered to an English concert violinist, the thirty-three-year-old Orrea Pernell.

Each of these partner clusters turned up in neighborhoods that money and capital had relegated to the margins. Each was also, not coincidentally, a queer neighborhood. According to George Chauncey in his book *Gay New York*, in Patrena Greco's district: "Many gay men moved into the railroad flats in the East Fifties and Sixties east of the Third Avenue elevated train, which allowed them to live close to the elegance of Park Avenue (as well as the gay bars of Third Avenue) at a fraction of the cost."[32] Meanwhile, Lillian Rita Davis's Greenwich Village was considered New York City's "most infamous gay neighborhood by outsiders."[33] And Harlem played host to the "riotous Black girls, troublesome women, and queer radicals" the historian Saidiya Hartman celebrates in her book *Wayward Lives, Beautiful Experiments*.[34] In each neighborhood, the existence of rooming houses and the possibility of renting a room—often a furnished room—as a single person or part of an unmarried pair created the conditions of possibility for queer communities to form, and the conditions of possibility for partners to cluster in the census.

Partners clustered on the other side of the continent too, on the West Coast, in San Francisco—where communities and enumerators negotiated a place in the data for Asian Americans, for people living in commercial districts, and for an avant-garde of office-working women.

Lodging, rooming, and apartment houses dominated the district in the city's northeast quadrant, where Rita Marie Ganzert knocked on doors, taking the census.[35] Her assigned spot also crossed a boundary line on a HOLC map. The western half bore a stain of red, a mark of its low status, its high risk. The accompanying description emphasized the "heterogenous mixture of industry, business, hotels, apartments, and flats, with a generous sprinkling of old residences many of which are in use as boarding or lodging houses." It warned of "a distinct threat of encroachment by business and apartment houses." It argued that neighboring Chinatown did not pose a threat, because of "topography."[36] The other half of Ganzert's district had already succumbed to an encroachment—it bore no color, no grade at all, just a series of crosshatches that indicated the area wasn't suitable for residence. This might have come as news to all the people who lived there in apartments above or around the various stores, bars, and other businesses at street level.

Ganzert enumerated Pauline Johnson and Frances Hamilton on April 18, both white women in their fifties with high school educations, one single and the other widowed. They managed an apartment house with fourteen residents, whom Ganzert also counted. Ganzert listed the residents as "lodgers," but Johnson became the "head" and Hamilton the "partner." Ganzert tended to list as "partner" the younger person in a pair, which is what she did in this case. Did Johnson or Hamilton have any say in the matter? Did they even know?

Ganzert labeled forty-one people as "partners" in total—many more than the three expected by a uniform distribution. Did I mention that partners came in clusters? Many of Ganzert's partners took notes or typed for a living—she ran into stenographer after stenographer, secretary after secretary, clerk after clerk. She even recorded a "comptometer operator," a divorced young white woman named Dixie Harmon who became a partner to the two secretaries she lived with. Comptometers were mechanical calculators, like typewriters but for math. Many of the women Ganzert interviewed worked as cogs in one way or another for one of the city's insurance companies or some other big business, and many of them were single, and many showed up in the census as partners.

A few blocks south of Ganzert's district, Hugh Randolph patrolled streets even farther into the no-man's-land on the HOLC maps.[37] But Randolph found plenty of people living outside the residential area, including more than twice as many partners as Ganzert. He, too, counted mostly two-women partnerships, with an abundance of typists and other office workers.

Some of Randolph's abundance of partners could have had as much to do with him as with his district. (Of course, this is always true.) In Randolph's case, he appears to have transformed a number of possible siblings or cousins into partners. Like Erich Vools and Louise Vools, a man and a woman, both white, both born in Germany, forty-six and forty-two, respectively, put down as "head" and "partner." What it looks like is that Louise got married, then got divorced and moved in with her brother. But Randolph made them partners, not "head" and "sister." Similarly, Robert Maempe was a "delivery boy," living with three women, all typists—he was the youngest of the four, and so the honor of being head went to the eldest, the twenty-three-year-old, white, single Anita Fuss. Fuss's "partners" were Roberta Millar, Thelma Maempe, and Robert Maempe. Thelma and Robert both hailed from Montana, by way of Nevada City, California—they must have been related, probably siblings. But Randolph made them partners, and that label stuck.

William W. Young patrolled a district just to the east and north of Ganzert's and Randolph's, and he counted more partners than both combined—151 in all.[38] Young's district didn't get any detailed description; it didn't receive a score—crosshatches marked it on the map as a nonresidential place. But it was packed with partners, and packed with cultural significance—Young, a Chinese American, was counting in Chinatown.

Young's partners constituted a cluster and came in clusters. Most were smallish, business-sized groups, so sized because the household and the business were one and the same. Gim Hong Wong (forty-eight years old, born in China, M7) owned a restaurant and so served as "head" for a household with nine partners, all born in China, all M7s (their brides presumably still in China), who served as cook, baker, waiter, porter, dishwasher, cashier, etc. Other partner clusters operated laundries or groceries, a printing shop or an herb store. One grocery operated through a series of neighboring households: a group of four partners and a head, all from China, all M7s, worked in sales, buying, and bookkeeping, while a salesman, Lin Juen Ng, lived next door with his wife, Lee Shee, and their three Chinese American children, Betty, Jackson, and Sally. The grocery's manager shared the building with the married salesman, living with his wife and their Chinese American children, Yam Too and Kai Foy (and Kai Foy's wife, Young). Some of the partnerships brought together men working in a variety of fields and trades. Sai Shenung Lee, a forty-two-year-old M7, a recent migrant to the United States who presumedly left a spouse behind in China, worked as a cigar maker while his fellow partners in a Spofford Alley house worked in a laundry, labored in a cannery, clerked at a grocery, manned a bar, and kept the books for a wholesale herb supplier.

If every normal household is the same, every peculiar one is peculiar in its own peculiar way.[39] "Partner" labels made it possible to place every household by absorbing those peculiar households that otherwise wouldn't fit. The "partner" label made it possible for a household census to count at the margins of society. It created a big tent filled with an enormous variety of arrangements for living together.

Big cities like New York and San Francisco had wide margins and plenty of people—and many rooming houses: they were bound to abound with partners. But they didn't have the largest clusters of partners. That honor went to a different kind of margin: the margin of the nation, the colonial edges of the American empire. The census's most remarkable and extensive collection of partners lived in Hawaii.

There are no HOLC maps for Hawaii. Not yet a state, still a colonial possession, a territory, Hawaii did not qualify for HOLC loans. The entirety of the territory counted as a marginal, peripheral place for the Question Men.

The partners of Hawaii don't figure in the total numbers of partners I've quoted so far, either. The approximately two hundred thousand reported by IPUMS draw on the data set for the United States, but not Hawaii, Alaska, Puerto Rico, the Panama Canal Zone, the Philippines, Guam, or the Virgin Islands—all of which used slightly different census forms or procedures, ensuring their data would be kept separate from and less comparable to mainland data. Hawaiian data moldered on the margins of American democracy's data.

Hawaii alone had thousands of partners. A database search for "partners" in Hawaii turns up over 6,700.[40] A researcher in my history lab at Colgate University, Ethan So, counted nearly 4,000 partners in his in-depth analysis of a wide swath of the territory's census sheets. The census determined the entire population of Hawaii to be about three-tenths of 1 percent of the entire U.S. population—and so we would expect the number of Hawaii's partners to also be around 0.3 percent of the U.S. total. Instead, it was a wildly disproportionate 2 to 3 percent—as much as ten times as many partners as one would have expected.

In America's colonial hinterlands, the "partner" label served as a tool for incorporating people whom empire and capitalism had drawn into distinct kinds of households.

On April 1, 1940, George Fong started counting heads for the territorial census on the north shore of the island of Oahu in Honolulu County.[41] On April 4, he recorded his first partner: Engnacio Aquilar, a thirty-six-year-old widowed Filipino man, became partner to Silvester Alejandro, also thirty-six, also a widowed Filipino man—both of whom did some of the hardest work on the island or anywhere else, toiling on a sugar plantation. Fong labeled 112 partners in all over the course of the next thirty days. The vast majority of those partners resembled Aquilar: Filipino men living in pairs or small groups consigned to the worst jobs on Hawaiian plantations.

Fong lived in a nearby town, working as an auto mechanic for the government's Road Department when he wasn't taking the census. He had been born in Hawaii, but the census recorded his race as Chinese. As Fong toured the surrounding sugar and pineapple plantations, he captured in his census sheets the changing hierarchies of race and labor on the island. With immigration from China banned when Hawaii became a U.S. territory, planters sought new sources of cheap labor among Japanese and Filipino migrants. In time, though, as historian Moon-Kie Jung explains, "Filipinos were relegated to the most labor-intensive unskilled jobs, while the Japanese could increasingly be found in supervisory, skilled, and semiskilled positions."[42] Nearly all Filipino migrants to Hawaii in the early twentieth century were men, which made them even cheaper to employ, since plantations gave some extra benefits to married workers. For all these reasons, Fong and his fellow enumerators were most likely to label as "partners" unmarried Filipino men. "Partner" served as a tool for explaining the relationship of men living together in plantation camps. The "partner" label made the masses of a colonial proletariat look like members of a household.

On April 30, Fong completed his enumeration among the gangs of

Works Progress Administration workers fixing the region's roads. Fong made sense of these workers with the "partner" label too, but they were far from typical. Consider the household headed by John Vierra, a forty-five-year-old divorced Puerto Rican man living with three partners: a sixty-year-old widowed Black man from Kentucky named Eph Young, a thirty-nine-year-old widowed Puerto Rican man named John B. Parker, and a forty-five-year-old single white man from Canada named Charles Flanagan. Other partners in this mini-cluster were Chinese, Native Hawaiian, Mexican, and Filipino. Partnerships in Hawaii were usually used to describe same-sex and same-race pairings or small groups, but there were notable, fascinating exceptions—like these men pouring pavement in Oahu.

In early 2020, *Washington Post* reporters investigated Margaret Scattergood's partnership with Florence Thorne. The reporters weren't interested in the census; they were interested in the Central Intelligence Agency. Thorne and Scattergood had been in bed with the spies, in a manner of speaking. The pair sold their house to the CIA in 1948 on the condition that they could go on living in it until they died. (Thorne died in 1973; Scattergood died in 1986.) The house has since been turned into a conference center for the CIA's Langley headquarters (the Scattergood-Thorne Conference Center).[43]

The reporters dug up the 1940 census record and pondered its possible meanings. They wrote, "If that partnership included romance, it was a well-kept secret." According to their investigation, "Scattergood's family members, who have diligently kept records of her life, say the pair had separate bedrooms and never acknowledged a relationship beyond friendship." The problem is that the "partner" designation cannot really tell us that much about the people it was applied to. It wasn't meant to reveal intimate details.

After Richard Gray enumerated Margaret Scattergood, one of the few women among the Question Men, her record would have made its way back to a Virginia district office, then on to Washington, D.C. There, a punch card operator would have translated Gray's handwritten observations into holes in a tabulating card. The column on the card for "Relation" had a limited number of options, because the card had only so much space. The options were: Hd, Wif, Chi, Par, GrC, OtR, Lod, Ser, Ot, Inm. "Hd" for "Head" is clear enough, and so is the second option: "Wif" for "Wife"—not spouse, but wife.[44] (Even the punch cards enforced the norm of the patriarchal family.) The other abbreviations stood for "child," "parent," "grandchild," "other relative," "lodger," "servant," "other," and "inmate." That "Par" is tantalizing, but isn't for "partner." Scattergood, as a partner, would have been punched in and tabulated as "Lod," as a "lodger." When it came to making statistics, all the partners of this chapter simply disappeared.

That is why their stories cannot be found in the published numbers.

It had never really been about the partners; the point had never been to single out partnered households.

The philosopher Ian Hacking has explained how "Enumeration demands *kinds* of things or people to count." He continued, "Counting is hungry for categories." If suitable categories don't yet exist, the designers of data must invent them. The language of class that defined the political economy of Karl Marx began as the language of worried bureaucrats counting people. The idea of poor revolutionaries climbing the barricades (possibly singing)—call them "Les Misérables"—that too began as a "standard set of pages in statistical reports" produced by nervous officials in early-nineteenth-century Europe. Hacking has shown that the categories created to keep track of a worrisome group, the categories printed in blue-ribbon reports and official statistics—those categories can take on a life of their own.[45]

That didn't happen with partners in the census. Concerns about adults living together outside of marriage did not inspire or require the partner label. In fact, the government cared so little about this group that it never tabulated or printed any data about partners. With no partners on the punch cards, a tabulation wasn't even possible.

So then why bother labeling Margaret Scattergood as a partner in the first place?

Partner labels preserved the social structure and the data structure. The "Relation" column persisted on into 1940 by bureaucratic fiat: officials believed it helped to tamp down fraud in the enumeration process. They banked on being able to sniff out abnormal household patterns, or just thought requiring a relation label would help deter false enumerations. But not everyone enumerators encountered at the nation's doorsteps measured up to the official ideal of a normal household—one with a clear head, usually male. The partner option provided a release valve for enumerators encountering queer couples, colonial laborers, rent-sharing roommates, or recent migrants from other counties or other countries—recognizing that in many cases, "partner" labeled people who might fit more than one of those descriptions.

The "partner" was an "other" option, but one that might have been easier for enumerators to use in doorstep negotiations. The way the label appears in clumps also hints that some census takers and some communities took to it on their own, perhaps because the term already made some sense to them. Though we have seen the tremendous variety of people and circumstances encompassed by partnerships, the job of making statistics rests on smoothing out variations and abstracting away difference. Back in D.C., the bureau decided to subsume the variety of partners and the specificities of its use within the category of "lodger." They charged its editors and card punchers with that translation. Such are the sorts of choices that statisticians must make—though there seems to have been little chance for public discussion of this choice.

Enumerators at over two hundred thousand doorsteps judged people to be "partners." Those judgments made those people countable and allowed them to show up in final statistics, though not as partners. Reading beyond the numbers, we can recover a series of lost histories, of communities of people who did not otherwise seem to fit, from Harlem to Hawaii.

Margaret Scattergood became a partner, then dissolved into the mass of the nation. Reading the data deeply now, we can see her and acknowledge her, and her choice to live outside the bounds of a patriarchal household, and the unseen negotiations that made her, maybe only briefly, a "partner."

MAPS REVEAL MARGINS, WHERE PARTNERS CLUSTER

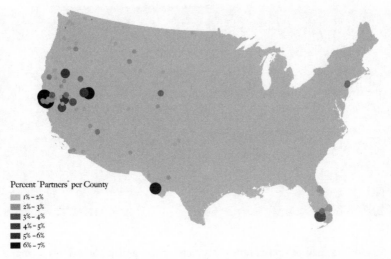

Percent "Partners" per County
- 1% – 2%
- 2% – 3%
- 3% – 4%
- 4% – 5%
- 5% – 6%
- 6% – 7%

This map, prepared for me by the data scientist Stephanie Jordan, nicely illustrates the occurrence of "partner" labels across the nation (but excluding territories, like Hawaii): they come in clusters.

I went looking for "partners" in marginal (edgy) neighborhoods, which could be seen on maps created by risk evaluators for the Home Owners' Loan Corporation (HOLC) to support federal mortgage lending.

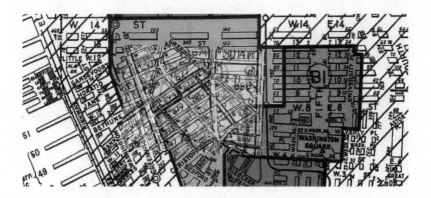

Here is a map of enumeration districts (E.D.s) superimposed on a HOLC map in New York's Greenwich Village neighborhood. Enumerator Lillian

Rita Davis labeled 13 partners in E.D. 31–879, marked simply by 879 in this map.

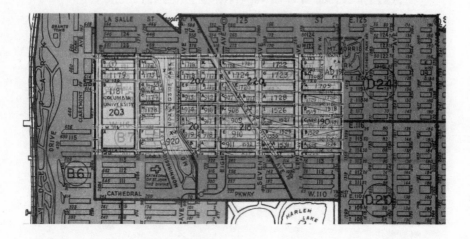

Here is a map of enumeration districts superimposed on a HOLC map in New York's Harlem neighborhood. Enumerator Vera Maude Smith labeled 15 partners in E.D. 31–1723B, marked simply by 1723 in this map.

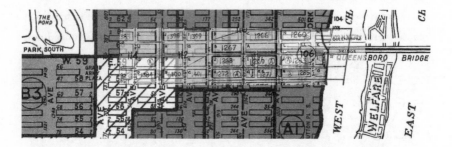

Here is a map of enumeration districts superimposed on a HOLC map in New York's Upper East Side neighborhood. Enumerator Patrena Greco labeled 13 partners in E.D. 31–1272, marked simply by 1272 in this map.

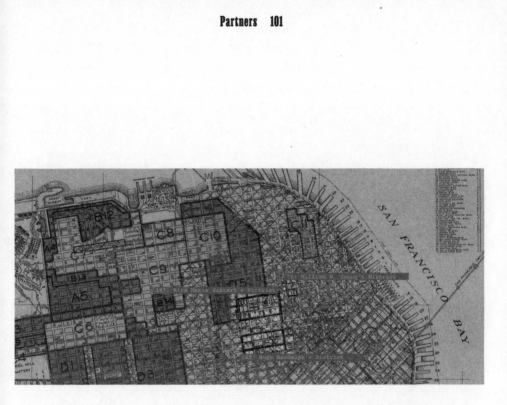

Here are three maps of enumeration districts superimposed on a HOLC map in northeast San Francisco. Rita Marie Ganzert in E.D. 38–157 counted 41 partners; Hugh Randolph in E.D. 38–168 counted 93 partners; and William W. Young in E.D. 38–18 counted 151.

4

Counting with Friends

Published numbers are scrubbed and stripped, as much as possible, of the personalities and politics that made them possible. But make no mistake, personalities and politics are involved. There are no census numbers without the people who make them and the political organizations that support them. The same could probably be said of any data set.

Reading the data in search of the people behind the numbers thus far, we have focused on the folks who designed the census and the folks who answered the questions. Standing between those groups, central to the project of preparing data that will serve a democracy, are the workers whose stories showcase the interweaving of science with both personality and politics.

A room filled mostly with white men could come up with a list of questions for the census, but those men alone could never ask those questions of a hundred million people. That roomful of men could not appear on millions of doorsteps, apply a name to each person, and find a way to wrestle each into a label they had previously deemed suitable. No, the Question Men could get answers only by relying on enumerators, and they needed a hundred thousand of them.

All enumerators left their own unique mark on every census schedule. At the very least, they left their own name, signed or printed, on the top right corner of every sheet.

Eudora Carpenter left her mark.

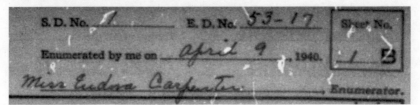

Clara Triplett Doss left her mark.

Lucile McCollum left hers too.

These are marks of data makers.

Millions upon millions of people influenced the data, ranging from those who wrote the questions and instructions to those who answered the questions to those who punched those answers into paper cards. But the hundred-thousand-plus enumerators left the clearest evidence of individual authorial contributions.

The census depended on the ingenuity, creativity, and local knowledge of these enumerators. The census was thus saddled with their foibles, misconceptions, and prejudices. Reading a census sheet, every line filled in by the same hand, feels like contemplating a profoundly personal project.

So why did these names appear on the top right corner of each census sheet? Why were these people granted the right and responsibility to make the data?

Seeking answers to those questions reveals much that is truly personal, about individuals struggling to get by, pitching their potential, begging for help, peeking over shoulders, or calling in favors. But it also turns out that seeking the stories behind the selection of enumerators allows us to see clearly the delicate dance of powerful political and technical forces.

The census was never just about counting. It was and is a part of the process of governing, a massive enterprise many would fight to control. Let us turn to Mississippi's census takers, to see how a president's ambitions, a congressman's friendships, a seasoned bureaucrat's maneuvers, and the texts and tests of reforming social scientists intertwined, and occasionally clashed, in choosing the country's counters.

"I have submitted an application to the U.S. Census Office in Tupelo," wrote Clara Triplett Doss.[1] Eudora Carpenter, whom her sister could recommend as an "old maid" with "her own car," also submitted an application. Lucile McCollum, widowed with two children, did too. The three women were savvy, well aware that politics would influence their fates, as would the stories they told about themselves and the skills they demonstrated. I wonder if they realized, though, that the politics of selection in Mississippi were particularly fraught and, for us, particularly revealing. Did they know that, apart from leaving a mark on the census sheets, they would also leave traces of themselves in presidential archives and a congressperson's papers? Those traces allow us to reconstruct Mississippi's process in detail.

The trouble started—and the records started accumulating—in August 1939, when Census Bureau director William Lane Austin informed President Roosevelt's people that he desired to make the Mississippi appointments himself.[2]

Making those appointments meant deciding which local congresspeople and which senators would be granted the opportunity to hand out plum managerial positions in the census to key supporters, who would, in turn, hand out more jobs to all those enumerators. The position of district supervisor was a plum job indeed, even if not an easy one. It paid a base salary of $2,000 for less than a year's work, and, on top of that, the supervisor got a small bonus for every person counted.[3]

The position also came with the privilege of handing out jobs in the thick of a still terribly depressed economic era.

Director Austin would need nine district supervisors in Mississippi and a total of 1,833 enumerators.[4] The supervisors would need assistants and secretaries, clerks and special agents too. These were all to be part of Mississippi's "field force," the workers responsible for making data from the state's people. When folks at the time talked about the census takers as a group, they marshalled military metaphors: they referred to the "army of enumerators" marching out to count the nation. Only the language of war could describe the sort of mass mobilization that made the census possible. (This still holds true today.)

David Niles was on the receiving end of Austin's request to take care of the Mississippi appointments. Niles worked for Harry Hopkins in the Commerce Department. Before that he had worked for Hopkins in the WPA, where he specialized in trading favors (especially "patronage," or the right to hand out jobs and other opportunities). After World War II, Niles won the ear of the president and advocated that Truman desegregate the military and support a Jewish state in Palestine.[5] But in 1939, Niles had his hands full doling out jobs and favors to those the administration favored.

The Mississippi issue—the Austin issue—appears to have been serious enough that Niles wanted the big boss to know what was happening. He wrote to the White House.

Niles did not think Austin should be allowed to take care of the Mississippi appointments himself. In fact, Niles concluded that Austin was someone he (Niles) needed to "handle."[6]

In Niles's letter to Roosevelt's office, he described Austin as "a nice old guy."[7] That seems to have been the greatest praise he could muster for the man. Niles thought that Austin's age and the ways of doing things he had learned over his sixty-nine years of life had made it harder for him to appreciate how the times and the politics around the census had changed.

Niles may have been right, but he also may have underestimated just how many revolutions in census taking and in census politics Austin had adapted himself to already.

The census that he would one day direct first counted William Lane Austin as a child of nine years old in 1880.[8] That 1880 census also began the enumerator era of the census. The enumerator John E. Miller who found Austin's parents on June 14 belonged to the very first cohort of census takers organized in Washington, D.C.[9] Before that census, the job of counting the nation's population had been subcontracted out through law enforcement: each U.S. marshal took up the task of appointing a band of census takers. For decades, the local census takers then posted the full list of everyone counted so that neighbors could approve whatever stories their fellow householders had told about their households.[10] But Austin was born, and then counted, under a new, modern regime that believed gathering data was its own special art, maybe even a science. And that regime slowly shifted toward greater confidentiality, working on the assumption that people would reveal more about themselves and more honestly if they thought their private data was not going to be broadcast widely.[11] That regime insisted that the people charged with doing the counting be carefully chosen and carefully trained.

Austin saw firsthand the Census Bureau's transition from an every-ten-year ad hoc operation to a permanent scientific agency. Having grown up in Mississippi, Austin went to college there too—a well-heeled young man assuming his place as a future leader of the state's white elite at Ole Miss. In his senior year he was elected president of his class.[12] He received a law degree, but he did not become a practicing lawyer. He became a teacher and then a Washington, D.C., bureaucrat instead, joining the 1900 census office as a clerk whose specialty would be America's plantations.[13] What began as a job with the 1900 census transformed into a long-term gig working for the newly established permanent Census Bureau in 1902.

Austin did not only work for the 1900 census. He was recorded in it as well and appeared in the manuscript data at age twenty-nine as a "book-keeper." His enumerator signed her name to the sheet as S. D. Austin, as in Susan Austin, William Lane's mother. Clearly, the census was in Austin's blood.[14]

The census operation that Austin headed in 1940 would employ many white women, women following in Susan Austin's footsteps, women like Eudora Carpenter, Clara Triplett Doss, and Lucile McCollum. Mississippi's regiment of enumerators eventually included 938 white women and 890 white men. It included just 3 African American men and 2 African American women. The state had the fewest Black enumerators despite having one of the largest populations of African Americans.[15]

In 1939, the selection of those enumerators was still to come, and the control of their selection was what David Niles had written to the president to discuss. Niles elaborated on what he saw to be the reasons William Lane Austin could not be trusted with the Mississippi appointments. Niles judged Austin to be oblivious to how the political ground had shifted underneath his feet. Austin believed "a Democrat is a Democrat." Niles claimed that Austin didn't see how Roosevelt was working to remake the Democrats into a more liberal party. The actual party that Roosevelt controlled had been built as an alliance of Southern conservatives with a liberal wing that believed in a more powerful, more interventionist government. Roosevelt at the time of the 1940 census sought to secure the legacy of his New Deal by rewarding liberals and by, when possible, freezing out those less enthusiastic about his agenda. To make that happen, Roosevelt needed to tighten his control over the dispensing of the spoils of government, centralizing some of the powers of patronage that the Congress traditionally enjoyed. Austin, in contrast, persisted in respecting congressional privileges, including the patronage powers of conservative Democrats. Niles had scolded Austin, explaining to him the new order of things in the Roosevelt White House: "appointments to the Census were not the province of the Congress but are to be determined by the President and Secretary Hopkins for whom we are working." Austin had to be shown the new channels directing the flow of power through the executive branch.[16]

David Niles's appraisal of Austin may have been correct. Austin might not have understood precisely how alliances were shifting within the Democratic Party. But Austin certainly understood that the success of the census depended on his tacking with the prevailing political winds. By that point, Austin—who was a lifelong Southern Democrat—

had seen his fortunes rise and fall with the Democratic Party's. When the Democrat Woodrow Wilson had become president, Austin had gotten a promotion to chief clerk of the Census Bureau and then again to head statistician of the agricultural census. But he had paid for that when the Republicans won the presidency in 1920.

The just-completed 1920 census had been plagued by delays, caused mostly by a very tight labor market that had made it hard to hire enough enumerators in rural areas. The new, Republican-appointed census director chose to single out bad weather—especially in January, when the count had begun—as a cause for the delays. This was a swipe at Austin, and Austin knew it. He had been key in pushing for a January start date, because he believed a winter count would yield better farm data. Austin could see that he—the Democrat—was being scapegoated.[17]

Bureaucrats at the time tended to be formal and civil in the letters they wrote, so it took me a long time to realize how much Austin distrusted his new Republican boss. He was clearly indignant about being blamed for the 1920 delays, but perhaps, I thought, that was just a one-time thing? It wasn't. I found a handwritten letter from 1928 that Austin had sent to a fellow Mississippi Democrat, John E. Rankin, who held a senior position on the House Committee on the Census. Austin was offering Rankin "one word of caution": Austin identified a "so-called democrat" who was working secretly as Census Director William Mott Steuart's *personal representative.* "Do not tell him anything you would care to keep from the Director and the Republican crowd," he warned.[18]

With Franklin Roosevelt's election to the presidency in 1932, Austin's fortunes turned again. At that point, Roosevelt still needed to shore up the support of the more conservative Southern wing of his party, and so he appointed Daniel C. Roper to represent the South in his cabinet.[19] Roper in turn raised his old census friend, Austin, to the bureau's directorship. However, the ground shifted again under Austin's feet, just as planning for the 1940 census was ramping up, when Roper stepped down as secretary of commerce after two consecutive four-year terms of service, clearing the way for one of Roosevelt's most trusted liberal advisors, Harry Hopkins, to take up the position.

Harry Hopkins was a spendthrift and a do-gooder, a man with rich tastes, a ready wit, a knack for responding well to crises, and a long history of creating jobs for the unemployed. Hopkins loved spending federal dollars to put Americans to work, and (according to some) he didn't mind directing a few more of those dollars every once in a while toward states and politicians who could help the administration. Hopkins thought he had a shot to succeed Roosevelt as president, and Roosevelt (in service of that dream) installed him at Commerce, where he could get to know the nation's business leaders better.[20] From December 1938 on, Hopkins would be Austin's boss. Austin owed his position to his ties to Roper and the big-tent, conservative-friendly Democratic Party that first elected the president. But by his third term in office, Roosevelt was seeking to build a party more committed to him and his New Deal. The fiercely loyal Hopkins would use his position and his own men, especially David Niles, to help. Austin would be in trouble if he got in the way, and it was Niles's job to be sure that Austin appreciated that.

Niles chided Austin for having made "promises to those who are not friendly to the President."[21] Niles was probably most upset about the appointment of the area manager in Mississippi, an appointment that Austin had promised to his longtime political mentor, the state's senior senator (and Democrat), Pat Harrison.

The area manager was a new invention for the 1940 census. The role interposed a new layer of control between the bureau in D.C. and the hundreds of district supervisors around the country. Crucially, in the eyes of the bureau, area managers oversaw the training of politically appointed district supervisors, but did not themselves hire those district supervisors, local enumerators, or any other patronage positions. (Area managers also solved unexpected problems, such as the one we saw when Elijah Lewis had to deal with rumors of Communist infiltration in California.) But to the president and to Congress, the new positions still looked like new opportunities for patronage. David Niles explained the bureau's official stance in a phone call to fend off an angry Texas senator: "The area supervisor has no more to do with the hiring of personnel in your state than [does] the man in the moon." But the senator worried, with good reason, that even a technical position had political value. "It is simply a political machine that you are building up," he said.[22] Another senator, from Delaware, complained first that his state had been passed over completely in this regard. Most states had one or two area managers, while the biggest states, with their larger number of supervisor districts, got a few more. But tiny Delaware had been (understandably) assigned an area manager from Maryland to oversee its sole supervisor district. That senator was not appeased when Delaware eventually got a separate area manager, but one whom he had no say in choosing: "You have no idea how embarrassing it is to the Senator to read in the local newspapers the names of these men who were selected contrary to his wishes," lamented the senator's secretary to Roosevelt's office.[23]

Niles kept insisting to livid senators that area supervisors had nothing to do with hiring and that each was an office worker, a "technical man," all of which was true.[24] Niles held back a key detail, though. Roosevelt himself signed off on each and every such appointment. "We have appointed approximately 120 area supervisors in accordance with the President's wishes," wrote Niles to Roosevelt senior aide and friend General Edwin "Pa" Watson in late September 1939, "but no one but you, Secretary Hopkins and myself know that I went over that list with the President."[25] These were good jobs being handed out in the thick of a depression, and every legislator wanted the loyalty such a job would yield, and so did the president. When Niles slighted a senator and denied him that patronage, the slight came directly from the president, just as many suspected. Roosevelt wasn't exceptional among presidents in using patronage power this way—he was just the first president to have the new position of area manager to bargain with, and he planned to use it as part of his unusually ambitious plan to transform his own party.

The problem with Austin's telling the senior Democratic senator from Mississippi, Pat Harrison, that Harrison could pick the area manager was that Niles (with the president's okay) had already promised that selection to the state's junior senator, Theodore Bilbo. Harrison was a Southern conservative and a onetime New Dealer who had fallen from favor when he resisted Roosevelt's turn toward a greater and wider distribution of wealth in the late 1930s.[26] Roosevelt and Niles threw their hats in with Bilbo instead. Bilbo was a racist demagogue, but despite that flaw, he was a valuable ally to Roosevelt as a populist who supported more aggressive economic policies (well, he supported such policies as long as the wealth being redistributed was shared only among whites).[27] So what was the solution for Mississippi? Two senators could not each get the single selection they were both promised.

Or could they? Austin proposed a compromise: give Mississippi two area supervisors, one for each senator.[28] And that is what happened.

The area manager position—and the controversies and compromises it inspired—illustrate well the way that the political and the technical could not be disentangled. The separation of politics and statistics is idle fantasy, a rationalist's dream. In reality, statistics depend on politics (and politics on statistics).

Before there could be a census, there had to be legislation authorizing that census, legislation that set broad rules regarding important questions, like how long the census could last, and legislation that made crucial logistical decisions, such as what to pay the enumerators. (Paying enumerators too little when work was plentiful and labor scarce had made Austin's life miserable in 1920, so he knew firsthand that Lucifer lurked in the logistics.) No census legislation could succeed without first winning the approval of the Census Committee of the House of Representatives. So census directors had to get cozy with that committee's members. In 1930, under a Republican administration, the Mississippi Democrat John E. Rankin wrangled an appointment for his brother, Ethelbert Rutledge Rankin, as the district supervisor in Tupelo, Mississippi. Rutledge (as he was called) sold cars for a living, which couldn't have been easy in 1930 as the Depression deepened. So he must have enjoyed the padding from that supervisor's salary he got thanks to the favors his brother did in getting a 1930 census bill passed.[29] (Now, Title 13 of the U.S. Code provides standing authorization for the census, but it used to be that every census needed to be authorized by a special bill passed before the census could begin. The bill authorizing the 1930 census was significant in part because it set a precedent for also authorizing future censuses ahead of time.) Austin's predecessor—Director Steuart—

had protected the census and ensured a well-supported count by throwing an appointment to Rankin's brother.

In 1939, Austin needed the promise of appointments to secure his own upcoming census. To get a crucial census bill approved (which would amend the standing authorization), he made a deal with Leland M. Ford, a California Republican on the Census Committee. Ford voted to approve Austin's special census of housing in 1940, and in return he got to choose the census supervisor and assistant supervisor for his district, the 16th in Los Angeles. Ford got what he wanted—the privilege of parceling out patronage, a privilege ordinarily reserved for representatives belonging to the administration's party. Austin got what he wanted—the housing census. But there are no everybody-wins propositions in patronage. The loser in this case was California's junior senator, Sheridan Downey, and he was not happy.

This time Niles took Austin's side. He had no sympathy for Downey. There were eight Republican congresspeople in California, and the state's senior senator was also a Republican, which meant that none of them was guaranteed any say in appointing census officials. The upshot was that, by Niles's counting, Downey was already "getting more appointments out of the Census than anybody in the Senate or the House." Congressman Ford pressed his own case with Niles, too, giving him a phone call to ask about that district supervisor appointment *before* he went out to say anything on the House floor that would help the administration. Still, Niles feared the trouble being sowed by Downey (or more precisely, Downey's "tough secretary"). He ran the situation by General "Pa" Watson. Niles wanted to give the appointment to Ford and stand behind Austin's deal, but he waited to be sure he had (via Watson) the president's support.[30]

In the meantime, Downey's camp caught the ear of James Farley, the postmaster general—visitors to Penn Station in Manhattan who admire the massive, classically styled former post office across the street might recognize Farley's name from its facade. Farley was one of the most powerful men in Washington (and rumored to be a leading presidential candidate if Roosevelt didn't run again). That wasn't because he controlled the mail. It was because he controlled the distribution of most patronage jobs among the Democratic faithful. What David Niles did for Secretary Hopkins, Farley did for the entire party. So it's hardly surprising that Farley stepped in for Downey to find out why Democratic patronage had been diverted to a Republican. Niles defended the decision. Farley knew, didn't he, that an effective bureaucrat needed sometimes to "make gestures of appeasement and even commitments on his own account"? As Niles told it, this had been one of those times for Austin. Niles appealed to the patronage king, trying to convince him that the Democratic Party's interests weren't being neglected. Congressman Ford had agreed to pick men who were acceptable to his district's local Democratic leaders, Niles explained.[31] And that was enough. California's 16th would be run by the Republican Ford's chosen, Democrat-approved man.[32]

Complex political negotiations like these have shaped, in one way or another, every census and probably every big data set.

William Lane Austin did not win total control of the Mississippi appointments, nor did he walk away empty-handed. He secured an area manager slot for his patron, and the deals necessary to secure a housing census too. And, as we'll see, he assured that the other Mississippi power broker he was indebted to—John E. Rankin—was also taken care of.

In 1930, the Mississippi congressman John E. Rankin wrangled a district supervisor position for his brother Rutledge—the only Democrat to get an appointment under a Republican administration. In 1939, Rankin topped the list of congresspeople Austin wanted to reward.[33] Rankin represented Mississippi's northeasternmost congressional district, on the border with Alabama and Tennessee. He had also served on the House Census Committee for most of his congressional career, where he was ruthless. Rankin appears to have understood that from his seat on the Census Committee, he could secure a prime spot in the patronage line and also protect the political power of Mississippi while preserving a commitment to xenophobia and white supremacy. He made the most of the power he accrued in committee.

Austin wrote Rankin a letter in mid-September 1939 soliciting a name for the supervisor in Mississippi's first district. It was mainly a form letter, but Austin scrawled "Personal" at the top and underlined it. It laid out the qualifications for a district supervisor: a local who could work full-time, an able-bodied person between the ages of twenty-five and sixty with at least a high school education and some experience running a large office or business. And it invoked the Hatch Act, which prohibited employees in the executive branch of the federal government from engaging in certain forms of political activity—the enumerators who a district supervisor was charged to hire would be patronage positions that would be distributed in an election year, but the patron (the district supervisor) wouldn't be allowed to actively run a candidate while also handing out jobs.[34]

Rankin tapped a newspaperman, Harold B. Sanders, owner and editor of the *Aberdeen Examiner*, to oversee his district's census and hire all its enumerators. Sanders was thrilled. The pay, he said, made the difference "in educating my girls, in a trying time."[35] (Many Mississippi men were anxious about educating their "girls"—daughters who might be nearly fully grown—as evidenced by letters later sent to Sanders begging for enumerator jobs.) Sanders gushed with gratitude, then acknowledged who the real boss was. When it came to hiring, there were "two or three men that I [Sanders] would like to help" but only "in case you [Rankin] have no preference," and even then, Sanders promised to consult Rankin before doing anything.[36] Rankin in turn sent Sanders the name of "two of my best friends" to serve as the district's assistant supervisor and clerk.[37] A "friend" in this case didn't have to be a buddy—it usually meant a political ally. Rankin said these two friends "know everybody in the county," and they presumably knew who Rankin thought should be favored and trusted with a job.

The job was a lifeline for one of those "friends" and really a lifeline for an entire family. Rankin chose a former sheriff (and former census district supervisor) named Oscar Trapp to be the assistant supervisor, only to learn that Trapp was too old for the job. He was sixty-six, and the Census Bureau refused anyone older than fifty-nine.[38] So Rankin threw his weight behind young Wendall "Wib" Trapp, Oscar's son. But Wib got another, better (and more permanent) job with a different New

Deal agency, the Home Owners' Loan Corporation. He begged Rankin to get the census supervisor job for his father, who was unemployed with an ailing wife. "I do not know of any other means of my parents remaining in their home at this time," wrote Wib, and he promised that Oscar would, as always, ensure that "your friends are used."[39] In the meantime, a swell of letters from other "friends" arrived to make Oscar's case. Rankin finally used his pull with the Census Bureau to make an exception, and Oscar Trapp got the position.[40] Rankin had done his best for an old, influential friend.

In the age of Facebook, which has made "friend" into a verb, a click, it might be easy to think that there was some completely uncorrupted past when friends were, well, friends, who knew each other fully and liked each other's company, not just their social media posts. Of course, such true friendships did and still exist. But the corruption of "friend" is much older than Facebook. As the historian Richard White explains in his chronicle of the construction of the transcontinental railroads, the robber barons of that era called each and every congressperson they paid off and every lobbyist they employed "friends."[41] "Friends" to Rankin, Sanders, and Trapp were allies in the internecine squabbles that scarred Mississippi's Democratic Party. And those men talked about "friends" incessantly.

Rankin wanted Sanders to look to "friends" across his district for advice: "I should like to have some friend who is worthy and qualified selecting [enumerators] for each county."[42] He recommended one man who "knows practically every person in the county, and knows who are my friends and who are worthy and qualified to do this work."[43] To another man, Rankin wrote: "You know who our friends are in that county, and who are worthy and qualified, and I know you will help select the best people for these places."[44] To the man he had installed as clerk in the district office, Rankin wrote: "I have not forgotten . . . your loyalty and continued friendship."[45] It was only natural for Rankin to enlist his allies in this important project, and he didn't see why he couldn't help them out and also get good workers: "Of course we want our friends to do this work, and we also want thoroughly capable and deserving people who will do it right."[46] Sanders agreed: "While I hope to get capable men and women in every case, [I] see no reason why I can't find them among your friends."[47]

One prominent state politician asked Rankin to "befriend" a woman who wanted to take the census.[48] He didn't want Rankin to get to know her—he wanted Rankin to get her a job. Another job seeker opened a request to Rankin "Dear Sir + Buddy." He had "one grown Girl" who had finished high school and wanted to go on to college, but the crops were bad, and he didn't have the money.[49] Rankin wasn't about to get it for him, though; Rankin might become this man's "friend," but he wasn't his buddy.

Congressional representatives had every incentive to see that their districts were fully counted—they wanted to protect their seats in the House, and they wanted the resources and prestige that came with size—so Rankin truly wanted to see enumerators hired who were capable and who would be dogged in their pursuit of every Mississippian in District 1. "We are not trying to make this a political machine, but are trying to make the best possible job of taking the 1940 census," wrote Rankin to one of his "friends" charged with identifying other worthy "friends" for enumerator jobs.[50] In the case that a "friend" had to be turned down because he was likely to be a very bad census taker, Sanders took the heat and the blame for the hiring decision; Rankin could stand back and claim he wasn't in charge. There was also another strategy available for dodging angry, unqualified "friends": blame the tests!

Before anyone could get an enumerating job, they had to pass a series of exams. Sanders got a local college professor to put together and grade a first round of (simple) tests in Tupelo. But the next round—"a very thorough examination" designed by census experts—went to Washington, D.C., to be graded. That unnerved Sanders. He had his secretary write to Rankin to explain that "he [was] doing his best to carry on a good job and treat everybody right." The letter thus winked in the direction of efforts to put in the fix for some "friends" before sending the exams to D.C.,[51] but Sanders couldn't control how Washington graded Rankin's preferred candidates. He wanted that point to be clear.

The more difficult tests hailed from D.C., where the men responsible did not talk about friendship. They talked about their doctorates.

A group of highly trained scientists had designed the second round of tests. They worked in the Census Bureau's Division of Statistical Research (DSR), led by the chief statistician, Calvert Dedrick. Cal, as he was known to his friends and colleagues, had earned a Ph.D. in sociology from the University of Wisconsin, one of the nation's premier programs. Wisconsin instilled in its graduates a desire to make science serve the public, while Franklin Roosevelt's New Deal created a sudden wealth of opportunities to satisfy such desires. Dedrick's government career had begun with an effort to count the Great Depression's unemployed, but he was soon lured away by an offer to join and then lead the fledgling DSR.[52] Dedrick surrounded himself with others who dreamed of rebuilding the Census Bureau and the census itself using the most sophisticated statistical techniques. At the top of their list of tasks was improving the quality of their enumerating "field force."

In a document he wrote discussing the Census Bureau's director, Dedrick didn't call William Lane Austin "a nice old guy," but he might as well have. Austin, he wrote, belonged to the "slow-moving tradition" of the "class of 1900"—by which Dedrick referred to all bureau staffers who had begun their service with the 1900 census. Among the strikes against this class for Dedrick was that "only three had Ph.D.'s." Dedrick nonetheless admired Austin for his pride in the bureau, his fierce defense of its honor, and especially his willingness to support experiments that he did not himself understand.[53]

The new generation of Ph.D.s in the Census Bureau spoke in an academic argot, so it's hardly surprising that when they set out to reform the system for training enumerators, they talked about founding "the country's most remarkable 'university.'"[54]

This "university," as it appears in a bureau publicity shot, looks less like a college than like a warehouse with vaulted ceilings, an open floor, and thick structural beams. In the photo, long tables are organized in a series of semicircles, at which sit mainly white men, many balding or graying, in suits. There are also two women, both wearing dark hats. The blinds on the space's tall windows have been drawn, and the whole crowd looks toward a man in a dark suit standing beside a film projector. This was where the DSR conducted its two-month-long training for area managers, who would in turn oversee the instruction of the rest of the census field force. The very best performers stayed in Washington to help, while the dullest of the dull (26 of 180) were dropped from the program; even having been handpicked by Roosevelt couldn't save them.[55] Somewhere in that mass of men (and two women) in Washington, D.C., were Mississippi's two area managers, Pat Reily and Eugene P. Lacy, who would have had to fight for one job, were it not for the compromise brokered by Niles. (One of these two was chosen by Roosevelt's man, Senator Bilbo, and the other by Austin's, Senator Harrison, but the records don't indicate which was which.)

While area managers went to "university," ordinary enumerators just went to school. The DSR called itself "a sort of grammar-school principal"—there to check in on the area managers and district supervisors who were, in this analogy, the trainer-teachers and the grade-school teachers, respectively. Dedrick boasted that the DSR had brought to the census the tools of modern "class-room instruction": they gave lectures, they administered multiple-choice "objective" tests, they even showed filmstrips.[56] The job of turning the newspaper editor Harold Sanders into a teacher fell to the area manager in Greenwood, Mississippi, Eugene P. Lacy. Sanders promised his patron, Rankin, he'd do him proud and "turn in a good grade at the close of school."[57]

Sanders's test would have been sent to Washington in early December 1939.[58] He must have at least passed, since he got to keep his job. A census of business and manufacturers began first, in January 1940, with just a few enumerators wandering the district asking shopkeepers and factory owners to open their books, so the instruction focused on that census. Sanders and his peers completed a correspondence course, reading a detailed manual, taking more tests. These tests were no longer meant to weed out the weak. They were about finding and fixing problems. Sanders met his peers in Atlanta—while others gathered at one of nine other regional training centers—where an expanded census "university" reconvened for a few days to clear up any problem areas exposed by all the testing.[59]

Testing placed constraints on "friendship." Tests were often tools that bureaucrats used to seize control of hiring from politicians. (Congress had repeatedly considered making census jobs subject to civil service examinations, which generally worked to constrain patronage, but Congress had repeatedly refused to give up its privilege.) Tests graded in Washington by the DSR, outside the civil service, were a compromise. Still, they made Sanders nervous. He couldn't control the outcome, and that meant he couldn't be sure he was doing what his patron wanted.

It is important to remember that the meritocracy promised by testing would not necessarily lead to better or fairer outcomes. In Britain the first great coup for testing had come with the requirement for civil service exams for selecting officials to staff the growing imperial apparatus in the middle of the nineteenth century. Its supporters lauded a new, rational system for rewarding the best and brightest, while its detractors noted that the tests seemed specially designed to privilege those who could afford an elite education.[60] Americans soon afterward installed their own system of civil service exams. With World War I, intelligence testing conquered the U.S. Army—where it is not clear what good the tests did in sorting soldiers but very clear that they were designed with native-born whites in mind, providing effective fodder for justifying the exploitation of African Americans and immigrants.[61] The DSR's tests employed by the census weren't IQ tests, though. They were tests for selecting and fine-tuning a legion of human sensors for the census.

A district supervisor like Sanders could use a simple test of their own choosing to make initial selections. After that, two more rigorous tests designed by the DSR stood sentry to protect the quality of the count from enumerator incompetence. The first DSR test, Test I, consisted of thirty-three questions and served to weed out the weakest of the force hired through the patronage system.[62] Test-takers faced questions like:

9. A white man is married to a Japanese woman and they have one child. What is the correct symbol for designating the color or race of the child?

Possible answers are "W" for white; "Chi." for Chinese; "Neg." for Negro; or "Other (fill in) _____."

Then comes:

10. Mrs. Green left her husband in February 1940, and has just filed suit for divorce. What is the correct symbol for designating the marital status of Mrs. Green?

Possible answers are "S" for single; "M" for married; "Wd" for widowed; or "D" for divorced.

Or consider, a bit later, this head-scratcher:

12. Mr. Simmons was born in Warsaw when it was part of the Russian Empire. After the World War this city became the capital of the free Republic of Poland. In 1939 it came under German control. What country should be entered as the birthplace of Mr. Simmons?

Possible answers are "Russia"; "Poland"; or "Germany."

In each case, more than one answer is not only plausible, but perfectly reasonable. A child born to a white father might well count as white. Or, knowing the power of the "one-drop rule" in early-twentieth-century America—a rule that said an individual with even one drop of "Negro" blood should count as "Negro"—one might decide a Japanese mother would disqualify the child from whiteness and settle on either "Negro" or "Chinese" as a non-white category. The test-taker did not have the option to "phone a friend," as if this were a TV game show but could reference an abridged set of enumerator instructions, and those made clear that the right answer was "Other," specifically "Jp" for Japanese.

Similarly, Mrs. Green could well be married, since her divorce had not gone through; single, since she was living on her own; or divorced, since that was in process in the courts. Only widowed seems entirely implausible. The Census Bureau's rules, though, allow only one right answer: "M" for married.

Finally, there's Mr. Simmons, the onetime immigrant to the United States who presumably entered the country before the immigration restriction laws of the 1920s would have made his entrance highly unlikely. Labeling Simmons German, since Warsaw had been conquered by

Germany, seems the most straightforward answer. Apart from that, calling him Russian, since it was in the Russian Empire that he had been born, would be equally reasonable. But the right answer was that Simmons was born in Poland, a nation that did not even exist when he was born or when he was enumerated (and we're not told in the question where Simmons's loyalties lay).

What these three examples illustrate well is that Test I was not an intelligence test, nor a measure of the applicant's judgment. It didn't want to see how well an applicant reasoned. It only sought to determine how well the enumerator could follow the Census Bureau's instructions. It determined how accurately each enumerator could record for the state what the state wanted recorded.

The final question of Test I seemed different. It asked for five sentences describing what the applicant would do "if someone refused to give you any information." This, it would seem, was a test of something substantial. Here was a question that probed the applicants' skill at communication and persuasion, their judgment and acumen. Right?

No. The answer key revealed that there was not only no officially correct answer, but that neither the substance nor the style of the answer mattered. The key read: "Grade handwriting as satisfactory; unsatisfactory." All that mattered was that the answer was legible. Test I sought to ensure that each prospective sensor could produce legible outputs.

Test II presented a series of even more complex scenarios. Each question presented a case amounting almost to a short story about a hypothetical encounter at an American's doorstep, one that the trainee needed to translate into data. The DSR dreamed up a fascinating cast of characters. There was the president of None-Such Products Co. and his two at-home servants, the farmer who depended on his son for labor, an unmarried woman working in a real estate office, the head of the sales force of Consolidated Leather Co., and an expectant mother, twice married with two living children and two who had not survived infancy.[63] The narratives corresponded perfectly to the kinds of things that enumerators were sent to investigate, but the DSR had created idealized training data. In real life, the people to be enumerated and the stories told on doorsteps would not line up so perfectly with the questions and categories set out by all those men (and two women) in a Commerce Department auditorium. That's why, for all the work they did to tune these sensors, the census would still ultimately depend largely on the existing strengths and limitations of the people—the "friends" and other employees—being sent out into the field.

It was a Tuesday morning in mid-March when a desperate Clara Triplett Doss arrived at the county courthouse in Macon, Mississippi. Pen and ink in tow, she entered a room that must have been packed. Harold Sanders had anticipated that his office would be inundated by "more applications than ever before known," and he hadn't been far off.[64] Drought had hit northeastern Mississippi hard. The cotton harvest disappointed. The Great Depression seemed to deepen. The federal government tossed lifeline after lifeline to help devastated (white) families stay afloat. The latest lifeline came through the census. For the first round of hires in January, to take the business and manufacturers census, Sanders had about five hundred applicants for only a dozen positions.[65] Triplett Doss might have been one of the many who were disappointed, but there was reason to hope for a better outcome with the population census. Sanders would end up hiring nearly twice as many people in Noxubee County alone for the population census—eighteen hires from the crowd of people Triplett Doss now sat surrounded by.

A WPA bookkeeper named Lucile McCollum—herself just barely surviving on temporary government work—sat in that room too, waiting to take part in the morning's "competitive examinations."[66] This wasn't the DSR exam. It was the initial screening test that Sanders and the Tupelo Office had put together to test more basic skills, like whether the test-taker could work out percentages or spell correctly. A professor, who also worked as the chief census clerk for the district led the design and did all the grading.[67] Taking even a simple test can be stressful, but McCollum had completed high school, and Triplett Doss had four years of college under her belt.[68] Their chances were good.

The quest to secure a census job began long before that March morning and it did not necessarily begin with a formal application. In June

1939 Lucile McCollum had sent a handwritten plea to Congressman Rankin's office asking that he secure her a census-taking position. She was, she wrote, a "widow with two small children."[69] She supported herself and those children (thirteen-year-old Patricia and eleven-year-old Gerald, according to the census)[70] with the pittance she earned at the WPA, but she would soon lose even that pittance when her current project ended. She needed a new job.

In that missive McCollum fit her life story into a well-established genre: "the begging letter,"[71] casting herself as a worthy object of Rankin's pity and patronage. Her application, submitted soon after, required a different set of contortions. She had to cram herself into a form with preprinted questions that brooked no silences.[72] How much did McCollum weigh? How tall was she? Did she "use" intoxicating beverages or habit-forming drugs? McCollum's answers allowed Census Bureau officials to identify her congressional district (since she was, after all, to be a patronage appointment—in Rankin's District 1, in this case), to determine if she held a public office (or was related to an officeholder) in any way that would disqualify her from census taking (not that we know of), and to see if she might qualify for a preference for employing wounded veterans or their wives/widows—again, no. It asked if McCollum had a car, or access to a car, because the Census Bureau wouldn't be providing one. Question 23 might have been the most practically important one: "Was this application filled out in your own handwriting?" This was crucial: A good sensor must create legible records. Could officials read what McCollum wrote? (I am certain they could—McCollum's first letter to Rankin had used a simple, clear cursive.)[73]

McCollum wrote again to Rankin on December 30, 1939, this time typing out her case: that she was a widow with two children, that she had useful experience counting people for the WPA.[74] She nevertheless received a letter, dated January 4, 1940, that explained the job had gone to a man named Hunter Scales George.[75] It said that the highest scorer on the test usually got this job of taking the business and manufacturers census.

But there were exceptions. Just ask Hollis Imes of Lowndes County (where McCollum lived). According to Sanders, Imes "made the highest grade and seemed qualified." Rankin signed off on him. But Rankin's chief "friend" in Lowndes nixed the appointment. Sheriff Propst said he "could not recommend the party," and with that Imes lost not only the business census, but also the population census job.[76] Hollis Imes provides evidence of the limited power that the local, non-DSR tests had. And Imes probably never knew he had been denied a place on Sheriff Propst's word. He might not even have known when the person hired instead of him came around on April 14 to count him. Hollis's mother, Millenium, answered the door and answered the questions, sparing Hollis. But her answers give us one clue to explain Hollis Imes's exclusion. He was divorced.[77] Had marital scandals sunk him?

Good test results couldn't guarantee a position, but bad results made it difficult to hire even a favored individual. Rankin got a telegram in December 1939 urging him to intercede with Sanders for a young man in Tupelo named Jimmie Patrick. The telegram came from Christobel Patrick, Jimmie's older sister.[78] The Patricks seem to have been powerful figures. "Miss Christobel" and her mother both held county clerkships, according to census records, and Rankin sprang into action when Christobel wired him. "I have . . . written Mr. H. B. Sanders at Aberdeen [on] Jimmie's behalf," he promised.[79] But Jimmie Patrick didn't get the business census job for January. It went to another man who had scored a "higher grade" on the test.[80] He also failed to get a job in Sanders's office when one opened up in late January. (The Patricks weren't the only Tupelo powerhouses fighting for that clerkship, which ended up going to a man from Aberdeen, one who'd "made a fine grade" and didn't anger the rival factions.)[81] Finally, Jimmie Patrick failed to secure a job with the April population census. His score must have been terrible. Or maybe he himself was terrible, and his score was but a useful excuse for holding off the wrath of Miss Christobel.

A month before she entered that courthouse, Clara Triplett Doss submitted her application to Sanders and got her entire family involved in a campaign of coordinated begging for Rankin's favor. Their letters set up Triplett Doss as poor but worthy and suggested that Rankin's support for her would help support an entire clan. Triplett Doss's mother explained that she was a widow, that her husband had left her with "no insurance to help me along," and that her daughter did "the best she can to take care of me and the baby too."[82] (He was a nine-month-old, according to census records.)[83] She also told Rankin that she wished he'd pass legislation to see that "all the able bodied lazy folks go to work. That would be more benefit to the world than any thing." It was an odd sentiment for a letter premised on the fact that work was impossible to find, but its message was really: we're not the lazy folks; we want to work. Triplett Doss's brother, Howard, proved his worth by a different tack. "As you perhaps know I am a world war veteran not receiving any pension from the Gov't," he began. Howard supported his mother—"as I should"—and had been "practically supporting my sister" (Triplett Doss) for fifteen years. A job for Triplett Doss would therefore lift a burden from Howard too. "I am not asking for charity," he stressed; he wanted a job—a census job—for his sister.[84]

Neither Triplett Doss nor McCollum left a record of their experience taking the first screening test. But we can guess they were scoping out their competition. Perhaps Triplett Doss was looking for, and comparing herself with, the other worthy poor. McCollum may have been looking for other widows in need. Veterans looked for other veterans and called on the American Legion to complain if an enumerator job went to a civilian.[85] People with census-taking experience looked for others like them and wrote Rankin or sent angry telegrams when noncensus veterans were chosen over them.[86]

In the exam, in tight quarters, test-takers may have let their eyes drift to other people's papers too. Lovie W. Moore wrote John E. Rankin an indignant letter after she learned she had been denied a position. She insisted that it couldn't be the test results that held her back. "I must have made the grade ok," she wrote. How did she know? Moore's trump card was that she had "sat together" with another woman who did get hired, "and our answers were exactly the same."[87]

Back in Noxubee County, Lucile McCollum fired off another letter to Rankin after passing the first exam and on the way to finishing the DSR tests. She had no meaningful connections, no claim on Rankin's attention, beyond being a widow.[88] Some of the other letters Rankin received drew on *very* close connections. One of his cousins successfully prevailed upon him to reserve a job for her "Mamma," who had been nearly ruined by the spring floods.[89] Another cousin wielded the Rankin name like a cudgel, bullying Sanders into a scheme to rearrange the census maps solely to get him a job; John Rankin had to send his brother out to put the raging cousin in his place.[90] The man got an ordinary census-taking job, though not the reorganization he'd demanded. In a similar situation, though, when the nephew of a Clay County supporter was rejected, Sanders did change the enumeration maps to carve out space for the young man to get work.[91] Family couldn't always be accommodated, but Rankin and Sanders did their best for important, influential "friends."

Eudora Carpenter didn't have a personal connection to either man. Her sister, in a begging letter meant to engender sympathy, called her "an old maid."[92] According to the 1940 census she was fifty-seven years old, living with her eighty-four-year-old-parents, helping to manage their farm. Carpenter tried flattery. "We are very grateful to you," she wrote to Rankin "for the splendid work you did in getting the T.V.A. over our county as well as your entire district."[93] By the "T.V.A." she meant the Tennessee Valley Authority, a publicly funded New Deal program to generate hydroelectric power that would be used to bring cheap electricity to poor, rural residents in surrounding regions—people like Eudora Carpenter. Rankin had managed to get his corner of Mississippi—the northeast corner—included in the TVA's electrical networks. By praising this accomplishment, Carpenter showed herself to be well informed, gracious, and of a favorable political bent. Meanwhile, her sister wrote to the state's lieutenant governor, explaining that Carpenter had three years of college and had experience taking the census, which was a job that ran in the family. Plus, she had a car! That was enough to get a letter from the lieutenant governor to Rankin asking him to "befriend Miss Eudora Carpenter."[94] She got the job.

Lucile McCollum did too, by some unknown mixture of begging letter and test-taking skill. So did Clara Triplett Doss. But Lovie Moore, Jimmy Patrick, Hollis Imes, and many others were denied the license to pry into other people's lives.

Roosevelt, meanwhile, got to reward loyal New Dealers who were helping him build a more liberal Democratic Party. Rankin got to solidify "friendships" in northeastern Mississippi. Director Austin got his army of enumerators and a little extra patronage for his political mentor. And the Division of Statistical Research advanced its vision of a process organized around teaching and testing instead of political patronage.

The census was never merely a count. It produced more than tables of numbers. It generated jobs. It raised a statistical army and trained its soldiers to appraise people the way the Question Men wanted them to—at least, it tried. It also cultivated competitions for influence and resources.

And though the politicians, bureaucrats, scientists, and enumerators seldom talked about it, the census also authored silences. It created statistical holes alongside statistical wholes, deciding which Americans would be seen, represented, and governed.

5

Silences and White Supremacy

eople sometimes say that the data speaks for itself. We know what they mean. Even if data cannot actually speak, much less speak autonomously, data points together can paint a convincing picture that invites a conclusion, that authorizes or justifies some decision.

But data never speaks for itself. People work hard to make data appear capable of speech and also to set limits on that speech. They struggle to control what things a data set will encompass, what questions it can answer, and on what topics it will be silent. That work and those struggles matter a great deal when what the data appears to say, or seems incapable of saying, has potent political consequences.

One way to uncover the political forces that shaped a data set is to look to that set's silences. Those silences often have political implications, and those silences themselves are often the product of politics. We can read data—both the process that generates the numbers and the numbers themselves—and be on the lookout for the things the data set, as constructed, is unable to say.

As a cultural historian, I have been trained to read texts for silences, to think about what a text might say but does not. In his landmark collection of essays on historical method, anthropologist Michel-Rolph Trouillot explains in detail how and why silences are produced in the making of history, and he says of censuses: "he who counts heads always silences facts and voices."[1] Applying Trouillot's methods to the 1940 census can expose the politics of those silences, explaining who counted and how in a system operating under the shadow of white supremacy, an ideology that valued the voices, votes, and lives of those labeled "white" more highly than all others.[2]

I read for silences with the tools of the humanist: through archival excavations and close scrutiny of the manuscript census. Others use statistical methods to read for silences in the census. Let's begin there.

Daniel O'Haver Price was, in 1947, a sociology graduate student at the University of North Carolina who had already authored an important paper on advanced methods in mathematical statistics.[3]

World War II had interrupted Price's graduate studies, sending him to the Pacific theater, where he served on a PT (patrol torpedo) boat. Upon returning to school, though, Price turned to wartime data to continue his studies.[4] To raise its armies for battle, the U.S. government had generated a database, the draft records created by the first Selective Service System's registration on October 16, 1940, which Price now probed.

Price compared the total numbers printed by the census in April 1940 to those reported a few months later in this special set of administrative records encompassing men between the ages of twenty-one and thirty-five in each state. Price had reason to believe that the registration data presented something close to a gold standard, that it approximated the truth even better than the census could. The government, he reasoned, meted out steep penalties for avoiding registration—for "dodging the draft"—and on top of that, the patriotic fervor of war generated enormous social pressure on men to register. Unlike the census, which relied on a seldom-used threat of punishment (and the slogan "cooperate"), the draft registration had teeth, decreasing the possibility that anyone might escape its jaws. Since the registration made its count just six months after "census day" (which was April 1, when the count officially began), Price could compare the two sources (after some minor adjustments) relatively easily. The draft data made possible a natural experiment, an unplanned test of the census's completeness.[5] Did the data set designed to describe every person in the United States succeed in doing so?

Price published his findings in the nation's leading sociological journal in 1947. In clear but dense and detailed prose illustrated by towering tables of numbers, Price informed his academic and technocratic colleagues that the 1940 census had done a very poor job of counting

African Americans. Price's analysis suggested an "underenumeration" of about 3 percent of the entire U.S. population, which was possibly troubling in its own right to those (like academic demographers or government officials) who relied on census data, though Price did not think that worth too much hand-wringing. The numbers looked much, much worse, however, when compared with those of Black draft registrants. That comparison suggested that the census had underestimated the Black population by about 13 percent.

Price aimed his paper at people who could work to redress this undercounting in coming years. Published in the *American Sociological Review* and based on research conducted with the support of the prestigious Social Science Research Council, the paper had what it took to be taken seriously, and it was. Today, histories of controversies over census "undercounts"—undercounting that is still with us today, though less severely so—usually point to Price's paper as the beginning of the story.[6]

Apart from its technical importance, Price read another implication into the census's silences. In the closing line of his paper, he informed "the advocates of 'white supremacy' in Mississippi" that they were due for some disappointing news, that they may "have been celebrating prematurely when the 1940 Census showed that Mississippi for the first time had more whites than Negroes." If Price's calculations were correct, "then actually in 1940 Negroes still predominated in that state."[7]

One day in the National Archives, I stumbled upon a silence in Price's paper itself. Working through a box of bureau records, I found a folder titled "Negro Enumeration of 1920" containing a typed reply to a scholar who had, in 1922, made a reasoned case for a significant undercount of African Americans.[8] This surprised me. I had never heard of serious scientific estimates of such undercounting before Price, and Price's paper hadn't said anything about Black researchers who had previously uncovered this. Price's paper hadn't prepared me for Kelly Miller.

At the turn of the twentieth century, mathematician Kelly Miller began devoting his time and attention to explaining how missing African Americans in the census endangered the race and all its members.

Flawed census counts, he came to believe, fueled a false narrative about Black inferiority. Undercounting lent credibility to those who claimed African Americans could not survive in the United States, or in the modern world, outside of slavery—a claim first voiced when slavery still reigned and long contested by Black intellectuals.[9]

Kelly Miller became one of that claim's most potent adversaries at the dawn of the twentieth century.

Miller first joined the fight while a young professor of mathematics at the Washington, D.C., flagship school for freedmen, Howard University. Miller jumped into the fray in response to a work that he himself called "the most thorough and comprehensive treatment of the Negro problem, from a statistical standpoint, which has yet appeared."[10]

In 1896, a statistician at New Jersey's Prudential Insurance Company—a German émigré named Frederick Hoffman—published one of the most influential works of American scientific racism. Hoffman's book *Race Traits and Tendencies of the American Negro* presented hundreds of pages of data that purported to prove the innate degeneracy and criminality of African Americans and that predicted the eventual extinction of the Black race in the United States.[11] Hoffman built his case on census data and then, thanks to the support of a Census Bureau statistician, published his book with the stamp of approval of the American Economic Association.[12] Hoffman worked hard at making racism look like a reasonable, objective stance, and his work heralded a new conversation for a post-slavery nation that sought to cast African Americans throughout the country as a problem. As the historian Khalil Gibran Muhammad put it: "The first modern race-relations expert to evince the statistical connections between black migration to the North, urbanization, and criminality, Hoffman helped to certify the nationalization of the Negro Problem."[13]

Miller took Hoffman very seriously but thought his conclusions wrongheaded and his methods mistaken. Miller argued that Hoffman had buttressed his conclusions with faulty data from an incomplete prior census; as Miller demonstrated, the Black population had grown in earlier censuses, though its rate of growth gradually decreased every decade. Then the 1890 census Hoffman referenced appeared to show that rate of growth fall off a cliff. "When a number of observations follow with reasonable uniformity a fixed law, but a single result deviates widely from this law," wrote Miller, "it is usual to suspect the accuracy of the discrepant observation." Hoffman had not done that. He hadn't blamed "the probable imperfection of the eleventh [1890] census" for the slowing growth of the Black population; he had blamed Black people, their physiology, their bodies. Hoffman blamed Black bodies, Miller wrote, even when his own evidence suggested that poverty and discrimination or imperfect statistics lay behind the problems he claimed to be revealing. "The colored race," wrote Miller, "most stubbornly refused to be argued out of existence on an insufficient induction of data and unwarranted conclusions deduced therefrom."[14] Hoffman could wish all he wanted, but he could not, via statistics, bring extinction to a race.

He could do harm, though. In the way they credited racial discrimination and justified the abandonment of any and all sorts of aid for northern Blacks, Hoffman's statistics tried to bring about the extinction they predicted.

As the years passed, however, Miller stubbornly refused to let census statistics erase his people.

In 1922, Miller advanced his undercount thesis again, reading for silences in the census with a method that was a close cousin to the one that Daniel O'Haver Price would later employ. Miller argued that the 1920 census missed African Americans at an alarming rate. A few years earlier, in 1918, a census report had admitted the possibility of significant undercounts and argued for their existence in both 1870 and 1890. (That report depended on the intellectual labor of "a corps of Negro clerks" supervised by three African American census officials: the statistics specialist Charles E. Hall and his fellow civil servants Robert A. Pelham and William Jennifer. It seems possible, maybe even likely, that Miller knew these fellow D.C. intellectuals personally.)[15] The bureau's 1918 report published corrected figures for 1870 and 1890. In 1922, Miller again analyzed rates of growth between censuses and found an abrupt slowing of the Black population. Miller demanded a correction for the 1920 figures too. As he mused in a popular scientific magazine, in his characteristically baroque style: "The irregularities of these figures are as whimsical as if produced by the sport of the gods."[16]

Miller's study postulated a new kind of undercounting. Earlier undercounts, like that in 1890, primarily stemmed from people missed in the rural South. The new undercount resulted from a "mobile negro population" that had been "greatly upset by the world war."[17] The new undercount missed African Americans living in cities.

The Census Bureau appears to have assigned to a white official named Le Verne Beales the task of answering Miller's critiques. I first encountered Miller's article after finding a draft of Beales's reply in bureau files. Where Miller argued for a burgeoning problem of Blacks being undercounted in cities, Beales blamed abnormal conditions: lower birth rates among Black migrants and excessive deaths from the 1919 influenza pandemic. The population really had changed in a startling way, he claimed. This wasn't the same as Hoffman blaming Blacks themselves, but it was a refusal to acknowledge a systematic flaw in the counting. To top it all off, Beales attacked Miller for making a "miscalculation"—one that he admitted didn't much matter for the undercounting debate—and impugned Miller for "the lack of care and occasional disregard of mathematics displayed in the preparation of his article."[18] Miller had questioned the scientific reputation of the Census Bureau, and now its representative returned the favor.

Miller had not set out to embarrass the Census Bureau. He had set out to protect people. He challenged any and every census that gave unfair fodder to those who still followed Hoffman, to those who still prophesied extinction, to those willing to just let African Americans suffer. "It is particularly unfortunate that such loose and unscientific propaganda can be bolstered up by data from governmental documents which the uninquiring mind is disposed to accept with the authority of holy writ," lamented Miller. "The thought, and perhaps the conduct, of the nation may be misled on the basis of erroneous data, backed up by governmental authority."[19] Miller resisted statistical erasures because he knew that they made political, economic, and social erasures that much easier.

Miller lost that fight. No correction came.

Mexican Americans in the 1930s also faced the possibility of a statistical erasure, and they too knew that statistics had political, economic, and social consequences. But in this case, a transnational alliance embraced erasure as a strategic goal. The allies sought the cover of whiteness, fearing the administrative implications of being segregated in official statistics.

Evidence of their success lives on in 1940 census sheets taken in southwestern states, especially Texas, New Mexico, and California. On such sheets, we can read the erasure directly and see how a silence can be orchestrated.

I can illustrate these elisions with the sheets prepared by the enumerator Ann G. Robinson, who sported an Anglo name and who surveyed the eastern outskirts of Houston. There, she encountered the Diaz household and similar families.[20]

The Diazes had lived in Texas for decades. Both parents were born in Mexico but had become naturalized American citizens (as indicated in the census). Their oldest child, Lupe, twenty years old, was born in Texas, as were the other six Diaz children. It was, in other words, an American family, through and through.

Robinson saw these Americans and categorized them as Mexicans (writing "Mex" in the "Color or Race" column), marking them Mexicans by race, by blood.

After she finished her rounds, after she packed up all her census sheets and shut them in her leather portfolio, Robinson released her data to join the thousands upon thousands of other such contributions flowing into a converted warehouse in Washington, D.C. There, the Diaz family underwent a transformation.

An unnamed, unknown—unknowable—census data editor put a thin line through each of Robinson's "Mex" inscriptions in the "Race" column. Above each crossed-out abbreviation, the editor wrote simply "1."

That "1" translated to "white," the default option, the default race, as the census saw it then and had seen it since the very beginning. (Enumerators in the field wrote in "W" for white, but editors in D.C. employed the numerical equivalent that would be used in later steps for processing the count.)

The Diazes were far from the only people made into racial Mexicans by enumerators, only to be made racially white back at headquarters. The same shifts swept over a few thousand others at least, according to a count made by Andrea De Hoyos, a researcher in my history lab. As we will see, those Americans stood still while the lines of race swept over them, pulled to and fro by the tidal forces of the privileges of whiteness and the power of white supremacy.

After Ann G. Robinson knocked on a door, she must have wondered who might come to greet her, who would stand face-to-face with her on that threshold. She must have looked carefully at each person who agreed to speak with her, because that was her job—to look at people closely and turn them into data. Some of what she needed to write down, her interviewees had to tell her. But other things, about some of the most consequential labels that could be applied in American society, she was supposed to figure out herself.

On April 2, on her very first visit, she probably took a long look at Gustav Reimers.[21] Without asking any questions she likely decided to write an "M" for male. She probably guessed that he was middle-aged, but she needed to ask him directly to find out that he was forty-five, that he had been born in Texas, and that he built and rented trailers for automobiles. Looking at him, at his skin and his hair, listening to his voice, and looking at the people out and about in his neighborhood, Robinson probably also decided on Reimers's race: she marked him down with a "W" for white.

Enumerators seldom asked people to name their race, and likely they were not particularly interested in racial self-conceptions. They had a job to do, putting Americans in their census-approved categories, making certain that each had one and only one census-approved race. A person could be "White," "Negro," "Indian," "Chinese," "Japanese," "Filipino," "Hindu," or "Korean." In exceptional cases, the enumerator could write in a different race (or "color"—the two words were used interchangeably by the census). That's what Ann G. Robinson did when she enumerated the Diaz family, making them Mexican.

Many people in the United States might have been labeled with more than one census-approved race or color. In such cases, the Census

Bureau instructed enumerators to defend the purity of the white race, although not in so many words. Instead, they gave instructions that would almost seem to require going out into the field with syringes and glass vials, kitted out to take blood samples from each American: "A person of mixed white and Negro blood should be returned as a Negro, no matter how small the percentage of Negro blood." Those were the instructions Robinson would have read.[22]

But Robinson did not draw anyone's blood. For one thing, blood doesn't actually work that way, bearing from generation to generation some fixed racial quanta, but blood was and is a potent metaphor for parentage or ancestry, and one frequently invoked by law.[23] Enumerators did not use needles to assess race—they used their eyes and their ears. They might also ask around about a person when they were unsure of their "color," letting the community that person lived in settle on a race. This way of thinking about race wasn't illicit; these enumerators weren't breaking any rules. The Census Bureau instructed them to ask neighbors about each person's race if there was any uncertainty: By what race was that person generally known and accepted? What race did the community ascribe to them? Race, in census practice, proved to be profoundly social.

Politics and law, though, could trump social norms, local practices, or an enumerator's judgment. That's what happened in the case of those Robinson had labeled "Mexican."

Politics made Mexicans white by default or, to borrow a phrase from the legal scholar Ian Haney López, "white by law."[24]

Politics dictated this line in Robinson's instructions: "Mexicans are to be regarded as white unless definitely of Indian or other nonwhite race."[25]

The path to that decision, though, is quite a story.

It begins with the Mexican-American War, when U.S. soldiers occupied what is now the U.S. Southwest. The initial invasion spilled little blood, until some among the hundred-thousand-plus Mexicans living in the region rose up, assassinating officials and plotting insurrection. Then the bloodshed came. U.S. cannons boomed, and guns fired. After the conquering army and the violence swept over the land and its people, a new border followed. The Treaty of Guadalupe Hidalgo ended the war in 1848, ceding from Mexico half of its territory to the United States: an enormous 1.3 million square miles of land. Mexicans who remained in the ceded region, simply by staying in place for a year, became American citizens. "We didn't cross the border," as the saying goes among Mexican Americans, "the border crossed us."[26]

By making Mexicans into citizens in 1848, the government conferred on all Mexicans the possibility of claiming whiteness. The existing naturalization law, passed in 1790, allowed only "free white persons" to become citizens. Therefore, Mexicans, as they became citizens, also became white. (In 1870, after the Civil War, an amended naturalization act allowed people of "African nativity or descent" to gain citizenship as well.)[27] But, as the legal scholar Laura E. Gómez has explained, many in the United States couldn't see Mexicans as fully white, or even fully American—Mexicans seemed too clearly to be a people of mixed or Indian descent.[28] Mexicans in the newly ceded lands gained citizenship by treaty, but most still languished in a kind of political purgatory—another sign of the racial stigma imposed upon them. They were stuck living as colonial subjects in the New Mexico Territory, waiting to become citizens in fully recognized states. They waited a very long time. New Mexico and Arizona became states only in 1912.

Mexicans also crossed the border into the United States, where the demand for fresh produce and mineral resources drew workers by the thousands north in the early decades of the twentieth century. The violence and disruption accompanying the Mexican Revolution of 1910 further encouraged migrants to flee to the United States, where restrictions on immigration from China, Japan, and eventually Europe made agricultural and mining interests hungrier for migrant Mexican labor. According to the historian George J. Sánchez, "For Mexico, the migration [of approximately one and a half million over thirty years] resulted in the loss of about 10 percent of its total population by 1930."[29] Meanwhile, the character of the border was shifting. Mexican migrants needed permission to enter the United States after 1919, with new migrants subject to medical inspections (like those developed earlier to screen migrants from Europe at Ellis Island) at major sites of entry (like

El Paso) or even treatment at bathhouses or "disinfection plants" that required migrants to strip down, endure a visual inspection, and then shower while their clothes were fumigated with pest-killing chemicals. Tens of thousands did not bother to get formal permission; they crossed the border as they had their entire lives, as generations of border dwellers had. It's easy to see why many would choose to avoid the indignity of mass disinfection.[30]

Border patrols soon sprang up, though their first job was to stop the Chinese and Japanese trying to circumvent the racist exclusion laws in the United States. (On the border with Canada, talk turned to the danger of "bootlegged" aliens; it was the era of Prohibition, when more than whiskey might be bootlegged.)[31] In 1924 Congress lifted the statute of limitations on unlawful entry to the United States and in 1929 made it a felony—henceforth, migrants who entered without permission became felons for life, and soon enough the border patrol turned its attention to Mexicans. The border, as far as policing went, widened and widened. Mexicans crossed back into Mexico too, many as part of an ordinary pattern of work and life, while somewhere from a few thousand to over ten thousand were forced out by formal or informal deportation every year in the late 1920s and into the '30s.[32]

After the physical deportations began in earnest, a symbolic deportation followed. In 1930, the Census Bureau ousted Mexicans from the "white" column in its statistical tables. The bureau's chief statisticians had for years favored and supported immigration restrictions, working hard to make the size of the American immigrant population and the nationalities of those migrating visible to policy makers. Now, as Mexican immigration became a controversial topic, as Mexicans became the prototype for a new class of person—the "illegal alien"—bureau statisticians made "Mexican" into a racial category. The formal instructions said that only first- and second-generation migrants should count as "Mexican," but in practice the bureau counted as Mexican a quarter of a million people who had been born in the United States and whose parents had been too. Seeing this treatment, the historian Paul Schor concluded that "applying the 'Mexican' category was a very clear case of racialization of a minority group."[33]

For the most part, Mexicans and Mexican Americans in places like Ann Robinson's Houston thought of themselves as thoroughly Mexican in the 1920s. They devoted themselves to México Bello, "Beautiful Mexico," as a prominent cultural club in Houston was called. They didn't necessarily see themselves as white or think that whiteness was, in itself, much to brag about. But they hadn't asked to be removed from the white category either.[34]

When the news broke that "Mexican" would be its own non-white racial category in the 1930 census, many Mexicans and Mexicans Americans simply shrugged. What was it to them?

However, pushed out of the "white" column in census tables, Mexican Americans soon felt the consequences. That statistical shift intensified their already growing vulnerability, and mass deportations of people deemed to be in the United States illegally followed, casting thousands of Mexicans and Mexican Americans out of the country after they had been cast out of whiteness. And the number of these deportations was dwarfed by the "repatriation" of hundreds of thousands of people—many, long-time residents, indeed, many even citizens—who were packed off to Mexico by local U.S. authorities with the cooperation of the Mexican government. The deepening economic depression had made jobs scarce and burdened local relief rolls, and Mexicans and Mexican Americans provided a convenient scapegoat population, one whose racial "otherness" made them expendable. "The movement [to deport and repatriate] did not distinguish between legal immigrants, illegal immigrants, and American citizens," explains historian Mae Ngai. "Mexican Americans and immigrants alike reaped the consequences of racialized foreignness that had been constructed throughout the 1920s."[35]

By 1935, it looked like the census categorization might cause a cascade of legal and bureaucratic consequences that would cement in place the idea of a distinct Mexican race, with all the limitations and discrimination that would entail.

A circuit court judge that year ruled that Timoteo Andrade, a Mexican immigrant, was not white and so could not be naturalized. The Mexican consul general pulled some strings to undo the decision, and Andrade did become a citizen, but the episode had terrifying implications. Not only were thousands being shipped out of the country, but all future Mexican immigrants stood a court decision away from losing their path to citizenship.[36] (Similar decisions of the U.S. Supreme Court a decade earlier had removed any possibility of naturalization for South Asians and Japanese, ensuring both groups would be prevented from immigrating to the States for decades to come, so the consequences of a court taking away any hope of the label "white" had been made very clear.)[37]

The Social Security Board rolled out its first forms in 1936 and suggested "Mexican" as a race category.[38] As a Social Security card became a prerequisite to getting a job, the forms threatened to racialize every Mexican American worker. This time, the League of United Latin American Citizens (LULAC)—a Mexican American group committed to promoting citizenship and assimilation—fought back. A Texas congressman—representing Ann Robinson's Houston—helped out by insisting that Mexican Americans were "white" since they "descended from the Spanish."[39] The Social Security Board apologized, but it refused to trash the forty million forms it had already printed.

In El Paso in 1935, the local official responsible for the registration system that kept track of births and deaths ordered that Mexicans should be recorded as non-white.[40] The official cited the Census Bureau precedent, and, it's true, the bureau wanted such registrars to follow its lead. But this official appears to have had ulterior motives. Segregating Mexican Americans in registration records would make the city's white population suddenly seem much healthier. The registrar wanted to improve the infant mortality rate for Texas whites without anyone having to bother to actually save more Mexican American infants. Such was the danger of segregated statistics in the Jim Crow South: they made it that much easier to ignore the unequal treatment of people living in segregated neighborhoods subject to substandard housing, poorly supported schools, and inadequate health care.

Marking a subpopulation and making it visible *can* lead to policies that aid oppressed groups and support the systematically marginalized—the Civil Rights movement made that possibility clear. But without the political will for equality, marking a subpopulation as racially other can—and in the 1930s did—justify continued inequality, neglect, and discrimination.[41]

And so Mexican American leaders—with the help of Mexico—began clawing their way back to statistical whiteness. The census was key. Groups like LULAC appealed to Census Bureau officials to do away with the Mexican racial category. The bureau's statisticians resisted the pleas—they viewed Mexicans as a distinct race and wanted to maintain continuity in their figures. That's when the State Department got involved. Mexican diplomats insisted that Mexican Americans be "white" for the purposes of the census, and in late 1936, Director William Lane Austin sent a series of strongly worded memos to his staff ordering them to classify all Mexicans as white going forward.[42] That he wrote multiple such memos and said repeatedly that his order brooked no argument suggests just how unpopular it was with his staff. They went along, though, and so in 1940 the menu of races no longer included "Mexican," and the instructions to enumerators said explicitly that Mexicans were white. And so foreign policy came to dictate statistical policy.

The same conditions that spurred Mexican Americans to insist on their statistical whiteness may have convinced Ann G. Robinson to label them Mexicans. She saw and enumerated racially segregated spaces. The first person she enumerated—Gustav Reimers—was white. So was the rest of his household, and everyone in the next household, and in the next one after that. For the entire month of April, as Ann Robinson worked her way through her jam-packed district, she wrote down only "W" for white except for a few instances of "Neg" for "Negro" (the proper census term at that time) for members of a couple of Black households and for a few Black servants in white households. Then, in early May, Robinson crossed a street, turned a corner, and entered a new section of town.

"Here ends Kashmere Gardens and begins Englewood," she wrote.

The first person Robinson spoke with in Englewood was Mary Sheffield, whom Robinson classified as "Negro." She was a fifty-two-year-old woman, married and living with her husband, Solomon. Both had been born in Texas. Mary was a homemaker. Solomon had a good job as foreman in a creosote factory. A young cousin lived in the house too.

Most who followed the Sheffields on that census sheet also bore a "Neg" marking. In the sheets that followed, throughout Englewood, Robinson enumerated mostly Black residents. But she also counted hundreds of Mexicans and Mexican Americans—including the Diaz family. Against her instructions, Robinson wrote "Mex" for race in each such case. She probably thought to herself: In segregated Houston, in the segregated South, in a deeply segregated country, how could any of these folks living in a mainly Black neighborhood possibly be classified as white?

It is also possible that the Diaz family, among others, might have identified themselves as racially Mexican. Census Bureau officials believed, in the words of Director Austin, "the wealthy class of Mexicans called themselves white, while the peon class will return itself as Mexican."[43] In this poor, segregated neighborhood, Austin and his peers might well have expected the people Robinson encountered to see themselves as something other than white.

It is impossible to know for sure. But I suspect that Robinson—not the Diaz family or their peers—chose the "Mexican" racial label. A sort of natural experiment in the data supports this suspicion. Robinson's district had split in two, each half of which remained very large. She enumerated one half: district 101–4A. Another census taker, Eugene E. Conner, took care of 101–4B.[44] Conner, too, encountered some Mexican Americans (although not nearly as many), but he followed his instructions and labeled them all "white." Even if some of them identified as Mexican racially, that didn't determine Conner's classifications. So I think Robinson's "Mex" labels—like most of the thousands of them that appear in the handwritten census sheets in 1940—tell us more about the assumptions and identity of each enumerator than about the assumptions and identities of those they counted and classified. (This is frequently true of surveys even now. The sociologists Aliya Saperstein and Andrew M. Penner have discovered that the way surveyors identify the race of a single individual from year to year changes much more frequently than one might expect, and it changes in part as that person's context changes or their social status shifts. Individuals' racial self-identifications also shift surprisingly often.)[45]

Today, the census honors racial self-identifications, but in 1940, enu-merators ascribed race more than they asked about it. That made the struggle over the possible categories all the more important. That's why so many Mexican American leaders and the Mexican government saw to it that Ann Robinson's "Mex" labels would disappear. The official returns of the 1940 census reported no racial Mexicans; they did not even admit the possibility of a Mexican race. Whiteness (statistically speaking) had swept back over Mexican Americans, like those in Ann Robinson's Englewood, even if their neighbors in Texas—including their enumerator—would deny them many of the other privileges of that designation.

The census affixed racial labels and operated according to racial defini-tions that, over the course of U.S. history, it played a significant role in designing. In 1940, there would be no label for Mexican, but enumera-tors could choose from five Asian categories (Chinese, Japanese, Fili-pino, Hindu, and Korean were the allowed terms), the Black/White binary (White or Negro), or they could indicate "In" for "Indian." (There was also an "Other.") We can read many intertwined silences if we con-sider now those Native Americans the census counted and accorded the racial status of "Indian." That racial label said something, but—it turned out—not enough to meet the census's constitutional role in determining congressional representation. Into the void left by the census data, other administrative records rushed in, only to prove lacking themselves. A question hung over the census: How were Native Americans to count in the United States in 1940? A new and significant silence—the removal of a very old statistical label—would be the most definitive answer.

In 1939, Francis Case began his second term in the House of Repre-sentatives, having been elected as one of South Dakota's six members.[46] He was, it seems likely, already thinking about his next election when he conferred that year with the attorney for the Sioux Nation, a man named Ralph Case.[47] (I would not be surprised to discover that Francis and Ralph were related.) Ralph had, at that time, already spent nearly twenty years engaged in a landmark lawsuit to seek redress from the U.S. government's seizure of the Black Hills from the Sioux—in the end, Case, working closely with his clients, would devote "almost forty years . . . pursuing a moral and historical argument that consistently failed in court," as historian Philip Deloria has written.[48] (The attorneys who succeeded Case won a settlement from the U.S. government now valued at over a billion dollars, but tribal governments insist the Lakota's stolen lands be returned and have refused to accept the money. They maintain that "the Black Hills are not for sale."[49]) Both Cases shared an opinion when it came to congressional apportionment: all Sioux should count toward the total population of South Dakota for the purposes of allocating seats in the House for the next decade. Francis presented their arguments to Director Austin.

South Dakota's Sioux should be removed from the column in the data labeled "Indians not taxed" and should instead be subsumed into the state's general population. The Cases argued that for the Sioux Nation the legal and statistical distinction implied by "Indians not taxed" had lost all practical meaning.

The attorney Ralph Case emphasized a series of sharp breaks and landmark shifts in policy: the termination of "the treaty-making period" in 1871, the allotment of reservations of 1887, the granting of citizenship to all Indians born in U.S. territory in 1924, and finally the extension of taxes so that they burdened Native Americans. Speaking specifically of South Dakota, Case pointed out that Sioux Indians on reservations had "registered as voters and voted in the 1924 Presidential election." (The Census Bureau, doing its due diligence, would find laws on South Dakota's books in 1938 that barred people from voting "while maintaining tribal relations," suggesting that Case was not entirely forthcoming.)[50] Finally, Case reported that the South Dakota legislature had just passed a sales tax, one that "our Indians are paying."[51] Others made similar arguments: that voting rights, formal citizenship, and sales or income taxes all adhered to Native Americans and obviated the Constitution's exclusions.

The "Indians not taxed" phrase was as old as the U.S. census (older, really) and had served as an active data label for nearly half a century by 1940. But as the Cases and bureau officials knew, it was also a legal and statistical quagmire.

The phrase "Indians not taxed" first appeared in the years leading up to the writing of the U.S. Constitution.[52] Those responsible for transforming rebellious British colonies into new settler states faced the problem of whether or how to count the members of other nations who lived on lands those states now claimed. The framers of the Constitution settled on a policy of exclusion, and the people they would exclude were those labeled "Indians not taxed." As Article I, section 2, put it: "Representatives and direct Taxes shall be apportioned among the several States which may be included within this Union, according to their respective Numbers, which shall be determined by adding to the whole Number of free persons, including those bound to Service for a Term of Years, and excluding Indians not taxed, three fifths of all other Persons." The inclusion of the phrase "Indians not taxed" might be taken as a recognition of the sovereignty of Native American nations, even as that sovereignty was frequently transgressed. It was, at the very least, a recognition that taxation should not be demanded from those to whom representation was not allocated.

The census mostly excluded Native Americans to begin with, up through 1870. But that did not mean they went uncounted. The Cherokee Nation conducted its own census in 1825 to aid in self-governance. Ten years later the U.S. government conducted a special census of the Eastern Cherokee—one that would serve as a prelude to the violent expulsion of approximately sixteen thousand of them from their homes, a quarter of whom died on the "Trail of Tears" forcing them west.[53] In the nineteenth century, the U.S. government often counted Native Americans as a prelude to seizing their lands.[54]

The phrase "Indians not taxed" survived the Civil War and the Fourteenth Amendment, which excised the part that counted the formerly enslaved as three-fifths of a person each but left in the exclusion of thousands upon thousands of Native Americans. "Indians not taxed" still did not count when it came to apportioning representatives. A few decades later, that exclusion became more clearly, statistically, and administratively visible: the silence was spoken aloud when, in 1890, a new column heading ("Indians not taxed") appeared in the data tables presented to Congress to allow it to apportion seats in the House for the following decade. The census reported 90,455 Indians not taxed in 1890. Of all the states' counts, South Dakota's tally showed up on the table as the one most diminished by the new column. The census labeled as "Indians not taxed" 19,792 people in the state and for that reason deducted that number from the state's official constitutional total.

"Indians not taxed" needed to be labeled and then subtracted in the statistics because Indians were now being counted. From 1870 on, the census extended its purview to encompass every Native American—instead of counting only those who had "renounced tribal relations" or those who could "exercise the rights of citizens," as it had done previously.[55] The census added "I" for Indian as an acceptable label for the race column. Instead of counting Indians living in tribal communities and polities as members of sovereign nations, the census data lumped all of them together in an indiscriminate racial category. The census produced data that spoke aloud a racial distinction and silenced assertions of tribal sovereignty.

A parallel data system arose that did think in terms of tribes and nations, however. In 1885, superintendents of Indian reservations received instructions to submit annually a census roll listing each person under their supervision. These Indian census rolls (some of which continued through the 1930s)[56] aided in the dispossession of land from tribes. But as the Native studies scholar Kim TallBear points out, because those censuses acknowledged tribal citizenship and belonging, tribes in recent decades have been able to reappropriate them (and the concept of "blood quantum") to enforce citizenship rules that privilege tribal identity over or alongside the generic racial identity (Indian) that the census and the federal government had worked to impose.[57]

Competing logics of enumerating Indians and competing data sets would ultimately play a crucial role, alongside the political and legal arguments of people like the Cases, in removing the "Indians not taxed" column from the census.

In preparing for the 1940 count, the Census Bureau anticipated that determining a true or even reasonable number of "Indians not taxed" would be a problem, and one that Congress members would make a fuss about. So earlier in 1939, bureau scientists began digging into the institution's own archives. How had their predecessors handled the classification of "Indians not taxed" in prior censuses? The answers they found did not prove comforting. Defining an "Indian not taxed" turned out to be a persistently thorny problem, one that bedeviled statisticians every ten years and resulted in strange and arbitrary outcomes.

Solving the problem involved attempting to integrate two mismatched data sets. First, in every census, the bureau began with its doorstep data. That data included a judgment of whether a person's "color or race" was "Indian." That judgment followed its own arcane rules, blending genealogical and social reasoning with the strictures of white supremacy. For instance, the 1940 instructions to enumerators declared that any person of mixed "Indian and Negro blood" would be labeled "Negro," while "a person of mixed white and Indian blood should be returned as Indian, if enrolled on an Indian Agency or Reservation roll; or if not so enrolled, if the proportion of Indian blood is one-fourth or more, or if the person is regarded as an Indian in the community where he lives."[58] One thing this judgment did not consider was whether a person was "taxed." Once, in 1910, the census attempted to use enumerators to decide if a person was an "Indian not taxed" by asking them directly, but the bureau declared the results meaningless.

Hence the need to consult a second data set, one derived from the records of the U.S. Indian Office. As a 1910 census expert explained, "the laws governing allotments and the Indian Office data" provided "better evidence as to what Indians are taxed or untaxed than the reports of enumerators and Indians themselves, who are ignorant of the law."[59] No individual was allowed to declare themselves an "Indian not taxed." That declaration had to come from the bureaucrats, who, even after careful study of laws and records, struggled to decide who counted and who didn't.

Perhaps inevitably, the two data sets combined to produce new problems. In 1920, the Census Bureau's chief statistician compared the numbers of Native Americans enumerated that year to the numbers supplied by the Indian Office for 1919. The two numbers "never agree," he reported, and "sometimes differ widely."[60] The statistician attributed the difference to the different logics of the data sets: "the figures of the Indian Office being the Indian population cared for by the school on the given reservation or locality, while the census figures of course give the number actually residing in the locality."[61] The difference could have also been the result of flaws in the count, a possibility that seems likely when we consider recent studies showing a persistent undercount of American Indians on reservations, one that reached as high as 12 percent in 1990 and was just under 5 percent in 2010.[62]

In 1930, the mismatch spawned an absurd error: it deducted Native Americans who had never even been counted by the census. The chief statistician caught the problem too late. After the enumeration had been completed, the bureau accepted from the Indian Office total numbers of Indians who were the "wards" of the U.S. government in each state. Those numbers were then deducted from each state's total to generate an official apportionment population, which was then shipped off to the secretary of commerce, who sent it to the president and then to Congress. A little while later, the bureau finished doing its tabulations of race data and from that produced a count of the number of "Indians" in each state. For five states, the number of people deducted to determine the state's apportionment population was greater than the number of people counted as Indian in the state.[63] There was no way to fix the error at that point, and the statistician comforted himself with calculations showing that the errors were not large enough to shift a House seat from one state to another. Still, the debacle could hardly inspire confidence in the project of classifying and counting "Indians not taxed."

In April 1940, as enumerators did their work—on reservations as well as off them—Case and his fellow members of Congress from states that in 1930 had suffered large deductions of "Indians not taxed" pushed for a change.[64] According to a bureau study, the percentage of Native Americans labeled "not taxed" had steadily declined from 76.3 percent in 1890 to 24.9 percent in 1920, only to spike to 58.6 percent in 1930, a result less of demographic shifts than of the legal and statistical arbitrariness involved. South Dakota had seen 5,308 persons deducted from its totals in 1920, which was about half of its Native American popula-tion.[65] Then in 1930, the number taken away from South Dakota's count soared to 19,844. No wonder Representative Francis Case and his colleagues—and Sioux voters—wanted to free themselves and their states from this statistical volatility.

After the politicians made speeches on the House floor, the Census Bureau called in the lawyers. In an earlier letter, an official had told Case that the bureau did "not wish to become involved in the legal issues on this subject"—but now there seemed no alternative.[66] Director Austin asked the secretary of commerce to request legal opinions on what the bureau could or should do.[67] Eventually those requests wended their ways to the department's solicitor and on to the attorney general of the United States. The attorney general's response came on the eve of the Census Bureau's deadline for delivering population totals that could be used for apportioning representatives and seemed to avoid taking any side: the courts and Congress, he said, had not made clear their intentions. The at-torney general concluded: "It is recommended, therefore, that you [the bureau] at this time follow your former practice, giving to the Congress full information with respect thereto."[68]

What were they to do with that advice? Top bureau officials met on November 28, 1940, in an emergency conference on the day before they were to deliver the apportionment numbers to the secretary of commerce. A hastily written note, literally scrawled on the back of an envelope, re-veals the choice the bureau confronted. They identified "two lines of ac-tion open under the Atty. General's opinion."[69] On the one hand, the bureau could report total population and explain why they had not ex-cluded any Indians. On the other, they could report the numbers of In-dians on reservations but then offer "explanations of unsatisfactory nature of data on Indians." The exact deliberations are not recorded, but the decision is evident from the data transmitted the following day. In the in-troduction to the data table, the bureau wrote: "The Director of the Cen-sus has included all Indians in the tabulation of total population since the Supreme Court has held that all Indians are now subject to Federal tax-ation (*Superintendent v. Commissioner*, 295 US 418). The effect of this upon apportionment of representatives, however, appears to be for determination by the Congress, as concluded in the Attorney General's opinion of November 28, 1940."[70] The attorney general's opinion was appended and would go on to be printed, while Congress did nothing, tacitly accepting the bureau's decision. "Indians not taxed" vanished from the statistical table, never to return.

All Native Americans counted by the census now counted toward a state's representation—they all became visible, though indistinguishable within a state's total population. In 1948, one of those who had been counted in New Mexico and who thereby contributed to New Mexico's gaining a second seat in the House, brought suit in court because he had been denied the right to vote by an "Indians not taxed" provision in the state's constitution. His name was Miguel Trujillo.[71]

A 1940 census enumerator listed him as thirty-four years old, college-educated, and working as an elementary teacher in a government school alongside his thirty-four-year-old, college-educated wife, Ruchanda. That enumerator had not asked if he was an Indian not taxed, nor if he had been denied the right to vote. Thanks to Trujillo's activism, he and his neighbors would not only count for the state they lived in, but they would have a direct say in how it was governed.

Silences have political implications, so people fight to make them or to end them.

Kelly Miller shone a light on the silencing of his fellow African Americans, because he knew their statistical absence supported a dangerous, fallacious story that endangered all Black people. His fight highlights the discursive, symbolic politics of data and the silences within it.

Such symbolic politics combined with concerns about the administrative impacts of data when the Mexican government joined with Mexican American advocates to ensure a silence. That transnational coalition sought to temper the political consequences of being seen statistically as not white by seeing to it that all of Ann Robinson's "Mex" race labels (and those of her peers) were edited to indicate official, statistical whiteness.

When data used primarily to administer clashed with data that shaped political representation, the result was the shifting, unstable, and ultimately indefensible count of "Indians not taxed." Congress members who sought the power that came with fully counting all Native Americans in their states successfully pressured the Census Bureau to create a new silence by removing that entire, noisy column of data.

The census is central to determining how political power gets distributed. That is, after all, its constitutional purpose. So a set of stories focused on the politics of silences in representation is where we should now turn, by way of returning to the social scientist Daniel O'Haver Price.

When Price read statistically the silences in the 1940 count, he judged that they would disappoint "the advocates of 'white supremacy' in Mississippi." It would seem he was thinking along the same discursive lines that Kelly Miller had. Price's study showed that African Americans still predominated in Mississippi, their numbers edging out those of whites, upsetting any story of inevitable decline, of a steady road to oblivion for Black people outside of slavery. There is another way to read those silences, though—in light of representational impact—and then the results look less disappointing to the cause of white supremacy.

Proponents of white supremacy—the ideological fruit of slavery— had long worked to game the census to the disadvantage of African Americans. At the moment of the census's origin, in the Constitutional Convention, those who most stood to benefit from counting enslaved Black persons fully were the enslavers and the slave interests. Anti-slavery forces or Northern states stood to benefit politically from preventing the enslaved from being counted. The Constitutional Convention landed on the Three-Fifths Compromise. Each enslaved individual counted as three-fifths of a person for the purpose of "direct" taxation and the apportionment of representatives in the House and electors in the Electoral College. In practice, though, Congress would seldom issue direct taxes (relying instead on tariffs on imports) and so including taxes in the deal mostly obscured the degree to which this compromise served the interests of the slave states.[72]

After the Civil War, the architects of the Fourteenth Amendment tried to protect the rights of newly freed African Americans by inserting a clause that could—if invoked—use the apportionment process to penalize states that denied any freedman his rights. White elites were at that moment working to claw back some semblance of the racial order of slavery, instituting laws and intimidating with violence to push freed Blacks down. So African Americans and their allies aimed with this provision to defend the Black ballot and the protections that came with political power.

The first section of the Fourteenth Amendment granted citizenship to persons born or naturalized in the United States—even people of color, even the formerly enslaved.[73] (It also kept the language excepting "Indians not taxed.") The amendment's second section undid the compromise that made the enslaved count as fractions of people—it transformed the once-enslaved from three-fifths of a person each to full persons. With that transformation, the onetime slave states grew in official, constitutional population by about 14 percent overall—Mississippi's population grew by more than 25 percent.[74] The transformation granted increased power and influence to a group of states that had very recently been in open insurrection against the U.S. government, which was understood to be a problem unless newly freed African Americans were allowed to vote. So section two of the amendment included a threat: if the right to vote of men who were twenty-one years or older was "in any way abridged, except for participation in rebellion, or other crime, the basis of representation therein shall be reduced in the proportion which the number of such male citizens shall bear to the whole number of male citizens twenty-one years of age in such state." In other words, if states stripped the right to vote from Black voters, the representative power of the state would be diminished in proportion to the scale of the disenfranchisement.

The census experimented with gathering data to enforce the disfranchisement penalty in 1870. It added two questions appearing in the final two columns of the questionnaire. The first assessed the default voting population. Like the Fourteenth Amendment, it imposed serious limitations on who could be a voter, excluding all women, all noncitizens, and all young people—serious exclusions that were generally in keeping with U.S. practice, although some states did allow some noncitizens to vote, and a handful of Western states would fully enfranchise women in the 1890s.[75] These exclusions shaped the data's frame. Enumerators only tallied "Male Citizens of the U.S. 21 years of age and upwards" in their search for possible voters.

The second question counted the unfairly disenfranchised (or tried to). It counted any people who had been counted in the previous column "whose right to vote is denied or abridged on other grounds than rebellion or other crime."

The superintendent of the census in 1870 gave the questions a mixed review in his post-census report. Knowing the total number of eligible male citizens of voting age struck him as very useful—and as something that enumerators could reliably count. He in turn printed a series of statistical tables showing those numbers for states and counties. He cared much less for the second question—the crucial one for any scheme to punish a state that robbed its freedmen of their ballots. According to the superintendent, that inquiry "mixed questions of law and fact" beyond the powers of judgment of his enumerators. "No particular value is attributed to results of these questions, so far as the original object is concerned," he wrote. The data weren't good enough "to be used in reducing the representative rights of a sovereign State."[76] He does not even appear to have bothered placing the number of those deemed to have had their voting rights denied in the final census publications, although members of Congress did receive the tallies and then ignored them. (The results singled out Rhode Island, which had stringent property requirements for voters, as a state deserving a penalty, while it counted a preposterously small number of disenfranchised in the states of the former Confederacy.) The data on disfranchisement were not used in apportioning representatives in 1870 and were never collected by the census again.[77]

While the census takers labored in the field in 1870, the Fifteenth Amendment won ratification and so prohibited any limitation on voting based on "race, color, or previous condition of servitude." The amendment left open a wide variety of possibilities for limiting voting—poll taxes or literacy tests, for instance—and in the ensuing decades states took advantage of those possibilities to create constitutionally plausible pretexts for stealing the franchise from nearly all southern Blacks.

Despite the Fourteenth Amendment with its disfranchisement penalty and the Fifteenth Amendment's proscription of race-based limits on voting, efforts to disfranchise Black voters intensified and occasionally succeeded. By the mid-1870s, well-armed, whites-only Democratic groups formed militias, overthrew or intimidated local Republican officials (who had been duly elected by Black and white voters), and terrorized Blacks in their churches or Republican-club meetings or when they came to the polls to vote. "Across the Deep South in the states where Republicans still had power," writes historian Justin Behrend, "Democrats took notice of the 'Mississippi Plan' and the violence that 'redeemed' the state."[78] When even violence did not intimidate Black voters, the job of stealing elections could be completed by local officials who made it nearly impossible for African Americans to register to vote or who simply rigged the results. After the 1876 bargain that handed the presidency to Rutherford B. Hayes, even Republican presidential administrations gave up on policing elections.

In the following two decades, when violence and manipulation had failed to fully suppress Black voting and political action, Southern states completed their coup by establishing whites-only primary elections and new voting restrictions based on literacy and a hefty poll tax. As Behrend writes, "Because of the persistence of black politics and freedpeople's insistence throughout the 1880s that an open and grassroots democracy be restored, exasperated Democratic leaders turned to disfranchisement as the ultimate means to stifle freedpeople's collective power."[79] In the final decade of the nineteenth century, advocates of white supremacy won greater power while stripping Black men of the right to vote. Congress did too little to protect the voting rights of African Americans, and it did not take away representatives from the states that had suppressed those rights.

In 1920, a team of Black activists fought to invoke the Fourteenth Amendment. If African Americans could not vote in the South, they would not allow their numbers to be used to prop up the power of white rule.

"We all know very well that the colored people generally throughout the Southern States are not allowed to vote under the same qualifications and under the same requirements as the white citizens," said James Weldon Johnson, a prominent intellectual and activist appearing before a congressional committee.[80] Johnson prophesied a coming disaster if nothing was done. "We are standing on the crater of a volcano. How long can that situation go on?" he asked. Then he cautioned the assembled members of Congress: "You have got to meet it with wisdom."[81] (Dear Reader: They did not meet it with wisdom.)

In 1920, an enumerator named Lillian Chappell counted Johnson living in Harlem as a lodger with a young doctor and his family. She labeled him "Mulatto"—then an officially acceptable racial category. She put down his occupation as "author," an apt enough term but hopelessly far from capturing the whole person.[82]

Johnson was most certainly an author—he penned an anonymous but celebrated novel, *The Autobiography of an Ex-Colored Man*; composed a powerful poem, "Lift Every Voice and Sing," that became a song widely known today as the "Black National Anthem"; and, with his brother, wrote dozens of songs for Broadway too. Through all his works and his influence as an activist, Johnson helped kindle the literary phenomenon called the Harlem Renaissance. So, yes, he was certainly an author. But he was much more too. He was a political organizer, a diplomat, and, beginning in 1916, the field secretary of a recently founded organization that fought the indignity of Jim Crow segregation, the bloody rule of lynch law, and the theft of political power from formerly enslaved people and their progeny. That organization was called the National Association for the Advancement of Colored People, the NAACP.[83]

Johnson came to Congress as an NAACP representative, and he brought with him data that made disfranchisement visible. His team took preliminary results from the 1920 census and combined them with public vote totals from the 1920 presidential election. The juxtaposition revealed some remarkable facts. The ratio of actual voters to potential voters dropped precipitously in the former Confederacy. In Georgia, only 9.2 percent of twenty-one-year-old citizens (women could vote now) voted, which made Florida at 28.6 percent look quite good. Mississippi and South Carolina brought up the rear, at 8.2 percent and

7 percent respectively.[84] No states outside of the South performed anywhere nearly as badly.

Those figures made a damning case. One member of the committee
from Louisiana tried to keep them out of the official record. "This Congress is very strong on economy," he said. "We ought not to print all of
this. It is extravagant."[85] But the figures did get printed, which is how we
can read them now.

Johnson's table evidenced the disastrous and continued efficacy of the
preceding half century's disfranchisement campaigns. That was Johnson's
point, and he called on Congress in 1920 to use the power granted it by
the Fourteenth Amendment to bring about justice. Johnson and his colleagues did not really want to see the South lose representation. They
preferred to see the voting rights of all Americans respected. But failing
that, the South should certainly lose some House seats. The NAACP
would rather exclude African Americans from the apportionment count
than remain pawns of a white supremacist regime.

But Congress never acted, blaming its inaction—in no small part—on
the silences in the data, on the fact that no official numbers could be
found of people whose rights to vote had been denied. The census hadn't
asked that question for half a century. It did not ask that question—or
anything remotely like it—in 1940 either. White supremacy and its congressional proponents or accomplices had made sure it wasn't even attempted. And they, in turn, wanted to ensure that their Black constituents
were at once counted and silenced.

Few Mississippi politicians believed in white supremacy as sincerely
and overtly as John Rankin. His career in Congress and the example of
census counts from his district illustrate well the care that racist politicians put into counting every one of their constituents.

When Rankin first came to Congress two decades earlier, in 1921, in
the wake of World War I, things had not gone back to the way they were
before the war, and it was far from clear if they ever would. Before
Rankin arrived in Washington, his colleagues decried "special trains
carrying thousands of Negroes and a great many white people to the
northern cities" in prior years.[86] They described what would come to be

called "the Great Migration," but they insisted (wrongly, it turned out) that the tide would come back in, that Mississippians—Black and white—would return. As Rankin put it from his seat in a congressional committee in 1921, there was "a great song that went throughout our section among the Negro population to the effect that they could get better wages elsewhere" during the war. He insisted, however, that "for the last 18 months these negroes have been pouring back into Mississippi and begging the landlords to take them back."[87] Rankin needed that to be true. He needed African Americans to need their white landlords.

Rankin made these arguments while attempting to safeguard Mississippi's eleventh seat in the House of Representatives. The Republican leadership sought to cap the House at 435 seats, which was an unconventional stance. Traditionally, the House grew as the population grew—which meant that, traditionally, few states ever lost a seat, which pleased incumbent legislators, who more often than not got to keep their positions. Rankin's Mississippi stood to lose a seat, and Rankin fought back. He aimed to pass a bill for an expanded House, and if he couldn't do that, he would kill the whole operation, impugning the accuracy of the census and undermining any apportionment at 435 seats. In the process, he appealed to white supremacists.

In the debate over reapportionment in October 1921, for instance, Rankin surpassed all his colleagues in the overt expression of racism, tarnishing the debate with rumors of white women raped by "brutal" Black men, warning that white women would vote out of office any who stood up for "Negro equality."[88] Rankin did not know how to talk about a fair distribution of power without asserting a racial hierarchy. For Rankin, good governance entailed the necessary suppression of the rights of African Americans or anyone else not classified as "white."

Rankin's racism—and the racism of many of his peers among Mississippi's political elite—ensured a lily-white census operation. In 1940, when all was said and done, 1,833 enumerators walked Mississippi's paths to count its people. Only 5 of those enumerators were Black—3 men, 2 women—just 5 out of 1,833, or 0.27 percent. This wasn't the way of things in the rest of the United States. Michigan employed 177 Black enumerators (33 men and 144 women), Missouri employed 203 (82 and 121), New York employed 233 (67 and 166), and Pennsylvania employed 239 (100 and 139). That worked out to 3.6 percent, 6 percent, 1.7 percent, and 2.9 percent, respectively.[89] Black enumerators were underrepresented everywhere, but in Mississippi and other states in the former Confederacy they were practically excluded.

So white enumerators were sent out to be sure that all the state's Black residents were counted. One of those enumerators, whom we've already met, was Clara Triplett Doss, counting in Noxubee County. Her mother and brother had vouched for her: she was poor but able, educated and hardworking—and she was white.

Reading down one of the first columns on Triplett Doss's sheets suggests a story about her journeys through Noxubee County. Column 4 required the enumerator to write "O" if a household owned its home and "R" if it rented. Triplett Doss's sheets read like this over the first few days:[90]

OOO RRRR O RR O R OO RRR O RR O RRRRR O RRRRRR RRRRRRRRR OOOOOO RR O RRR O RRR OO R OO R O.

Alternating "O"s and "R"s weave a patchwork quilt of ownership and tenancy. Scanning to the right a few columns, where Triplett Doss ascribes a race to each person, the pattern stands out. Ownership almost always came paired with a "W" label. Renters were much more likely to be labeled "Neg"—although there were also quite a few poor white families farming on shares.

The very first family Triplett Doss enumerated, however, broke this rule entirely and by its exceptional qualities proved the rule. The first family Triplett Doss enumerated defied all sorts of expectations. Jennie Hinton owned a modest place, valued at $350. She was widowed and long-lived, at seventy-four years old. Jennie's granddaughter, also Jennie, lived with her. The younger Jennie—also widowed—usually worked as a cook in someone else's home, but just then she had no work. Triplett Doss recorded one final member of the household, four-year-old Ethel Eloise Orr, as the matriarch's "great, great grand daughter." One wonders if an extra "great" slipped in there. Regardless, what a family: three generations, possibly spanning four generations—all Black women living in a home and on land that they themselves owned. What further stories might they have told if asked different questions than those asked by this census?

The owners Clara Triplett Doss interviewed seven households after the Hintons' more closely fit the archetype of those who owned: marked as white, identifying as farmers, in a home valued at thrice that of the Hinton house. These folks also happened to be named Triplett.[91]

Was Clara related to these Tripletts? There is no direct evidence one way or the other, but it's hard to ignore the possibility. Clara counted these folks, these close or distant cousins. They would have been able to inform Clara in definite detail about those to whom they rented (if they rented), about who lived where, about those the community counted as Black and those as white (regardless of how light or dark their skin).

Reading Clara Triplett Doss's data gives a feel for her district, which resembled Noxubee County as a whole. Most people farmed. The vast majority were Black. Four-fifths of all farmers worked as tenants on someone else's land.[92] As tenants, they likely lived at the mercy of cycles of debt—borrowing from a landowner or the local store for seed and supplies and maybe food to get through the harvest, hoping for a good year, when they might not fall too much deeper into debt. The landlord, whom Clara Triplett Doss would more often than not label as white, kept a close eye on tenants, on their land, and on their crops—the eye of someone who expected to make a living off the people working that land.

White enumerators may have been at a disadvantage trying to win information in Black neighborhoods and regions, but they were being asked to spy on people already very much used to intrusive spying by local white elites. The surveillance the census built itself upon (and probably paled in comparison to) was the everyday surveillance of tenant farming and Jim Crow social organization.[93]

Mississippi's white elites enforced a racial hierarchy, a system intended to keep Black farm laborers in place and in places where they could be readily counted. At the same time, politicians like John Rankin wanted desperately to wield the power that came from representing the entire Black population of his district, while he wanted just as desperately to ensure that none of his Black constituents had any say in choosing him.

That is another story in Daniel O'Haver Price's undercount analyses: of the places that Price studied, Mississippi boasted the *lowest* rate of undercounting among Blacks, only 5.4 percent.[94] In Northern states, by contrast, the rates sat in the twenties or higher. This was not some accident of percentages, either, not a false picture made possible by the admittedly very large Black population in Mississippi. In fact, the total number of Black people missed in Mississippi in Price's sample was also relatively small, quite a bit smaller than the totals for most of the other states on the list.

Political will and the social structures set in place by white supremacy work to explain why Mississippi's undercount of African Americans appears to have been relatively small. But the rate of undercounting for Mississippi's Black residents still more than doubled the undercounting rate for the state as a whole; digging into the numbers a bit more deeply, it becomes evident that the state's entire undercounting rate of 2.4 percent total could be explained by the undercounting of African Americans. Perhaps those missing Black Mississippians can be explained by the way poverty drove some of the state's Black residents out of their homes and onto the streets, where enumerators had greater difficulty finding them; or maybe the enumerators missed those then fleeing to cities to escape the oppressive surveillance that came with tenant farming. I wonder, too, if it can be explained partly politically, as an act of resistance by various individuals who didn't care to be counted by a system in which they had no say.

Washington, D.C.—Kelly Miller's city—was the opposite of Mississippi.

By Price's calculations, states on the receiving end of the Great Migration, states most likely to be the terminus of the flight from tenancy, were haunted by rates of undercounting reaching truly terrible levels: 25 percent in New York and New Jersey, 34 percent in Illinois, and, worst of all, 40 percent in Washington, D.C.[95] These percentages weren't necessarily precise, and they were premised on comparisons of a particularly hard-to-count group—young Black men—but the basic picture they presented was probably true. That was one difference between D.C. and Mississippi.

There was another: D.C. employed many more Black enumerators, 58 in all (out of 503 total, so over 10 percent).[96]

One of them was Richard Leach. He had been, prior to the census, waiting tables in a cafeteria—not the sort of work he'd gone to college to prepare for. The twenty-six-year-old was an architectural draftsman by trade—a training manifested in the dark, firm lines he used to letter the names on his census sheets.[97] Truly, his sheets read beautifully.

In the very first household he enumerated we find in miniature the makings of D.C.'s massive undercount. Leach found nine people crammed into a single rented home: there was Emma Handy, a forty-two-year-old African American woman, living with her mother, a nephew, a brother, and a cousin and with four "lodgers" to boot.

Cities drew in people from all over, many having recently moved or still on the move, and crammed them together—sometimes in a simple rented house or apartment. That held true especially in poorer neighborhoods, where low-wage workers (as here, a gaggle of domestics working in other people's homes) chipped in what little they had to keep the water running and the heat on. When people move frequently, they're harder to catch in an enumeration. Who claims the urban wanderer for their household? Even today, census advocates within civil rights groups point to poverty and housing insecurity as enduring root causes of a persistent, disproportionate undercount of African Americans.[98]

Leach made it to this house on May 18, a full six weeks after the census began, and it was his job to determine who had lived there on census day, April 1. Would the members of this household, or of similar ones, recall everyone who had happened to be staying with them precisely six weeks earlier? Had another cousin been staying there then, looking for work? When did that lodger who had just arrived from the South find a new place to live? These were the sorts of questions that the people who Leach interviewed might have to ask themselves. Someone might easily have been forgotten. Many, many were.

While the District of Columbia faced these ordinary challenges of counting the poor, mobile masses of a great city, it also struggled to overcome one exceptional deficit. No powerful figures had a direct interest in a complete count of its population. It had no senators, no representatives—not even a say in presidential elections (until 1961, when the Twenty-Third Amendment to the Constitution took effect).

This enumerator, Richard Leach, was born in D.C., but his widowed mother, Carrye, came from Mississippi. When Carrye Leach left Mississippi, she left behind the John Rankins of the world, the politicians who wanted to count her body but refused to respect her rights. She landed and made a life in a political void, gaining the security of a position as clerk in the Treasury Department at the expense of any and all representation.[99] Washington, D.C., had no John Rankins of its own, no congressperson bent on counting Carrye Leach and her neighbors.

Richard Leach did his best, though, and he ended up counting Kelly Miller's family.

He counted Kelly's wife, Annie Mae Miller, noting her graduate studies. He counted their daughter, Irene, and her husband, James, a teacher and a dentist, respectively. He counted a widowed daughter-in-law and two nearly grown grandchildren. Theirs was a textbook example of the Black bourgeoisie. But Richard Leach didn't count Kelly Miller, which was entirely appropriate, because Kelly Miller had died in December 1939. But even if Miller had still lived, he would not have been represented in the congressional apportionment. He and his neighbors lived in a gaping silence that persists even today.

There are stories in the data, and also silences. And silences, like stories, suffused with politics, can be searched out and read.

A census data editor in Washington, D.C., probably made each strike through the "Mex" labels that Ann G. Robinson wrote in column 10. Robinson ascribed a "Mexican" racial identity to the entire Diaz household. The D.C. editor, following bureau instructions, recoded them all as "1" so they would be counted and tabulated as white.

Enumerators like Ann G. Robinson sometimes noted spatial transitions on their sheets, indicating when a block ended or a new neighborhood began. In this case, Robinson reports, "Here ends Kashmere Gardens and begins Englewood." The transition shows up as a transition in the race column too.

The enumerator who filled out this form in D.C., Richard Leach, had a background in architectural drafting that shines through in his census lettering. Just as important, the African American households he enumerated, like this one, point to the crowding of homes and apartments with people who were often on the move: in this example, one woman's rented space houses her, her mother, a brother, a nephew, a cousin, and four lodgers (all of whom had been born in the South). That crowding and mobility—alongside the District's lack of representation in Congress—at least partly explain the undercount for that city.

6

Uncle Sam v. Senator Tobey

In mid-March 1940, Director William Lane Austin received a very strange envelope in the mail. The envelope contained no letter. The envelope *was* the letter, its front and back both covered, corner to corner, with curious calligraphy.

"Lady, shun the Census Taker," read its first line, beginning a seven-stanza satirical poem (followed by a postscript and a "comic supplement").[1]

Mordantly funny, the poem mocked the census and each enumerator who roamed the streets "with his questions, queer and quaint." It took lighthearted digs at the temerity of asking if a person received relief payments from the government, or about family finances more generally: "Can your sister earn a living, / With dancing lessons she is giving?" But a dark, violent streak also ran through it. Its first stanza ended with: "You will wish the under-taker, / Undertook the Record Maker." The poem's second stanza closed with the couplet: "You'll think his quizzes are all rot, / You'll surely say, he should be shot."

(When I showed this letter to a colleague who studies the modern internet, she said: "Oh, that's trolling!" And so it was.)

With his questions, queer and quaint,
you'll surely say, he's not a saint
As you'd shun the under-taker,
Lady, shun The Census Taker!

One obnoxious troll, even one with a fine hand, could hardly trouble the Census Bureau. Director Austin, though, whatever the reason, kept this peculiar missive. Did he smirk or even laugh out loud at it? Maybe.

But if he did laugh, his laughter might have vented a deep well of increasing unease. This letter writer had made threats, even if in verse. At that same moment, a much more imposing—and dangerous—opponent challenged the Census Bureau and the census. A Republican senator decided to score some political points at the census's expense, challenging the up-for-reelection president's administration, accusing it of prying improperly into Americans' private financial lives. He saw the census (even before it published any numbers) as a field for political combat, a place to fight for the presidency and to fight about policy, about whether and how government should be responsible for individuals' economic opportunity. And while he did not achieve his chief aims—Roosevelt still won, and the questions on income persisted—his efforts made their mark on the census data, as series of zeros, nulls, silences.

The senator, too, said to shun the census taker, and people listened.

Herbert Mace lived on a rural strip of road just outside Artesia, a ramshackle suburb of Los Angeles. Mace had once been a preacher, but by 1940 no flock of souls sought his shepherding.[2] (And unlike his neighbors, most of whom were dairy farmers, he didn't look after a flock of any other living creatures either.) Mace had a wife (at least he said he did), and yet in 1940 he also claimed to live alone. He eventually told the Census Bureau that he made a living as the proprietor of a "retail gift shop."[3] It's not clear that this was true. Every response recorded on a census sheet deserves a fair bit of skepticism, and that goes triple for someone like Herbert Mace, as unreliable a narrator as we've encountered in this book, and—as we'll see—no fan of the census taker.

If Mace ever made it into town in the early months of 1940, if he ever entered the local post office, he probably saw a big, bright poster. Bold white letters, outlined in red, stood out against a deep blue background—they read "It's Your America!" with the "Your" underlined for emphasis. A man's bespectacled face floated near the center of the poster, its skin stark white, a goatee and bushy white eyebrows outlined in red, "with a pronounced twinkle in his eye."[4] The head wore a tall top hat, its blue band decorated with white stars, accenting the stovepipe made of thick red and white stripes. Herbert Mace and all his neighbors would have known who this spectral figure was: it was Uncle Sam, an avatar for America, the boss of the bureaucracy, a caricature of the country in its celebration of whiteness and masculinity. In his hand, Uncle Sam gripped a pencil and a thick sheaf of papers, ready to write. Uncle Sam was coming, the poster told Herbert Mace and all his neighbors, to take the 1940 census. "Help the Ten-Year Roll Call," it instructed.

Looking at that poster, Mace probably agreed that it was his America. Mace had a bit of Uncle Sam's charismatic good looks, his wavy hair, and his light skin. Mace didn't walk around in a suit made from pieces of the American flag, but he valued his citizenship, his country, and his rights. It *was* his America: would he answer the roll call?

At other places around town Mace might have seen a flyer advertising a contest: guess the 1940 population of Los Angeles, the closest answers to receive prizes organized by the city's business elites in the Chamber of Commerce. The winners would stand next to the mayor and other local bigwigs and have their pictures taken, memorializing their keen population prognostications—and publicizing what everyone assumed would be a big increase in the city's count.[5] Did Mace submit a guess? Did he think about it?

When Mace got home, when he rested his feet and tried to take his mind off the day's troubles, did he pick up a copy of *Reader's Digest* (like millions of his fellow Americans) and flip through its contents, plucked and pruned to bite-size lengths from popular magazines or newly published books?[6] (When I was a child, my grandparents, who were Mace's contemporaries, still read *Reader's Digest* religiously, or rather, they read it regularly—on the toilet, to judge from where I usually found a copy.) In the February 1940 issue, Mace could have read about the "World's Greatest Quiz Session," a story about the "polite enumerators" setting out to ask questions in "every city, town, hamlet, lonely ranch house and trailer, all day long, Sundays and evenings." He would have read in that article about the widely held conviction that the population of the

United States was headed toward stagnation, that it might even be headed toward a decline. (This turned out to be spectacularly wrong.) He would have already read that the census would deliver "facts, instead of the guesses we have had so far, about our chief problem— unemployment."[7] It would also determine if President Roosevelt had been right, when, in his second inaugural address, he declared, "I see one-third of a nation ill-housed, ill-clad, ill-nourished."[8]

In the final paragraph of that *Reader's Digest* piece, Mace would be made to understand how crucial he was to the entire endeavor. It read: "The 1940 census depends for its success on the truthfulness and cooperation of those to whom the questions are put." It stated directly the census's promise that individual answers would never be used as anything other than "impersonal statistical totals," and it noted that "heavy penalties" awaited any census employees who violated that promise. More ominously, it explained that a penalty also awaited ordinary Americans who didn't help out. "Uncle Sam can fine or imprison any one of us who refuses to answer or does so falsely."[9] I wonder if Uncle Sam still had a twinkle in his eye when he set about the fining and imprisoning.

The article writer reassured his readers that "such extreme measures have never been necessary."[10] The Census Bureau insisted on this point too. But it was not strictly true. In 1890, for instance, at least a couple dozen people were arrested in New York City for refusing to even identify themselves to the census taker (in part as a protest of new questions about family mortgages and diseases suffered).[11] In 1930, at least one person had been detained after refusing to cooperate as well.[12] There were probably more examples, maybe many more—it simply wasn't true that extreme measures had never been necessary. It was true that they were *almost* never employed.

Events in 1940 further made clear that the threats of punishment were real, even if rarely pursued. In early March, toward the end of the business census and on the eve of the population count, a Kenosha cobbler got into a scrap with his census taker. James Rosselli owned three shoe-repair shops and looked every bit the shoe smith, with his massive arms, wide frame, and striped apron. Without fail, reporters listed him as weighing 250 pounds, as if they were discussing a prizefighter instead of a disobedient citizen. The conflict escalated toward violence. "We grabbed each other by the coats," Rosselli said. But he insisted, "I would have answered questions if he had asked them politely."[13] The enumerator and his supervisor brought charges against Rosselli. The Census Bureau—fearing bad publicity—just as swiftly asked that all charges be dropped and sent out a different census official, whom Rosselli obliged.[14]

In that *Reader's Digest* piece, as in much of the Census Bureau's own press, the legion of enumerators—120,000 plus—marched forth as an "army," one "officered" by census district supervisors and "rapidly assembled."[15] We don't know if Herbert Mace encountered the bureau's own language touting its civilian army, but we do know that he heard the protests of New Hampshire's junior senator, Charles W. Tobey, as the senator became the public face for counter-mobilization to resist the census. As Mace's letters to Tobey would eventually reveal, Mace not only heard Tobey—he took him very seriously.[16]

Tobey had been New Hampshire's governor at the start of the Great Depression and then went to Congress for three consecutive House terms. In January 1939, Tobey started spending his days at the other end of the Capitol Building, having been elected in the prior year to the Senate.[17] He got there just in time to raise a fuss over the census.

The first public hint of political trouble for the new census came in late January when a New York Republican in the House of Representatives recast the census army as an occupying force. Daniel A. Reed, who hailed from Upstate New York, urged his colleagues to "take immediate steps to prevent the army of 120,000 census enumerators from invading the privacy of our 30,000,000 families."[18] Reed wanted to defund the special census of housing that Congress had previously added to the 1940 count, but he couldn't swing the votes for that in a Congress controlled by Democrats. But he may have inspired his former House colleague, Charles W. Tobey, to take the fight to the Senate.

On February 1, Tobey stood on the floor of the Senate and expanded the Republican assault on the census beyond the housing census. He cut deeply into the heart of the census, attacking the population count directly. Tobey rose and read aloud a letter he had just sent to Secretary of Commerce Harry Hopkins. Tobey inveighed against the questions in the 1940 census that, for the first time, inquired into each American's income. The questions violated an inherent right to privacy, he said. They were to be asked, Tobey claimed, by miscreant minions of Democratic political machines. And, to make matters worse, ordinary people were compelled to answer under threat of imprisonment. Tobey condemned this "great inquisitorial and snooping campaign."[19] The galleries of the Senate erupted in applause. A week later, Tobey introduced a resolution calling on Harry Hopkins to order the deletion of the income questions.[20]

Perhaps Herbert Mace read about Tobey's speech in the papers. Or maybe he read about all the speeches and all the politics that followed. Tobey and his allies managed to keep the census—framed consistently as a politically motivated inquisition—in the news week after week. On February 7, Tobey introduced a Senate resolution calling on the Department of Commerce and the Census Bureau to remove the offending income questions.[21] Over in the House of Representatives the next day, Daniel Reed pivoted away from his failed effort to torpedo the housing census and joined Tobey's crusade against the income questions.[22] In late February, a Senate subcommittee held three days of public hearings on Tobey's bill. It voted (3–2) to advance the resolution with a favorable report, and then the full Senate Commerce Committee also approved it (9–7).[23] Meanwhile, in early March, a Republican-controlled Senate in Roosevelt's home state of New York seized the opportunity to embarrass their longtime foe, passing a resolution to abolish "personal questions" and any criminal penalties associated with not answering such questions.[24] Tobey kept pushing for his resolution to come up for a final vote late into March, while his colleagues in the House announced they, too, would vote for it.[25] Democratic leaders ensured, however, that neither chamber ever voted on the resolution.

It seems more likely that Mace heard Tobey on the radio. That was where Tobey made his really big splash with a fifteen-minute spot broadcast nationally in prime time on Monday, February 19.[26] That appearance put "census snooping" on the lips of Americans across the country in the week leading up to the first hearings on Tobey's resolution to remove the questions. The networks pushed his next few broadcasts out of prime time, and by Tobey's count for one of those spots, only 29 percent of local stations decided to air his speech.[27] (He sometimes speculated about a conspiracy to limit his reach.) Still, access to the airwaves made a difference. On March 21, speaking to the Senate, Tobey tallied the letters he'd received concerning the income questions at over fifteen thousand.[28] In the coming weeks that number climbed by a few thousand more. (I had assumed this was hyperbole until I visited Tobey's archives and leafed through thousands of letters that still remain from that haul. Even if he exaggerated the exact number, Tobey's point remained true.)

Among those letters is one from an Illinois farmer who underlined every word he wrote—the pre-digital equivalent of sending an email composed in all caps. In the opening passage of his February letter, his anger and enthusiasm manifested as *multiple* thick underscores, as he wrote to Tobey: "We farmers heard your talk over the radio about Census Snooping, and we wish to say that the farmers of this country are in no frame of mind to take any 'monkey business' of any kind from Washington, Wall Street, or the Chicago Board of Trade and we mean Republicans, and Democrats alike."[29]

On April 1, the day before the army of enumerators set out to either reveal America's truths to itself or invade its people's privacy, depending on whom you asked, Tobey got another prime-time spot: a full half-hour on NBC's radio network, beginning at 8:00 p.m. EST.[30] In the performance he encouraged Americans to join together in an act of civil disobedience, refusing en masse to answer the income questions. He promised to support them if they did. For taking that stance, Tobey won himself an unlikely honorific: the "Mahatma Gandhi of the census."[31] Herbert Mace could well have seen "Mahatma" Tobey talked about in his hometown paper.

In Washington, D.C., Tobey terrified the officials responsible for counting people. They worried about the prospect that he might turn the country against them. The Census Bureau's chief statistician confided the staff's fears to a young scholar who happened to be the future Nobel Prize–winning economist and conservative icon Milton Friedman, writing, "We are under extremely heavy fire because of the income question." He continued, explaining: "We fear that the public opinion aroused by the deliberate misconstruction of this question will seriously affect public cooperation with the Bureau, and will make it very difficult and expensive for us to carry through our plans. . . . Some of our men feel rather bitter on this subject."[32] That was in early March. Soon enough, some in the bureau stopped bothering to conceal their bitterness, referring in telephone conversations with Tobey's son (who was also his secretary) to "the Tobey Baloney Works" and "Blitzkrieg Tobey."[33]

Herbert Mace enlisted in Tobey's resistance and proved himself its most zealous adherent.

An enumerator named Mary Brown Bryant may or may not have found Mace at home on April 18. On that day, according to the census records she made, Bryant worked her way down West Sixth Street in Artesia's outskirts. She passed the dairies that stretched west of Pioneer Boulevard and enumerated sundry "hands," "milkers," and "operators" who worked the land and looked after the cows. She also passed—and left unmarked—the address of Mace's home.[34] Since Bryant's census sheets suggest a diligent and careful worker, the silence in this situation probably indicates her failure to find Mace or to get him to cooperate on her first pass through—such silences weren't really that uncommon; sometimes people weren't home, sometimes they needed some extra convincing. Months later, Mace would claim that Bryant encountered him the day before, on April 17.[35] It could be, but, then again, Mace's story had a way of shifting.

The ensuing news reports and Mace's own testimony offer a hazy outline of what happened that goes like this: sometime in late April, Bryant visited Mace's home, found him there, and asked him the ordinary census questions. Mace refused to answer some or all of them. According to Mace, she threatened him. The nature of those threats isn't clear. According to a letter Mace wrote to the *Los Angeles Times* (published on April 25), the enumerator (indicated by the male pronoun "he") "left with a veiled threat to the effect that I would be reported and government men would call on me."[36] All the evidence suggests that such a threat—were it real—would have delighted Mace. He was spoiling for a fight.

Mace didn't just write to the newspapers to report his act of civil disobedience. (The *Los Angeles Times* titled his letter, perhaps too grandly, "A Conscientious Objector.") He wrote to the U.S. district attorney as well to request "aid against the census takers infringing upon my rights and the rights of others and reporting the threats made by the census taker." The district attorney gave no such assistance. Mace was the one who had broken the law. To the D.A., it looked as though Mace had written a letter turning himself in, and he would receive whatever punishment there was to be meted out.[37]

It took a while for the authorities to come after Herbert Mace—the only person for whom the arrest was a priority was probably Mace himself. The details are sketchy, but it seems Mace spent a little over a week in prison. He later described his state when he learned he'd be arrested: "I was tired, sick, had had a very disappointing letter from my wife," and that was when he read the warrant against him. When the police arrived, he attempted to passively resist: "I stepped over by my typewriter table & pulled out a small chair and started to sit down; when the larger fellow rushed at me like a mad-bull and the other one said to put the handcuffs on me." The handcuffs bruised and chafed. The food in prison revolted Mace. He came to the conclusion that the prison system did nothing to reform a person. The drafts in his cell gave Mace a nasty cold.[38]

He finally relented. As a reporter put it: "A rugged individualist for a day, the 48-year-old former preacher succumbed to the full majesty of the law, interested relatives and the hot weather and decided he would answer the questions of the census enumerator."[39] Mace pleaded guilty before a U.S. district judge and then went to the local census office. I wonder if Mary Bryant was there for the occasion—I don't believe she was. Eventually, Mace's information would be recorded on Bryant's census sheets, but not in her handwriting. The *Los Angeles Times* printed only Mace's photo from that day at the census office—Mace had succeeded in making himself the protagonist in his own farce. The reporter concluded: "He was no longer a rugged individualist, he was going back in the great American mold."

The papers either did not notice or did not announce Mace's partial parting victory, but it is recorded in the data.

The census sheet shows that Herbert Mace avoided saying how much his house was worth (that field is blank) or how much money he had earned (it just says "0"). He resisted to the end.

After he got out of prison, after he submitted his (incomplete) census response, and after he once again wrote to the newspapers, Mace wrote to Senator Tobey.

"This case," he wrote, meaning *his* case, "has the ear-marks of being dirty politics; the work of would-be dictators."[40]

The accusation that the census—any census—had been politicized was hardly novel. Every ten years, in one way or another, the census has gotten swept into political debate. In the antebellum years it became fodder for those fighting over slavery. In the following decades it drew attention to and channeled concern over immigration to the United States. Amid the greatest depression in the history of the nation, at the dawn of a new, aggressive welfare state, it's hardly surprising that those for and those against a more economically interventionist government would contest their points through the census.

What's more, the census necessarily veered into politics. Its results determined the distribution of political power in the federal government for each decade.

Every twenty years, the inherently political census attracted even sharper partisan attention when the ten-year census rhythm coincided with the four-year cycle of presidential elections. Every second census overlapped with every fifth national election, and chaos ensued. Imagine what it must have been like to take the census in 1860, on the eve of Abraham Lincoln's election, on the eve of the Union's fracture. More recently, in 1920, the twinned aftermaths of the world war and the global flu pandemic cast a deep pall over the census, but the fact of the presidential election still aroused partisan spirits, spurring suspicions about flawed census counts made by enumerators chosen to press for political advantage over statistical quality.[41]

There was nothing accidental in the way the census became a partisan flashpoint. In early February, Senator Tobey gloried with his colleague Daniel Reed in the House about the possibility of making political hay with the census. "I think," wrote Tobey, "that this whole issue will, before we are through, create quite a bit of embarrassment to the administration, and it certainly should."[42]

Herbert Mace's choice of words, his reference to "dictators," followed the developing Republican playbook for the 1940 elections—when all eyes were on Roosevelt, about to announce his candidacy for an unprecedented third term. Tobey led the way in drawing parallels between the U.S. president and the tyrants of Europe. In a March 31 radio broadcast, Tobey blended the words "Democrat," "dictator," and "bureaucrat" to summon a new monstrous threat to American freedom: the "dictocrat."[43]

Republicans and other critics of Roosevelt's New Deal hammered home the risk of the "regimentation" of American society. "Regimentation" did not mean any one specific thing, but it evoked associations of jackbooted Nazi thugs marching through the streets and of innocents imprisoned in Soviet purges. "Regimentation" came paired with "planning"—hardly a dirty word among progressives but a term conservatives used as a slur. Planning, to their minds, meant Stalin-esque centralized control of all economic activity, which meant the death of freedom. As Tobey said in his first attack on the income questions: "In this day of impermanence in governments, in this age of 'social planning,' when disastrous inroads in the liberties of the individual are perpetrated in the name of greater efficiency, a questionnaire of this kind is, to say the least, untimely."[44] The implication was clear: First they come for your economic data. Next they come for your freedom.

The fear of looming dictatorship resonated with many people who wrote to Senator Tobey after his radio addresses. "We have had about all of the Hitlerism we can stand," wrote Charles B. Chase of New Hampshire on March 18, 1940.[45] A Lackawanna, New York, Presbyterian minister sent Tobey a clipping from a Buffalo magazine with a picture of Heinrich Himmler, having underlined a portion of the caption: "Himmler has a complete dossier on almost everyone in Germany." The minister made his meaning clear: "It is patent to any student of history that the first weapon of any dictator is the Secret Police with their dossiers."[46] Mace struck the same notes when writing to Tobey, while also borrowing Tobey's own language of an invading census: "The census law to start with was an insult to the American people; an invasion of their homes and private lives; and has every appearance of being intended to card-index the people on behalf of would-be dictators."[47]

Here was a forerunner to today's database politics. Before the advent of the digital computer, card indices allowed governments and businesses to keep track of thousands or even millions of individuals. The same people who developed the card catalog for making a vast library's holdings accessible realized in the late nineteenth century that stiff paper cards could create searchable inventories of entire populations. Melvil Dewey—of Dewey decimal system fame—started a company that got into the business of secretly sharing medical records among big U.S. insurance firms.[48] Soon enough, the federal government also realized the power of the index card.

That is nowhere better illustrated than in a photograph from the offices of Roosevelt's crowning achievement: the Social Security Board (later renamed the Social Security Administration), where men in suits, suspenders, and vests leaf through card files containing wage records for tens of millions of Americans.[49]

Ordinary Americans could well be forgiven their fears that the government had gone dossier mad. Breathless news coverage of the new Social Security system called it "the biggest bookkeeping job in history." By the middle of 1938—less than two years after the first Social Security numbers were issued—the card files held records for forty million workers, and almost half a million new worker records entered those filing cabinets every month.[50]

But critics who blamed this giant information-gathering operation on a desire for left-wing dictatorship missed the point. Other countries—like Britain—installed an even more extensive and generous welfare state without the same sort of data surveillance that the United States employed. By contrast, the U.S. government built card indices because it modeled its chief welfare program on private insurance practices and borrowed technologies from private insurance corporations. It was not a coincidence that the rows of file cabinets in the Social Security offices so closely resembled those in the Metropolitan Life or New York Life towers. In the end, Roosevelt's preferred model for old-age insurance depended on the U.S. government keeping track of each worker's wages over the course of their entire life—an extraordinary data project.[51] When a worker retired, those wages and the contributions made from those wages through Social Security payroll taxes decided on the level of the worker's old-age pension. The formulas were broadly redistributive, leaning slightly in favor of poorer workers, but the system still awarded larger total pensions to workers who had been paid more over the course of their lives—and, as many noted, even in the administration, relying on payroll taxes (instead of taxes on other forms of wealth) laid a disproportionate burden on poorer wage workers than on the well-off. Roosevelt's welfare system and its data systems aimed to shore up American capitalism, not to overthrow it.

Behind all the talk of regimentation, dossiers, dictators, and card indices, a more mundane fear lurked: the fear of taxation. Promises of statistical confidentiality ensured that no income figures collected by the census taker could be used to tax a particular individual—just as they also protected against conscription or any other harm. Roosevelt reaffirmed the promise in his census proclamation: "No person can be harmed in any way by furnishing the information required. The Census has nothing to do with taxation, with military or jury service, with the compulsion of school attendance, with the regulation of immigration, or with the enforcement of any national, state, or local law, or ordinance."[52] But Tobey and his tribe worried that the statistical data being collected by the census could still be used to define and justify new tax brackets, expanding the reach of the still-fledgling, relatively tiny Internal Revenue Service.

The federal income tax took deep root only with the ratification of the Sixteenth Amendment to the U.S. Constitution in 1913. Up until that time, the Constitution required Congress to assess direct taxes from each state in proportion to census totals. The income tax amendment severed the relationship of taxation to population. Counting dollars would determine tax receipts, not counting heads.

In its first few decades, the federal income tax grew slowly, burdening only a tiny portion of all Americans. In 1939, only 3.9 million individuals paid any income taxes—well under 5 percent of the entire population. In contrast, after World War II caused a massive expansion of the income tax to fund the mobilization, 42.6 million people paid income taxes—a greater than tenfold increase.[53] No one in 1940 knew that the income tax would soon encompass so many, but Roosevelt's critics expected something was coming; to them, the income questions on the census looked like a first step. On the air, Tobey quoted a like-minded associate who made this argument: "The underlying purpose in gaining the information, of course, is to prepare a tax plan, from that they will extract taxes from the low-income groups."[54]

The limited reach of the income tax also caused—or exacerbated—another point of conflict for Tobey. The final census instructions required any person who made less than $5,000 in wages in 1939 to declare their precise income to the census taker. But those who made more than $5,000 only had to say they made more than $5,000. Their income would appear on the census sheet as $5,000+. (For a host of examples, see the incomes of nearly all the "Question Men" displayed in the tables after chapter 1.) Tobey cried: "Discrimination!" Why, he asked, did the poor have to tell the government their precise income, while the rich could hide their wealth in a big bucket?

Certainly, there was a kind of discrimination here. The rich were, well, rich—and powerful too. Bureau officials worried that they, in particular, might complain or refuse to answer the census questions. The "$5,000+" label was intended to mitigate those concerns.[55] But even with that label, preliminary Census Bureau dress rehearsals of the census in Indiana determined "those in the higher brackets" to be most likely to resist a request to release their income information. Despite the later talk about the income data being used to target those who earned less, the bureau in 1939 reported "little difficulty experienced in getting answers to the income question from persons receiving small salaries and wages."[56]

Resistance among the wealthy was (superficially) harder to understand, too, because the government already knew the incomes of the well-off. For everyone who made at least $5,000, the U.S. government already had a very precise figure accounting for their wages, because those individuals all paid income tax. As we'll see, the wealthy were probably less anxious about the government knowing their incomes than they were worried about divulging their high wages to their (probably poorer) enumerators. But because the government possessed tax data, it could afford to let the wealthy give a vague "$5,000+" response. As a former Census Bureau official explained it: "It would obviously be unnecessary, if nothing else, to repeat in the higher income brackets what the government already knows."[57]

Apart from the wealthy, some among the working and middle classes also ended up protesting the income questions in 1940. One cluster of letters, from Berlin, New Hampshire, to Senator Tobey suggests a reason that some such folks objected—viscerally—to a request for their income: such questions violated unwritten rules, in an era before widespread income taxation, about who was expected to reveal their household finances when the government came knocking.

The letter writers congratulated their senator. "Freedom of Speech moves me to say: 'I am against the personal questions on the 1940 Census,'" wrote Caroline Anderson. Yvette Gunn asked Tobey to "add my name to the list of those protesting such questions as the personal ones on the 1940 Census." Jeanette Mailhot exclaimed: "The 'Bill of Rights' should be upheld, down with the personal questions of the 1940 Census." And Paul Morin said, "What this country needs, is more men like you in the U.S. Senate and House to stop such things as the 'Snooping Census' of 1940." Some in the group mentioned having read a pamphlet outlining Tobey's objections. Others had heard him on the radio. They mailed their letters together, but they did not reveal the real-life ties that bound them to one another.[58] The manuscript census, however, offers some clues.

A researcher in my history lab, Emily Karavitch, found those clues while looking for this group to see how they had responded to the census enumerator. She discovered a deep irony.

Mailhot had told an enumerator on April 19 that she worked as a "relief investigator" earning $540 over thirty-six working weeks. Caroline Anderson, a widow born in Finland and now age sixty-two, no longer worked, but she reported on April 9 that her nineteen-year-old native-born daughter, Evelyn, was a typist for the "City Relief office," earning $168 the prior year. The forty-two-year-old French Canadian–born Morin listed his occupation as "overseer poor," reporting $1,800 in income. Yvette Gunn, twenty-four and married to a machinist, described herself on April 9, 1940, as an "interviewer" for the city of Berlin, making $1,040 the previous year. It would seem that these letters had been mailed by a group of city employees administering relief programs, for which the city's needy had to submit to investigations and interviews to prove their poverty. Did Tobey notice that this group of New Hampshire citizens so concerned about government snooping all, at least indirectly, earned their living by prying into the personal finances of the poor?

It would be easy to condemn this group, calling them hypocrites. But here's one way to think about their stance: who knew better than they the indignity suffered by those compelled by law or circumstance to admit to local officials their private financial data? They knew better than most that the people most commonly forced to reveal their incomes to politically powerful neighbors were the very poor. They probably also knew that a corrupt or incompetent government and powerful neighbors could abuse such data. To have one's income investigated bore the stigma of poverty and dependence and threatened further harms.

In his retellings of the first encounter with his enumerator, Herbert Mace couldn't decide what pronoun to use. The enumerator started out as a "he," then became a "she." Maybe Mace used "he" at first because that was his go-to generic term, in a time when the singular "they" had less purchase on our speech. Or maybe Mace intended the misgendering. "I felt the actions of the census taker very unladylike," he wrote to a San Diego paper. When the Census Bureau had demanded that he write to Mary Bryant and supply his census answers (which he refused at that time to do, leading to his arrest), he stated, "I did not consider a woman a lady who would come into a man's home and demand with a threat of injury private information; that therefore I did not care to have any correspondence with her."[59]

As was usual, Mace proved himself to be an unusual case, even while expressing common concerns. Mace didn't like the enumerator he met— Mary Bryant—possibly because of who she was or how she looked, or possibly because he didn't think a man should have to submit to a woman. Since Uncle Sam couldn't knock on any actual doors, Bryant and 120,000 other enumerators each did their best to gather data for the nation. For the duration of the census, they were the government made flesh. And sometimes the person being counted did not like the guise in which the government arrived.

It did not help that Senator Tobey deliberately sowed fear and distrust of the enumerators. In his very first speech, he asked: "Why should [a person] be compelled to divulge the amount of his income to political appointees who may reside in his neighborhood, who may be his next-door neighbor, in fact, or even an enemy."[60] He hammered on that question—and its threatening implications—for months, and it struck a chord with many of those who wrote to him.

The fears most consistently confided to Tobey reflected these local concerns. C. C. Harley told Tobey she was "a widow and live[d] alone." She continued: "I do not care to have all my affairs known to every one, especially Money matters."[61] Moments later, Harley divulged her income of $265 a year to Senator Tobey. She could trust her Republican senator but not the local enumerator—who, it turns out, was Frank B. Shea, whom she presumed (maybe correctly, maybe not) to be a Democratic Party hack. Shea never did find Harley: he enumerated 47½ East Pearl Street but not 48, where Harley hid.[62] Harley thus avoided the census, but she did a poor job of keeping her financial details away from our prying eyes. Writing to a U.S. senator is a great way to leave a record for posterity, and Harley's letter reveals something surprising: many

Americans resisted the census income questions not because they feared dictatorial rule, but rather because they did not trust their neighbors. They feared local gossip more than the specter of a centralized state.

Such mistrust motivated Mina H. Dearborn of Bristol, New Hampshire, a seventy-seven-year-old widow, who wrote that "for certain reasons I do not wish to make my private business known to a local census taker" and asked what options she had to avoid answering the income questions out loud. She did not seem to care if the federal government learned of her income but feared it being revealed in town.[63] Still, when an enumerator named Winifred E. Goodhue (a forty-seven-year-old housewife with a high school education and two children) finally caught up with Dearborn on April 23, 1940, the widow joined the ranks of many Americans (and several of the other women on Prospect Street in Bristol) who said they had not worked any weeks in 1939, had earned $0 in wages, and had received more than $50 from some other source. With those answers, Dearborn kept her business about as private as she could.[64]

Some letter writers—following Tobey's lead—saw enumerators as patronage appointees serving the interests of a Democratic Party machine. Harold J. Stewart of Portsmouth, New Hampshire, insisted to Tobey (in a letter typed on the letterhead of the Board of Street Commissioners) that he'd rather pay the $100 penalty than open his records to "the questioner," one of "the notorious local Democratic ward-heelers and so crooked he cannot lie straight in bed."[65] He didn't object to divulging financial information to the federal government; Stewart noted that both his and his wife's incomes were reported on tax returns. His problem was with passing to local Democrats data that might be used for nefarious purposes. Nonetheless, on April 23, 1940, he reported his income as $1,872, earned working fifty-two weeks as the office manager of a waterworks.[66]

At other times, concerned letter writers just saw enumerators as neighbors whose judgment they wished to avoid. William H. Brooks, also of Portsmouth, New Hampshire, feared that his enumerator would get the wrong impression of him. "As a retired marine," he wrote, "I object to having it whispered about that there is so and so much government money coming to my house." He disliked being called a "Government pauper." But he objected even more "to telling the census taker that the only education I ever had was at a country schoolhouse." After all, he had "shook with the malaria fever and suffered from the yellow fever in Cuba, hiked in the Phillipines [*sic*] on inadequate and not very fresh rations" and had risen to the rank of acting assistant quartermaster during World War I. The marines had been his school. His pension now only just made up for his poor pay in earlier years. Why, he wondered, must he "be insulted by telling a provincial that I am an uneducated ninny to satisfy the whim of a sensational [*sic*] loving politician."[67]

When an enumerator, David A. Tober, came to Brooks's door a couple of months later and talked to his wife, Carrie, on April 10, 1940, the family could cooperate (mostly) without divulging that which William most wanted to keep secret.[68] Tober recorded Brooks as having had four years of high school education (which may have been an exaggeration) and reported zero weeks worked in 1939, zero dollars in wages, and an income of $50 or more from other sources. In the end, Brooks did not have to lie (much), because the census schedule had no place for discussing the size of one's school, and pension income didn't count as wages.

Every letter writer my history lab managed to find in the 1940 census sheets bore the mark "W" in the race column, for "white." A large number came from Tobey's home region of New England, and for these writers, the dangers of centralized government appeared much less worrisome than the corruption or gossip of community members and the stifling prospect of sanctioned local surveillance. Uncle Sam creating dossiers concerned them less than did their nosy (and possibly unladylike) neighbors.

As Senator Tobey's influence grew, massive resistance to the upcoming census seemed possible, even likely. On February 29, 1940, at the Senate hearings on Tobey's resolution, a group called Women Investors in America prophesied a public revolt. As *The New York Times* reported it,

Cathrine Curtis, the group's director, said Congress should set aside money "to enlarge the jail accommodations throughout the country to house those millions who will go there rather than to disclose their wages or income, and their matrimonial adventures."[69]

One month later, immediately before the counting started, Tobey's opponents worried that the furor imperiled the very institution of the census. One of his colleagues across the aisle in the Senate, Claude Pepper of Florida, warned a national radio audience of "the seriousness of this attack [by Tobey] upon the integrity of the census, made by a United States Senator." Pepper continued, explaining just how high the stakes seemed to him: "Upon the integrity of this census will depend the number of representatives that the states have in the House of Representatives for the next 10 years. Upon its integrity will depend the reliability of our knowledge about our country and its people for the next decade. If the integrity of one census is destroyed, it weakens the integrity of all censuses." On that same broadcast a high-ranking government statistician scolded one of Tobey's allies, insisting that the census was "one of our most important non-partisan inquiries upon which every individual in the United States depends for basic information for the next ten years, and you would destroy it."[70]

Soon, though, the Census Bureau decided to declare a (possibly preemptive) victory. At the end of the first full week of its enumerators asking questions around the nation, the bureau issued a press release filled with stories from the field. An initially reluctant woman in Wisconsin ended up enjoying her census interview so much that she "phoned to [a] dozen friends to assure kindly reception," while a San Jose citizen offered to tell all his neighbors that the census had been much simpler than the furor would suggest. An Oakland, California, household invited their enumerator to stay for lunch, while a Kansas City housewife offered hers coffee, and a Philadelphia woman handed the census taker a dozen eggs. Many people expressed confusion that the questions seemed so innocuous.[71] For many, perhaps, Tobey's controversy backfired by preparing Americans to expect a greater outrage than the census would actually deliver.

In coming years, the Census Bureau brushed aside Tobey's tirades, judging them inconsequential tantrums. A retrospective analysis prepared in 1948 determined that there were only 81,500 "absolute refusals" to answer any questions the first time an enumerator came to the door in 1940. The Census Bureau guessed that some portion of those refusals probably did end up getting counted on follow-ups. That would mean that less than 0.2 percent of all people contacted by an enumerator refused to answer the census's questions.[72] An official procedural history of the 1940 census (prepared, again, long after the count had been completed) claimed that only 2 percent of all respondents refused to answer the income questions.[73] Another Census Bureau study put the figure up as high as 2.56 million people, or nearly 5 percent.[74] However one sliced it, though, after the fuss that Senator Tobey had raised, this looked like a huge win for the Census Bureau.

Herbert Mace, though, would not have believed such minimalist claims. He told Tobey: "There were literally thousands of people who refused by various methods to answer census questions—even among the men who took a part in my arrest and imprisonment." He recounted the story of a Justice Department official who said he withheld information about his income from his wife so that she could not tell it to the census taker. "He is a part of the law agencies that have branded me as a criminal for doing the same thing that he did," wrote Mace, adding bitterly, "except he was a sneak and a cheat in his refusal to answer the questions—while I openingly [sic], honestly told the census taker that certain things were my own private affairs."[75] The distinction played to Mace's desire to be seen as a political prisoner, and his story leaves plenty of room for doubt and suspicion, yet something about his accusations rings true.

The more closely I read the census responses, looking at the original census sheets, the more it seemed that those who wanted to resist the income questions may have found subtle ways to do so, ways that would have been easy (or convenient) for the Census Bureau to overlook. Most resistance didn't involve outright refusals or violence and didn't end in imprisonment. As the stories of some of Tobey's letter writers make clear, even those who anticipated a showdown on their doorstep found quieter ways to protect their privacy and fend off the Feds.

Florence Doud, who lived on rural route 2 in Michigan City, Indiana, wrote that she supported all government efforts that would "in every way . . . prove a blessing to all." She wanted it to be clear that she was a good citizen. Still, she worried that there was "a limit" to what could or should be asked of citizens by their government. The census questions, she wrote, threatened to "breed a nation of prevaricators," a legion of liars. "Over ambitious leaders" with their intrusive census questions threatened the freedoms that Americans bragged about, and words alone couldn't fully express the anger, the righteous indignation, she felt about that. So she doodled a housewife in the act of kicking a census enumerator squarely in the rear end, launching him into the air and sending a portfolio, helpfully labeled "census," flying too. Doud even gave her valiant white housewife an action-hero-style one-liner: "I had these brass toes made for just such [an] occasion."[76]

Now, I have never heard of brass toes. Have you?

I have no evidence that Florence Doud owned any brass footwear either, but I do know that she registered her protest to her enumerator.

When a census taker named Donald Myers came around, he managed to get Doud to answer some questions without any kicking. She revealed herself to be a forty-eight-year-old white woman, born in Michigan, with an eighth-grade education, living in a rented house.[77]

On the economic questions, Doud identified her and her husband Ray's occupations as grocery clerk and barber, respectively, but claimed to have earned no wages from such work in 1939 (but to have earned more than $50 from some other source). In the manuscript data, those answers appear as "52/0/yes" for Ray (weeks worked/income from wages/more than $50 other income) and "8/0/yes" for Florence.

It is possible that Ray earned no wages; if he owned his own barbershop, he wouldn't have had to report his profits as pay. Did Florence, however, receive nothing in return for her grocery store work? Or were her answers, as she herself had suggested, "prevarication"? Without brass toes, perhaps that was the best weapon she could muster.

How common were such tactics? Had the census truly bred the "nation of prevaricators" that Doud feared? How many enumerators had endured a metaphorical kick in the pants by crafty folks who figured out how to answer questions and yet not answer them?

I searched the census for more of these possible acts of resistance.

I found them in many places all across the country, especially in Montevideo, Minnesota. I first started looking at Montevideo—a small midwestern city surrounded by countryside—because I had evidence already of organized political protest there. A concerned Montevidean wrote to the Census Bureau's chief statistician in 1940 to inform him that local Republicans were distributing handbills that excoriated the census questions and aimed to stir up both census resistance and votes for the Republican ticket in 1940.[78]

"YOU'VE GOT TO GET MAD," screamed handbills in bold block letters, and they were distributed along the same blocks census enumerators roamed in early April 1940. "STAND FIRM ON YOUR Constitutional Rights," it warned. The Constitutional Rights Republican League of Minnesota jeered at "Washington Bureaucrats" and their "snooping,"[79] and they called on individuals to refuse to cooperate.

The April handbill amplified Tobey's overheated political rhetoric. Census questions became "super-snooping," and New Deal officials were transformed into "fake Americans" aiming to "hogtie American industry" and "impose an Alien scheme of regimentation" that amounted to "class discrimination" against the poor. A GOP elephant holding aloft the Constitution anchored the handbill, its weight supported by a foundational aspiration: "LIFE BEGINS IN '40."

Montevideo had been inundated with such flyers. So I wondered: what impact might such a coordinated local campaign have on the data?

The answer was mixed. As did most of America, Montevideo cooperated. Still, I discovered, and was intrigued by, a surfeit of entries that answered the enumerators' questions while revealing almost nothing—just as the Douds had done, just as Herbert Mace had done, just as the Bristol widow Mina Dearborn had done.

The folks reporting zero wages appeared to cooperate with census taker Mary Rupp—but without disclosing other possible income.

There were some true cyphers among them, like two individuals for whom no occupation or industry appears. Others worked outside the system of wages, as was the case with George Harstad, who worked fifty-two weeks at "care of invalid," probably looking after his seventy-four-year-old father, Hogan.[80] George made it clear to Rupp that he worked a full-time job, even if he wasn't paid.

Others owned businesses or were self-employed and so technically didn't earn wages. But some folks appear to have gamed the census, claiming to be self-employed to hide their hard-won, and precious, pittances. That's my read on the local carnival manager, the laborer, and the county fair horse racer. Did they truly work on their "own accounts," (indicated by an "OA" in column 30), or might their income have been construed as wages? The same goes for the gas station "attendant." Those cases raise my suspicions, but there is even more reliable evidence of gamesmanship. Inconsistencies within Mary Rupp's district demonstrate the interpretive possibilities open to clever, possibly wary, Americans.

Take garbage collecting. Lloyd H. Eschen, a married, thirty-two-year-old white man with twin four-year-old sons, said he earned $400 for forty-one weeks of work as a garbage collector.[81] He admitted to being a paid worker, and so his wages became visible to the census. But a few blocks away lived Therlo W. Torrey, a thirty-seven-year-old white native Minnesotan and his wife, Mabel, and daughter, Phyllis Rae. Torrey worked fifty-two weeks as a garbage collector but claimed to work on his "own account," which meant he received no wages. Mary Rupp dutifully reported $0 in wages and "yes" to indicate that Torrey earned more than $50 by some other means—presumably the proceeds from his independent trash pickup.[82]

Cases like these suggest to me that in the process of gathering answers to the income questions, Mary Rupp collected some garbage too.

And then, finally, there's the question of Charles W. Tobey. What did the census's most vocal critic do? Did he answer?

I don't know.

Tobey pledged (loudly enough that reporters could hear him, loudly enough to get a rebuke from the White House) that he would evade the income questions. He practically begged the Census Bureau to arrest him for his noncooperation. As far as I can tell, though, he (intentionally or not) did not appear in the census at all. At least, I did not find him.

But I found Charles W. Tobey, Jr., a lawyer for the federal government living in Arlington, Virginia. By all indications, this was the senator's son, who worked as his father's personal secretary. What did he do? The usual thing: he cooperated without cooperating. The rightmost three columns of his entry read: "52/0/no." Tobey Jr., reported working fifty-two weeks as a lawyer for the Feds while earning $0 in wages and less than $50 in any other income. Government work might not pay great, but it pays better than that! Tobey Jr. was so committed to refusing to answer the income questions that he wouldn't even tell the government how much it was paying him.

I found few clearer examples of outright resistance on a census sheet.[83]

The honor—or maybe shame—of being the private person who resisted the census most publicly would go to Herbert Mace. He tried his best to be a martyr for freedom and privacy. But even so, not many people noticed.

Among those who did was Weldon F. Heald, another Los Angeles resident (from Altadena). To Heald, Mace's protest missed the point. "Mr. Mace," he explained in a letter to the editor of the *Los Angeles Times*, "as far as the census is concerned, is a digit who is arrogating to himself a personality out of place in statistics."[84]

To know America, each American had to submit to being known. Promises of confidentiality tried to assure these individuals that their particularities would not be subject to indiscreet scrutiny—no one (apart from the Census Bureau's employees) would even ever see Mace's answers, or anyone else's. Such promises were a means of securing reliable statistics.

But Mace and Tobey—and (perhaps more sympathetically) Doud and Dearborn and many, many others—worried more about their privacy than about the nation's statistics. So they prevaricated or held their tongues or fudged or hid the truth.

In the coming years, fears that personal data might be misused proved to be devastatingly reasonable—but it wasn't the people who wrote to Charles W. Tobey whose data was turned against them, and the income questions weren't the problem. War was coming, and the census was about to be weaponized against people it was meant to serve.

One of the 1940 census slogans is breathtaking in its bald simplicity: "Cooperate." In short, cooperate with the census, answer your enumerator. It's hard to believe, today, that such a command would have any chance of working. In this image, we see the slogan paired with a stick-figure Uncle Sam filling out a census scroll. The implication is clear: the enumerator who comes to a doorstep is not just some person from the community—they are a manifestation of Uncle Sam, come to take attendance. The image and slogan told Americans that to cooperate with the enumerator was to cooperate with Uncle Sam.

This widely distributed poster put Uncle Sam front and center. This was "Your America" and his count.

People who heeded Senator Tobey's warnings saw the situation differently. Florence Doud of Indiana drew an enumerator who looked nothing like Uncle Sam and then gave that enumerator the boot. (Well, gave the enumerator the brass toes.)

When the actual enumerator came calling, Doud and her husband revealed much of the requested information. But when it came to the final columns, where sensitive financial data was to be recorded, they managed to avoid revealing anything. The zeros in column 32 indicate that Mr. and Mrs. Doud claimed to have been paid no wages in 1939 despite working fifty-two and eight weeks, respectively, or a combined sixty weeks between them. This would have been the appropriate response for people who were self-employed (and so were not paid wages by an employer), but those people would then have an "OA" for "own account" listed in column 30—but here that column is left inexplicably blank.

In just one enumeration district in Montevideo, Minnesota, I found fifty-nine instances of people reporting working some number of weeks while also earning zero wages. In most of these cases, though not all, individuals managed to shield their income by claiming in column 30 to be employers (E) or working on their own account (OA).

Look at all those zeros! (Note: these entries did not occur one after the other as they appear here but were interspersed throughout the schedules.)

Occupation	Industry	Class			Weeks	Wages	Other
Proprietor	Hotel + Apts	PW			52	0	Yes
Proprietor	Hotel + Apts	PW			52	0	Yes
					42	0	Yes
Laborer	Odd Jobs	PW			48	0	Yes
Proprietor	Cafe	PW			52	0	Yes
					52	0	Yes
Proprietor	Retail Impl	E			52	0	Yes
Sheet Metal Worker	Sheet Metal Works	OA			52	0	Yes
Saleslady	Retail Ladies Items	PW			48	0	No
Joint Proprietor	Auto Sales Repair	E			52	0	Yes
Shoe Shiner	Shoe Shine Parlor	PW			40	0	Yes
Shoe Repairer	Shoe Repair Shop	OA			52	0	Yes
Shoe Repairer	Shoe Repair Shop	OA			52	0	Yes
Plumber	Plumbing	OA			52	0	Yes
Radio Repairer	Radio Repair	PW			26	0	Yes
Attendant	Oil Station	OA			52	0	Yes
Tinner	Hardware	OA			52	0	Yes
Laundress	Home	OA			22	0	Yes
Carpenter	Bldg Constr	OA			34	0	Yes
					11	0	Yes
Butcher	Retail Meat Store	OA			52	0	Yes
Plumber	Plumbing	OA			52	0	Yes
News Trucking	Newspapers	OA		14	52	0	Yes
Auto Elec Mechanic	Auto Elec Co	PW			52	0	Yes
Proprietor	Retail Meats	OA			49	0	Yes
Proprietor	Lunch Room	E			52	0	Yes
Proprietor	Lunch Room	E			52	0	Yes
Manager Parts	Retail Auto Parts	E			52	0	Yes
Proprietor	Billiard Parlor	OA			52	0	Yes
Garbage Man	City	OA			52	0	Yes
Care of Invalid	Home	NP			52	0	Yes
Tinner	Tiny Hardware Store	OA			52	0	Yes
Attendant	Oil Station	OA			52	0	Yes
Bus Driver	Bus Line	OA			52	0	Yes
Garbage Collector	City Homes	OA			52	0	Yes
Janitor Helper	Office Bldg	PW			26	0	Yes
Farmer	Farm				52	0	Yes
Farm Manager	Farm	OW			52	0	Yes
					52	0	Yes
					8	0	Yes
					26	0	Yes
Theater Manager	Movie Theater	E			52	0	Yes
Traveling Salesman	Wholesale	OA			26	0	Yes
Proprietor	Gas Station	OA			52	0	Yes
Proprietor	Gas Station	OA			52	0	Yes
Proprietor	Gas Station	OA			34	0	Yes
					13	0	Yes
Carnival Manager	Carnivals	OA			20	0	Yes
Proprietor	Auto Top Shop	OA			52	0	Yes
Shop Keeper	Auto Top Shop	PW			52	0	No
Proprietor	Cafe	E			52	0	Yes
Proprietor	Retail Furniture	E			52	0	Yes
Proprietor	Farm Loan	E			52	0	Yes
Laborer	Carnival	PW			13	0	Yes
Horse Racer	County Fair	OA			4	0	Yes
					34	0	Yes
Hotel Proprietor	Hotel	OA			52	0	Yes
Cook	Hotel	OA			4	0	No
Live Stock Trucker	Trucking	OA			52	0	Yes

7

The Inventory and the Arsenal

In 1947, a former Census Bureau statistician looking back on World War II emphasized how crucial population data had proved to the war effort. "The most essential commodity for the prosecution of the war was people," he said, "people to fight the war, people to produce war material, and the people to whom critical material had to be diverted for the production of civilian goods." To deal in that most essential of commodities—its people—the U.S. government needed "current knowledge" and a "future picture" of "the population, its composition and distribution, as well as the forces affecting it."[1] And the census offered that.

The statistician who authored those lines began working for the Census Bureau in 1940. He arrived just in time to see that decade's inventory of democracy take shape, to see it manifest as hundreds of thousands of paper certificates, as billions of holes punched in rigid paper cards. He arrived just in time to see how the U.S. military enlisted the inventory as part of its arsenal, to see the census weaponized.

His name was Iwao Milton Moriyama. He had earned a B.S. from the University of California, Berkeley, and both a master's of public health and a Ph.D. from Yale. He would go on to work for the federal government for the next thirty-five years. He would become widely honored and respected in the census's Division of Vital Statistics. In his retirement, he would serve on the international commission evaluating the long-term health effects of exposure to the two atom bombs that the United States dropped on Japan. But all of that was still to come.[2] In

1940, Iwao Moriyama joined the Census Bureau as a new employee, alongside thousands of others.

He and his fellow employees received a handbook, and if Moriyama read his to the end, he encountered this picture, an image representing the ultimate end goal, the final product and promise of the census.

The Published Results   (41)

A democracy's data, bound in leather.

This was how the census was supposed to end. Then came the war, and it became impossible to pretend the census could be simply and neatly bound in leather. It became impossible to pretend that the data, like the democracy it served, could do no harm.

A year after the Question Men convened in the Commerce Department's auditorium, Moriyama walked into that same colonnaded building to begin what would be a long and distinguished career as a government statistician. As he sat down to his first day of calculations, as he wrote his first memorandum, trying on his official status as a "biometrician," the ongoing world war may have felt far away.

Maybe Moriyama thought about his younger brother, Hisashi, a trumpet player who had reversed their parents' migratory path, returning to Japan in search of opportunities as a musician that America had withheld from him. (He succeeded too. Hisashi would later be called the "Father of Japanese Jazz" and was the literal father of a celebrated Japanese singer, Ryoko Moriyama.)[3] I suspect the war felt more immediate to Hisashi Moriyama in 1940 than it did to his older brother.

Iwao Moriyama's new colleagues in the Census Bureau offices worried more about the battle being waged at home against their operations by Senator Charles W. Tobey. Their attention was occupied planning their own domestic "invasion" (as Tobey would have put it)—they needed to get 120,000 enumerators into the field and then process the billions of answers those enumerators gathered.

That would not be easy. Even apart from Senator Tobey's challenge to the census, this new inventory of democracy suffered from serious deficits: of time, of money, of people, and, notably, of office space.

The gleaming halls of the Department of Commerce building couldn't (and weren't meant to) accommodate the churn of paper and the incessant ticking of mechanical calculators that the census required. Since World War I, the Census Bureau had housed its messier operations in structures in D.C. originally built to meet emergency wartime needs. They were always meant to be temporary, always slated for a short life. So when the government finally demolished those buildings in the 1930s, it left the bureau in the lurch, starved for space. The Roosevelt administration promised a building (dubbed, without fanfare, the "New Federal Office Building")—one that wouldn't have a fancy facade but that would have big windows, good lighting, air-conditioning, and specially wired outlets for running power-hungry machinery. That building was supposed to be ready for the bureau in July 1939, but when that date rolled around, the government had not even broken ground at the construction site.[4]

As a result, the 1940 census's key operations began in a rented warehouse. The massive space usually stored goods for a downtown Washington, D.C., department store: Woodward & Lothrop, or Woodies, for short.[5]

The Census Bureau's Geography Division set up shop there, drafting and then printing the hundreds of thousands of maps necessary to guide the count. Four hundred civil servants filled the warehouse's makeshift map factory, toting their drafting tools: compasses, scissors, T squares, and magnifying glasses.

Those geographers divided the country into roughly 147,000 enumeration districts, attempting to ensure that no place (or person) would be missed or counted twice.[6] Their handiwork has appeared throughout this book to illustrate the areas each enumerator patrolled. They divided so census takers could quantify.

The bureau's Field Division also supplied the country's enumerators from the Woodies warehouse; the Division alone would have required an entire warehouse worth of capacity. It "occupied 36,000 sq. ft. of floor space [three-quarters of the size of a football field, not counting the endzones] for assembling, packing and shipping supplies, schedules, instructions, etc." According to a report compiled later in the decade, Field Division employees in that makeshift base in Woodies' warehouse "placed 27 different items in each of 147,000 portfolios, packed and shipped 29,500 shipping cases." The Field Division shipped "160 million forms, 2½ million letterheads, 33 million envelopes, 350,000 blotters, 18,000 pen points," and more: over 2 million pounds of shipping all told, processed by 287,292 person-hours of labor over the course of 16 months, beginning in August 1939.[7]

In a photograph taken in the warehouse, an unidentified census employee with polished shoes and a natty vest is moving a small packet between a rolling handcart and a wall of wooden cartons. Most of the cartons in the foreground say simply "census" on them. In the background white tags dangle from a wall of large containers set to be shipped somewhere. The stamps on the middle boxes name people and addresses in New York and Chicago—perhaps they are en route to the "area managers" responsible for training and supporting the many district supervisors in those cities and their surrounding areas. The caption, pasted to the back of the photo, provides more context: "These are some of the 29,000 boxes which are being used to ship questionnaires for the 1940 census. Fifty-six mail cars will be needed to transport supplies for the census."[8] The bureau wanted it to be clear that the census required a lot of everything to generate all the numbers in an inventory of democracy.

The Woodies warehouse postponed the Census Bureau's real estate crisis but did not resolve it. About six hundred employees occupied the warehouse, making maps or shipping supplies. But more than ten times that many employees still needed space to do the work of translating Americans' answers into reliable facts. The Commerce Department's offices could accommodate around 1,600 census workers.[9] That number included highly trained and credentialed newcomers like Iwao Moriyama, whose jobs also entailed the ordinary office activities of preparing reports, writing memos, and attending meetings. Neither the warehouse nor the Commerce Department had enough room to house the thousands of remaining employees, though. That was why Director William Lane Austin pressed so insistently for a new building.

In 1939, an architect drafted a picture of this new home for the census's factory of facts. It would be a six-story structure with three extended wings. The drawing imagined tree-lined sidewalks, making the building look like part of a suburban college campus.[10]

In fact, the federal government decided to situate the building in the southwest section of Washington, D.C., on Virginia Avenue bounded by Second, Third, and D streets, which was, in Austin's words, "in the middle of Negro town."[11] A certain racist logic makes this choice seem almost inevitable. D.C. was then, as it is now, a segregated city. Beginning in the 1920s, the federal government built new and elegant spaces for white employees and visitors, like the beautiful and monumental structures of the Federal Triangle. It shipped its more congested, louder, or dirtier work elsewhere. That's how the Census Bureau's thousands of workers (including many African Americans) and their heavy machinery ended up in "Negro town."

The new building opened on March 28, 1940—just days before the population count began—thanks to construction crews working around the clock. Those crews mounted steel racks specially built to withstand the weight of all the completed census paperwork flowing back in from the field. After the racks came the "robots." A Census Bureau press release announced the installation of a "huge battery of mechanical robots which will tabulate the returns of the 1940 census."[12]

The Census Bureau loved its tabulating machinery, its "robots." The handbook for new employees waxed poetic about the census's computing capacities. "The tabulation of the enormous mass of data assembled by the Bureau is made possible by the use of punched cards and electric tabulating equipment." The people punching those cards or running the equipment, the people who made the tabulation possible—the people reading the handbook—did not warrant a mention. Instead, new employees read paragraph after paragraph extolling the "amazing speed" and overwhelming power of "these almost superhuman machines."[13]

The Census Bureau had played a singular role in the invention of those superhuman machines, so the pride and enthusiasm are understandable. The census could take credit for inventing the punch card, thereby preparing the way for the computer and the information age. Inspired by the practice of conductors punching tickets with information about a railroad journey, the young engineer Herman Hollerith (who had experienced firsthand the enormous volume of information that a census had to process while assisting a bureau statistician on the 1880 count) realized that personal information could also be stored on a paper card, and so for the 1890 census he designed the first machines to sort and calculate using punched cards.[14]

In 1940, each individual's data would be punched into a forty-four-column, twelve-row rectangular card. Once these paper cards were punched, cleverly designed machines could read the inscribed data and add it all up. The population of the United States had grown steadily, as had the desire of its people and its politicians for more and better data.

Before Hollerith's invention, the Census Bureau had reached the absurd point where it had not yet finished processing all of the previous census's figures when the new one began. Mechanical sorters and tabulators, as well as the punch cards they fed upon, did more than make an expanding, data-hungry census viable. They formed the basis for what would become IBM and then an entire industry. This enthusiasm for the most up-to-date calculating capacity would make the Census Bureau the first civilian purchaser of an electronic computer (the room-size UNIVAC), which it used to process the 1950 census.[15]

In 1940, the Census Bureau's mechanical laboratory continued to invent new machines and techniques. A publicity photo showed two women operators, both working on adding tabulators. The woman in the background used a machine fixed in place, while the woman in the foreground showed off a new invention: a tabulator on wheels, literally being rolled out for the coming count.[16]

In years to come, bureau technicians developed optical mark recognition (OMR) technologies (a cousin to the pencil-shaded-bubble forms that were to become the bane of generations of students and SAT-takers), as well as pre-GPS, nation-spanning digital maps. According to the historians Steven Ruggles and Diana Magnuson, the Census Bureau lost ground as an innovator only because of a four-decade-long effort to trim the size of the government, which gutted the bureau's technical staff, leaving gaps to be filled (often poorly) by private (usually military) contractors.[17]

Today's internet giants rely on the hidden labor of low-wage workers to make their "smart" systems actually smart: so-called ghost workers perform simple, repetitive tasks that will later be credited to ineffably high-tech "AI."[18] In these practices, too, the Census Bureau helped lead the way—although their workers enjoyed greater protections.

Behind each tabulation machine or card-punching-device stood a census worker, usually a white woman wearing a dress. That was true in the Census Bureau's offices and true in its publicity photos.

Examining one such photo, my gaze flies first to a person's face, to a ruffled collar, to meticulously styled hair. I see she wears a nicely pressed short-sleeved jacket. I see painted fingernails. Then I notice the papers she's grasping in her left hand—a thick stack, marked up all over. Finally I notice a small mechanical device. In sum, I see a census clerk preparing paper punch cards—she's grabbing one such card with her right hand, about to place it into her punching device. I see a working woman in a knowledge factory, one individual in the human chain that transformed enumerators' completed schedules into bound volumes of printed statistics.

In contrast to my experience of the photo, its official caption says: "This is a card puncher, an integral part of the tabulation system used by the United States Census Bureau to compile the thousands of facts gathered by the Bureau. Holes are punched in the card according to a prearranged code transferring the facts from the Census Questionnaire into statistics."[19] To Census Bureau officials, the subject of the photo was the machine, not the person.

You might be thinking: Maybe "card puncher" was just an old-timey job label. After all, people (primarily women) used to be "typewriters"— that is, people whose job was to work a typewriter, which was itself a kind of light machine). People used to be "computers" too (the word "computer" began as a term for a person who made computations, sometimes with the aid of calculating devices).[20] So why not "card puncher"?

While possible, the rest of the evidence argues against that interpretation. For one thing, the series of photos in which I found this one displays and names pieces of machinery, not workers. For instance, another photo shows a white woman in a dark dress with short hair placing cards in the top of a machine. The caption begins, "This electric tabulator" and goes on to describe only the machine.[21] The captions never reference the (mainly women) workers who appear with the machines. The only nod to the labor of those workers comes through passive-voice constructions such as "Holes are punched" or "The electric machine tabulator is fed statistics."

By August 1940, the new Census Building housed 5,650 workers, workers who operated the machines, who did the most crucial of census work, and who, in myriad ways, could not be adequately encompassed by the passive voice.[22]

They bowled, for instance. They bowled a lot. The Census Bureau's bowling league was its "oldest organized activity" (apart from counting people), and it regularly attracted over four hundred participants in multiple men's and women's leagues. For all those card-punch and electronic tabulator operators there were a pair of "Machine Tabulation Leagues."[23] Iwao Moriyama had some skill as a bowler and would in later years drag his fellow Division of Vital Statistics teammates to a middling record.[24]

The census workers played softball too. (Moriyama covered shortstop, next to a future Census Bureau director.)[25] Some rode horses. Others pitched horseshoes. And these were all official, organized activities for census office staff, as were debating and dramatics, dancing and taking boat rides.

The dances were racially segregated, like almost everything in the Census Building. Black men played in the Afro-Government Softball League. African American men and women attended the "Negro" dances or played bridge, table tennis, and swam at local high schools for Black children.[26] The new Census Building had a cafeteria—and next to it was a smaller "Colored" cafeteria.[27]

One crucial census worker activity did cross the color line: union organizing.

Moriyama might at some point have walked past a flyer hanging on a census office bulletin board, from January 1941, that read: "Democracy Begins at Home." Director Austin definitely saw the flyer—a copy ended up in his archival papers. The flyer's authors were affiliated with the United Federal Workers of America (UFWA), one of the three unions that represented census workers. They asked their colleagues a question: "Today with the world at war, with the United States launching a gigantic program to defend Democracy, is it not our first task to preserve Democracy right here at home?" And they considered discrimination based on "race, color, sex, religion, or anything else" a dire threat to "democracy at home." The flyer concluded: "Democracy cannot be maintained by proceeding to deny it to any group in America."[28] I wonder if Moriyama got involved in the fight.

The UFWA did not appear to prioritize getting rid of segregation in the cafeteria or at dances. It sought economic justice before social equality: the UFWA prioritized securing better jobs for African American census workers. By the union's reckoning, there were no African Americans in the well-paying ranks involved with the sorting and tabulating machines, and none worked in the cushier jobs available in the Commerce Department building either. (Which is to say, none of Moriyama's office mates were African American.) Black workers could get jobs only as "card punchers" or census data "editors" (those who fixed errors in census sheets and prepared them to be punched into cards)—and on those lowest rungs of the ladder, nearly a thousand African Americans languished.

Being stuck on those rungs left Black workers in a precarious position. Jobs with the census tended to be temporary, coming and going as the glut of data flowed in and out. African American editors and punchers were among the first workers dismissed when demand slackened, while their white colleagues stayed on or got transfers to other good government jobs. An investigation by the American studies scholar J. D. Schnepf recently uncovered the mechanisms by which the Census Bureau used apparently objective error rates and efficiency ratings to justify these discriminatory hiring and firing patterns; in fact, as Schnepf shows, the bureau engineered a system where workers created data records tracking fellow employees' errors and productivity "to establish grounds for employee dismissal, a practice that disproportionately affected the bureau's black women workers" since those workers were the most recently hired and as a result usually less efficient and more prone to beginner errors.[29] The unions fought alongside African Americans against these practices that set worker against worker, and the African American press drew attention to the controversy, with some success. A few dismissed employees got their jobs back, and finally a change in federal policy in 1942 cleared a path for many of the "temporary" African American census workers to find more permanent perches in the wartime government.

Although tabulating machine operators made more money and enjoyed greater prestige than punchers or editors, arguably the most important job in Census Building was done by hand. As each enumerator's portfolio of work arrived in D.C., a clerk combed through each and every census sheet to make sure the right ones had been included, that all the right places had been enumerated, and that all the blank lines or lines filled in accidentally had been "canceled." Then the clerk counted up all the lines that had people's names on them, counted all the canceled lines, checked to be sure the sum added to eighty for each sheet, and wrote down the total.[30]

A very simple technology—a paper form, called Form P-113a—controlled this operation. To look at it, one would not guess this form had constitutional significance.

But it did.

It had two simple columns: one for "Entries" and one for "Blanks."[31] The clerk counted the number of filled-out entries on each sheet in each enumerator's portfolio (a number of eighty or fewer) and wrote it down before counting the number of blank lines (which could be used as a check—adding the blanks to the entries should add up to eighty for every sheet). At the very bottom, the clerk wrote the district's "total population," which could be found by summing up all the values in the "Entries" column. That work then got handed with the portfolio to a section chief. All those forms, clipped to their respective portfolios, made their way to still more clerks, who gathered all the P-113a forms together, placing them in manila envelopes marked for the state and county they counted. Someone in this process added up the totals on each of those pieces of paper for each state and ultimately for the United States as a whole.

Those figures—the total populations of each state and of the nation—made possible the every-ten-years process of reapportioning representatives among the states. Reapportionment was the reason there was a census in the first place—the framers of the Constitution needed a census to make congressional representation proportional to population. So it is ironic, and possibly surprising, that for all the hullabaloo and publicity surrounding the mechanized work of the Census Bureau, its most important, most fundamental work happened quietly, without fanfare, and by hand.

The bureau's factory of facts depended more on the ingenuity and energy of its workers than was usually acknowledged.

If Moriyama or any other new census employee picked up the May 1940 special feature on the census in *The Washington Post*, perhaps in the hope of finding himself photographed or mentioned, he would have read that all the bureau's thousands of new employees were delighting in "the prospect of spending possibly three years reducing what we told the census man to statistics on punch cards." The reporter continued, explaining the work a card puncher did: "Each hole represents a single fact, such as age, color, or sex. Thus the individual identity is lost and each American becomes a statistic."[32] Over and over, audiences encountered different versions of the same message: in the census, the individual dissolves into the statistical.

(If Moriyama did look for himself in the *Post*, it was in vain. The paper only printed pictures of the bureau's white employees.)

When Moriyama or any other new census employee read the employee handbook, they would have read this line, italicized for special emphasis: "*Nothing is ever published which will disclose information given to the Bureau by any individual person or business concern.*"[33] In a similar vein, new employees (along with the rest of the country) could not help but run into President Roosevelt's 1940 census proclamation, reprinted repeatedly in the papers and plastered on posters everywhere. It read: "No person can be harmed in any way by furnishing information required. The Census has nothing to do with taxation, with military or jury service, with the compulsion of school attendance, with the regulation of immigration, or with the enforcement of any national, state, or local law, or ordinance." Not only were individual responses confidential, but the president's proclamation (following a tradition established by Taft a few censuses earlier) insisted that while it was compulsory to answer the census, each set of answers was not to be used to achieve other kinds of compulsion.[34]

War challenged these ideas and commitments.

The war created a series of incentives to view the inventory of democracy differently, even before the United States formally entered the conflict. The mobilization for war set in motion processes that reconceived of the census as a factory of reliable and official data that were also fundamentally personal, individual facts.

The war crept into backroom conversations about the census as early as September 1939. At that point, officials in the Department of Commerce still spoke of a war that the United States wasn't fighting in—at least not directly—yet they nonetheless requested that the Census Bureau consider how it could reorganize itself or shift its priorities to contribute better to the nation during wartime. Director Austin did his best to dodge the request, insisting that the best way the Census Bureau could help in a future war was by completing the census it was currently planning.[35] This does not seem to have been the answer the administration hoped for.

A few months later, the U.S. Attorney General's office started contemplating means to make the census useful to war preparations. What about using the data to sniff out possible subversives or saboteurs? The AG's office passed around a proposal to amend existing legislation so that the FBI and the military intelligence agencies could gain access to individual census responses for investigations of suspected espionage. President Roosevelt immediately denied any "unrestricted access to Census files" for military intelligence or for the Federal Bureau of Investigation. But he was open to the idea of providing investigators with "information regarding a specific person" if they could state a good reason for wanting the information. He left it to his staff to work out possible legislation along those lines.[36]

The AG's proposal surfaced again in early March, but the census was by that time under fire on the grounds that it invaded individual privacy. Thus, it wasn't a great moment to publicly expand the census's invasive capacity. Indeed, the people working in the census trenches resisted the proposal (when word of it reached them) with particular vehemence. Officials in the Departments of Labor and Agriculture—who depended on aggregate census data for their work—resisted too. Farmers and workers, those departments said, might lose faith in the census if it were used so overtly for surveillance. The strength of the census, according to the Secretary of Labor, "depends largely upon its universality and the cooperation of the public in giving full and truthful information."[37] You could kiss that "universality" and "cooperation" goodbye, officials feared, once ordinary Americans (and private businesses) knew that their answers to enumerators might end up on the desk of the FBI's chief, J. Edgar Hoover.

As Roosevelt entertained the proposal, his advisors reminded him that he had released a proclamation insisting the census would not be used by any sort of law enforcement. The official charged with evaluating the proposal advised Roosevelt: "It does not seem to me, that the enactment of the legislation proposed by the Department of Justice should be considered as being in accord with your program."[38] He recommended killing the bill.

Roosevelt scrawled out his reply: "I agree with you. FDR 3/2/40."[39] That ended (for the time being) the plan to let the FBI and military intelligence obtain targeted information about individuals from the census.

But the plan still came back to bite the administration. Senator Charles W. Tobey somehow got wind of the proposed law and started digging. His son reached out in early April to the FBI, which acknowledged its desire to peek into the census files. Yet the FBI stated that the Census Bureau felt "very strongly on the subject; they don't want anything to be done to weaken the confidential character of the census records for any purpose."[40] That assurance didn't prevent the senator from taking more shots at the census, though—just as bureau officials had feared. One national newspaper ran a headline (quoting Tobey) saying that the plan was "to make census into police list" and that the decennial survey really served as "One Gigantic Spy System." Tobey raised the specter that the administration could change course at any time, saying: "When the census inquisition has been completed, we may well expect the administration to exert its efforts for this new power."[41] (And as we'll see, he was not wrong—the shift would take a couple of years, though.)

In 1940 and 1941, the threat of war did not prove powerful enough to actually turn the Census Bureau into a *secret* supplier of private personal data. Instead, the threat of war turned the bureau into a very *public*

supplier of such data. The threat of war and the fear of sabotage in particular made census records appear suddenly quite valuable.

In a May 1940 address, President Roosevelt warned his radio audience about the possibility of "new methods of attack." He warned "a
nation unprepared for treachery" to watch out for "spies, saboteurs and
traitors" out to undermine the United States' preparations for war. Roosevelt worried about the wrenches that possible saboteurs might throw
into the gears of American factories producing tanks or planes or bul-
lets.[42] He needed those factories, and many more factories besides, to
turn the United States into "the great arsenal of democracy," as he would
put it later that year.[43] Without committing American military forces to
war directly, Roosevelt sought to commit American productive capacity
to war. That required safe factories. That required many, many workers,
and, to prevent sabotage, Roosevelt's administration required that all
defense workers be U.S. citizens.

Requiring workers to be citizens was one thing; proving to the government that they were citizens was another. Many people who were old
enough to be war workers were also old enough to have never had a birth
certificate; it's hard to imagine now, but the reasonable assurance that
every baby in the United States comes home from the hospital with a
birth certificate is less than a century old. The Division of Vital Statistics
that Iwao Moriyama joined in 1940 had previously played a leading role
(alongside the Children's Bureau) in establishing and mapping the "birth-
registration area," which was ideally exactly as large as the United States
and within which (nearly) every baby would be registered. If a U.S. state
passed new birth-registration laws and proved that at least 90 percent of
all new births were, in fact, registered, then its territory joined the birth-
registration area's territory. All forty-eight states finally joined in 1933,
auguring a future where the overwhelming majority of people born in the
United States would receive an official birth certificate.[44]

That bright, well-registered future did not, however, do much good
for the millions of adults in the 1930s who needed proof of their age to
get a work permit or to register for the new Social Security old-age insurance program. The Census Bureau's "Age Search" section came to the
rescue, sorting through prior census records for evidence of a person's

age. For the fee of $1, the bureau transmuted an enumerator's long-ago jottings into a formal, official certificate proving a person's age and citizenship status. The bureau's staff received a request with a person's name (and, ideally, at least a rough address) and consulted a special index, called a "Soundex" because it was organized phonetically. The Soundex had been a Depression-era WPA project and seemed like it would come in handy with the advent of Social Security and other retirement programs.[45] No one realized just how essential the Soundex would become. No one foresaw the massive demand for personal census data about to be unleashed: the arsenal of democracy demanded more workers, who demanded the census bureau's data. Iwao Moriyama, looking back from 1947, thought the entire operation might collapse under the weight of the war: "The unprecedented load imposed upon the vital statistics registration system threatened to break down the system completely," he wrote.[46]

The Census Bureau joined the supply chain of the arsenal of democracy by becoming a supplier of personal data. The factory of facts got into the business of world war. In a July 1940 press release, Director William Austin revealed that the Census Bureau supplied to individuals who requested them two thousand records every week while even more requests piled up, "taxing the capacity" of existing staff, who were also (of course) trying to continue all the work on the 1940 census.[47] (Those individuals could then use those records to prove their age or citizenship and so secure a job.) Seeking extra funding and more staff, Austin complained that requests from workers trying to get or keep jobs related to national defense had "snowed [the bureau] under."[48] The requests arrived as a blizzard that refused to let up.

In the first six months of 1940, well over one hundred thousand requests came in. By the end of the year that number had doubled—resulting in an unprecedented volume of searches. The requests doubled again in just the first five months of 1941. By September 1941, the bureau was on track to receive eight hundred thousand requests a year. It sucked up staff and resources to chip away at that pile, at a rate of about thirteen thousand a week—which meant the bureau would still end up disappointing more than one hundred thousand people seeking defense jobs that year. A bureau official lamented the "thousands upon thousands of citizens, lowly workers trying desperately to hold jobs they already have or struggling frantically to obtain jobs they sorely need" who "have been unable for weeks, now running into months on end, to obtain from their government and this Bureau information which the very government itself requires them to have."[49] He also worried that the failures of the bureau to provide timely responses might do damage to the government more generally. He—and those around him—judged it crucial to do whatever was possible to make the Census Bureau a fast, reliable broker for individuals of their own personal data.

Fears of spying or sabotage drained bureau staff and attention in other ways too. The bureau's chief statistician and one of his trusted employees (the same person who wrote the new employee handbook) lent their services full-time to the Immigration and Naturalization Service (INS) in August 1940 and to a lesser degree in the following few months. At that point some field offices were still finishing up their counts and shipping in portfolios to D.C.; resources in the bureau were stressed, and the census demanded expert attention. But concerns about seditious immigrants persisted even after all noncitizens had been excluded from defense industries. Congress decided that all "aliens" (that is, noncitizen immigrants) must register with the government, submitting to being fingerprinted and committing to update their addresses whenever they moved.[50] The resulting database could then be searched by law enforcement or military intelligence looking for suspicious individuals, which in effect made all unnaturalized immigrants suspicious by default. The Census Bureau lent its experts to the INS to help design the alien-registration forms, to facilitate the nationwide process of getting immigrants to register (at their local post office), and to assist in building the infrastructure to process and maintain the new registry.[51]

Some immigrants then sought to secure new opportunities or fend off suspicion by pursuing citizenship, which meant they needed official records of their age or proof of residence; some immigrants needed official records of their age or proof of residence for their registration as aliens. Such immigrants landed among the hundreds of thousands begging the Census Bureau to dig up their data.

The bureau statisticians finished their alien-registration work just in time to dive into supervising work on the apportionment of congressional representatives. That work depended on the outcome of the hand count of state populations. Those figures were then to be fed into a (mostly) automated algorithm that would determine how many seats in the House of Representatives went to each state. The purpose of that automated algorithm (established in law in 1929) was to make the system work while holding the House at only 435 seats, breaking well over a century's worth of precedents during which each census that demonstrated an increased population was followed by an increase in the size of America's legislative branch. The Census Bureau succeeded in completing the hand count in time for the automated system to swing into motion.[52] But in almost all aspects of its work on the 1940 census, the bureau kept falling further and further behind.

Mobilization for war placed new pressures on the Census Bureau to deal directly in personal data. While bureau officials had resisted the efforts by the FBI and intelligence officials to get secret access to census files, a larger sea change opened the floodgates, and census records poured out. Technically, that flood abided by the bureau's strict rules about confidentiality: each person could request a certified copy only of their own record or some data from that record, such as age, address, or citizenship. Yet those people requesting their own data had in many cases been compelled, if not coerced, into making such requests. Individuals who had suffered through years of unemployment during the Depression faced a future of plenty in wartime industry—but only by making data given under a promise of confidentiality available to their employers. Immigrants facing intense suspicions found themselves subject to new registration laws that many could obey only if they granted INS officials access to responses given under a pledge of privacy. Even before the United States formally entered World War II, the war was prying open access to data in the Census Bureau's vaults and forcing the bureau to sacrifice its ambition to process and publish a nation's statistics in the name of mass-producing facts about individuals.

———

Bombs fell on Pearl Harbor on December 7, 1941, as the Japanese Empire tried to preemptively paralyze the United States' military in the Pacific. The surprise strike succeeded in sinking ships but failed in its larger aim. The United States declared war the following day.

The Census Bureau had already shifted to a wartime footing. Indeed, after he had assumed the directorship from William Austin earlier in 1941, J. C. Capt appeared before a congressional committee and argued for a provision that would ease confidentiality protections for data useful to national defense activities. Congress did not (yet) grant him that request.[53] Still, he was ready. When war came, the bureau got "to work on the Japanese thing" before Roosevelt even made it to Congress on December 8. "We didn't wait for the declaration of war," bragged Capt, a month later.[54]

Getting to work on "the Japanese thing" meant putting the sorting and tabulating machines to work. The bureau pulled paper cards for major American cities, especially on the West Coast. It sorted those cards by race, separating out those coded 5 or "Jp" for Japanese. Over the next month, it printed up tables showing the number of Japanese by race, those who weren't U.S. citizens, and those who were—and the bureau shared those figures with the military, with the FBI, and with local authorities. They printed up tables down to the level of the census tract—a census geography that broke down big cities into "tracts" containing three thousand to six thousand people. The bureau got to work making similar tabulations for Germans and Italians, even before Germany or Italy declared war on the United States.[55]

The Census Bureau's advisory committee—a group of outside academics and former census directors—cheered on these efforts, suggesting that the bureau should show that same kind of initiative regarding other aspects of the war, anticipating what the military might need and having it ready. If the bureau anticipated correctly, it could stay relevant and keep its staff and its funding.

No one in the advisory committee voiced any concerns about the ethics of the tabulation of Japanese in the country. No one appears to have discussed if it was right to single out a racial group, a subgroup of Americans—many of whom were citizens—for special military attention.

The closest anyone came to expressing any doubts stemmed from questions about the relevance or accuracy of the 1940 census data about that subgroup. Did it really matter? Could it really help? Capt replied: "We think it is pretty valuable. Those who got it thought they were pretty valuable." He elaborated the point: "If they knew there were 801 [Japanese] in a community and they only found 800 of them, then they have something to check." And then, Capt said, if there were still difficulties tracking down Japanese Americans, "I would give them further means of checking individuals."[56]

The recently retired William Lane Austin, who sat in on the meeting, appeared to champion using census data to help track down subsets of individuals more generally. He asked if the Selective Service had requested access to individual cards for men of an age to serve in the military, and he mused that the census records could be used to identify those of draft age, presumably to ferret out any shirkers. Bureau officials replied that they hadn't yet been asked for such data. Austin did not mention that it would have been illegal to share data about particular individuals—though it would have been. He said nothing about his earlier resistance, before the 1940 census, to letting the FBI or military intelligence review individual files. No, Austin's only comment about the hypothetical prospect of handing over millions of census cards to the draft boards was that it "would be an immense job." His colleagues changed the subject.[57]

It was a telling exchange, though, a sign of how the bombing of Pearl Harbor, the entry of the United States into the war, had changed things. Austin called it "total war," and he argued, "If we are going to win this war it's got to be an all-out effort."[58] He meant that the Census Bureau might have to abandon some of its ordinary work, and it appeared that he may have also been willing to set aside the bureau's commitment to confidentiality. Also important was the fact that the 1940 census had entered a new phase, having shifted out of data-collection mode and into the tabulating and processing phase. In March 1940, Austin had worried that news about the bureau giving data to the FBI might make it harder to count and canvass. In January 1942, he seemed to think that the same sorts of acts, now at a massive scale, would make the bureau look patriotic.

Austin's was an extreme position in that meeting. Generally, in the months after the declaration of war, bureau officials balanced a competing set of priorities and concerns. They feared the enemy: the German, Italian, and Japanese militaries. They feared the United States could lose the war. They also feared that the United States might win without the bureau's help, that the country might survive but that the Census Bureau could perish, starved of funding, drained of talent, and displaced by statistical institutions that had been more helpful to the war effort. To solve the bureaucratic problem of navigating a "total war," officials tried to make the bureau as useful to the war effort as possible, while keeping up with the ordinary tasks of census tabulation.

That wasn't easy to do. Other agencies wanted to hire away highly trained bureau staff to help with war-related data issues. The government was tightening its belt when it came to activities that weren't directly war-related. And even when the bureau managed to cobble together the resources to complete a tabulation from the 1940 census, it faced enormous challenges getting those results published. The Government Printing Office (GPO) had other priorities, war work got first dibs, and when paper and presses became available, they cost much more to operate in wartime. Already behind in the massive task of processing the 1940 census results and fearing that the rug might get pulled out from under the entire operation at any moment, bureau officials begged for more money and did as much war work as they could manage while still plugging away at the census.[59]

That strategy worked for the bureau, ensuring its funding and survival.[60] When a constituent wrote to President Roosevelt in 1942 to complain that spending money on nondefense operations wasted money, the president replied in a telegram that many civilian agencies had proved their worth by "orienting themselves to the war effort." He offered the Census Bureau as a prime example.[61]

It is easy to see why. The Census Bureau served as a statistical standing army. A report prepared by the bureau a year after the bombing of Pearl Harbor listed every single example of "gratuitous work" the bureau did to help the war effort. It ran to seventy-six pages, each page covered with examples of bureau scientists lending their skills, of the bureau's tabulating machines processing other agencies' data, or of bureau workers producing special tabulations from original census data.[62] There were another nineteen pages listing similar contributions for which the bureau had been reimbursed.[63] Much of that work involved tracking the prices of essential goods and keeping tabs on the productive capacity of American industry. The Census Bureau generated report after report meant to allow more centralized command and control of the wartime economy.

Iwao Moriyama would later argue that the most essential commodity for the war effort was people, and, sure enough, the bureau generated report after report for war agencies inventorying the American people. Some of that work went toward manpower planning for war and production: how many people could be drafted into the war, and how many could be enlisted into wartime factories? But much of the effort to inventory people focused on immigrants, particularly immigrants and their children from "enemy" nations: from Italy, Germany, and Japan—especially Japan. For instance, the paid-for efforts included "machine work on alien registration" for the Department of Justice, indicating that the bureau ran tabulations from the alien-registration cards for law enforcement. One of the first pieces of pro bono work listed was a count of "Japanese, Germans and Italians in the United States" for the U.S. Army, followed by a count of "naturalized and foreign-born citizens" for the Navy. Over the course of the year after the attack on Pearl Harbor, the bureau volunteered information specific to Japanese Americans to the Army, Navy, and War departments, the Office of Naval Intelligence, the Army War College, the Department of the Interior, the Agricultural Adjustment Administration, the Federal Security Agency, the Treasury Department, the War Relocation Bureau, and the Office of the Provost Marshal General. And that is not even a full list; nor does it capture the volume of work and data the bureau transmitted to help the U.S. government's many various arms as it considered, debated, and eventually forcibly removed, relocated, and imprisoned one hundred and twenty thousand innocent Japanese Americans.

When the bureau oriented itself to the war, when the inventory joined the arsenal, people got hurt.

On April 2, 1940, a San Francisco enumerator visited his first household and counted his first three people: Saburo, Reki, and Kazu Moriyama.[64]

He found them on Sutter Street near Laguna, in an area marked deep red on HOLC maps, undoubtedly because the Moriyamas and their neighbors were Japanese Americans. The parents, Saburo and Reki, were "Issei," first-generation immigrants—they had been born in Japan and were barred by racist laws from becoming U.S. citizens. Their children, by contrast, were "Nisei"—Kazu and her siblings became citizens upon their birth in California.[65] The enumerator did not list the two Moriyama sons, one of whom had departed for Japan while the other had landed in D.C., working for the Census Bureau. Iwao, this elder son, lived in a lodging house. Census records indicate that an enumerator interviewed him there.[66]

Back in the D.C. offices over the next few months, clerks edited and coded the Moriyamas' census sheets. Others tallied up the Moriyamas during the hand count, incorporating the San Francisco Moriyamas into the total for the entire California population. Since the 1920s, white nationalists in Congress (including, very prominently, John Rankin) had tried to exclude noncitizens from the counts that were used to determine each state's allotment of congressional representatives, but most accepted that to do so would require passing a constitutional amendment, and they lacked the political might to achieve one. As a result, Saburo and Reki counted toward California's sum—they did their part to win California three more seats in Congress for the next decade.

Iwao contributed another head to the District of Columbia's total in the hand count, and the Census Bureau duly reported the district's population to the secretary of commerce. But none of that mattered—Iwao Moriyama and his neighbors did not matter—in terms of representation, because D.C. was not allowed any seats in Congress.

In the second half of 1940—after Senator Tobey's tantrum had died down—Saburo and Reki had to submit themselves for further, more invasive (and possibly punitive) enumeration. They submitted more data, including their fingerprints, on the forms for "alien registration" designed with the cooperation of Census Bureau statisticians. Once the United States entered the war, Iwao's colleagues in the bureau's tabulating-machine division contributed both human and machine labor to process the data gathered by registration. The Moriyamas submitted their data because they could not do otherwise, because to resist would risk prosecution and deportation. Saburo and Reki both subsequently received an "alien registration number."[67] The Census Bureau aided in the program because it believed in registration processes in general, approved of gathering more data in most cases, and because it wanted to prove the bureau's worth on the eve of war.

The day after the attack on Pearl Harbor, the bureau started churning out new reports, and the Moriyamas' data lurked somewhere in most of them. The Moriyamas were, for instance, subsumed in the published report of the Japanese population in the Pacific states: Reki was represented in San Francisco county's 894 female Japanese aliens, while Saburo showed up next to her in the column reporting 1,362 male Japanese aliens. The figure reporting 1,536 female citizens encompassed Kazu.[68] This report, and others like it, passed through the hands of military officials and politicians debating what to do. Military leaders pointed at 1940 census facts: that 92.5 percent of the "Japanese" population (marked as Japanese by race) lived in the states of the Western Defense Command; that 88.5 percent of the entire population actually lived in the coastal states of California, Oregon, and Washington; and that well over half of the entire Japanese population lived near one of five major cities or ports—like the Moriyamas in San Francisco.[69] From these facts, military leaders fomented unfounded fears of mass sabotage, conjuring up the specter of nonexistent legions of disloyal Japanese Americans waiting to aid invading armies. President Roosevelt accepted those arguments, despite the paucity of evidence supporting them, and succumbed to pressure to allow even citizens to be removed from their homes and relocated. He issued Executive Order 9066 and empowered the army to create military areas that encompassed the entire region in question—an enormous swath of the country transformed into a military zone from which could be excluded anyone the army wished, on grounds of "military necessity." Exclusion orders soon targeted those of Japanese ancestry—citizens and noncitizens alike—who were henceforth to be barred from the entire West Coast. (A commission created in 1980 by the U.S. Congress conducted a thorough investigation and insisted there was never actually any military rationale for exclusion: "the record does not permit the conclusion that military necessity warranted the exclusion of ethnic Japanese from the West Coast.")[70]

Japanese Americans would be forced out of their homes. Exclusion would uproot whole communities and disrupt thriving businesses and productive farms. It would cast a pall of unearned dishonor over loyal Americans—citizens and noncitizens alike—who had built their lives, families, neighborhoods, and more on the West Coast.[71]

A Census Bureau statistician left for San Francisco in late February 1942, the same statistician lent out to aid in alien registration in 1940. The Provost Marshal General's office at first intended to use him to register enemy aliens on the West Coast. Instead, the army choose to force a mass evacuation of all Japanese Americans from the area. The statistician's brief stay turned into a full year of intense statistical and organizational work. He arranged for his assistant—a woman with good statistical training—to join him. They received detailed printouts of data showing numbers of Japanese and related information, down to the level of the city blocks where they lived in some cases.[72] The statistician undoubtedly captured the Moriyamas in those tabular cells and translated them into new forms too. The three Moriyamas (and seven of their neighbors) combined to make one black dot on a map that plotted the location of every group of ten Japanese in the American West. The map had a cutout focusing on the Bay Area to make the Moriyamas' group easier to see. Those dots, in the context of deeply rooted anti-Japanese sentiment, further argued for or justified a policy of exclusion; they also provided fine-grained data that could be used to organize the process of forcibly removing over one hundred thousand people from the area.

The Moriyamas had to leave behind everything. Saburo's photograph gallery would have to be shuttered and possibly sold at a severely depressed, fire-sale price. His career would be paused indefinitely, with him losing all at once his hard-won goodwill, artistic reputation, and clients. Reki lost her home, her friendships, her reputation in her community, and who knows what else.

On March 2, 1942, General John DeWitt declared Military Area 1, spreading across the westernmost regions of California, Oregon, and Washington, including San Francisco. All people of Japanese ancestry were instructed at first to "voluntarily" move out of the region, but few had the resources or capacity to move at a moment's notice, even if they had been willing. With voluntary evacuation foundering, a new policy was announced on March 27, effective two days later, that prevented people of Japanese descent from leaving Military Area 1 on their own; instead, the U.S. government began systematically rounding them up—citizens and noncitizens alike—to incarcerate them indefinitely in concentration camps. In the two days between the March 27 announcement and the beginning of the mandatory evacuation, a rush of people (about 2,500 in all) sought permission to relocate elsewhere in the United States.[73] The Moriyamas were among them. The U.S. Employment Service in San Francisco, working as an agent of the organization set up to implement the removal, the Wartime Civil Control Administration (WCCA), issued a "travel permit" to Saburo and Reki Moriyama. It authorized them to move to Washington, D.C., to 1771 Massachusetts Avenue, NW, the same address where an enumerator had counted Iwao two years earlier.[74] Saburo and Reki, forced to leave everything behind, fled to the shelter of their son's room in a D.C. lodging house.

Many of their neighbors had no sons working for the federal government to turn to. Those neighbors the Moriyamas left behind were sent first for as much as six months to a temporary assembly center—such as the Tanforan in San Bruno, a converted racetrack that would eventually incarcerate more than eight thousand Japanese Americans, mostly from San Francisco.[75] Some of those thus unjustly detained were forced to live in former stables permeated with the stench and filth of horse manure. From the assembly centers, the Moriyamas' onetime neighbors would have been shipped inland to newly constructed concentration camps, where they would work hard for minimal wages until some months into

1945.[76] I have not been able to find a record of what happened to Iwao's sister, Kazu; perhaps she was among those deprived of their liberty in the camps.

In Washington, D.C., the Moriyamas lived beneath a shroud of state—and statistical—surveillance. The only reason I know that Saburo and Reki made it to D.C. is because they were stopped and interviewed by FBI agents in March 1943 for the suspected crime of living in the city without a permit. The FBI made a record of their every prior trip to Japan, including lists of family members who lived there. It must have been terrifying for the pair who had left so much and come this far, only to now face the threat of imprisonment. It must have been humiliating, as well, to be falsely accused of disloyalty. They kept what freedom they had, though, when proof of their permits arrived from San Francisco.[77]

The humiliations and surveillance persisted despite the sacrifices and the service of Japanese Americans supporting the war efforts. Across the Atlantic, Japanese Americans—tens of thousands of U.S.-born Nisei—fought for the United States in the European theater with the segregated 442nd Regimental Combat Team, one of the war's most decorated combat units.[78] In the Pacific, thousands more second-generation Japanese served in military intelligence in the Pacific theater.[79] In D.C. the Moriyama's son, Iwao, was working as a key official in the Census Bureau.

But even his own record of service to the nation's chief statistical office could not save Iwao from suspicion or the violation of his data privacy. In August 1943, the U.S. Secret Service requested information on every person of Japanese descent living in the Washington, D.C., metropolitan area, ostensibly to protect the president.

The Census Bureau handed over a typed list of seventy-nine names, each supplemented by the individual's address, age, citizenship status, employment, and other such details that the 1940 census had been built to capture. One name had been given a strange number: 65½. The name next to that number was Iwao Moriyama.[80]

Since the Second War Powers Act, passed in late March 1942, had removed the prohibition on sharing personal census records with other government agencies, the transmission did not break any laws, even if it broke the bureau's and the president's promises of confidentiality. Some scholars, activists, and former evacuees have charged that other such records were shared even before the Second War Powers Act made it legal.[81] Certainly, we've seen that top Census Bureau officials expressed a willingness and desire to share such data if it would aid in the war. But no hard evidence, no proof, has yet surfaced of any illegal data transmission.

Still, in 2007, the researchers Margo Anderson and William Seltzer—who have in recent years led the investigation into the role of the Census Bureau in forced Japanese evacuations and imprisonment— found the 1943 document that listed Iwao Moriyama as 65½.[82]

When Anderson and Seltzer first discovered this list that the Census Bureau had supplied to the Secret Service, they speculated that Moriyama's colleagues in the bureau had left him off it intentionally to shield him from scrutiny. Bureau staff would have known that it wouldn't matter to the government that Iwao Moriyama had nothing to hide, that he was a loyal citizen, because loyal Japanese American citizens had been languishing in concentration camps for well over a year by that point. Anderson and Seltzer thought that someone higher up the chain of command in the bureau must have noticed Moriyama's name missing and then added it by hand to an already ordered sequence—hence the "½." That hypothesis appealed to me; it seemed proper for the bureau's employees to be protecting one another.

Then I looked more closely at Moriyama's 1940 census record. (Anderson and Seltzer couldn't do that in 2007, because the original 1940 census documents had not yet been opened to researchers.) And I realized that the enumerator had recorded Moriyama's race as "white," rather than as "Japanese." Who knows how or why that happened? I suspect that a census taker in segregated Washington, D.C., simply couldn't imagine that anyone who wasn't white would be living in a lodging house full of white people. Perhaps, for the purposes of D.C. segregation, Moriyama was white. We know that he played on the Census Bureau's white softball team and bowled in the white league rather than using the facilities or playing on the teams that African American census workers had to.

Whatever the reason, Moriyama's classification as white offers another explanation for why he was overlooked at first in 1943. The machines used by the bureau to fulfill the Secret Service request by sorting the census cards for Japanese individuals in and around Washington, D.C., would not have found Moriyama. That's likelier why he didn't make it onto the Secret Service list at first. He hadn't been protected by a colleague. He'd been temporarily saved by an enumerator's judgment call three years earlier.

Moriyama's colleagues may still have tried to defend him; we cannot know. All we can know for sure is that someone in the bureau added Moriyama's name to a list that endangered him. Iwao and his family, despite their contributions to the country, remained under surveillance, stigmatized and suspected for no good reason.

Through it all, Moriyama remained at his post with the bureau, building the data infrastructure for what he called the most precious of wartime commodities: people. Iwao Moriyama became the chief of the planning and analysis section of the bureau's Division of Vital Statistics. In that position, he and the Census Bureau inadvertently served the internment authorities one more time. A study prepared by the successor to the War Relocation Authority (the entity that ran the concentration camps) highlighted Moriyama's supervision of a "large staff" as proof that the war had created opportunities for Japanese—even to oversee "Caucasian crews." That study argued: "By earning the respect of both fellow workers and community leadership for wartime service . . . Americans of Japanese descent have gained a degree of economic acceptance hitherto unknown in the United States."[83] It was a self-serving and perverse claim, one that highlighted Iwao Moriyama's success but diverted attention from the many more Japanese Americans who lost government jobs (and much more) to racism and hysteria.

One of the hundreds of Japanese Americans who lost a position in California's state government, Mitsuye Endo, who had been a typist for the Department of Motor Vehicles, became the named plaintiff in a suit for her own freedom that reached the Supreme Court. The court decided that the United States had no right to keep loyal citizens in the internment camps.[84] That decision followed quickly on the heels of Public Proclamation No. 21, issued on December 17, 1944 (timed to ensure Roosevelt had already secured his reelection in November), which allowed Japanese American "evacuees" to return to their homes and declared that the camps would close within the coming year.[85]

Two years later, in 1947, the Second War Powers Act provisions allowing the release of individual census data to aid in the "conduct of the war" lapsed.[86] Strict confidentiality became the standard once again. The sort of data that the Census Bureau had released about Iwao Moriyama and other Japanese Americans in and around D.C. could not be released in the future. In coming decades, Congress tightened confidentiality laws further, and the Census Bureau put in place procedures and internal review boards meant to protect against the release of data that could identify individuals or single out small groups. In 2000, the Census Bureau's director, Kenneth Prewitt, apologized for the role the bureau had played in the internment camps and emphasized the "important safeguards to protect against the misuse of census tabulations" that had since been instituted and which he insisted would "preclude a repeat of the 1941/42 behavior."[87]

In the end, the Census Bureau's strategy for bureaucratic survival in a time of "total war" had succeeded—albeit at a terrible cost. It took longer than expected, but the results of the 1940 census were finally released. The bureau managed to publish the most basic counts of people and their characteristics, as well as statistics on the labor force, in 1943—which, given the circumstances, was impressive. The bureau published its other studies piecemeal—on fertility rates in 1944 and 1945, on migration within the United States in 1946, and on education in 1947. Among the last pieces to come out in 1946 was a study of the life expectancy of Americans. One of its architects was Elbertie Foudray, who first inspired me to write this book. Another key contributor was Iwao Moriyama. Neither Foudray nor Moriyama got formal authorship credit, however; that went to Thomas Greville, a white male actuary hired—despite Foudray's decades of experience and success—to be her boss.[88] As ever, census data informed the nation's course, but it often resulted from less than democratic practices. The decisions the census informed—in war or peace—could not overcome the limits of the society the data described.

Democracy's data is only as good as the democracy it serves.

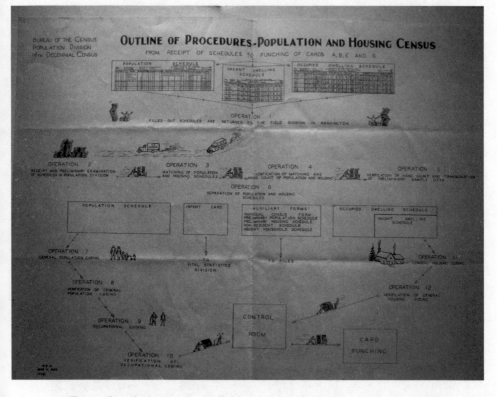

Even after the count in the field was completed, the census remained an enormous undertaking. This diagram attempted to outline just some of the steps that remained in translating filled-out census sheets into statistics—the processes that preceded card punching. Note the towering piles of census sheets weighing down desks or tottering on handcarts, making clear the physical heft of the data and the exertion necessary to advance it through the system.

Census Bureau photographs like these two show the makeshift offices built
in the Woodies warehouse space to house the Geography and Field Divisions.

This new six-story building will house the approximately 7,000 clerks needed to compile the returns of the 1940 census. Population, housing, agriculture, irrigation and drainage, business, manufacturing and mines and quarries will be covered in this census which is the sixteenth time a national census has been taken since the first one in 1790.

Processing the nation's data required an enormous amount of space—for people, paper, and machines. With the 1940 census enumeration about to begin, the bureau required a new office, here shown first as an architectural design from 1939 and then as it was finally constructed. (It was finished just in time to process and tabulate the census results.) The architectural drawing has been altered so that the caption, on the back in the original, is visible on the front.

Inside this office, workers (mainly women) labored on machines. In one photo, a woman worker punches cards. In the next, two women workers operate adding tabulators. The caption for the second photo, like all the others, ignores the workers in the photo. It begins: "The machine in the foreground is a new adding tabulator developed in the experimental laboratories of the United States Census Bureau."

To process the nation's data, the Census Bureau needed to hire a lot of workers very quickly. Many of those labor needs were to be filled by African American workers (mainly women), like the census data editors shown in this photo. Bureau offices were segregated spaces, just as the census data itself was rife with strict racial boundaries. Still, that did not stop workers from organizing in unions across color lines, with white workers joining their colleagues to fight for stable government jobs for Black employees, who were often the last to be hired and first to be fired.

Among the documents being processed were the next two excerpts from census entries. The first comes from San Francisco and shows the enumeration of the Moriyama family. Note that column 10 indicates that all three family members were marked "Jp" or "5" to indicate their "race" was Japanese. Column 15 shows that Saburo and Reki, the parents, were born in Japan, and column 16 indicates that both were "aliens," or noncitizens, which is hardly a surprise, since Japanese immigrants were barred from being naturalized. The blank in column 16 for Kazu's entry indicates that she was a citizen by virtue of having been born in the United States (in California).

LOCATION	HOUSEHOLD DATA	NAME	RELATION	PERSONAL DESCRIPTION	EDUCATION	PLACE OF BIRTH	YEARS OLD AND OVER—EMPLOYMENT STATUS		
		Name of each person whose usual place of residence on April 1, 1940, was in this household	Relationship of this person to the head of the household			Where in the United States; give State, Territory, or possession. If foreign born, give country in which birthplace was situated on January 1, 1937. Distinguish Canada-French from Canada-English and Irish Free State (Eire) from Northern Ireland.	OCCUPATION, INDUSTRY, AND CLASS OF WORK		
							OCCUPATION	INDUSTRY	
1	2 3 4 5 6	7	8	9 10 11 12 13 14		15	28	29	30
51	1711 18 R 200	Mira, Sara	Head	F W 71 S 4 6		New York			
52		—, Kate	sister	F W 70 S 4 6		New York			
53		Peterson, Hugh Jr	lodger	M W 25 S M C-1		Mississippi	Salesman	Printing Sales	
54		Kirk, William	lodger	M — M M C-5		Indiana	for Clerk	Civil Service	
55		Beckholt, Henry J.	lodger	M W 29 S M C-4		Penna	Maint Man	Corps Ascen	
56		Herrington, John E.	lodger	M W 28 S M C-5		Massachusetts	Adjudicator	Social Security	
57		—, James M.	lodger	M W 31 S M C-5		Massachusetts	File Clerk	Army Dept	
58		Moriyama, Iwao	lodger	M W 31 M M C-4		California	Vital Statistics	Census Dept	
59		Newman, Robert	lodger	M W 26 S M C-4		Penna	Auditor	Res Fin Corp	
60		Hanley, John C.	lodger	M W 32 S M C-5		Massachusetts	Personnel Classifier	Civil Service	
61		Lyons, Robert B	lodger	M W 42 S M C-5		S Dakota	Administrator	H S Farm	
62		Riggle, Cavin	lodger	M W 17 S M C-4		Texas	Translator	H S Farm	
63		Bechler, Robt. E.	lodger	M W 26 S M C-5		Ohio	Statistician	Rail Ret Board	
64		Blum, Paul E.	lodger	M — 31 S M C-5		Texas	Economist	Dept Commerce	
65		Riley, John Stephen	Lodger	M W 43 S Yr3 C4		Connecticut	Draftsman	Navy Department	
66		Spith, Winfield Churchwell	Lodger	M W 42 S 16 C4		Tennessee	Mechanical Engineer	Navy Department	
67		Tuggle, Allen Owen	Lodger	M W 30 S 16 C5		Korea	Technician	Government	
68		Lackey, Frank	lodger	M W 33 S M M		Virginia	Personnel Clerk	Armed Services	

The second excerpt enumerates Iwao Moriyama and his neighbors in a Washington, D.C., lodging house. The lodgers hail from all over the United States, from Mississippi to Massachusetts to Texas to (in Iwao's case) California. There's even one person who was born in Korea, though the enumerator took pains to write "Am Cit" next to his name, meaning he was likely the child of citizens living abroad. The occupations listed indicate that all of the lodgers worked in one way or another for the government. The enumerator also indicated, in column 10, that the race of all of the residents (including Iwao) was "W," meaning white. When the Census Bureau later produced for the Secret Service a list of all people of Japanese descent living in D.C., that racial designation initially kept Moriyama off the roster. After the war, and in succeeding decades, Congress tightened confidentiality provisions, and the Census Bureau developed new procedures and institutions to prevent census data from being weaponized against those it was meant to serve, as it had been in the case of Japanese Americans during World War II.

8

The Data's Depths

here are stories in the data.

Having "read" quite a bit of this data, what do you think it tells us about the society that brought it into being? What is the democracy that is revealed by this data?

The answer depends on where and when you look.

When democracy took shape on a blank census sheet, it looked as neat and tidy as could be. It was a bureaucrat's dream for democracy, as was fitting for a form designed in a government auditorium. It was the sort of democracy devised behind closed doors. Officers of the labor unions talked calmly but insistently with captains of commerce and industry, who rubbed elbows with scholars who lived off the largesse of philanthropic fortunes, and around them milled the visionaries and the functionaries of a newly vigorous American state. The representatives of these competing institutional interests compromised their way to a completed questionnaire—one that could be mass-produced and one that could be explained clearly by a brief census takers' handbook governing the entire process of counting the country's people—democracy reduced to a series of well-constructed queries culminating in a detailed database. I will not lie: I feel much affection for this vision. It appeals to the part of me that believes that good design can produce good systems. It appeals to the order I learned to love as a student. It appeals to me, I'm sure, because I could very easily see myself in that room, worrying about technical criteria, pretending that whatever we're doing, it is not political.

A different picture of democracy in the United States in 1940 emerges from an examination of completed census sheets. The hand-writing on one sheet—a flowing cursive—differs starkly from the style of another—in dark, scratched black caps. The names on the lines also, obviously, differ. The data reminds me of all the people and interactions involved in completing a census. The blank census form and the census takers' handbook and curriculum and training films all sought to re-move the individuality from each census encounter—but they clearly fell short of that goal. Democracy in the completed census sheets looks di-verse and unruly. In the profusion of handwritten answers, many of which break the predetermined rules or defy expectations, the limits on centralized control become clear. And this realization appeals to me even more: that the American people could never fit neatly within a fixed set of pre-drawn lines. I also admit to the romantic appeal of the doorstep encounter. I read each census entry as evidence of a meeting somewhere—on a threshold or in a living room—and I muse that those millions of conversations evoke what I want from democracy far better than the order imposed by the elites on their big lined sheets.

The census interview could be, at its best, a moment of cooperative civic action: a meeting of a pair of people (often with some children in tow) to add a few more strokes to the grand canvas of "America." The individuals might exchange smiles and even get to know one another a bit, maybe even share a cup of tea. We know that such encounters did happen, that relationships, however fleeting, did form. In internal mem-oranda, census officials relayed to one another the story of a reluctant Kansan who was so won over by the interview that he invited his enu-merator to stay for dinner (though no one said what they ate). A Denver enumerator, in a similar tale, had to choose from among multiple dinner invitations![1] But even as friendly encounters doubtless occurred more frequently than was ever reported, the census still seldom led to a shared supper. My romantic longing for the census to serve as a point of con-nection cannot make such connections real, and, more important, not all connections lead to happy endings. Closer readings make it harder to overlook the problems plaguing doorstep democracy.

Enumerators held the power of the pen, the power to decide what answer to write down in each blank, but the folks they interviewed could reveal (or not) the truth as they knew it. Doorstep encounters often became negotiations or even contests playing out across the gaps between classes and groups in the hierarchy that structured American society. Onetime Communists might disguise their identities to avoid persecution. Widows with pensions hid their incomes out of fear of neighborly gossip, or worse. The Margaret Scattergoods of the country labored to explain themselves and their unconventional households. The real-life Alberta K. Johnsons of the country, like Langston Hughes's poetic invention, asserted their dignity in the face of racism compounded by sexism by seeking control over what got written down. The Herbert Maces and Charles W. Tobeys also scrapped and fought over the doorstep, but they broadcast their evasions, seeking public acclaim and political advantage, which I am loath to laud. On the other hand, I celebrate all who by effort and cleverness found a way either to be themselves in the census or to protect themselves from the census. I revel in the chaos and uncertainty each introduced to the process. I take not a little pleasure in the sheer volume of tiny subversive maneuvers that the census sheets hint at. Still, that profusion also points to bigger problems—to the many ways that doorstep democracy fell far short of America's promise.

After the 1940 enumeration, census officials in Washington, D.C., sought to assert their control. The census sheets flowed back to the bureau in their leather cases and in wooden crates, and industrial democracy took over. Unionized employees pored over the census sheets—when they weren't bowling or attending segregated dances or fighting against discriminatory hiring practices. They took responses that did not fit the expectations of the census and made them fit it nonetheless, one way or another. Ghostly marks haunt census sheets, showing where unknown and unknowable census data editors replaced each "Mex" designation with a "1," indicating official whiteness, or coded a "7" in a different column to indicate married people living apart from their spouses. Card punchers punched holes in paper cards corresponding to those coded entries, taming the data from the wild, turning "stepchilden" into simply "children" or "partners" into "lodgers." Machines clattered and clinked,

sorting and grouping the paper-card population over and over on the way
to the official printed reports of the 1940 U.S. census, a process that war's
exigencies extended longer than planned.

The bureau stripped away all evidence of any chaos and confusion
that had accumulated in earlier phases. It generated definite numbers,
precise numbers, like 131,669,275. That was the U.S. population on
April 1, 1940, according to the 1940 census.[2] Not 131,669,274, nor
131,669,276. Not even *around* 131,669,000. The official number is ab-
surdly precise. I always laugh a little when I see such a number, though
not with any malice. The statisticians know their precision outstrips
their certainty, but the government requires a number, and the bureau
works hard to produce a good one, ideally the best one.

Bureau officials did not erase the chaos. They kept careful records of
the entire count, with all of its hiccups. Those in charge of the census
often acknowledged publicly some of the grander challenges that had
been faced and—to one degree or another—overcome. In 1820, the U.S.
secretary of state (who then administered the census) had had to write
to Congress to explain that the total population given for Alabama (at
that point a new state) was surely very wrong, because many of the enumeration sheets had been delayed too long to be included in the count.[3]
In 1850, the official report noted that the new state of California had
suffered a data catastrophe, with multiple counties' worth of figures
(including San Francisco County) burned or lost in transit.[4] In 1870, the
census director informed Congress that he deemed some of the data
collected—on whether or not people had been denied the franchise—of
such low quality that he was not even reporting it. Such examples
abound.[5]

Beginning with the 1890 census, statisticians quantified the confusion. They tried to confine the chaos within careful studies and measures
of error. The first significant effort to do this came in 1899, when Walter
Willcox compared the federal census counts to separate censuses made
by a variety of states. He argued from the comparison that "the last federal enumeration was probably within one per cent of the truth."[6] Willcox thus quantified the census's errors and made them public, with the
expectation that this would actually increase faith in the count. Willcox

believed—with good reason—that people who observed the messiness of an actual enumeration came away from the whole process more distrustful of the data than they ought to be.

Some subsequent researchers followed Willcox in quantifying census errors but produced more alarming results, particularly when their analyses looked at race. Kelly Miller called out an undercount of African Americans after the 1920 census. In 1947, Daniel Price discovered a similar undercount in the 1940 census, and this time, with the information coming from a white scholar, other statisticians paid attention. Henceforth the estimation of differential undercounts of African Americans, as well as of other groups (including young children), became a fixture of every census evaluation. Even as the census perpetuated some forms of inequality and ignorance, it at least got better at acknowledging those shortcomings.

Quality had been on the mind of statisticians as they prepared the 1940 census count. Bureau statisticians contemplated a kind of "check" on their count that would give them more insight into how and why they succeeded or failed in counting people accurately.[7] It would be another decade, though, before the bureau succeeded in implementing a "postenumeration survey"—a mini-census conducted by specially trained enumerators for a small sample of households and locations, which was then compared with the results of the actual census to create an estimate for how many people had actually been missed nationally. In 1950, the bureau's survey suggested a net under-enumeration of 1.4 percent—so the final total population fell short of the truth a bit over the 1 percent level that Willcox had asserted.[8] Yet the kinds of analyses that Miller and Price had used revealed that larger errors lurked within. A net 1.4 percent error could result from members of some groups being missed repeatedly while others were counted more than once. Who is most likely to be missed: the marginalized, those who in 1940 might (when not simply statistically invisible) end up labeled a "partner."

When I contemplate a number like 131,669,275, I think about the chaos lurking in it, inexorably. Bureau officials designed questionnaires to channel the counts, implemented training programs for enumerators, hired a few thousand editors and card punchers to clean and buff the data returning from the field, and then, when all that was done, they tried to estimate the errors still embedded within. One of the lessons of reading data closely, though, is that no amount of effort can remove or even accurately quantify the profound uncertainties that plague something as complex as a census. That's why it's so important to tell the stories behind the numbers alongside efforts to quantify the errors within them. The stories and the numbers highlight the errors and inequity that trouble democracy in the United States.

Willcox had a point when it came to the dangers of inviting outsiders in to see what the process of making an official count really looked like. You, Dear Reader, have likely experienced a few moments of shock, surprise, or even revulsion in this book's extensive accounting of some of the stories behind the numbers. You may have ended up, from time to time, rather down on the data.

This is a feature of reading data, not a bug. The shock and surprise subside with time, and feelings of revulsion can be directed toward reform. But one cannot change a data system or remake the society that produces such data without first looking squarely at the data, without examining precisely how the numbers get made. And the more we read data, the more we play in the muck from which all good data is made, the more resilient we will be to looking squarely at complicated data-making processes, to seeing them clearly without shrinking away or overreacting. And looking squarely at complicated data-making processes is becoming an essential activity for all those who wish to have a say in shaping our world, from activists to policy makers, and for every person striving to remain an informed citizen.

The exuberant embrace in recent days of Big Data and new analytical tools like machine learning too often point in a different direction. The cry of the innovator is, Don't worry about where the data came from, just mine it algorithmically for potent predictions. This book has made clear how foolish, even dangerous, a cry like that is.

We need more investigations into data histories, not fewer, and more people willing and able to read the stories behind the numbers. Otherwise, data will be more apt to train algorithms and models to perpetuate biases or inequalities, as the computer scientist Timnit Gebru and her colleagues point out while explaining why there should always be "data-sheets for datasets."[9] Otherwise, data that should be personal and protected will instead be more readily extracted and exploited—as the historian of science and medicine Joanna Radin warns in an exemplary study of a data set used widely to "train" algorithms to "see" patterns in Big Data, a data set built from medical records originally intended to fight diabetes among Akimel O'oodham people living on a reservation in Arizona.[10] When data sets represent people, those who want to use that data should have to think long and hard about how those "datafied" persons can continue to be faithfully and justly represented. Reading data encourages just such thinking.[11]

The Census Bureau completed the hand count of state populations and transmitted those figures to the secretary of commerce and then to the president on November 29, 1940.[12] That transmission revealed the number 131,669,275 for the first time. Once transmitted and published, that number and the rest of the census figures produced in the bureau's factory of facts went on to live multiple parallel lives, lives that statisticians could try to influence but could seldom control. Published data, like data being collected in the field, has a tendency to turn feral.

Consider the story of the apportionment data—the data demanded by the Constitution, the reason there is a U.S. census in the first place.

The printed data table transmitted in November 1940 also included the results of two different methods for dividing up a 435-seat U.S. House of Representatives. One method, called "major fractions," favored large-population states a bit more, and the other method, "equal proportions," favored smaller-population states a bit.[13] The major-fractions method had been used for the past two apportionments and stood to be the automatic default. Census Bureau experts claimed neutrality but clearly favored the equal-proportions method (which had been devised in part by a former bureau official). They testified before Congress on both methods but made the stronger case for equal proportions. A bureau statistician went to a Harvard mathematician's Berkshires vacation home to coordinate a campaign for the method.[14] (Those plans included separately imploring the Harvard mathematician to stop writing to Congress: "If I may be perfectly frank with you, and I feel that I can, I would advise that you not send further mimeograph letters to members of the Committee on Commerce. . . . I feel that efforts of this type on your part will not further sympathetic understanding by the Senate of the essential issues of the problem of reapportionment," wrote another bureau statistician.)[15] Debate over the Lend-Lease Act to aid Allied nations took precedence in the Senate in 1941, and so the war gave the victory (temporarily) to the default method: major fractions.

Later in 1941, Congress revisited the question and passed a new bill, switching to equal proportions. The Census Bureau's arguments had not been the deciding factor. By choosing equal proportions, a Democrat-controlled Congress could shift a seat in the House from predictably Republican Michigan to solidly Democratic Alabama—and so it chose equal proportions, a choice that to this day gives a slight advantage to states with smaller populations. (In 2020, by my calculations, equal proportions gave seats to Rhode Island and Montana that would otherwise have gone to New York and Ohio.) The bureau's experts had their say, but ultimately they could not force Congress or any other data users to interpret the data in any one particular fashion.

What sort of democracy did census data evoke in the debates over the House? Numbers might keep Congress honest but also left room for politics. In the end Congress stuck with a valid method for dealing with the fact that whenever you try to divide seats up in proportion to each state's size, there will be some fraction left over. When all was said and done, the apportionment guaranteed proportional fairness by some, but not by all, measures. And that's where politics crept in. Congress picked its method to suit the ruling party's interests and made the whole system entirely automatic, pointing to a shift toward automatized, algorithmic government.[16] That says something about American democracy too, because the reason Congress needed to automatize this process was because of the decision that the House should no longer expand. Even if the people of the United States continued to multiply, their number of representatives would stand still, guaranteeing that the government held in place by an automized algorithmic system would become less and less representative every decade if the country continued to grow.

Published census data showed up all over and was turned to many purposes. It could be used to advance many visions of American democracy. District of Columbia residents brought census totals with them to Congress in 1941 to protest their taxation without representation, for instance.[17] They armed themselves with census statistics to fight a political battle. In another case, a pundit took advantage of the income question returns to argue that too many Americans still lived at or below subsistence levels. He depicted a democracy still hampered by inequality. A national magazine, in contrast, pointed to evidence of new suburban affluence in an advertisement that used census data to claim that migration to suburbs amounted to "America's Greatest Population Movement Since the Covered Wagon!"[18] The census's data helped call into being what the historian Lizabeth Cohen has called "a consumers' republic.[19]

Some commentators also used census results to justify new ways of thinking about the nation as a whole. An enterprising reporter in South Bend, Indiana, for instance, used census publications to go in search of the "average American" in 1940. The reporter sought to replace Uncle Sam with Statistical Sam. The bureau's calculations placed the center of the U.S. population in Indiana, and so the reporter hired a local busybody in the average-size town of Plymouth, Indiana, to go looking for a white, U.S.-born, twenty-eight-year-old man (just over 50 percent of the U.S. population at the time was male) who earned between $1,000 and $1,250 and who had a wife and two children. Together they discovered a "mechanic's helper" named Ralph C. Suter and granted him the title of "America's average man." (The newspaper noted that the man lived with his family in a house that did not have central heating, and it printed a menu for the simple meal that Suter's wife served the reporter.)[20] Census statistics were supposed to define groups instead of individuals, and the idea of naming a single "average American" is ridiculous, but once the data was out the door, people could do all sorts of things with it, whether it was a good idea or not.[21]

The profile of Mr. Average American ended by relaying another inference drawn from census data: the United States would be growing older in coming years, but not growing larger. Ralph C. Suter, at twenty-eight, hardly seemed aged, but he and his wife had only two children. The reporter argued that "taken together, these facts indicate a day when the United States will no longer be growing." Lower average fertility rates and restricted immigration would slow the population's reproduction, he wrote, while advances in medicine and public health lengthened lives. The final line of the story quoted a Minnesota Planning Board document declaring that the United States stood "face to face with the sober and thought-provoking necessity of developing a way of life for a maturing community."[22]

This "maturity" trope appeared everywhere, over and over, in the 1940s. (Some population researchers had been foretelling slowed growth and a graying nation for decades, but it really caught on during the Depression as birth rates fell.) The journalist Stuart Chase (who was responsible for popularizing the term "the New Deal" to describe Franklin Roosevelt's policies) wrote: "The 1940 Census is one of the great landmarks of American history." He continued: "It proves that we have grown up."[23] The United States had grown to be a "mature" nation with a "mature" economy. But the price of this maturity was a need for management. In the past, it was said, population growth had driven economic prosperity; if the population remained stable, something else would have to fuel the economy. In the past, larger and younger generations rose up to care for those who had aged out of work. A United States that grew more slowly, in order to thrive, would therefore require its government to pick up the slack. That was Chase's argument, and it was made by many others too.

Chase and his peers found in the 1940 census good reason to believe that government could succeed in managing the country. Chase called the census a "statistical drama" and then added that "some people would call it a statistical miracle."[24] The "miracle" part stemmed from the way the census could be read as confirming prior predictions. In the last couple of decades, leading researchers had devised new techniques for foreseeing future population growth: they looked at statistics showing prevailing rates of birth, death, and migration for various age groups, and then used those to model how the actual U.S. population (with its distinct distribution across those age groups) would change over time if those same rates persisted. This approach was cutting edge and models of this style are still used widely today. Leading up to the 1940 census, researchers used data from the 1930 count to project three possible futures (a high-growth, medium-growth, and low-growth future, each dictated by the assumptions the researchers built into their model). The 1940 results landed squarely between the low and medium predictions, and Chase called it a miracle: "They hit the bull's-eye."[25] Whether it was miraculous or not, or even a bull's-eye, the results as interpreted by Chase conferred greater credibility on the idea that populations could be forecast—if not perfectly, then at least within a range of possibilities. The promise of a more predictable future gave Chase and many of his contemporaries reason to believe that a technocratic government could make informed and effective plans for a "mature" United States.

There was a hiccup, though. Even as they celebrated the prediction's success, conditions were shifting. Americans began to have more babies again. By late 1941, *Life* magazine could croon about a "Boom in Babies" and make its own predictions: "If the trend goes on, next year may see the U.S. winning the baby war against Hitler, in birth rate as well as total production."[26] The U.S. population did not settle into maturity—it kept on growing throughout the twentieth century. It took the researchers quite some time to catch up to that reality, though. They made the bulge in births into an anomaly, one that would upset carefully planned institutions, from hospitals to schools to universities to pension plans. Because they were certain that "maturity" was coming, they cast the continued growth of the U.S. as a problem and so helped invent the idea of a profoundly disruptive Baby Boom generation. Boomers, as they came to be called, challenged the premise of the statistically sophisticated, data-driven, prediction-powered welfare state, simply by being born.[27]

Finally, while the results of the 1940 census played many and varied roles in political processes (like congressional apportionment) and arguments (over, for instance, the nation's future), while they were interpreted and reinterpreted by commentators (like Stuart Chase), the way census publications came to be used against Americans in the course of the war demonstrates the destructive potential of the nation's data and of American democracy itself. The Census Bureau, keen to survive the war and to do its patriotic duty, rushed into the fray, publishing data about so-called enemy aliens. It churned out data on Germans, Italians, and Japanese living in the United States. And it distributed special reports and tabulations to military authorities, thereby helping to justify and facilitate the mass incarceration of 120,000 Japanese Americans. That number itself eerily echoes the number of enumerators in 1940. Imagine the outrage if the United States had corralled its approximately 120,000 census takers behind barbed wire for years. In its militarized, weaponized form, the 1940 census (and the government it served) fell far short of being "the greatest inventory of the world's greatest democracy."

We have, over the course of this book, traced out the full story behind (and beyond) the published census numbers. The 1940 census's data began as a tightly controlled thing—a mass-produced questionnaire—engineered in a government office by representatives of the New Deal coalition. Over one hundred thousand enumerators carried those sheets across the nation, from the top floors of bustling tenements to the far reaches of Indian Country to the patchwork shares of tenant farmers to the midwestern towns where the so-called average American might live. Census data in the field was subject to millions of negotiations and compromises, varying from person to person, enumerator to enumerator, place to place. Back in D.C., the factory of American facts spun into motion to bring officially sanctioned order to the count, revising each set of responses to fit predetermined bounds of possibility, reducing each person to a punch card. With the published results of the census, the government exerted its authority once again and with its most enduring force. But no sooner were the results released than they, too, went off to live a thousand different lives far beyond the controlling reach of the Census Bureau or of anyone else.

Such is the story of all data. It weaves in and out of line, sometimes sprawling, only to be drawn back into a tight, neat package. Each stage of the census process produced data, from the conference room to the doorstep and beyond. The data generated by the census runs far deeper than the published results or the spreadsheets of figures anyone can download today.

The same could also be said for other kinds of data that serve democracy, that there are hidden stories to be told in the records of the Internal Revenue Service or the Social Security Administration, though neither could match a decennial population census for its inclusiveness and scope. There are other censuses with stories to tell too, in the United States and around the world.

One could also go looking for communism's data, fascism's data, or colonialism's data. One could pick through files scheduling shifts in a state-owned factory overseas, or reverse-engineer a detailed population register tracking the movements (and race or religion) of every individual, or scan scientific land surveys drawn to erase the lines drawn earlier by Indigenous rulers or local custom. One could uncover important stories here too, as in the suppressed Soviet census of 1937. Stalin ordered it, the state publicized it, Stalin read its results revealing the true, terrible cost of his policies in millions of lives lost, and then Stalin ordered the statisticians slaughtered and their findings forgotten. The 1953 Chinese census would also stand out: the first modern count of the Chinese people, all 583.6 million of them, compelled to report to local offices where 2.5 million census workers enumerated each person (as an individual and not as part of a household), noting only each one's name, age, sex, and nationality—a truly astounding endeavor. Ironically, Soviet experts had advised the new Communist regime, making possible such an enormous enumeration. These are just some of the stories to be read in communism's or fascism's or colonialism's data, glimpses of which have surfaced in this book—the 1940 census was, after all, also a census of the U.S.A.'s colonies, like Hawaii, with its abundance of "partners."[28]

It takes time and patience—sometimes decades or longer—just to get the opportunity to read a significant data set like the U.S. census in all its layered complexity. Much of the 1940 census data entered a period of hibernation once all the tabulations were complete. The records for each individual slept, carefully preserved, in bureau files and then in the National Archives for seventy-two years. Some records awoke briefly from time to time when called upon by a person seeking proof of age or residence to get a Social Security account or a job. Most records slumbered, though, in climate-controlled, fire-retardant vaults. Precisely how long they were to persist undisturbed was unclear in the 1940s. Some in the bureau had expected the records would be made available in fifty or sixty years, at which point they would be "thrown open for individual research by historians, genealogists, and students of sociology."[29] With the opening of the National Archives and then the release to the public from that new building of the 1870 census results in 1942, a seventy-two-year precedent was set.[30] Some in the government wondered if census confidentiality laws prevented records from *ever* being released, but a new federal records law in 1950 made fifty years the legal period for keeping the data confidential. Finally, in 1978, Congress passed a law that settled the matter: all census data about individuals would remain confidential for seventy-two years.[31] The 1940 manuscript data would remain private until 2012.

The seventy-two-year rule tells its own story about American democracy. It speaks to an ideal that protects individual privacy, one that would become more remarkable every year of the twentieth century, as individual data became more and more valuable. By the late twentieth century, scholars sought individual-level data so as to better understand, model, and predict big complex systems like economies or populations; governments around the globe also sought such records in order to augment their police powers and fine-tune their own predictive systems for managing the economy and public services; and businesses caught on to the power and promise of data gathered, used, and often sold at a heretofore unknown scale. In an age of big, commodified data, a commitment to confidentiality that spans decades deserves some wonder.

At the same time, that preservation speaks to the value of individuals—no matter who they are—to a democracy. A bureau official expressed this line of argument in the 1930s: "Every person in the United States, however insignificant he may be, has a permanent place in the history of the country, for a record of his personal life is made by the National Government every ten years and filed away in the government archives. Nobody need feel that he merely lives and dies without the facts about this existence permanently recorded."[32] The bureau official skated over an important caveat: some people never got counted, whether because they chose to avoid the enumerator or because the census failed to look for them in the right place. Those people, who tended to be very young or poor and unhoused or from disenfranchised racial minorities, don't appear in the records. In this case, as with the preservation of confidentiality—which was violated to such devastating effect during World War II—the actual practice fell short of the ideal. Yet the ideals still mattered, and the census strove to attain them. That, ultimately, was what drew me to study the census in the first place. This data teems with the stories of Americans from all walks of life, the sort of stories that a historian cannot find anywhere else. In telling such stories, I aim above all to affirm each person's dignity and advocate for the inherent, equal value of every individual, even or especially when the census itself did not.

Epilogue

A letter arrived in our mailbox in the middle of March 2020. It bore a Census Bureau logo and—in bold all caps—shouted **"YOUR RESPONSE IS REQUIRED BY LAW"** / **"SU RESPUESTA ES REQUERIDA POR LEY."** The letter didn't have our names on it, or anyone else's either. The bureau addressed it to whoever resided in our apartment. In March 2020, that meant our little family. This was how the census arrived. This is one important way that American democracy manifested for us, for me. This letter heralded an opportunity to participate in that democracy by helping to fit our household into the nation's data. It also heralded an opportunity to read the census in real time.

The goal of the census is that every resident of the United States be represented in the data. I think they all should also have the tools—if they want them—to understand that data, how it is made, and how it influences our society. They should also have the tools they need to negotiate their place in that data and to make the census represent them better. Democracy's data is too important to be reserved for experts in quantitative methods. Democracy's data is too political, too messy, too human to be understood solely through numbers.

We cannot yet read the 2020 census as deeply as we can the unlocked 1940 version. We don't have the full manuscript entries. We don't have access to all the bureau's records and deliberations. I do, though, have my own experience filling out that form, and some evidence from others' similar experiences. That's something. Every time we encounter a form or answer a survey, we're given a chance to read into the data, at least a little.

Reading the 2020 census, beginning with that letter in our mailbox, I'm struck by how much has changed over the last eighty years.

No person came to our door to count us. That's a change.

It was a lucky one too, because we were living through a pandemic by then, and I was in no mood to have a sustained face-to-face conversation with a stranger. (So much for my romantic ideas about the doorstep encounter!) I had once stumbled upon a newspaper clipping from 1940 containing two black-and-white photographs showing the aftermath of a tornado. One showed a small house torn in half, the walls thrown to the ground. The other showed an automobile on its side. The automobile belonged to a census taker who had chosen the worst possible moment to try to enumerate that homeowner; both the counter and the counted were injured.[1] In 2020, it felt like the entire world had been hit by that tornado, and I couldn't imagine trying to be an enumerator in those circumstances.

The envelope we received included a code that I could input in a government website where I could fill out a census questionnaire through an online form. (There was also an option to submit a form by mail or to answer the questions by phone.) It was the first time the Census Bureau had allowed everyone to fill out the census online—and what timing! (That form has its own story, according to my collaborator, the ethnographer danah boyd: the sleek, well-functioning form I filled out had been designed by Census Bureau career staff, but it almost didn't exist. The federal government had hired a private contractor to build the self-response form, but the result proved clunky and unreliable. At the last minute, the bureau substituted in its in-house backup plan and saved millions of Americans from a frustratingly dysfunctional Web interface!)

So, what does it say about American democracy that no enumerator came to our door?

Between the 1940 census and the 2020 census, enumerators did not disappear—in fact, their number increased substantially, growing even faster than the U.S. population. From around 120,000 enumerators to count around 131 million residents in 1940, the number rose to 635,000 census takers to count over 308 million residents in 2010. In 2020, the bureau hoped to get away with only about 500,000 enumerators.[2] Even then, we're talking about a fivefold increase in census takers, while the U.S. population itself had merely tripled. So why didn't anyone come to our door?

Oddly enough, the overarching reason an enumerator didn't come to our door was because American democracy had grown more committed to the principle that every person really, truly counts—and because the U.S. bureaucracy needed precise data to direct the flow of trillions of dollars meant to improve the lives of each of those people.

The truth is that the Census Bureau probably would have preferred to send out zero enumerators. Over the course of the twentieth century, enumerators had come to be seen as a necessary evil: they carried the stink of patronage politics; on a very few occasions, they lied; when they didn't lie, they made mistakes or idiosyncratic judgments; they weren't always nice. In 1940, we've seen how the bureau worked to standardize or mechanize their army of enumerators through tests and training films and detailed instructions. But we've also seen that those efforts had significant limits.

Leading up to the 1960 census, bureau officials studied the possibility of shifting toward "self-enumeration"—every person their own enumerator! The results came out more mixed than was probably expected. Self-enumeration didn't, on the whole, generate more accurate answers. There were trade-offs. As one bureau study noted in a close examination of responses to occupation questions: "although the worker himself is undoubtedly more familiar with his occupation than is his wife [who was often the one answering an enumerator's questions], he does not understand the type of detail we need (it is difficult enough to teach this to enumerators in formal sessions) or is unable to express himself adequately in writing."[3] But the bureau reasoned that self-enumeration could allow something closer to a "one-day" census, when everyone answered the questions on more or less the same day. (Even before self-enumeration, the census asked people to answer all questions as if it were census day, which was April 1 in 1940, so that everyone's answers could be more easily compared.) They also believed that self-enumeration would eliminate error "clusters" caused by an enumerator's particular tendencies.[4] Essentially, by introducing large-scale self-enumeration in 1960, the bureau decided that error on the whole wouldn't decrease but that it preferred the random, unpredictable errors of hundreds of millions of Americans to the lumped-together errors of better-trained census takers. That's one important reason that I was sent to a website in March 2020 and no enumerator knocked on our door.

The quest for a complete count is the other big reason that I didn't talk to a census taker. A complete count—one that counts every person once and in the right place—is the holy grail of census taking. It's long been the bureau's goal. But since 1940, it has become more and more important. The count must be complete because so much is at stake now. In 1940, the big thing that would be swung by the census count was the apportionment of representatives in the House and votes in the electoral college—which are both big deals, but they don't require too much local precision. Two developments in the 1960s put much more pressure on census data and especially on what is called "small-area data."

First, Civil Rights advocates won major victories in a series of Supreme Court cases that together established the principle of "one person, one vote," while the coordinated pressure throughout the South of protestors marching and resisting (and registering voters) alongside Martin Luther King, Jr., Fannie Lou Hamer, and John Lewis pushed President Lyndon Johnson and the U.S. Congress to pass into law the Voting Rights Act of 1965. Practically overnight the census was transformed from a tool that had long reinforced white supremacy into a mechanism for dismantling it.[5] And to fight racism and discrimination with census data, that data had to be complete and more accurate than ever before; the long-standing undercounts of African Americans had to be addressed, as did similar undercounts of Mexicans, Puerto Ricans, Cubans, and other "Hispanic" people—undercounts that were uncovered and protested in the early 1970s.[6]

Second, the "Great Society" legislative agenda of the Johnson administration ramped up the distribution of federal dollars to programs that fought poverty, improved housing, or provided medical insurance and care to the underserved.[7] Congress passed laws that tied federal funding to populations at the state and local levels. Presidents Richard Nixon and Gerald Ford's administrations scaled back the amount of federal spending but kept those funds closely tied to census counts.[8] Cities and states noticed the new implications of accurate censuses, and they let the Census Bureau and Congress know that they would not stand for the status quo when it came to undercounts: the bureau received 1,900 formal complaints in 1970.[9] With the 1940 census, the bureau had begun preparing detailed "procedural histories" after every census; since 1980, those histories have devoted entire chapters to discussing legal challenges to the census. Bureau statisticians devoted significant energy toward mathematical methods that could adjust for and correct errors in the census—an effort that succeeded in some respects but also generated much controversy and many lawsuits, leading eventually to the conclusion that statistical methods couldn't fix undercounts.[10] Enumerators had to do that.

So the bureau sent out enumerators to find the 30 to 40 percent of the population that didn't self-respond. It scaled up programs to count people in homeless shelters and other spots transients might frequent. It invested in hiring more diverse groups of enumerators, including people who spoke languages besides English. And it kept hiring more and more enumerators. That's why the size of the census-taking army has grown fivefold over the last half century, even though many people will never encounter an enumerator.

The 2020 census was different from 1940's: no one knocked on our door, and the sheet of questions I faced had shrunk from its previous incarnation.

In 1940, enumerators had to work through more than thirty columns for each person. In 2020, most people only had to fill in seven blanks. The census now wanted to know some things about the size of our household, whether we rented our apartment, and our answers to questions about relation, sex, age, ethnicity, and race. That was all.

What does it say about American democracy that there are so few questions?

Did the U.S. government get less curious over that eighty-year span? Or less driven by data?

No.

Another data revolution had intervened, one that had begun in 1940.

If you asked someone what technology fundamentally changed the census in the twentieth century, I bet almost everyone would answer, "the computer." It's not a bad guess, and the introduction of the electronic computer to census making (beginning in 1950) certainly shaped the process ever since. But the use of computers for the census probably helped advance computing more than computing remade the census. In the end, the census used electronic computers to do many of the same kinds of tabulations that older tabulating machines had done. Computers changed the media of the counting—trading in paper cards for magnetic tapes or discs—but they did not change the structure of the census.

So a better answer to the question of what technology changed the census the most in the twentieth century is "sampling," or selecting part of the population to extrapolate the characteristics of the whole. The technique that the Question Men in 1940 turned to in order to squeeze in a few more questions about, among other things, women's fertility gradually overtook the census. Government innovators in 1940 invited the casino into the census. Today, most of the facts of American life start in that casino.

In 1950, the income question—after generating so much heat in the previous decade—led the march of questions to the portion of the census asked only of a partial sample of the population. The Question Men in charge of that 1950 census decided to ask only one in every five people about income. That one in five, or 20 percent, sample was also asked questions about education and migration within the United States. The possibility of asking questions of a smaller sample allowed the form enumerators used to shrink to twenty-two columns—about a third of its size in 1940.[11]

Then, in 1960, the number of questions asked of everyone shrank even further. All Americans were asked to reveal their sex, age/birthdate, race, marital status, and relationship to the head of household.

These questions came to be called the "short form" in 1970, because households received them on, well, a short form. In 1960, a sample of 25 percent, or one in four households, had to answer many more probing questions, which elicited information about employment status and income, education, fertility, mobility, birthplace of parents, and citizenship status—most of which had been basic questions for everyone in 1940.[12] That sample came to be called the "long form" in 1970. The bureau used mathematical techniques to generate from that sample a picture of the entire nation. With some clever analysis and the fruits of reasoning with probability, the answers of one person could be used to guess quite well what three other people would have answered.

Sampling saved time and money. Fewer people had to spend time filling in a form, and the bureau could devote fewer resources to chasing answers or processing those results, which allowed them to commit more resources to chasing people. Those benefits bore real costs, though: sampled data would never be as precise as a full enumeration, and the space reserved for each individual in the data decreased. Readers of censuses after 1950 will find less and less recorded about *every* person.

But sampling also offered new options for deeper investigations. This was true in 1940, when the bureau first used probability theory to cheat the constraints of the questionnaire, and it remains true today. In 2010, the Census Bureau leaned into sampling and leveraged its capacities. Instead of sending out a "long form" to a quarter, fifth, or twentieth of all households every ten years as it had in prior censuses, it relied instead on the annual American Community Survey (ACS), which had begun five years earlier interviewing about a 2 percent sample. The new survey could stay up-to-date with changes in people's lives and the nation's circumstances.[13] It could also be nimbler, adding or adapting questions from year to year. (In 2013, for instance, the ACS acknowledged the internet and began asking questions about whether people had access to the Web.)[14] With the advent of the ACS, the sampling revolution that began in 1940 entered a new phase, shifting the role played by the every-ten-year count: for many questions and forms of social knowledge, the decennial census would no longer be the direct tool for making an investigation. Instead, it would henceforth provide a baseline "ground truth" count of the population, from which could be constructed the "sampling frame" used to construct samples, and those samples would be asked the desired questions. The census and the census's "master address file" provided the underlying data necessary to pick a "representative" sample of Americans who could be made to stand in for the nation.

The ACS, as the apotheosis of the sampling ideal, is not without its critics. Some researchers have cast the shift to the ACS as part of an extended effort to limit the census—one driven by conservative, small-government politics.[15] Others mourn (or at least acknowledge) that something substantial is lost when mass participation gives way to probabilistic modeling.[16] The 1940 census and the subsequent long forms depended on the active cooperation of hundreds of millions of people in order to get firm knowledge about the country. The ACS requires input from only a few million people. That is surely more efficient but may not generate the same satisfaction or democratic commitment that total enumeration did. With the 1940 census, most knowledge about the United States came through Americans representing themselves and engaging directly in the work of democracy. Today, when it comes to the production of knowledge about the nation, most households and most individuals will be represented instead by a group of people no one voted for. Statistical representation is undoubtedly valid as science, but can it be counted on to build reliable national truths?

Sampling made the 2020 census sheet much shorter than it would have been otherwise. But it very nearly was a little bit longer.

In March 2018, President Donald Trump's secretary of commerce, Wilbur Ross, announced his decision to add a new question to the 2020 form.[17] It was new but quite similar to a question asked in 1940, one that had, in the intervening years, been sloughed off into the sampling sphere. Trump and Ross wanted all individuals to submit their citizenship status.

Secretary Ross claimed that the Department of Justice needed that information to carry out the provisions of the Voting Rights Act. Court documents would eventually reveal that Ross persuaded the DOJ to make a request along these lines only after he'd decided to add the question. Unlike the income question in 1940, the 2020 citizenship question did not win the approval of the new era's Question Men—who were now very likely to be women and no longer universally white. On the contrary, Census Bureau officials, experts who advised on the census, state government officials, and civil rights advocates cried foul. They all argued that the question would likely dissuade people from cooperating with the census, fearing that they or members of their household might be labeled (rightly or wrongly) noncitizens or as people with an unlawful immigration status. Indeed, the question seemed designed to depress the counts of immigrant communities and looked in particular like a means of intimidating (and erasing) Latinx people.

States concerned that their residents might go uncounted and civil rights groups committed to counting everyone filed lawsuits to prevent Ross from adding the citizenship question to the 2020 census. In June 2019, Chief Justice John Roberts wrote the decision for the Supreme Court ruling against Secretary Ross. Roberts's ruling did not address the fact that the question's inclusion would likely depress response rates and lead to undercounts. Rather, Roberts ruled against Ross because the record had revealed Ross's stated explanation for adding the question to be "contrived" and, even worse, a "distraction."[18] The DOJ had no real need for the data Ross wanted—to enforce the Voting Rights Act or anything else—and Roberts and a majority of the court refused to accept a contrived, distracting reason for adding the intrusive question.

As I read that decision, I couldn't help but see it as an invitation of sorts. It seemed to me that the Supreme Court might be saying that Ross could, in fact, get the question into the census if he would admit his real reasons for wanting it, that if he confessed his desire to single out noncitizens or to depress immigrants' response rates, perhaps the question would be allowed. Initial reports suggested that Ross had given up the cause in the face of the defeat, but a tweet from President Trump labeled those reports "FAKE!" and insisted that Commerce was not "dropping its quest to put the Citizenship Question on the Census."[19] I, like many others, was on the edge of my seat, anticipating that the administration would challenge the ruling and try again. But it turned out they were already out of time. An issue of logistics had saved the day: the Census Bureau's printing schedule demanded the questions be settled right away. The government needed to start producing documents and questionnaires for those many Americans who would not respond online and that necessity inadvertently protected the integrity of the 2020 census (for a while, at least). The forms for the Web were also coded without a citizenship question.

The 2020 census was in many ways different from 1940's—enumerators no longer visited every home, and the census forms had shrunk—but one important thing did not change: fitting ourselves into the forms still required negotiations.

We received our letter in the mail. Then I went to my computer to grapple with the online census form that demanded I make our family known on its terms.

The first self-enumeration took place with the 1960 census. It represented a fundamental rupture in the nature of the count, one that can hardly be underestimated. It wasn't meant to be revolutionary, but it was. Before the 1960 census, the census taker held the pen, made judgments, and chose what to write down. After 1960, the power to define each person shifted to that person (or someone in the household, at least). The shift to self-enumeration came with a shift in worldviews. Henceforth, how a person understood themselves would matter more than how a bureau employee might understand that person. The Census Bureau instituted self-enumeration in order to limit the clustering of errors, but since the decision was made, census stakeholders—from civil rights groups to people on the streets—have embraced self-enumeration on different grounds. Self-enumeration has become crucial as a means to assert and protect people's right to determine how their identity will be recorded in the nation's ledger—a determination with personal and political consequences.

There are still limits to how much self-determination an individual filling out a census form has, even on the subject of personal identity. This is probably inevitable. The novelist Jesse Ball has imagined a census where census takers ask questions with an intent to stimulate self-examination and to trouble the census's own categories—in his radical vision, a census becomes a collection of people's reflections and stories and an unlimited expression of identity.[20] I find that vision appealing and beautiful as an exaltation of individuality, but democracy demands that we lump ourselves together with others, that we cram ourselves into categories, which can be hard work.

As I looked through my 2020 census form, I thought about how best to represent our family using the census's allowed terms. I would have to think a bit differently this year than I had in the past.

I filled in the code number sent via mail to my apartment and made my way through the initial steps, confirming my address and entering "3" for the number of people who lived in our household. Then came the first choice, which I did not at first register as a choice. Our child sat with me on our couch as I typed into the form's blanks on my laptop computer. He looked over my shoulder. My partner of nearly twenty years had gone out for a walk in the park. The time had come to enter the first person's name.

I began to type "Dan Bouk." What happened next gets fuzzy as I try to recollect my actions. I am kicking myself for not taking a screenshot.

Here's what I think happened. I think I caught myself, realizing that whatever name I entered first, that person would become "Person 1." All other people in the household would be defined as in some relation to Person 1. Gone was the old distinction of a "head" of the household, but the census remained a household census, and it was clear to me that "Person 1" meant "head." And that wasn't me.

So I think I backspaced, deleting my name, and typed in "Liz Bouk" instead.

It is, however, also possible that I realized my error too late and that I inadvertently became "Person 1" and then the form wouldn't let me go back and change it. I don't think this happened, but I cannot say for sure—and since I have strived to be honest and as precise as I can be in this book, I am sharing my uncertainty with you.

Maybe one of you will think to check back in 2092: someone, please riffle through the raw data files and find out what I did.

The task before me as I typed into those boxes was to express our family's conception of itself within the constraints imposed on me (and everyone else) by the form. At least fitting our queer household into the form's square fields was easier in 2020 than ever before. This was thanks to our LGBTQ forebears and advocates, who had campaigned for decades to get census options that acknowledged marriages or partnerships between people of the same sex. The "partner" label has a longer history, as we have seen, but with the move to self-enumeration, it had fallen out of use. In 1990, the census added an "unmarried partner" category, and the National LGBTQ Task Force saw an opportunity: leaping to action, it campaigned to get same-sex couples to check this new box—queering the partner option. The Census Bureau, though, edited out of existence all those same-sex partners, since it said it could not tell which were intentional and which simply errors. Advocates protested, and those same-sex partners survived statistically in the 2000 census tallies—while same-sex married people were edited to be opposite-sex married, again on the grounds that many were actually just mistakes. Queer advocates kept up the fight and made alliances in government and with other civil rights groups, and so in 2020, the census rolled out new boxes for partners and marrieds with options for same-sex or opposite-sex.[21]

Thanks to decades of protest and organizing, when it came time to check one box (and only one box!) describing my relation to "Person 1," I had an obvious answer: "Same-sex husband/wife/spouse." I clicked contentedly, even while knowing that the fight for sexual-orientation and gender-identity questions in the census continues.

I did not have any trouble finding boxes to click for the next question, the "sex" question, either. I clicked "Male" for me and "Male" for Liz and "Male" for our child. (The only other option was "Female.") This was an easy choice. It was also a consistent choice with the relationship answers. It should sail through when the Census Bureau goes looking for errors and inconsistencies to edit. The bureau wouldn't have any reason to dig deeper, which is probably for the best.

Were the bureau to dig into its records, things could get interesting. Back in the 2010 census, I would show up as "Male," while Liz would have been recorded as "Female." Between those two censuses, however, Liz came out as a transgender man. The transition our family went through inspired some of the questions in this book; it heightened my interest in the "partner" label and the history of the "relation" categories. Liz succeeded in getting his name changed officially to "Liz," and he performed opera professionally as Mr. Liz. He has since then changed his name to a more conventionally masculine one, Lucas. His driver's license and passport reflect his proper gender. His census records do now too.

Someone should go and confirm that in 2092.

In the box-clicking business, we had it pretty easy. That doesn't mean that I feel like the "me" recorded by the 2020 census speaks perfectly of my identity. "Male" works for me. That's how I was raised, and I am comfortable with folks referring to me as "he." But becoming a parent unsettled some of my own sense of my gender. I tended to do things with our kid that have usually been said to be mothers' jobs or roles: I liked being the caregiver, the one who got up in the middle of the night to replace soiled sheets or who soothed whatever needed soothing. My partner, meanwhile, enjoyed riling up the child and cracking bodily-function jokes. He liked being a conventional dad. We call him Dad. They call me Papa, but I feel more like Mom. For a while we each felt to some degree like we weren't doing things "right" and the way of being a family that we were improvising elicited a mixture of praise, concern, and disapproval. We argued and analyzed and adapted. I grew to accept and even like being Mom a few years before my partner took a much bolder step and came out as trans. We were queering together for a while, and sometimes it was very hard. But none of this will be reflected in our data.

When it came to filling in our census, though, we had it easy, thanks to queer activism. Some other queer folk, however, had to distort their conceptions of themselves more severely to fit into the form. Even without an enumerator present, negotiations still had to take place between a person and the questionnaire. On March 30, 2020, a Redditor posted about a strategy they employed when the census categories didn't fit. The poster was an agender nonbinary person married to another agender nonbinary person. As a result, the binary sex categories (by definition) excluded them both. But they wanted to be counted and to be counted as queer—they were here, they were queer, and they wanted to appear in the nation's statistics. So they chose a sex—"Female"—and then identified as a same-sex couple. They wrote on Reddit: "So I guess what I'm saying is now we're political lesbians. . . . Census lesbians. Censusbians."[22] They were surely not alone in making such compromises.

Those who most needed to contest or resist the census categories could resort to the paper questionnaire. That is what one person who posted to Facebook on May 1, 2020, apparently did, adding a photo of their entry as "Person 2." They handwrote "spouse" as their relation to "Person 1" and even drew a little checkbox next to the word, which they then put an "X" in. Next they wrote "Intersex"—again with the checkbox and X—next to "Male" and "Female."[23] For their troubles, Facebook removed the photo of their post—presumably deeming it misinformation rather than an act of protest. Back in its offices, the Census Bureau will likely edit this response to shoehorn this person into the binary conception of sex, picking for them one sex or the other—I don't know how that decision will be made. It shouldn't have to be made at all.

Next up, the census asked for the age of the respondent. This, too, was easy for our family. Every one of us has a birth certificate locked in a fireproof box with an official copy kept by the state of New York as well—the same is true of nearly everyone born in the United States now, thanks to the extension of birth registration by the census and its allies in the early twentieth century. It wouldn't have been true for nearly so many Americans in 1940.

Just two more questions remained to be answered.

First I was asked if I am "of Hispanic, Latino, or Spanish origin." The 1940 census had removed Mexican as a viable race, making all Mexicans white. The "Spanish origin" question emerged as a racial alternative for the 1970 census in the face of political pressure from Chicano and Puerto Rican activists who needed data to demonstrate the political potency and the particular needs of their communities.[24] Now, a person could click a box next to "Yes. Mexican, Mexican Am., Chicano" or "Yes" followed by another nationality. Then that person would be asked to pick a race, any race. Certainly Hispanics can be white, but the 2020 census did not force them to be.[25] I clicked the box next to "No."

"What is this person's race?" the final screen asked me.

I saw the answer I would give right there—it was the first option. This much had not changed between 1940 and now—between 1790 and now, for that matter: white got top billing.

I clicked the box next to "White." Below it I saw an empty rectangle where I was prompted to type a description of my "origins." Among the sample answers given are: "German, Irish, Italian, Lebanese, Egyptian, etc." Those examples suggested that the origins we were talking about were national origins of some sort. And they had been chosen with care to signal that white can or should include people from the Middle East or North Africa, a class of people who were nearly granted their own, separate checkbox for this census.[26] I was not certain what my origins were or should be. One uncle who does family genealogy had told me that his side of the family hailed from England and Wales, among other places. Another uncle on the other side of my family had explained that our ancestors hailed from, among other places, the contested region on the French and German border, the sort of place that makes the choosing of one national origin an uncertain task. Then there's the linguistic origins of my last name, which means "stomach" in Dutch. Should I enter "Big Bellied Northern European"? I didn't know. I don't know.

The internet confirms for me that I was not alone in my confusion. It also confirms for me that other people were cleverer than I am. One person tweeted out a photograph of "premium white sandwich bread" as their answer to the race question, while another person in the thread replied that they're "just store brand."[27] Another expressed surprise at being forced to "specify what flavor of white" she was, and said she settled on "vanilla."[28] Some joked about appealing to hue. "I'm eggshell white," tweeted one person—though it seems unlikely they actually submitted that to the bureau.[29] One of the most popular tweets I saw came from a person who wrote, "I got super overwhelmed and just put 'Becky' for type of white I am."[30]

While some joked, others wrestled with the choice and felt its weight. A scholar of medieval manuscripts whom I follow on Twitter observed that the field expected a "country" as an answer and explained what a difficulty this presented. She wrote: "For many Askenazi [*sic*] we're like [shrug emoji]."[31] A news story from early April revealed this to be a common sentiment, one that had "launched countless Jewish conversations."[32] It explained some of the varied responses. Many people, it seems, simply wrote "Jewish" or "Ashkenazi." Some went a step further, rejecting "white" as the proper race, and checked "other race." One person did what I suspect many, many other white people did and wrote "USA" as their origin. (Writing in "American" was also suggested by some conservative commentators.)[33]

I heard from some white friends who tried to make sense of their origins for the census and took the responsibility seriously. One wrote me saying she knew the census mattered and that researchers depended on its accuracy. But she couldn't figure out what to write. There were so many different European nations she could reasonably choose. She could seek greater certainty from a DNA ancestry test, but none of those, even if they proved reliable, would give her one right answer—they would return a set of probabilities and just more evidence of mixture. And while she felt overwhelmed by too many choices, she thought about an African American friend, who, as a descendant of enslaved people, had lamented the problem of tracing origins that the concerted efforts of the slave system had sought to erase or obscure.

African Americans stared into the same blank field beneath the checkbox marked "Black or African American." The census offered examples that were again national— "Jamaican, Haitian, Nigerian, Ethiopian, Somali"—as for whites, but the first sample option seems to have spoken to my friend's concerns about obscured roots for the descendants of the enslaved: the first sample option was simply "African American." That did not dull the sting for everyone—I read a tweet from a person who described herself as a "descendant of enslaved persons," and she described the origin box as "frustrating" because it was required and yet she and her fellow family members did not know where their origins lay.[34] Census records were a place that many Americans could turn to to discover possible answers to the question of their origins, but when those records failed (as they sometimes did with the enslaved), a newer technology—DNA testing—promised to provide answers.[35]

The scholar, sociologist, and essayist Tressie McMillan Cottom had racked up over one hundred thousand likes and over six thousand retweets when she posted her response to the origins question. "The Census asked me what kind of Black I am," she tweeted. "I listed 'AF.'"[36] (If the meaning isn't clear here, McMillan Cottom was using the text-message abbreviation for a profane way of saying "very much so.") I snorted when I read it, actually truly laughing out loud, and knew it would end up in this book. Thank you, Dr. McMillan Cottom, I thought. Her next tweet answered me preemptively: "You're welcome, future social scientists."

It will almost certainly be seventy-two years before any social scientist has a chance to see that "AF" response. It will be seventy-two years before we know if the whole thing was just a joke for Twitter. (I, for one, believe it is in there.) The tabulated results of the 2020 census will surely erase this response, hiding it in an "Other" category or subsuming it within the "African American" label. Like 1940's "partners," the Black "AF"s (if there are others out there) will never become official numbers. (Reader: If they are, I will be thrilled to have been wrong.) For that matter, I am sure that only a tiny fraction of all labels that people chose for themselves will ever be published.

What will certainly be published are figures for each checkbox race. If answering the origins question elicited talk of "identity crises" among white and Black people facing that demand for detail for the first time in 2020, then those people got a taste of the crises that the origins question and the race question had inspired for decades among Asians, Native Hawaiians or Pacific Islanders, American Indians or Alaska Natives, and multiracial individuals. In all such cases, the decision to choose a race or origin could have more significant implications than simply affecting one person's sense of self or expressed identity. Individual decisions could add up and make some groups visible, drawing the attention of politicians, researchers, and philanthropies.

That's the reasoning, for instance, driving groups like the Taiwanese

American Citizens League to run campaigns in their communities to get people to check "Other Asian" and write in "Taiwanese."[37] An "Other" group that gathers enough respondents stands a chance of getting published in the official statistics. A graphic spreading on Twitter with the hashtag #BlackLatinasKnow emphasized the larger point about the political nature of all such choices: "The Census is not therapy but a way to document race-based and other social and political inequalities." The person who shared the graphic online announced that she was checking "White" and only "White" on the census for the first time, having realized that she was usually treated as white.[38] So in that case a onetime person of color for census purposes transformed to white-only in an act of solidarity—but an act that I imagine would frustrate some politicians or civil rights leaders who win power for their communities through greater numbers, not fewer. Indeed, the option to check more than one box had been advanced by leaders of communities of color who were concerned that a separate "multiracial" checkbox or something similar would erase members of their group and make it harder to enforce civil rights legislation.[39]

A friend of mine who helped "get out the count" by advertising the census and organizing communities to cooperate shared with me her story of strategic self-enumeration. In entering her race, my friend could have checked multiple boxes. Her father is, in census terms, "Asian Indian." Her mother is Black Haitian. She could have reported both races, but she worried (with reason) that in some consequential tabulation down the line, that choice might land her in a "two or more races" bucket, where she would not represent either her Indian or Black communities. It was better, she reasoned, to pick a community that could use her representation and make sure she counted for them. In 2092, someone should be able to find her among those who clicked "Black or African American" on the screen and then typed in "Haitian."

I did not enumerate myself strategically because I did not imagine my origins answer would end up mattering. Indeed, I tried to leave the field blank. But when I clicked through to the next page, the website raised a flag and outlined the empty field in red. I got the message that I had to fill it out. (Mind you, that's the message I intuited. I didn't read closely enough the error message that sprang up—I later learned that it stated that "if this person does not have an answer, continue to the next page." Had I only been more persistent, I could have avoided the question, as I had intended.) I wasn't clever enough to figure out that I could skip the question, and I wasn't clever enough to type anything clever. I typed "German" because we had lived in Germany for a few years. Why not? But data users should take any data that includes my racial self-description with many grains of salt. You're welcome, future social scientists?

Why did I go to the trouble of fitting myself into the Census Bureau's form? (Which, admittedly, was not *that much* trouble.) Why do so many people put so much effort into trying to track down everybody in the country and fit them into such a form?

We fit ourselves into forms, in large part, to see that we are represented: We want to be made into statistics. We want to be a part of something bigger.

As I write this, evidence of our family's participation in the 2020 census has appeared in the numbers 20,215,751 and 331,449,281, the official populations of the state of New York and the U.S.A. respectively. Without us, those numbers would be 20,215,748 and 331,449,278.

Evidence that we exist will appear many more times in coming months as the Census Bureau publishes more tables of data—like the tables that New York State will use to redraw its boundaries for congressional districts, or the tables with aggregates according to race, sex, or age that will be used by the demographers in my city (New York) to decide where to open new schools or where to send help during the next emergency we all face. Our family will be in those totals, lurking in those spreadsheet cells, represented by the official results.

We will march forth in the mass of data, important because we are part of a group. This is, in part, what participating in democracy looks like.

Over the summer of 2020, my child and I stood in a socially distanced crowd gathering at 168th Street and Broadway in Northern Manhattan—farther north than you probably thought Manhattan went.

George Floyd had been murdered. So had Breonna Taylor. We met to march and say their names. We marched with people who marched for many reasons, some to call for justice to be served in holding accountable the police responsible for these murders, some to affirm that Black lives did indeed matter, some to demand the repeal of laws that protect police from prosecution and to demand a sharp decrease in New York City's budget for policing, and some to seek the total abolition of policing in order to cultivate more just, less racist, and actually equitable means of ensuring the safety of our communities. As we milled about, our numbers multiplying, and began to march, we made mass democracy happen and tried to make American democracy better.

As the crowd continued to gather, a person in a button-down shirt passed among the assembled with a clipboard and paused to talk to a group of older men wearing Malcolm X T-shirts. The buttoned-down one said that Black Lives Matter advocacy work meant getting everyone counted in the census. He pitched completing the census form as its own act of protest, or at least an act of democratic action. I overheard this conversation and thought about the two aggregates then forming: one a statistical mass, the other a moving, masked, chanting mass of flesh. I was proud to be a part of both aggregates, proud to be one of many, a person among people, all asserting our shared dignity and aspiring to equality.

Photographers captured countless snapshots of that and other marches over the summer. In all likelihood, the police did too. At one march, a reporter took down my name, but his paper never printed the picture of us. I was never arrested, but the police could have tied me to the marches through my social media posts if they chose to. For the most part, though, if I appear in any of those photographs, I blend in, probably unidentifiably.

The Census Bureau insists on an even higher standard of anonymity and confidentiality. It promises that no one who looks at a census aggregate—at any of its published tables—will be able to pick me out from the statistical crowd and learn anything about me as an individual. It was making that promise even in 1940. Back then it aimed to live up to its promises by refusing to publish some kinds of tables for small areas, like the census block or the larger census tract. After all, some people might be easily recognizable if classified too finely in too small an area. Back then an area of concern might have been exposing income information, for instance. Imagine an unscrupulous data hound reading her neighborhood's figures if too much were published: "The census reports there's a ninety-year-old person living in this block," she might say. "That must be Widow So-and-So, and now from this table I can figure out how big that job of hers really pays!" The Census Bureau bent and then broke its promises of confidentiality during World War II when it published finer-grained tabulations of Japanese Americans and then that list that included Iwao Moriyama with names and addresses. But after the war it redoubled its commitment to confidentiality and to providing accurate data, often even at the block level, that would help enforce the Voting Rights Act, draw fair voting districts, undergird research, and support local planning.

In 2020 and 2021, a long-simmering tension between these commitments to confidentiality and to fine-grained data has come to a boil.[40] Faster computers and ready access to private data sets mean that census tables that once would have been perfectly safe to publish have now become risky. If you possess the right algorithms and purchase the right database, you could sniff me out (or sniff out someone very likely to be me) and possibly learn more about how I answered the census. (Clearly, this is not something I personally am very concerned about, since I have revealed most of my answers in this epilogue. But things would be different if, for instance, I did not want to admit to my landlord how many people I had living with me or if I feared repercussions from an employer who discovered that I was queer.) New techniques make it possible to discern individuals within conventionally published census aggregates. The Census Bureau's response has been to develop a "Disclosure Avoidance" system based on a statistical method called Differential Privacy. It allows for fine-grained data to still be published while preserving the anonymity of individuals by adding just a bit of "noise" to the data; that is, if the census were a photograph of a march, then differential privacy would work by blurring that photo just enough so that no faces could be recognized, even as the mass of the march would remain clear.[41] It is a neat technical solution but one that has concerned and sometimes enraged some civil rights activists, local or state government officials, and social scientists. By the time you are reading this, the entire matter may have boiled over, or maybe not.

One way or another, we should each be represented in the numbers that are released, and yet no one should be able to find us in those numbers.

I have another reason for wanting to be counted by the census. I don't know how many others share that motive. I want to be counted so that my individual data (and the story it tells about me and my country) will survive. I appreciate that I and all of my neighbors will have some trace of our existence preserved permanently.

Unfortunately, I have grown less sanguine in recent years that those traces will truly survive the seventy-two years until 2092 or beyond. Can the U.S. government manage to keep our individual answers—in a viable, readable form—for that three-quarters of a century or even longer?

Both preservation and protection of individual data are old problems. Census records maintained on paper were susceptible to moisture, mold, deterioration, or slow oxidation. They could also fall victim to accelerated oxidation, to bursting into flames. That's what happened in 1921, when a fire tore through tightly bundled original responses from the 1890 census. Whatever responses escaped the flames suffered death by drowning in the water that gushed from firemen's hoses. That fire set off a series of events that ended in the decision to build a National Archives, a structure designed to hold paper safely in fireproof rooms behind walls made of stone. When, in the course of my research, I visited the archives, I engaged with an architectural technology designed to keep census records—and other government records—in good shape over decades and even centuries.

At the same time that thousands of workers set up machinery to tabulate the 1940 census, others freed the leather-bound past from its bookish fragilities. "Not always has the census been such a machine-age process as it has been in 1940," wrote a reporter in *The Washington Post*.[42] Enumerators in the past had recorded the personal details of earlier Americans in leather-clad ledgers, and over time, the paper flaked and chipped, suffering with every flip of every page. So a legion of census microphotographers used carefully mounted cameras to take pictures of every sheet from the entire census past. Nearly a century before Google descended on the nation's research libraries with scanning cameras to digitize everything, the Census Bureau produced its own "scans" onto microfilm sheets that were both durable and replicable—and easy enough to access, even without special equipment. When individuals today head to the library or log into Ancestry.com to search for their forebears, they engage with digitized versions of those earlier photographs; they look at scans of scans. The Church of Jesus Christ of Latter-day Saints—some of whose members employ genealogical research to identify ancestors and secure their salvation—works with electronic records but also maintains microfilm masters in its Granite Mountain Records Vault.[43]

How will the modern U.S. census be maintained? What is the digital-age equivalent of a fireproof vault? There are no paper census records anymore, at least none that will be saved. Beginning with the 2010 census, the National Archives moved to digital-only storage: no paper, no microfilm.[44] Much of the 2020 census will have been born digitally. A digital-only data set strikes me as particularly fragile. Digital records still live on physical media, whether optical drives or magnetic discs, and any physical media can burn or suffer water damage or breakage. Those aren't the most serious threats, though. The bigger problem is media obsolescence. Imagine trying to read the punch cards produced by the 1940 census. Because they're on paper, someone could actually still read them, even without access to a sorting and tabulating machine. But digital records may be legible only on a certain kind of device. Maintaining digital records means maintaining older devices, or it means regularly updating and translating old records to new formats. It's like the big move from paper to microfilm, but over and over again every ten years. That's a big commitment, and it leaves me wondering if my contributions to the 2020 census will still be around in 2092.

My United States just generated a new edition of democracy's data. Will anyone in the future get a chance to read it closely? What does it say about our democracy, that in our mad rush for what is efficient and innovative, we may lose track of the few actual traces left behind by generations upon generations of ordinary Americans?

A more immediate reason for being counted is the one most often touted in advertisements or mentioned to the wary, to those who'd rather not cooperate with the census: the census count guides the distribution of money and power.

According to a series of reports published in the years leading up to the most recent count—a series aptly titled "Counting for Dollars 2020"—the census numbers can be expected to inform the allocation of well over a trillion dollars every year. The study reported that census data guided the delivery of $1.5 trillion in 2017 alone.[45] That suggests that census numbers (and projections based on those numbers in future years) will play a crucial role in doling out $15 trillion or more to states, cities, towns, and communities over the course of a decade.

Census numbers—especially a data release known for the public law (PL) that guides its creation, the PL-171 files—will also lead directly to the redrawing of legislative districts for state and federal elections. "Redistricting" mapmakers will draw boundaries containing equal numbers of people (following Supreme Court mandates and the "one person, one vote" principle)[46] and take into account age, sex, and race data and their own understanding of places within each state to draw either fair or favorable lines. Ten states rely primarily on independent commissions to draw their congressional lines, while the rest rely on—to varying degrees—politically partisan processes that allow the parties that control state legislatures to "gerrymander," or draw lines that they believe will help them win more seats.[47] (Among gerrymanderers, the logic is: why bother waiting for voters to choose politicians when politicians can choose their voters?) Whatever lines are drawn are subject to challenges in court, particularly if they seem to run afoul of the Voting Rights Act by diluting the voting power of racial minority groups. Census data suffuse the entire process, providing fuel and fodder for debate in the offices of consultants hired by political parties to dream up viable gerrymanders, in redistricting commission conferences or state legislatures hashing out maps, and in federal courtrooms trying voting rights cases.[48]

The very first official numbers released by the 2020 census weren't intended to deal with distributing dollars or to be used in drawing district lines—at least, that was not their primary purpose. They were numbers that dealt out seats (and so votes) in the U.S. House of Representatives: in other words, apportionment figures.

On April 26, 2021, I tuned in to an official Census Bureau livestream to hear these first results of the 2020 count. I won't lie—I was psyched, and also nervous. After the citizenship question controversy, the Trump administration had kept up its efforts to generate data about citizenship status—a series of efforts that failed to produce any usable data but probably succeeded in dissuading many people from cooperating with any shape or size of census taker. And in early March, as the first round of census self-response invitations went out in the mail, the COVID-19 pandemic had crashed the party. Our family hunkered down in New York City. We sewed our first masks from old dish towels. The Census Bureau paused its operations in the field. People started talking about "delaying" the release of census data, which sounded crazy to me.[49] I didn't realize how serious this crisis was.

The delay happened. It had to happen. The bureau needed more time: more time to get enumerators out knocking on doors and time to convince people to answer those doors during a pandemic; more time to sort through all the responses received online, on the phone, or through the mail; more time to debug the tabulation software and check for errors. In 2021, the new Biden administration committed to allowing the Census Bureau the time it needed, and so for the first time census data dropped four months later than expected, four months after the existing statutes required. (I thought missing the deadlines would be a huge deal, but the courts in late 2020 had essentially shrugged and said: What are you gonna do? This is a pandemic.)[50]

I didn't know what to expect from the first numbers to be released. Those numbers would be population totals for each state and for the entire United States, as usual. But could anything else about this census be normal?

I laughed out loud when the bureau's acting director, Ron Jarmin, announced to an online audience the U.S. population: 331,449,281 people.[51]

Not 331,449,280 people. Not 331,449,282 people.

Nope: 331,449,281 people precisely.

I laughed as I messaged the number, with multiple exclamation points, to fellow geeks. This absurd precision was hardly new in 2021—all governments depend on a certain suspension of statistical disbelief at moments like this. Still, this year, I laughed more than usual.

A few minutes after the announcement, as journalists asked, one after the other, about the population totals for whatever state they covered, the precision got even more absurd.

Kristin Koslap, the Census Bureau's expert in charge of translating state counts into a number of guaranteed seats in the U.S. House of Representatives, fielded a question asking how close New York was to losing a second congressional seat. Population estimates had led most observers to predict a seat loss for the state; indeed, many thought that New York could lose two. But Koslap's answer made me gasp. She said: "If New York had had eighty-nine more people, they would have received one more seat." Eighty-nine people! Newspapers ran with that number the following day. Twitter trembled with the outrage of pundits who didn't realize that New York's performance in the census had been spectacular but instead complained that their state had been robbed. They blamed COVID—the interruptions it had caused, the people it had displaced or killed—for the loss of a House seat, and they blamed the Census Bureau for missing, somehow, those eighty-nine people. They talked about lawsuits or recounts. (Though, as of this writing, neither has happened.)

I shook my head in disbelief. The whole situation was absurd.

When the margin of error for this census is eventually estimated, it will (if it's like prior censuses) reveal an over- or undercount somewhere around 1 percent of the state population, and given that the bureau reported the official apportionment population of New York for 2020 to be 20,215,751 (not 20,215,750, mind you!), a 1 percent miscount would entail around 200,000 people, not 89.

The fact is that Census Bureau figures necessarily contain within them some error and uncertainty. That isn't a criticism. It's a fact. So it is absurd that we rely on these preposterously precise numbers to deny representation to some states and award it to others. It doesn't have to be this way. In 1929, Congress first passed legislation that made it possible to operate apportionment as a zero-sum game. That is, if New York won an extra seat, then another state lost one. Thus, if New York had kept that seat, Minnesota would be out of luck. But before 1929, Congress had a different way of dealing with apportionment, a practice that better fit the uncertainty baked into all such counts. More often than not, every ten years, Congress would increase the size of the House after each census, and no state (or only one or two states) would lose a seat. These findings were reported in a Web project called USApportionment .org that was designed by the media scholar Kevin Ackermann (who also provided invaluable research support for this book) based on extensive research directed by the historian Taylor Savell.[52] Letting the House grow lowered the stakes in the apportionment count while still rewarding more representation to faster-growing states (which might gain multiple seats while slow-growing or shrinking states just held on to theirs). Most important, it allowed the number of representatives to grow with the population. Even with that method, the average number of people represented by each House member grew from the 30,000 to 40,000 range in the first decades of the republic to over 200,000. But capping the House membership at 435 has caused that number to rise to more than 700,000. That's a lot of people for one person to represent. Too many, by far. So forget being outraged by 89. Be outraged by 700,000!

That number 89 rankles me for another reason too. This is the story that gives that number its meaning: Imagine a world in which New York found 89 more residents, while every other state's population remained exactly the same. In that case, New York would win the 435th seat. The problem is that this imaginary world doesn't correspond with our actual world. New York's number couldn't change while every other state's number stayed the same. Had the Census Bureau somehow improved its methods for counting people, those improvements would have affected other states too. This number 89 gets spit out as a by-product of the system that calculates the allocation of House seats. It shouldn't be mistaken for a fact. This number 89 looks precise, but it's more silly than serious as far as statistics go. The only thing that the 89-people figure tells us is this: the race for the final seat was very close.

And I am here to remind you that there's no particularly good reason to be racing for seats in the first place. Democracy shouldn't be a game of musical chairs.

A census is so much more than the numbers it reports, as important and crucial as those numbers are.

Every census is a remarkable accomplishment, a glorious dream, and a serious slog. Every census asserts the values of the government and the people that government serves. Every census disseminates to the entire nation a series of acceptable labels and categories, and it relies on households to adapt their identities to the census's constraints. Every census affirms, in principle, the inherent and enduring value of each person residing in the United States, regardless of their status, creed, or circumstance. Every census directs the course of American democracy, distributing dollars and seats for a decade to come.

For all these reasons, every census matters and needs to matter to every person committed to building a better, more equitable, more inclusive, and more democratic democracy.

Planning for the 2030 census starts right now. It's tempting in the wake of a census to sigh, take a breath, and sit back and wait: we can get back to this census thing in ten years, right? But no. The questions that will guide our future decisions, the categories that we will each have to fit ourselves into, and the mechanisms that will be put in place to preserve the full depth of the data—these will all be shaped by debates, discussions, and proposals taking place in the early years of the 2020s. Dear Reader, now's the time for us to start working to achieve a census capable of extending and improving this experiment in democracy, a census that lets us see ourselves and our country clearly enough to face our keenest problems and discover our greatest opportunities, in the numbers and beyond them.

Perhaps the past can ease us into new dreams for the future, getting the ball rolling, setting our tongues wagging. In 2022, all the manuscript census sheets from 1950 will be released. Millions of Americans will turn to those records to write new chapters of their family stories. If just a fraction of those millions also tries to read the 1950 census data a little more deeply, they can contribute to writing new chapters of this nation's story too. As we study the 1950 census, reading its data deeply, we can ponder how far the U.S.A. has come and how far it still has to go. While people who love numbers and spreadsheets are welcome to the party, no quantitative skill is necessary to contribute to crafting, improving, and even reimagining our democracy's data.

Maybe gathering to read the census together can also help us work together to figure out a way forward in a world now suffused with data and with talk of data. These days, it seems like one must either love data or fear it. Enthusiasts tout the possibilities for better understanding the human condition, for making our social and economic systems more efficient, and for making lots of money too.[53] In response, a growing chorus of critics smell something at once foul and nefarious.[54] Data won't save us, they say. It's more likely to ensnare us.

This debate misunderstands data by missing out on its depth. It focuses on just the numbers at the expense of the processes and systems and people behind them. The fact is that every data set has a doorstep, a place where plans and dreams of order meet the throbbing tumult of experience, and from such encounters, via eruptions of ingenuity, we get these strange texts that bear the label "data." They are texts with power in the world, texts that indeed should be treated carefully, debated in public, and sometimes regulated by governments. They are texts, too, that we can use to better understand ourselves, our political systems, and our societies. We just have to learn how to read them.

Notes

ARCHIVES CONSULTED AND CITED

RG 29, NARA, D.C.
Bureau of the Census Records, Record Group 29, National Archives, Washington, D.C.

HOOVER PAPERS
Secretary of Commerce Files, Herbert Hoover Presidential Library, West Branch, Iowa

HOPKINS PAPERS
Papers of Harry L. Hopkins, Franklin D. Roosevelt Presidential Library, Hyde Park, New York

NILES PAPERS
David Niles Papers, Harry S. Truman Library and Museum, Independence, Missouri

RANKIN PAPERS
John E. Rankin Papers, University of Mississippi Archives and Special Collections, J. D. Williams Library, University, Mississippi

TOBEY PAPERS
Charles W. Tobey Papers, Rauner Special Collections Library, Dartmouth College, Hanover, New Hampshire

Throughout the notes, 1940 manuscript census records are cited in the following form: City, County, State, Enumeration District, Sheet Number. Sheets can be found online at https://1940census.archives.gov/.

A NOTE ON METHOD

1. For most questions about U.S. census history, I start by consulting Margo J. Anderson, *The American Census: A Social History*, 2nd edition (New Haven, CT: Yale University Press, 2015 [1st edition published in 1988]). Many of the scholars who have led the way in investigating how politics, economics, and culture shape censuses have started by exploring the production of race and racial classifications, often in comparative national contexts. Interested readers should begin with Melissa Nobles, *Shades of Citizenship: Race and the Census in Modern Politics* (Stanford, CA: Stanford University Press, 2000); and Debra Thompson, *The Schematic State: Race, Transnationalism, and the Politics of the Census* (New York: Cambridge University Press, 2016). Important works on race and racial categories in the United States alone include G. Cristina Mora, *Making Hispanics: How Activists, Bureaucrats, and Media Constructed a New American* (Chicago: University of Chicago Press, 2014); Paul Schor, *Counting Americans: How the US Census Classified the Nation*, translated by Lys Ann Weiss (New York: Oxford University Press, 2017); and Kenneth Prewitt, *What Is "Your" Race? The Census and Our Flawed Efforts to Classify Americans* (Princeton, NJ: Princeton University Press, 2013).

0. STORIES IN THE DATA

1. Readers interested in pursuing this point further can start with Theodore M. Porter's classic *Trust in Numbers: The Pursuit of Objectivity in Science and Public Life* (Princeton, NJ: Princeton University Press, 2020). See also Deborah Stone, *Counting: How We Use Numbers to Decide What Matters* (New York: Liveright, 2020). Christopher J. Phillips uses baseball statistics to get behind and beyond numbers and data sets in *Scouting and Scoring: How We Know What We Know About Baseball* (Princeton, NJ: Princeton University Press, 2019). Ruha Benjamin defines a new discipline of race critical code studies to see how race and racism work in seemingly neutral numbers and data sets: *Race After Technology: Abolitionist Tools for the New Jim Code* (New York: Polity, 2019).
2. Field Division, Bureau of the Census, "Rough Draft: Historical Report of 1940 (16th Decennial) Census Made from the Records That Were Available in

1948 with Emphasis on the Field Aspects" (1948), 7 in Folder "16th Decennial Census 1940—Historical Report of 1940 Census," Box 2, Entry P 26, RG 29, NARA, D.C.

3. "Big Data" is a term of recent coinage used to discuss very large data sets that can be plumbed and prodded by statistical methods or machine learning algorithms to draw conclusions or make predictions. It is not a term that anyone in 1940 would have employed, and yet looking closely at something like the 1940 census can help us learn to think with Big Data today. Readers interested in thinking differently about Big Data will find much of value in Catherine D'Ignazio and Lauren F. Klein, *Data Feminism* (Cambridge, MA: MIT Press, 2020); and Jer Thorp, *Living in Data: A Citizen's Guide to a Better Information Future* (New York: MCD / Farrar, Straus and Giroux, 2021). Those interested in deeper histories of data and information can find valuable entry points in Ann Blair, Paul Duguid, Anja-Silvia Goeing, and Anthony Grafton, eds., *Information: A Historical Companion* (Princeton, NJ: Princeton University Press, 2021); and Elena Aronova, Christine von Oertzen, and David Sepkoski, eds., "Data Histories," *Osiris* 32 (2017).

4. This paragraph refers to material gleaned from the manuscript sheets of the 1940 U.S. Census. For all such references, I will provide information for the locality, county, and state, along with an enumeration district (E.D.) number and the sheet number where the material discussed appears. In this case, that reference looks like this: Rochester, Monroe, NY, E.D. 65–112, sheet 2A. Readers can find these sheets using the reference information through the U.S. National Archives' website: https://1940census.archives.gov/.

5. Folder "C-3 Census Records: 1930," Box 231, Entry 215, RG 29 NARA, D.C.

6. Numbers included in Jesse Jones to Franklin D. Roosevelt, November 29, 1940, in Folder "Speeches, Articles, and Papers," Box 4, Entry 229, RG 29, NARA, D.C.

7. I am driven in this book to explain what Michel Foucault called the "microphysics of power"—the mechanisms by which modern institutions discipline bodies and minds through tools like statistics. Foucault and those who have followed him have studied the construction of categories that shape the making of selves. The works of Ian Hacking and Sarah Igo are exemplary. But there remains much to be done in terms of looking at the labor that goes into translating abstract categories and instructions into actual data. See Ian Hacking, "Biopower and the Avalanche of Printed Numbers," *Humanities in Society* 5, nos. 3 and 4 (1982): 279–95; and Sarah E. Igo, *The Averaged American: Surveys, Citizens, and the Making of a Mass Public* (Cambridge, MA: Harvard University Press, 2007).

8. Robin Wall Kimmerer, *Braiding Sweetgrass* (Minneapolis, MN: Milkweed Editions, 2020), 164.

9. Peter Stallybrass, "Printing and the Manuscript Revolution," in *Explorations in Communication and History*, ed. Barbie Zelizer (New York: Routledge, 2008), 112.

10. Gerri Flanzraich, "The Library Bureau and Office Technology," *Libraries and Culture* 28, no. 4 (Fall 1993): 403–29; Rebecca Lemov, *Database of Dreams: The Lost Quest to Catalog Humanity* (New Haven, CT: Yale University Press, 2015).

11. Lorraine Daston, "Super-Vision: Weather Watching and Table Reading in the Early Modern Royal Society and Académie Royale des Sciences," *Huntington Library Quarterly* 78, no. 2 (2015): 187–215.

12. Jacqueline Wernimont, *Numbered Lives: Life and Death in Quantum Media* (Cambridge, MA: MIT Press, 2018); Michelle Murphy, *The Economization of Life* (Durham, NC: Duke University Press, 2017).

13. Some early and influential enthusiasts for Big Data were Viktor Mayer-Schönberger and Kenneth Cukier in *Big Data: A Revolution That Will Transform How We Live, Work, and Think* (New York: Houghton Mifflin Harcourt, 2013); and Christian Rudder, *Dataclysm: Who We Are (When We Think No One's Looking)* (New York: Crown, 2014). One of its most influential critics is Shoshana Zuboff in *The Age of Surveillance Capitalism: The Fight for a Human Future at the New Frontier of Power* (New York: Public Affairs, 2019). See also Cathy O'Neil, *Weapons of Math Destruction: How Big Data Increases Inequality and Threatens Democracy* (New York: Crown, 2016).

14. Lindsay Poirier, "Reading Datasets: Strategies for Interpreting the Politics of Data Signification," *Big Data and Society* (2021): 1–19; Caitlin Rosenthal's approach to reading the "frame" of the data informs the analysis of chapter 1 and is discussed further there. Her book is *Accounting for Slavery: Masters and Management* (Cambridge, MA: Harvard University Press, 2018). Other texts that discuss methods for "reading" data and data sets include Yanni Alexander Loukissas, "A Place for Big Data: Close and Distant Readings of Accessions Data from the Arnold Arboretum," *Big Data and Society* 3, no. 2 (2016): 1–20; and Melanie Feinberg, "Reading Databases: Slow Information Interactions Beyond the Retrieval Paradigm," *Journal of Documentation* 73, no. 2 (2017): 336–56.

15. Robert Pinsky, *The Sounds of Poetry: A Brief Guide* (New York: Farrar, Straus and Giroux, 1999).

16. Michael Baxandall, *Painting and Experience in Fifteenth-Century Italy* (New York: Oxford University Press, 1988).

17. Carol Willis, *Form Follows Finance: Skyscrapers and Skylines in New York and Chicago* (New York: Princeton Architectural Press, 1995).

18. On the development of the term "data" in the English language, beginning in the seventeenth century, see Daniel Rosenberg, "Data Before the Fact," in

Raw Data Is an Oxymoron, ed. Lisa Gitelman (Cambridge, MA: MIT Press, 2013), 15–40.

19. Donna Haraway's classic 1988 essay argued that "only partial perspective promises objective vision . . . this essay is an argument for situated and embodied knowledges and an argument against various forms of unlocatable, and so irresponsible, knowledge claims." (583) Donna Haraway, "Situated Knowledges: The Science Question in Feminism and the Privilege of Partial Perspective," *Feminist Studies* 14, no. 3 (1988): 575–99. Another work in feminist science studies has been even more important to my thinking in terms of trying to wrap my head around what the data I'm reading actually is, what it does, what it stands for, and how the way you set out to observe it changes its nature. The conclusion of this book in particular owes a debt to Karen Barad's exciting, mind-bending book *Meeting the Universe Halfway: Quantum Physics and the Entanglement of Matter and Meaning* (Durham, NC: Duke University Press, 2007). On objectivity and its history, see also Lorraine Daston and Peter Galison, *Objectivity* (New York: Zone Books, 2010); and Porter, *Trust in Numbers*.

20. The figures in this paragraph are from pages 10, 12, and an unpaginated appendix of Field Division, Bureau of the Census, "Rough Draft: Historical Report of 1940 (16th Decennial) Census Made from the Records That Were Available in 1948 with Emphasis on the Field Aspects" (1948) in Folder "16th Decennial Census 1940—Historical Report of 1940 Census," Box 2, Entry P 26, RG 29, NARA, D.C.

21. Anna Echterhölter, Sophie Ledebur, and Laurens Schlcht invited me to a workshop at the Institute for Advanced Studies in Vienna titled "Data at the Doorstep." I owe them a great debt for helping put the doorstep front and center in my thinking about data and the census.

1. THE QUESTION MEN

1. I have reconstructed the details of Dublin's role at the conference and his travel there and back from W. L. Austin to Louis I. Dublin, March 1, 1939; Louis I. Dublin to W. L. Austin, March 8, 1939; Louis I. Dublin to W. L. Austin, March 13, 1939; and William Lane Austin to Richard C. Patterson and Secretary Hopkins, March 14, 1939, in Folder 48C Population, 1940, Box 7, Entry 142, RG 29, NARA, D.C.

2. Kate Ascher, *The Heights: Anatomy of a Skyscraper* (New York: Penguin Books, 2011), 14.

3. On the Empire State Building, see Willis, *Form Follows Finance*, 90–101.

4. "Department of Commerce Edition," *The Washington Post*, December 31, 1931, in Box 234, Entry 215, RG 29, NARA, D.C.

5. The attendance roster for the meeting is drawn from a list at the end of the minutes titled "Conference on the 1940 Population Schedule," March 3–4, 1939, in Folder 48C Population, 1940, Box 7, Entry 142, RG 29, NARA, D.C.

6. "Sample of the Letter," February 17, 1939, appended to "Conference on the 1940 Population Schedule," March 3–4, 1939, in Folder 48C Population, 1940, Box 7, Entry 142, RG 29, NARA, D.C.

7. William Lane Austin to William Steuart, March 1, 1939 in Folder 48C Population, 1940, Box 7, Entry 142, RG 29, NARA, D.C.

8. Bureau of the Census, "Know Your USA" (1940), https://youtu.be/cImIlPSuyR8.

9. Highland Park, Lake County, Illinois, E.D. 49–14, sheet 6B.

10. These items all appear in the 1940 Sears Catalog, as it can be viewed here: https://christmas.musetechnical.com/ShowCatalog/1940-Sears-Fall-Winter -Catalog.

11. Justus D. Doenecke, "General Robert E. Wood: The Evolution of a Conservative," *Journal of the Illinois State Historical Society* 71, no. 3 (1978): 162–75 at 164.

12. Kim Phillips-Fein, *Invisible Hands: The Businessmen's Crusade Against the New Deal* (New York: W. W. Norton, 2010).

13. Doenecke, "General Robert E. Wood," 164–67.

14. Vergil D. Reed, "New Marketing Dividends for 1940," Eleventh Annual Boston Conference on Distribution, Boston, MA, October 3, 1939, in Folder Census, Exhibit K—Public Speeches, Box 111, Papers of Harry L. Hopkins, FDR Library, Hyde Park, New York.

15. Readers interested in Dublin can find much more in Dan Bouk, *How Our Days Became Numbered: Risk and the Rise of the Statistical Individual* (Chicago: University of Chicago Press, 2015). On the possibilities for radical social possibility that insurance once inspired, see Caley Horan, *Insurance Era: Risk, Governance, and the Privatization of Security in Postwar America* (Chicago: University of Chicago Press, 2021).

16. Jessica Contrera and Gillian Brockell, "In 1933, Two Rebellious Women Bought a Home in Virginia's Woods. Then the CIA Moved In," *The Washington Post*, February 14, 2020, https://www.washingtonpost.com/history/2020 /02/14/cia-women-neighbors-langley/.

17. David Brody, *In Labor's Cause: Main Themes on the History of the American Worker* (New York: Oxford University Press, 1993), quoted from 68.

18. David M. Kennedy, *Freedom from Fear: The American People in Depression and War, 1929–1945* (New York: Oxford University Press, 2005), 120.

19. Robert Lee, Tristan Ahtone, Margaret Pearce, Kalen Goodluck, Geoff

McGhee, Cody Leff, Katherine Lanphear, and Taryn Salinas, "Land-Grab Universities," *High Country News*, March 30, 2020, https://www.landgrabu.org/.

20. For more on these early German universities and how their model shapes academic life even today, see Chad Wellmon and Andrew Piper, "Publication, Power, and Patronage: On Inequality and Academic Publishing," *Critical Inquiry*, July 21, 2017, https://criticalinquiry.uchicago.edu/publication_power_and_patronage_on_inequality_and_academic_publishing/. On the seminar as a particular kind of space for research and teaching and its influence in the United States, see Bonnie G. Smith, "Practices of Scientific History," in *Gender of History* (Cambridge, MA: Harvard, 1998), 103–29. On German chemistry and its role in American agriculture, see Margaret Rossiter, *The Emergence of Agricultural Science: Justus Liebig and the Americans, 1840–1880* (New Haven, CT: Yale University Press, 1975).

21. This interpretation of Du Bois relies on Kwame Anthony Appiah, *Lines of Descent: W.E.B. Du Bois and the Emergence of Identity* (Cambridge, MA: Harvard University Press, 2014). On this era's intellectual exchanges more generally, see Daniel T. Rodgers, *Atlantic Crossings: Social Politics in a Progressive Age* (Cambridge, MA: Belknap Press of Harvard University Press, 1998). Saidiya Hartman offers an important, recent reinterpretation of Du Bois's social science and his Philadelphia study in "An Atlas of the Wayward," *Wayward Lives, Beautiful Experiments: Intimate Histories of Riotous Black Girls, Troublesome Women, and Queer Radicals* (New York: W. W. Norton, 2019), 81–120.

22. William R. Leonard and Walter F. Willcox, "Walter F. Willcox: Statist," *American Statistician* 15, no. 1 (1961): 16–19. A short obituary for Hill appears in W. L. Austin, "Memorandum for the Secretary of Commerce," December 13, 1938, in Folder 71 Statistical Research, Box 9, Entry 142, RG 29, NARA, D.C.

23. For more on eugenics, see Daniel Kevles, *In the Name of Eugenics: Genetics and the Uses of Human Heredity* (Cambridge, MA: Harvard University Press, 1995); and Alexandra Minna Stern, *Eugenic Nation: Faults and Frontiers of Better Breeding in Modern America* (Berkeley: University of California Press, 2005).

24. Emily Klancher Merchant, *Building the Population Bomb* (New York: Oxford University Press, 2021), 48.

25. Louis I. Dublin, "The Statistician and the Population Problem," *Journal of the American Statistical Association* 20, no. 149 (1925): 1–12 at 11.

26. For more, see Bouk, *How Our Days Became Numbered*, 186–97.

27. 1930: Manhattan, New York County, New York, E.D. 31–474, sheet 5A.

28. Quoted in Edmund Ramsden, "Carving Up Population Science: Eugenics, Demography and the Controversy over the 'Biological Law' of Population Growth," *Social Studies of Science* 32, no. 5/6 (2002): 857–99 at 894.

29. Bunzel and Dublin wrote, for instance, *To Be or Not to Be: A Study of Suicide* (New York: Harrison Smith and Robert Hass, 1933).

30. Washington, D.C., E.D. 1–11, sheet 2A. Mary Dublin appeared as General Secretary of the National Consumers League before a Senate committee in February 1939 to defend the income question on the census. She did not mention her father or his role in choosing that question. See U.S. Senate, *1940 Census: Hearings Before a Subcommittee of the Committee on Commerce United States Senate, Seventy-Sixth Congress, Third Session on S. Res. 231* (Washington, D.C.: Government Printing Office, 1940).

31. William Lane Austin to Mr. Kerlin, December 12, 1938, in Folder 48C Population, 1940, Box 7, Entry 142, RG 29, NARA, D.C.

32. Benjamin Wiggins, *Calculating Race: Racial Discrimination in Risk Assessment* (New York: Oxford University Press, 2020).

33. I expand this argument in chapter 7 of *How Our Days Became Numbered*.

34. "Conference on the 1940 Population Schedule," March 3–4, 1939, page 1 in Folder 48C Population, 1940, Box 7, Entry 142, RG 29, NARA, D.C. I cite specific pages from this document, which provided a summary of the conference and its discussions, when I offer a direct quote. For ease of reading, I have not dropped in a note each time I've used this document to reconstruct the debates and discussions that took place during the conference. Wherever the deliberations of the Question Men are discussed, without other attribution, this document is the source.

35. Readers interested in learning more should consult Mae M. Ngai, *Impossible Subjects: Illegal Aliens and the Making of Modern America* (Princeton, NJ: Princeton University Press, 2014).

36. U.S. House Committee on the Census, *Apportionment of Representatives: Hearings Before the Committee on the Census on H.R. 14498, H.R. 15021, H.R. 15158, and H.R. 15217* (Washington, D.C.: Government Printing Office, 1921).

37. William Lane Austin to Richard C. Patterson, April 20, 1939, in Folder 48C Population, 1940, Box 7, Entry 142, RG 29, NARA, D.C.

38. "Dunn, Matthew Anthony," *History, Art and Archives*, United States House of Representatives, https://bioguide.congress.gov/search/bio/D000551.

39. The 1830 census was the first to seek tallies of those deemed "deaf and dumb" or "blind." As Leah Samples explains, the difficulty of gathering stable statistics on disability and the desire of experts to control new data sources tied to the welfare state led to a discontinuation of counts of the blind in 1930. Leah Samples, "Calculating Blindness: The Role of Statistics in New Deal America," presented at Contested Data Workshop at Data and Society, New York, March 6, 2020.

40. Barbara Young Welke, *Law and the Borders of Belonging in the Long Nineteenth Century United States* (New York: Cambridge University Press, 2010), 11.

41. "Conference on the 1940 Population Schedule," March 3–4, 1939, page 3 in Folder 48C Population, 1940, Box 7, Entry 142, RG 29, NARA, D.C.

42. Article I, section 2, of the U.S. Constitution explained that representation in the U.S. House would depend on population and then said, "The actual Enumeration shall be made within three Years after the first Meeting of the Congress of the United States, and within every subsequent Term of ten Years, in such Manner as they shall by Law direct."

43. On the very early history of numbers and quantification, see Denise Schmandt-Besserat, "Tokens and Writing: The Cognitive Development," *Scripta* 1 (2009): 145–54.

44. Interested readers should consult Lorraine Daston, *Classical Probability in the Enlightenment* (Princeton, NJ: Princeton University Press, 1988); Ian Hacking, *The Emergence of Probability: A Philosophical Study of Early Ideas About Probability, Induction, and Statistical Inference* (Cambridge: Cambridge University Press, 1975); Ian Hacking, *The Taming of Chance* (New York: Cambridge University Press, 1990); and Theodore M. Porter, *The Rise of Statistical Thinking 1820–1900* (Princeton, NJ: Princeton University Press, 1986). For more on how the relationship of states to probability shifted in the twentieth century, see Theodora Dryer, *Designing Certainty: The Rise of Algorithmic Computing in an Age of Anxiety 1920–1970* (University of California, San Diego, Ph.D. Dissertation, 2019); and Arunabh Ghosh, *Making It Count: Statistics and Statecraft in the Early People's Republic of China* (Princeton, NJ: Princeton University Press, 2020).

45. For more, see Emmanuel Didier, *America by the Numbers: Quantification, Democracy, and the Birth of National Statistics*, translated by Priya Vari Sen (Cambridge, MA: MIT Press, 2020); Dryer, *Designing Certainty*.

46. Madge C. Crandell to Herbert Hoover, April 14, 1930, in Folder "E-2 Experiences of 1930 Census Supervisors and Enumerators. Criticisms of Census, Etc.," Box 231, Entry 215, RG 29, NARA, D.C.

47. The U.S. government funded Pare Lorentz's 1936 film about the Dust Bowl, *The Plow That Broke the Plains*. For an overview of the Dust Bowl and its causes, see Donald Worster, *Dust Bowl: The Southern Plains in the 1930s* (New York: Oxford University Press, 2004).

48. "Dust Bowl Refugee" is a song from Woody Guthrie's *Dust Bowl Ballads* (Victor Records, 1940). On Dorothea Lange, see Linda Gordon, *Dorothea Lange: A Life Beyond Limits* (New York: W. W. Norton, 2009). Lange and others' photographs were compiled and set alongside a poem (a "sound track") by the poet Archibald MacLeish in *Land of the Free* (New York: Da Capo, 1977).

49. Hartman, *Wayward Lives*, 108.

50. On wages and insurance and how the rise of each shaped ideas about freedom and self, see Jonathan Levy, *Freaks of Fortune: The Emerging World of Capitalism and Risk in America* (Cambridge, MA: Harvard University Press, 2012).

51. Bureau of the Census, *Know Your U.S.A.*

2. NAMES AND NEGOTIATIONS

1. In act 2, scene 2, Juliet says: "What's in a name? That which we call a rose / By any other name would smell as sweet."

2. Langston Hughes published the poem "Madam and the Census Man" on the Associated Negro Press (ANP) wires, for it to be picked up by African American newspapers, as it was in this case in 1944: "Madam to You," *Plaindealer* (Kansas City), January 7, 1944. It was republished five years later as part of a series of poems gathered under the title "Madam to You: The Life and Times of Alberta K. Johnson," in Langston Hughes, *One-Way Ticket* (New York: Alfred A. Knopf, 1949).

3. Manhattan, New York County, New York, E.D. 31–1804, sheet 9B.

4. Bureau of the Census, *Instructions to Enumerators: Population and Agriculture 1940* (Washington, D.C.: Department of Commerce, 1940), 41, paragraph 443.

5. Kasia Boddy, "The Great American Novel and the Census," in *Writing, Medium, Machine: Modern Technographies*, edited by Sean Pryor and David Trotter (London: Open Humanities Press, 2016), 52–66 at 60.

6. Dellita L. Martin, "The 'Madam Poems' as Dramatic Monologue," *Black American Literature Forum* 15, no. 3 (1981): 97–99 at 98.

7. Benjamin, *Race After Technology*, 3–4.

8. Ngai, *Impossible Subjects*; Stern, *Eugenic Nation*.

9. Susan J. Pearson, *The Birth Certificate: An American History* (Chapel Hill: University of North Carolina Press, 2021).

10. Herbert M. Bratter, "Can You Prove You Were Born?," *The Saturday Evening Post*, May 17, 1952, 170; Ann Herbert Scott, *Census U.S.A.: Fact Finding for the American People, 1790–1970* (New York: Seabury Press, 1968), 84–85.

11. Charlotte Braunstein enumerated and wrote "1 mile" or "1½ mile" descriptions in Judicial Twp 3, Kern County, CA, S.D. 15–44, sheet 8B. On this sheet Braunstein enumerated Florence Hills, who was the subject of Dorothea Lange's *Migrant Mother* photograph.

12. El Portal, Mariposa County, California, E.D. 22–12, sheet 11B, enumerated by Matthew E. Beatty.

13. Seattle, King County, Washington, E.D. 40–106, sheet 2A.

14. For more on the early history of house numbering in Europe, see Anton

Tantner, "Addressing the Houses: The Introduction of House Numbering in Europe," *Histoire et Mesure* 26, no. 2 (2009), https://journals.openedition.org /histoiremesure/3942.

15. Reuben Rose-Redwood, "'A Regular State of Beautiful Confusion': Governing by Numbers and the Contradictions of Calculable Space in New York City," *Urban History* 39, no. 4 (2012): 624–38 at 627.

16. Reuben Rose-Redwood and Anton Tantner, "Introduction: Governmentality, House Numbering and the Spatial History of the Modern City," *Urban History* 39, no. 4 (2012): 607–13 at 610.

17. Alexander Keyssar, *The Right to Vote: The Contested History of Democracy in the United States* (New York: Basic Books, 2000), 16.

18. For a fuller treatment of this story, see Patricia Cline Cohen, *A Calculating People: The Spread of Numeracy in Early America* (New York: Routledge, 1999), chapter 6.

19. Theodore M. Porter, *Genetics in the Madhouse: The Unknown History of Human Heredity* (Princeton, NJ: Princeton University Press, 2018).

20. Louis P. Masur, "'Age of the First Person Singular': The Vocabulary of the Self in New England, 1780–1850," *Journal of American Studies* 25 (1991): 189–211 on 205–206.

21. Keyssar, *The Right to Vote*, 33–34.

22. Anderson, *The American Census*, 43, 51.

23. Anderson, *The American Census*, 47–50.

24. Gaps in genealogical data don't just come from silences in the slave schedules. As Alondra Nelson writes: "For African Americans, this search [for ancestors and origins] is both more elusive and more fraught. A profound loss of social ties was an immediate outcome of the Middle Passage and racial slavery. The ravages of the Civil War left vital records and slave-plantation paperwork degraded or destroyed. Information about black families was also lost intergenerationally—an understandable impulse to forget traumas of the past. But today African Americans use genetic ancestry testing with the hopes of shedding light on precisely the kind of familial and historical information supplied by [the formerly enslaved person] Venture Smith's slave narrative and family tree" (5). Nelson's book explores the rise of genetic genealogy and its uses and meanings for African Americans, including in efforts to win reparations for slavery. See Alondra Nelson, *The Social Life of DNA: Race, Reparations, and Reconciliation After the Genome* (Boston: Beacon Press, 2016).

25. "Hughey" Auld enumerated on sheet 37 in Baltimore, Maryland. See records in "Frederick Douglass (b. 1818–d. 1895)," *Archives of Maryland (Biographical Series)*, https://msa.maryland.gov/megafile/msa/speccol/sc5400/sc5496/013800 /013800/html/013800sources.html.

26. 1840 Census, New Bedford, Bristol County, MA, sheet 411; Douglass and his whole household appeared named in 1850: Rochester, Monroe County, New York, enumerated by M. G. Warner on September 4, 1850.

27. Daughter Rosetta was born in 1839 after the Douglasses moved into a home on Elm Street. See National Park Service, *New Bedford Whaling: Frederick Douglass*, https://www.nps.gov/nebe/learn/historyculture/frederickdouglass.htm.

28. Frederick Douglass, *Narrative of the Life of Frederick Douglass, an American Slave* (Dublin: Webb and Chapman, 1846), 110–12.

29. Douglass, *Narrative of the Life of Frederick Douglass*, 112.

30. The Democrat was named Lee Geyer. "Census Men Here Named. Supervisors and Aides for Eight Congressional Districts Appointed," *Los Angeles Times*, December 18, 1939.

31. Census Bureau, "Addresses of Area Managers and District Supervisors. Sixteenth Decennial Census 1940," in Folder Census, Addresses of Area Managers and District Supervisors, Box 112, Hopkins Papers.

32. The story that follows of a search for census Communists relies on Carl Rogers, "Report on Investigation into Charges That Certain Employees of the Bureau of the Census, in the 17th Congressional District, Los Angeles, California, Are Communists," April 19, 1940, in Folder 1940 (1 of 2), Box 22, Niles Papers.

33. Quoted from page 6 of Carl Rogers, "Report on Investigation into Charges That Certain Employees of the Bureau of the Census, in the 17th Congressional District, Los Angeles, California, Are Communists," April 19, 1940, in Folder 1940 (1 of 2), Box 22, Niles Papers.

34. On number of Communists, see Robert W. Cherny, "The Communist Party in California, 1935–1940: From the Political Margins to the Mainstream and Back," *American Communist History* 9, no. 1 (2010): 3–33 at 7.

35. Page 1 of Carl Rogers, "Report on Investigation into Charges That Certain Employees of the Bureau of the Census, in the 17th Congressional District, Los Angeles, California, Are Communists," April 19, 1940, in Folder 1940 (1 of 2), Box 22, Niles Papers.

36. Bureau of the Census, "Application Form 1940 Census Field Service," Folder 3, Box 4, Entry P 15, RG 29, NARA, D.C.

37. The census recorded no income in 1939 for Wesley: Los Angeles, Los Angeles County, E.D. 60–1233, sheet 16A.

38. Philip Sutton, "Why Your Family Name Was Not Changed at Ellis Island," New York Public Library July 2, 2013, https://www.nypl.org/blog/2013/07/02/name-changes-ellis-island; Caitlin Hollander, "No, Your Ancestors' Names Were Not Changed at Ellis Island," Hollander-Waas Jewish Heritage Services, October 7, 2019, https://www.hollander-waas.com/blog/ellis-island-name-change.

39. Jennifer Mendelsohn, http://resistancegenealogy.com/.

40. Jen Deerinwater, "Paper Genocide: The Erasure of Native People in Census Counts," *Rewire News Group*, December 9, 2019, https://rewirenewsgroup .com/article/2019/12/09/paper-genocide-the-erasure-of-native-people-in -census-counts/. See also "Names" in U.S. National Archives, "Indian Census Rolls, 1885–1940," https://www.archives.gov/research/census/native-americans /1885–1940.html.

3. PARTNERS

1. John Milton, *Paradise Lost*, book 10, https://www.dartmouth.edu/~milton /reading_room/pl/book_10/text.shtml.
2. Margo J. Anderson, *The American Census, Second Edition* (New Haven, CT: Yale University Press, 2015). 94, 100–101.
3. Anderson, *The American Census*, 125.
4. W. C. Hunt to Joseph A. Hill, "Memorandum for Dr. Hill," October 30, 1917, Folder P-28 Fourteenth (1920) Census (Minority Report), Box 151, Entry 200, RG 29, NARA, D.C.
5. On 1890 and Minnesota, see Ronald A. Goeken and Diana L. Magnuson, "'I Hate to See the Evening Sun Go Down': Recounts and Padding in the 19th Century U.S. Decennial Census of Population," Social Science History Association Annual Meeting, 2019, 26.
6. Benedict Anderson, *Imagined Communities* (New York: Verso, rev. ed. 1991), 166.
7. There were 50,845 partners according to the totals in the IPUMS 100 percent 1880 Complete Count database. The total 1880 population was 50,189,209. These totals are drawn from the 100 percent sample for the 1880 U.S. Census in Steven Ruggles, Sarah Flood, Sophia Foster, Ronald Goeken, Jose Pacas, Megan Schouweiler, and Matthew Sobek, IPUMS USA: Version 11.0 [data set] (Minneapolis, MN: IPUMS, 2021), https://doi.org/10.18128/D010.V11.0.
8. Secret Cannōn, Eureka County, Nevada, page 39, June 28, 1880.
9. Richard White, *The Republic for Which It Stands: The United States During Reconstruction and the Gilded Age, 1865–1896* (New York: Oxford University Press, 2017), 380.
10. White, *The Republic for Which It Stands*, 380–381. For more, see Beth Lew-Williams, *The Chinese Must Go: Violence, Exclusion, and the Making of the Alien in America* (Cambridge, MA: Harvard University Press, 2018).
11. Carroll D. Wright, *The History and Growth of the United States Census, Prepared for the Senate Committee on the Census* (Washington, D.C.: Government Printing Office, 1900), 170–71.

12. Bureau of the Census, *Instructions to Enumerators*, 43, paragraph 451.

13. Bureau of the Census, *Instructions to Enumerators*, 37, paragraph 421.

14. "Illustrative Example of Completed Population Schedule," in Volume 4, Entry 238, RG 29, NARA, D.C.

15. Narrative and Illustrated Form in Folder "1940 Territories and Possessions—Forms + Schedules," Box 25, Entry 252, RG 29, NARA, D.C.

16. Census Bureau, "Objective Test for Census Enumerators—Hawaii," in Box 27, Entry 252, RG 29, NARA, D.C.

17. Census Bureau, "Illustrated Example of Completed Population Schedule" in Folder "1940 Territories and Possessions—Forms + Schedules," Box 25, Entry 252, RG 29, NARA, D.C.

18. "About Us," Central Council Tlingit and Haida Indian Tribes of Alaska, http://www.ccthita.org/about/overview/index.html.

19. Elizabeth W. Russell, "The 'Vanished American,'" *Expedition Magazine* 8, no. 4 (1966), https://www.penn.museum/sites/expedition/the-vanished-america/.

20. These totals drawn from the 100 percent sample for 1940 U.S. Census as registered on January 4, 2022, in Ruggles et al., IPUMS USA: Version 11.0 [data set].

21. Amy E. Hillier, "Redlining and the Home Owners' Loan Corporation," *Journal of Urban History* 29, no. 4 (2003): 394–420 at 394–95.

22. "Introduction," in Robert K. Nelson, LaDale Winling, Richard Marciano, Nathan Connolly, et al., "Mapping Inequality," *American Panorama*, ed. Robert K. Nelson and Edward L. Ayers, https://dsl.richmond.edu/panorama/redlining/#loc=5/39.1/-94.58&text=intro.

23. Manhattan, New York County, New York, E.D. 31–879.

24. See "C1" in Area Description Images for Manhattan, New York, in Nelson et al., "Mapping Inequality," *American Panorama*, https://dsl.richmond.edu/panorama/redlining/#loc=5/39.1/-94.58&text=downloads.

25. See "Biographical Note" for "Viola Wertheim Bernard Papers, 1918–2000," http://www.columbia.edu/cu/lweb/archival/collections/ldpd_5420220.

26. Manhattan, New York County, New York, E.D. 31–879, sheet 62B.

27. Manhattan, New York County, New York, E.D. 31–1723B.

28. See "D23" in Area Description Images for Manhattan, New York in Nelson et al., "Mapping Inequality," *American Panorama*, https://dsl.richmond.edu/panorama/redlining/#loc=5/39.1/-94.58&text=downloads.

29. For more context on the larger forces that might explain these relationships, see chapter 2 of Dianne M. Stewart, *Black Women, Black Love: America's War on African American Marriage* (New York: Seal, 2020).

30. Manhattan, New York County, New York, E.D. 31–1272.

31. See "A4" and "D15" in Area Description Images for Manhattan, New York, in

Nelson et al., "Mapping Inequality," *American Panorama*, https://dsl.richmond .edu/panorama/redlining/#loc=5/39.1/-94.58&text=downloads.

32. George Chauncey, *Gay New York: Gender, Urban Culture, and the Making of the Gay Male World, 1890-1940* (New York: Basic Books, 2008), 159.

33. Chauncey, *Gay New York*, 227.

34. Hartman, *Wayward Lives, Beautiful Experiments*.

35. San Francisco, San Francisco County, California, E.D. 38–157.

36. See "D5" in Area Description Images for San Francisco, California in Nelson et al., "Mapping Inequality," *American Panorama*, https://dsl.richmond.edu /panorama/redlining/#loc=5/39.1/-94.58&text=downloads.

37. San Francisco, San Francisco County, California, E.D. 38–168.

38. San Francisco, San Francisco County, California, E.D. 38–18.

39. For a deeper analysis of the people living in families that the census might deem odd or queer, and the role of state policy in making such families, see Nayan Shah, *Stranger Intimacy: Contesting Race, Sexuality, and the Law in the North American West* (Berkeley: University of California Press, 2012).

40. *1940 United States Federal Census* [database online], Ancestry.com, 2012.

41. Honolulu County, Hawaii, E.D. 2–187.

42. Moon-Kie Jung, *Reworking Race: The Making of Hawaii's Interracial Labor Movement* (New York: Columbia University Press, 2006), 94.

43. Jessica Contrera and Gillian Brockell, "In 1933, Two Rebellious Women Bought a Home in Virginia's Woods. Then the CIA Moved In," *The Washington Post*, February 14, 2020, https://www.washingtonpost.com/history/2020 /02/14/cia-women-neighbors-langley.

44. The punch card is reproduced on page 125 of Robert M. Jenkins, *Procedural History of the 1940 Census of Population and Housing* (Madison: University of Wisconsin Press, 1985).

45. Ian Hacking, "Biopower and the Avalanche of Printed Numbers," *Humanities in Society* 5, nos. 3–4 (1982): 279–95 at 280, 287.

4. COUNTING WITH FRIENDS

1. Mrs. Clara Triplett Doss to John E. Rankin, February 19, 1940, Series Jobs Folder Census 1940, Rankin Papers.

2. W. L. Austin, "Memorandum to Mr. Niles," August 10, 1939, in Folder 1939, Box 22, Niles Papers.

3. Salary information from page 18 of Field Division, Bureau of the Census, "Rough Draft: Historical Report of 1940 (16th Decennial) Census Made from the Records That Were Available in 1948 with Emphasis on the Field Aspects"

(1948) in Folder "16th Decennial Census 1940—Historical Report of 1940 Census," Box 2, Entry P 26, RG 29, NARA, D.C.

4. Nine district supervisors listed in Bureau of the Census, *Sixteenth Census of the United States: 1940. Mississippi Supervisors' Districts* (Washington, D.C.: Department of Commerce, 1940) in Folder "Field—Supervisor's Districts 1940," Box 211, Entry 210, RG 29, NARA, D.C.; 1,833 enumerators from Appendix to Field Division, Bureau of the Census, "Rough Draft: Historical Report of 1940 (16th Decennial) Census Made from the Records That Were Available in 1948 with Emphasis on the Field Aspects" (1948) in Folder "16th Decennial Census 1940—Historical Report of 1940 Census," Box 2, Entry P 26, RG 29, NARA, D.C.

5. On Niles, see "Niles, David K.," Harry S. Truman Library, https://www .trumanlibrary.gov/library/personal-papers/david-k-niles-papers. On Niles's Zionism, as described by an opponent in the State Department, see "Edwin M. Wright Oral History Interview," Harry S. Truman Library, https://www .trumanlibrary.gov/library/oral-histories/wright.

6. David K. Niles to Marguerite Le Hand, September 6, 1939, in Folder 1939, Box 22, Niles Papers.

7. David K. Niles to Marguerite Le Hand, September 6, 1939 in Folder 1939, Box 22, Niles Papers.

8. Leake County, Mississippi, E.D. 52, page 34.

9. For more on this era in census history, see Anderson, *The American Census*, chapter 4.

10. For an overview of confidentiality (or lack thereof) in the U.S. census, see George Gatewood, *A Monograph on Confidentiality and Privacy in the U.S. Census* (U.S. Census Bureau, July 2001), https://www.census.gov/history/pdf /ConfidentialityMonograph.pdf.

11. This was admittedly a halting development, which maintained some glaring holes even as more people gained some confidentiality protections. In World War I, for instance, "since the 1910 census law did not prohibit disclosure, the Census Bureau furnished many transcripts to the U.S. Department of Justice, local draft boards, and individuals, especially in connection with cases where the individuals had been arrested for draft evasion." Gatewood, *A Monograph on Confidentiality*, 11.

12. William Seltzer, "Replacing Austin: A Study of Leadership Change at the U.S. Census Bureau," Paper prepared for presentation at a session, The Census and Statistical Policymaking: Lessons from History, at the 2011 Joint Statistical Meetings, Miami Beach Florida, July 30 to August 4, 2011.

13. On Austin's early career and relationship to Roper, I rely on C. L. Dedrick's notes in "Notes from Dedrick files Re: Directors and 1920 Census" shared by

Sharon Tosi Lacey, chief historian of the U.S. Census Bureau in an email from August 7, 2019.

14. Scott County, Mississippi, E.D. 88, sheet 1.

15. Appendix to Field Division, Bureau of the Census, "Rough Draft: Historical Report of 1940 (16th Decennial) Census Made from the Records That Were Available in 1948 with Emphasis on the Field Aspects" (1948) in Folder "16th Decennial Census 1940—Historical Report of 1940 Census," Box 2, Entry P 26, RG 29, NARA, D.C.

16. David K. Niles to Marguerite Le Hand, September 6, 1939, in Folder 1939, Box 22, Niles Papers.

17. Austin wrote in 1920: "I wish to call your attention and the personal attention of the Director to the reasons given for the belief that future censuses should not be taken in the winter. If the statement is made for the purpose of excusing our delays and difficulties in taking the censuses of population and agriculture for this Census, my opinion is that the case made is a very weak one." W. L. Austin to Chief Clerk, September 15, 1920, in Folder C-21, Box 146, Entry 200, RG 29, NARA, D.C.

18. W. L. Austin to J. E. Rankin, April 5, 1928, in Folder "1928 Census," Series 1, Rankin Papers.

19. See C. L. Dedrick's notes in "Notes from Dedrick files Re: Directors and 1920 Census"; one researcher claims that Roper, a former campaign aide for William Gibbs McAdoo in 1924, was instrumental in getting California's delegation to swing to Roosevelt in the 1932 convention. The evidence is thin at best, but it is clear that Roper had strong ties to the old Wilsonian wing of the Democratic Party and worked hard behind the scenes for Roosevelt in the campaign. See Thomas T. Spencer, "Daniel C. Roper and the 1932 Presidential Campaign," *South Carolina Historical Magazine* 85, no. 1 (1984): 22–32.

20. On Hopkins's history and relationship to Roosevelt, I'm relying most on David L. Roll, *The Hopkins Touch: Harry Hopkins and the Forging of the Alliance to Defeat Hitler* (New York: Oxford University Press, 2013), prologue and chapters 1–2.

21. David K. Niles to Marguerite Le Hand, September 6, 1939, in Folder 1939, Box 22, Niles Papers.

22. Typescript of Niles's phone call with Senator [Tom] Connally, September 26, 1939, in Folder 1939, Box 22, Niles Papers.

23. Randolph Hughes to Edwin M. Watson, October 9, 1939, in Folder 1939, Box 22, Niles Papers.

24. Typescript of phone call with Ambrose J. Kennedy, October 5, 1939, Folder 1939, Box 22, Niles Papers.

25. David Niles to Edwin M. Watson, September 25, 1939, Folder 1940 (1 of 2), Box 22, Niles Papers.

26. On Harrison, see Martha H. Swain, "Senator Pat Harrison: New Deal Wheelhorse (1933–1941) Suspicious of His Load," *Mississippi History Now*, https://www.mshistorynow.mdah.ms.gov/issue/senator-pat-harrison-new-deal-wheelhorse-suspicious-of-his-load-1933-1941.

27. On Bilbo, see David G. Sansing, "Theodore Gilmore Bilbo," *The Mississippi Encyclopedia*, https://mississippiencyclopedia.org/entries/theodore-gilmore-bilbo/.

28. I don't have direct evidence of the decision to have two area supervisors, or of who picked whom, but I do know Austin suggested the compromise, and I know there ended up being two according to Bureau of the Census, *Sixteenth Census of the United States: 1940. Mississippi Supervisors' Districts* (Washington, D.C.: Department of Commerce, 1940), in Folder "Field—Supervisor's Districts 1940," Box 211, Entry 210, RG 29, NARA, D.C.

29. W. L. Austin, "Memorandum to Mr. Niles, 10 August 1939," in Folder 1939, Box 22, Niles Papers; J. E. Rankin to E. R. Rankin, April 7, 1930, Folder Census 1930, Series 1, Rankin Papers. Ethelbert was enumerated by James F. Dobbs (who put down "car salesman" as his occupation) on May 7, 1930, in Lee County, Mississippi, E.D. 41–15, sheet 27B.

30. David K. Niles to Edwin M. Watson, December 5, 1939, Folder 1939, Box 22, Niles Papers.

31. David K. Niles to James A Farley, December 21, 1939, Folder 1939, Box 22, Niles Papers.

32. Ford's Democrat-approved man was named Frank A. Helton.

33. W. L. Austin, "Memorandum to Mr. Niles, 10 August 1939," in Folder 1939, Box 22, Niles Papers.

34. W. L. Austin to John E. Rankin, September 15, 1939, in Series Jobs, Folder Congress 1939, Rankin Papers.

35. Harold Sanders to John E. Rankin, December 2, 1939, in Series Jobs, Folder Congress 1939, Rankin Papers.

36. H. B. Sanders to John E. Rankin, September 29, 1939, in Series Jobs, Folder Congress 1939, Rankin Papers. The two or three men being discussed were probably local office assistants or staff, as it's a response to Rankin's writing: "According to our conversation, I will send you recommendations for assistants, etc. Please do not make any commitments until you hear from me further."

37. John E. Rankin to Harold B. Sanders, October 3, 1939, in Series Jobs, Folder Congress 1939, Rankin Papers.

38. This was Trapp's age as recorded in the 1940 census: Tupelo, Lee County, Mississippi, E.D. 41–10, sheet 5B.

39. Wendall (Wib) Trapp to John E. Rankin, October 11, 1939, in Series Jobs, Folder Congress 1939, Rankin Papers.

40. John E. Rankin to O. T. Trapp, October 12, 1939, in Series Jobs, Folder Congress 1939, Rankin Papers.

41. Richard White, *Railroaded: The Transcontinentals and the Making of Modern America* (New York: W. W. Norton, 2011).

42. John E. Rankin to Harold B. Sanders, October 3, 1939, in Series Jobs, Folder Congress 1939, Rankin Papers.

43. John E. Rankin to H. B. Sanders, November 22, 1939, in Series Jobs, Folder Congress 1939, Rankin Papers.

44. John E. Rankin to W. G. Roberds, November 8, 1939, in Series Jobs, Folder Congress 1939, Rankin Papers.

45. John E. Rankin to A. L. Burdine, October 3, 1939, in Series Jobs, Folder Congress 1939, Rankin Papers.

46. John E. Rankin to H. B. Sanders, October 16, 1939, in Series Jobs, Folder Congress 1939, Rankin Papers.

47. H. B. Sanders to John E. Rankin, January 8, 1940, in Series Jobs, Folder Census 1940, Rankin Papers.

48. J. B. Snider to A. L. Ford, January 3, 1940, in Series Jobs, Folder Census 1940, Rankin Papers.

49. D. D. Pitts to John E. Rankin, September 22, 1939, in Series Jobs, Folder Congress 1939, Rankin Papers.

50. John E. Rankin to W. G. Roberds, November 8, 1939, in Series Jobs, Folder Congress 1939, Rankin Papers.

51. Daisy L. Green to J. E. Rankin, March 16, 1940, in Series Jobs, Folder Census 1940, Rankin Papers.

52. Anderson, *American Census*, 172. On the DSR's establishment in 1933, see "Memorandum Concerning the Proposed Establishment of the New Division of Statistical Research," June 9, 1933, in Folder 71 Statistical Research, Box 9, Entry 142, RG 29, NARA, D.C.

53. "Notes from Dedrick files Re: Directors and 1920 Census."

54. Photo with caption "Heading for the Big Round-Up" in Folder "Pictures Taken in Indiana Trial Census August 1939," Box 234, Entry 234, RG 29, NARA, D.C.

55. "Training Program of the 16th Decennial Census" in Folder "Field—Report on 'Training Program' to Census Adv. Comm. By Dr. Dedrick 3/29/40," Box 211, Entry 210, RG 29, NARA, D.C. For the number dropped from the program, see page 8 of Field Division, Bureau of the Census, "Rough Draft: Historical Report of 1940 (16th Decennial) Census Made from the Records That Were Available in 1948 with Emphasis on the Field Aspects" (1948) in Folder "16th

Decennial Census 1940—Historical Report of 1940 Census," Box 2, Entry P 26, RG 29, NARA, D.C.

56. "Training Program of the 16th Decennial Census" in Folder "Field—Report on 'Training Program' to Census Adv. Comm. By Dr. Dedrick 3/29/40," Box 211, Entry 210, RG 29, NARA, D.C.

57. Assistant to the Director to Harold B. Sanders, November 27, 1939, in Series Jobs, Folder Congress 1939, Rankin Papers.

58. Page 9 of Field Division, Bureau of the Census, "Rough Draft: Historical Report of 1940 (16th Decennial) Census Made from the Records That Were Available in 1948 with Emphasis on the Field Aspects" (1948), in Folder "16th Decennial Census 1940—Historical Report of 1940 Census," Box 2, Entry P 26, RG 29, NARA, D.C.

59. "Training Program of the 16th Decennial Census" in Folder "Field—Report on 'Training Program' to Census Adv. Comm. By Dr. Dedrick 3/29/40," Box 211, Entry 210, RG 29, NARA, D.C.

60. On U.K. civil service exams and critics, see Jon Agar, *The Government Machine: A Revolutionary History of the Computer* (Cambridge, MA: MIT Press, 2003), chapter 2.

61. John Carson, *The Measure of Merit: Talents, Intelligence, and Inequality in the French and American Republics, 1750–1940* (Princeton, NJ: Princeton University Press, 2007), chapter 6.

62. The following questions and answers for Test I are drawn from "P-104 Test I: Based on Abridged Instructions to Enumerators for Population Schedule," Volume 4, Entry 238, RG 29, NARA, D.C.

63. "P-106 Test II: Based on Instructions to Enumerators for Population Schedule," Volume 4, Entry 238, RG 29, NARA, D.C.

64. H. B. Sanders to John E. Rankin, October 21, 1939, in Series Jobs, Folder Congress 1939, Rankin Papers.

65. Daisy Lucile Green to J. E. Rankin, January 10, 1940, in Series Jobs, Folder Congress 1940, Rankin Papers.

66. "Dates for Examinations for Filling Places. Jobs Taking the Census." Stamped February 1940 in Series Jobs, Folder Census 1940, Rankin Papers.

67. Daisy L. Green to J. E. Rankin, March 16, 1940, in Series Jobs, Folder Census 1940, Rankin Papers.

68. Educational attainment per the census, for McCollum: Lowndes County, Mississippi, E.D. 44–6, sheet 3B; for Triplett Doss: Noxubee County, Mississippi, E.D. 52–21, sheet 26B.

69. Lucile McCollum to John Rankin, June 19, 1939, in Series Jobs, Folder Congress 1939, Rankin Papers.

70. Lowndes County, Mississippi, E.D. 44–6, sheet 3B.

71. Scott A. Sandage, "Gender and the Economics of the Sentimental Market in Nineteenth-Century America," *Social Politics* 6, no. 2 (1999): 105–30.

72. These questions are drawn from a sample application in Folder 3, Box 4, Entry P 15, RG 29, NARA, D.C.

73. Lucile McCollum to John Rankin, June 19, 1939, in Series Jobs, Folder Congress 1939, Rankin Papers.

74. McCollum to John E. Rankin, December 30, 1939, in Series Jobs, Folder Census 1940, Rankin Papers.

75. See attachment to Daisy Lucile Green to J. E. Rankin, January 10, 1940, in Series Jobs, Folder Census 1940, Rankin Papers.

76. H. B. Sanders to John E. Rankin, January 8, 1940, in Series Jobs, Folder Census 1940, Rankin Papers.

77. Lowndes County, Mississippi, E.D. 44–11, sheet 12B.

78. Miss Christobel Patrick to John E. Rankin, telegram, December 15, 1939, in Series Jobs, Folder Congress 1939, Rankin Papers.

79. John E. Rankin to Miss Christobel Patrick, December 15, 1939, in Series Jobs, Folder Congress 1939, Rankin Papers.

80. "List of Appointments of Census Enumerators-Census 1st District-Miss," in Series Jobs, Folder Congress 1939, Rankin Papers.

81. H. B. Sanders to John E. Rankin, February 2, 1940, in Series Jobs, Folder Census 1940, Rankin Papers.

82. Mrs. A. G. Triplett to John E. Rankin, February 20, 1940, in Series Jobs, Folder Census 1940, Rankin Papers.

83. Noxubee County, Mississippi, E.D. 52–21, sheet 26B.

84. Howard H. Triplett to John Rankin, March 12, 1939, in Series Jobs, Folder Census 1940, Rankin Papers.

85. J. E. Rankin to E. A. White, March 25, 1940, in Series Jobs, Folder Census 1940, Rankin Papers.

86. Louise A. Riley to John E. Rankin, telegram, March 28, 1940, in Series Jobs, Folder Census 1940, Rankin Papers.

87. Lovie W. Moore to J. E. Rankin, March 28, 1940, in Series Jobs, Folder Census 1940, Rankin Papers.

88. Lucile McCollum to John E. Rankin, March 25, 1940, in Series Jobs, Folder Census 1940, Rankin Papers.

89. Marcie Roberts to John E. Rankin, November 6, 1939, in Series Jobs, Folder Congress 1939, Rankin Papers.

90. Tracy Rankin was the cousin in question. J. E. Rankin to E. R. Rankin, December 26, 1939, in Series Jobs, Folder Congress 1939, Rankin Papers.

91. Harold B. Sanders to John E. Rankin, April 2, 1940, in Series Jobs, Folder Census 1940, Rankin Papers.

92. Vivian C. Terry to J. B. Snider, December 28, 1939, in Series Jobs, Folder Census 1940, Rankin Papers.
93. Eudora Carpenter to John E. Rankin, December 11, 1939, in Series Jobs, Folder Congress 1939, Rankin Papers.
94. J. B. Snider to A. L. Ford, January 3, 1940, in Series Jobs, Folder Census 1940, Rankin Papers.

5. SILENCES AND WHITE SUPREMACY

1. Michel-Rolph Trouillot, *Silencing the Past: Power and the Production of History* (Boston: Beacon Press, 2015), 51.
2. On the "value gap" in American society that values Black lives less than the lives of others, and the way that gap perverts American democracy more generally, see Eddie S. Glaude, *Democracy in Black: How Race Still Enslaves the American Soul* (New York: Crown, 2016).
3. Daniel O. Price, "Factor Analysis in the Study of Metropolitan Centers," *Social Forces* 20, no. 4 (1942): 449–55; "Daniel O'Haver Price," UNC Department of Sociology, https://sociology.unc.edu/daniel-ohaver-price/.
4. "Daniel O'Haver Price," UNC Department of Sociology, https://sociology.unc .edu/daniel-ohaver-price.
5. Daniel O. Price, "A Check on Underenumeration in the 1940 Census," *American Sociological Review* 12, no. 1 (1947): 44–49. The work of historian and religious scholar Judith Weisenfeld offers an interesting companion to Price's study. In researching her book *New World A-Coming* on religio-racial movements like the Nation of Islam and the Moorish Science Temple, Weisenfeld turned to draft registration records as a tool for, among other things, finding those who belonged to religious movements that denied race categories. Weisenfeld's work suggests that even Price's gold-standard data missed some people he would have classified as African American because they refused that racial label in the draft registration process. More generally, Weisenfeld reflected on her method and made a case for what I have called "reading data": "I came to understand the richness of government records for this sort of work accidentally," she wrote. See Judith Weisenfeld, "New World A-Coming, Author's Response," *Journal of Africana Religions* 6, no. 2 (2018): 308–15 at 313; Judith Weisenfeld, *New World A-Coming: Black Religion and Racial Identity During the Great Migration* (New York: New York University Press, 2017).
6. The scholar and former census director Ken Prewitt, for instance, called Price's analysis "the first reliable measure of how many people, at least among young men, were missed in the census." Prewitt, *What Is "Your" Race?*, 107. Ander-

son and Fienberg note that, since George Washington, "officials had been concerned about undercounting the population," but they, too, give pride of place to Price's study, discussing it under the heading "The Discovery of the Undercount." Margo J. Anderson and Stephen E. Fienberg, *Who Counts? The Politics of Census-Taking in Contemporary America* (New York: Russell Sage Foundation, 1999), 29.

7. Price, "A Check on Underenumeration in the 1940 Census," 49.

8. Folder N-2 Negro Enumeration of 1920, Box 150, Entry 200, RG 29, NARA, D.C.

9. John S. Haller, Jr., *Outcasts from Evolution: Scientific Attributes of Racial Inferiority, 1859–1900* (Carbondale: Southern Illinois University Press, 1996).

10. Kelly Miller, *A Review of Hoffman's Race Traits and Tendencies of the American Negro* (Washington, D.C.: American Negro Academy, 1897), 3, https://catalog.hathitrust.org/Record/100788175.

11. Frederick L. Hoffman, "Race Traits and Tendencies of the American Negro," *Publications of the American Economic Association* 11, no. 1/3 (1896): 1–329.

12. Walter Willcox, a Census Bureau chief statistician, championed Hoffman's piece for the AEA. Mark Aldrich, "Progressive Economists and Scientific Racism: Walter Willcox and Black Americans, 1895–1910," *Phylon* 40, no. 1 (1979): 1–14 at 8.

13. Khalil Gibran Muhammad, *The Condemnation of Blackness: Race, Crime, and the Making of Modern Urban America* (Cambridge, MA: Harvard University Press, 2010), 55.

14. Miller, *A Review of Hoffman's Race Traits*, 6, 19.

15. Bureau of the Census, *Negro Population 1790–1915* (Washington, D.C.: Government Printing Office, 1918), 13.

16. Kelly Miller, "Enumeration Errors in Negro Population," *Scientific Monthly* 14, no. 2 (1922): 168–77 at 169.

17. Miller, "Enumeration Errors in Negro Population," 172.

18. Le Verne Beales, "The Negro Enumeration of 1920: A Reply to Dr. Kelly Miller," *Scientific Monthly* 14, no. 4 (1922): 352–60.

19. Miller, "Enumeration Errors in Negro Population," 177.

20. Harris County, Texas, E.D. 101–4A.

21. Harris County, Texas, E.D. 101–4A, sheet 1A.

22. Bureau of the Census, *Instructions to Enumerators*, 43, paragraph 455.

23. See the discussion of "blood" in chapter 1 of Kim TallBear, *Native American DNA: Tribal Belonging and the False Promise of Genetic Science* (Minneapolis: University of Minnesota Press, 2013).

24. Ian Haney López, *White by Law: The Legal Construction of Race* (New York: New York University Press, 2006).

25. Bureau of the Census, *Instructions to Enumerators*, 43, paragraph 454.

26. In telling this story, I rely on Laura E. Gómez, *Manifest Destinies: The Making of the Mexican American Race* 2nd edition (New York: New York University Press, 2018). See also David G. Gutiérrez, "Migration, Emergent Ethnicity, and the 'Third Space': The Shifting Politics of Nationalism in Greater Mexico," *Journal of American History* 86, no. 2 (1999): 481–517.

27. Mae M. Ngai, "The Architecture of Race in American Immigration Law: A Reexamination of the Immigration Act of 1924," *Journal of American History* 86, no. 1 (1999): 67–92 at 81.

28. Gómez, *Manifest Destinies*.

29. George J. Sánchez, *Becoming Mexican American: Ethnicity, Culture, and Identity in Chicano Los Angeles, 1900–1945* (New York: Oxford University Press, 1993), 18.

30. Alexandra Stern, "Buildings, Boundaries, and Blood: Medicalization and Nation-Building on the U.S.-Mexico Border, 1910–1930," *Hispanic American Historical Review* 79, no. 1 (1999): 41–81.

31. See, for instance, U.S. House, *To Amend the Constitution: Hearing Before the Committee on the Judiciary, House of Representatives Seventieth Congress Second Session on H.J. Res 102 H.J. Res. 351* (February 13, 14, and 19, 1929), 28. "Contemporaries estimated that illegal immigration ran as high as 100,000 a year throughout the 1920s. Unofficial entry was not new, as migration across the border had had an informal, unregulated character since the nineteenth century," writes Ngai, "The Architecture of Race," 90.

32. I rely here on Ngai, *Impossible Subjects*, especially chapter 2. See also Kelly Lytle Hernández, *Migra! A History of the U.S. Border Patrol* (Berkeley: University of California Press, 2010).

33. Schor, *Counting Americans*, 212.

34. F. Arturo Rosales, "Shifting Self Perceptions and Ethnic Consciousness Among Mexicans in Houston 1908–1946," *Aztlan* 16, no. 1–2 (1987): 71–94.

35. Ngai, *Impossible Subjects*, 71.

36. Rosales, "Shifting Self Perceptions," 83.

37. The relevant cases are *Takao Ozawa v. U.S.* (1922) and *U.S. vs. Bhagat Singh Thind* (1923), discussed in Ngai, *Impossible Subjects*, chapter 1.

38. The form instructions read: "For other than white or negro, write out color or race to which you belong in the space provided. Typical examples of other color classifications are: Mexican, Chinese, Japanese, Indian, Filipino, etc." See "Social Security Numbers: Employee SSN Application Form," Social Security Administration, https://www.ssa.gov/history/ssn/ss5.html.

39. Rosales, "Shifting Self Perceptions," 80–81.

40. Rosales, "Shifting Self Perceptions," 82.

41. Brian Gratton and Emily Klancher Merchant, "La Raza: Mexicans in the United States Census," *Journal of Political History* 28, no. 4 (2016): 537–67.

42. See the contents of Folder "Popu.—Mexican Classification," Box 217, Entry 210, RG 29, NARA, D.C.

43. W. L. Austin quoted from CAC meeting minutes in Schor, *Counting Americans*, 215.

44. Harris County, Texas, E.D. 101–4B.

45. Aliya Saperstein and Andrew M. Penner, "Racial Fluidity and Inequality in the United States," *American Journal of Sociology* 118, no. 3 (2012): 676–727.

46. "Case, Francis Higbee," *History, Art and Archives*, United States House of Representatives, https://history.house.gov/People/Detail/10732.

47. Francis Case to Director, Bureau of the Census, October 16, 1939, Folder "Indians Not Taxed—Dedrick," Box 218, Entry 210, RG 29, NARA, D.C.

48. Philip Deloria, "Review of *Black Hills/White Justice*, *Great Plains Research* 3, no. 1 (1993): 127–28. Deloria's father, the scholar and Native American rights activist Vine Deloria, Jr., wrote an even more critical review in *American Historical Review* 98, no. 1 (1993): 227–28. The reviews agree that the book, written by the son of the attorney who succeeded Case, is still a useful account of the very long and complicated lawsuit: Edward Lazarus, *Black Hills/White Justice: The Sioux Nation versus the United States, 1775 to the Present* (New York: HarperCollins, 1991).

49. Delilah Friedler, "The Black Hills Are Not for Sale," *Mother Jones* (March/April 2020), 34–45 at 37.

50. "State Statutes Restricting Voting Rights of Indians," Folder "Indians Not Taxed—Dedrick," Box 218, Entry 210, RG 29, NARA, D.C.

51. Page 3 of Ralph H. Case to Francis Case, September 7, 1939, Folder "Indians Not Taxed—Dedrick," Box 218, Entry 210, RG 29, NARA, D.C.

52. Seltzer notes some early uses of "Indians not taxed," such as in a proposed amendment to the Articles of Confederation on page 5 of William Seltzer, "Excluding Indians Not Taxed: Federal Censuses and Native-Americans in the 19th Century," paper presented at 1999 Joint Statistical Meetings August 9, 1999.

53. See Seltzer, "Excluding Indians Not Taxed," 12–13; Dennis Zotigh, "The Treaty That Forced the Cherokee People from Their Homelands Goes on View," *Smithsonian Magazine*, April 24, 2019, https://www.smithsonianmag.com/blogs/national-museum-american-indian/2019/04/24/treaty-new-echota/.

54. As William Seltzer has explained, there were some exceptional examples, like the Cherokee of Quallatown, who successfully resisted the forced migrations of the 1830s to maintain their community through the 1840s. These Cherokee asserted their right to be enumerated, hoping that being counted would buttress their claims to citizenship. See Seltzer, "Excluding Indians Not Taxed," 9–10. Seltzer is drawing on John R. Finger, *The Eastern Band of Cherokees: 1819–1900* (Knoxville: University of Tennessee Press, 1984).

55. Language from instructions for the 1860 census; quoted from Seltzer, "Excluding Indians Not Taxed," 27–28. "By extending the coverage of Indians in the general census, their numbers were increased, although this did not mean growth in their population but rather an increase in the portion of the Indian population included in the general census." Schor, *Counting Americans*, 121.

56. National Archives, "Indian Census Rolls, 1885–1940," https://www.archives.gov/research/census/native-americans/1885–1940.html.

57. TallBear, *Native American DNA*.

58. Bureau of the Census, *Instructions to Enumerators*, 43, paragraph 456.

59. Daniel Folkmar to Chief Statistician, November 22, 1910, File 416, Box 3, Entry 227, RG 29, NARA, D.C.

60. Joseph Hill, *"In Re* Indians Not Taxed," November 3, 1920, File 416, Box 3, Entry 227, RG 29, NARA, D.C.

61. Joseph Hill, *"In Re* Indians Not Taxed," November 3, 1920, File 416, Box 3, Entry 227, RG 29, NARA, D.C.

62. Thomas Mule, "Census Coverage Measurement Estimation Report: Summary of Estimates of Coverage for Persons in the United States," May 22, 2012, 15.

63. Joseph A. Hill, *"In Re* Indians Not Taxed," n.d. (1931), in File 400, Box 1, Entry 227, RG 29, NARA, D.C.

64. Congressional Record, April 11, 1940, 4373–74.

65. Joseph A Hill, "Subject: Indians not taxed in Indian population as reported in census of 1920," December 11, 1920, File 416, Box 3, Entry 227, RG 29, NARA, D.C. This number also appears in the table on page 6 of House of Representatives, *Apportionment of Representatives*, 66th Congress, 3rd Session, Report no. 1173, January 8, 1921.

66. Vergil D. Reed to Francis Case, October 30, 1939, Folder "Indians Not Taxed—Dedrick," Box 218, Entry 210, RG 29, NARA, D.C.

67. Director of the Census to Secretary of Commerce, "Request for opinion concerning 'Indians Not Taxed' for purposes of apportionment report to the President," April 19, 1940, Folder "Indians Not Taxed—Dedrick," Box 218, Entry 210, RG 29, NARA, D.C.

68. J. J. O'Hara to William L. Austin, November 28, 1940, Folder "Indians Not Taxed—Dedrick," Box 218, Entry 210, RG 29, NARA, D.C.

69. "Indians Not Taxed and Apportionment 1940," Folder "Indians Not Taxed—Dedrick," Box 218, Entry 210, RG 29, NARA, D.C.

70. U.S. House of Representatives, "Sixteenth Decennial Census of Population: Message from the President of the United States Transmitting a Statement Prepared by the Director . . . ," January 8, 1941, 77th Congress, 1st Session, Document 45.

71. Keyssar, *The Right to Vote*, 203.

72. Anderson, *The American Census*, 11–13. For more on these debates, see Robin Einhorn, *American Taxation, American Slavery* (Chicago: University of Chicago Press, 2006), chapter 5.

73. In interpreting the reconstruction amendments, I am leaning on Keyssar, *The Right to Vote*, 69–83.

74. Bureau of the Census, "Report of the Superintendent," *Ninth Census: The Statistics of the Population of the United States* (Washington, D.C.: Government Printing Office, 1872), xiii.

75. Keyssar, *The Right to Vote*, 225, 337–39, 365–68.

76. U.S. Bureau of the Census, "Report of the Superintendent," xxviii. In the end, in Table XXIV, beginning at page 622, of the census, the bureau printed totals of persons "21 and up" for each state and for counties within states, divided by all males vs. only male citizens. The table does not include totals for "not able to vote" or similar.

77. Ethan Herenstein and Yurij Rudensky, "The Penalty Clause and the Fourteenth Amendment's Consistency on Universal Representation," 2020, page 16, https://ssrn.com/abstract=3684792. The IPUMS database reconstruction shows 125,000 people marked as having their votes denied or abridged. These totals are drawn from the 100 percent sample for 1870 U.S. Census in Ruggles et al., IPUMS USA: Version 11.0 [data set].

78. Justin Behrend, *Reconstructing Democracy: Grassroots Black Politics in the Deep South After the Civil War* (Athens: University of Georgia Press, 2015), 216.

79. Behrend, *Reconstructing Democracy*, 236.

80. Johnson's testimony appears in U.S. House of Representatives, Census Committee, *Apportionment of Representatives H.R. 14498, H.R. 15021, H.R. 15158, and H.R. 15217* (Washington, D.C.: Government Printing Office, 1921), 70.

81. U.S. House of Representatives, *Apportionment of Representatives H.R. 14498, H.R. 15021, H.R. 15158, and H.R. 15217*, 76.

82. 1920: Manhattan, New York County, New York, E.D. 1353, sheet 8B.

83. *The Autobiography of an Ex-Colored Man* (Boston: Sherman, French, 1912); "James Weldon Johnson," NAACP, https://www.naacp.org/naacp-history-james-weldon-johnson/.

84. Census Committee, House of Representatives, U.S., *Apportionment of Representatives H.R. 14498, H.R. 15021, H.R. 15158, and H.R. 15217* (Washington, D.C.: Government Printing Office, 1921), 74.

85. Census Committee, House of Representatives, U.S., *Apportionment of Representatives H.R. 14498, H.R. 15021, H.R. 15158, and H.R. 15217*, 73.

86. Paul B. Johnson in *Congressional Record* 60 (1921): 1625–56 at 1633.

87. Committee on the Census. U.S. House of Representatives, *Hearings Before*

a Subcommittee of the Committee on the Census House of Representatives Sixty-Seventh Congress First Session (Washington, D.C.: Government Printing Office, 1921), 65.

88. *Congressional Record* 61 (1921): 6307–49 at 6316.
89. Figures derived from appendix to Field Division, Bureau of the Census, "Rough Draft: Historical Report of 1940 (16th Decennial) Census Made from the Records That Were Available in 1948 with Emphasis on the Field Aspects" (1948), in Folder "16th Decennial Census 1940—Historical Report of 1940 Census," Box 2, Entry P 26, RG 29, NARA, D.C.
90. Noxubee County, Mississippi, E.D. 52–21.
91. Noxubee County, Mississippi, E.D. 52–21, sheet 1A.
92. "Noxubee County," *The Mississippi Encyclopedia*, https://mississippiencyclopedia.org/entries/noxubee-county/.
93. To see how Black studies can and should be made central to our histories and theories of surveillance, see Simone Browne, *Dark Matters: On the Surveillance of Blackness* (Durham, NC: Duke University Press, 2015).
94. Price, "A Check on Underenumeration in the 1940 Census," 47.
95. Price, "A Check on Underenumeration in the 1940 Census," 47.
96. Appendix to Field Division, Bureau of the Census, "Rough Draft: Historical Report of 1940 (16th Decennial) Census Made from the Records That Were Available in 1948 with Emphasis on the Field Aspects" (1948), in Folder "16th Decennial Census 1940—Historical Report of 1940 Census," Box 2, Entry P 26, RG 29, NARA, D.C.
97. Washington, D.C, E.D. 1–47, sheet 61A.
98. The Leadership Conference Education Fund and Georgetown Center on Poverty and Inequality, "Will You Count? African Americans in the 2020 Census," 2018, http://civilrightsdocs.info/pdf/census/2020/Fact-Sheet-African-Americans-HTC.pdf.
99. Washington, D.C, E.D. 1–47, sheet 61A.

6. UNCLE SAM V. SENATOR TOBEY

1. W.A.M. or W.H.M. Apt. 84 Franklin Park Hotel, DC, to William Lane Austin, March 12, 1940, in unlabeled folder Box 12, Entry 142, RG 29, NARA, D.C.
2. "Rebel on Census Questions Decides He'll Give Answers," *Los Angeles Times*, August 1, 1940.
3. Artesia, Los Angeles County, California, E.D. 19–124, sheet 64A.
4. "1940 Census News," February 12, 1940, in Folder Census, Exhibit G—Pamphlets, Box 111, Hopkins Papers.

5. "1940 Census News," February 12, 1940, in Folder Census, Exhibit G—Pamphlets, Box 111, Hopkins Papers.

6. "By the 1940s, the Digest had surpassed one million copies a month and was the bestselling publication in America—exceeded in sales only by the Bible and spreading its own gospel of 'America the Great,'" according to "About Reader's Digest," https://www.rd.com/about-readers-digest/.

7. George F. Willison, "World's Greatest Quiz Session," *Reader's Digest* (February 1940): 113–16 at 113, 114 in Folder Census, Exhibit H—Reprints, Box 111, Hopkins Papers.

8. Franklin D. Roosevelt, "Second Inaugural Address," January 20, 1937, http://historymatters.gmu.edu/d/5105/.

9. George F. Willison, "World's Greatest Quiz Session," *Reader's Digest* (February 1940): 113–16 at 113, 116 in Folder Census, Exhibit H—Reprints, Box 111, Hopkins Papers.

10. George F. Willison, "World's Greatest Quiz Session," *Reader's Digest* (February 1940): 113–16 at 116 in Folder Census, Exhibit H—Reprints, Box 111, Hopkins Papers.

11. David J. Seipp, *The Right to Privacy in American History* (Cambridge, MA: Harvard University Program on Information Resources Policy, 1981), 44, 49–50; Sarah E. Igo, *Known Citizen: A History of Privacy in Modern America* (Cambridge, MA: Harvard University Press, 2018), 46–47. I have confirmed that news reports agree that at least twenty-five were arrested in New York City or the Northeast for refusing to agree to everything, and there seems to be evidence of arrests in a few other places, including San Francisco.

12. Typescript, "Conversation between Mr. Tobey and Mr. Moran on March 22, 1940," in Folder 10, Box 108, Tobey Papers.

13. "'Snoop Census' Fight Grows. Citizen Battle Is Launched to Resist Prying. Shop Owner Faces Jail Sentence," *Chicago Daily Tribune*, March 6, 1940.

14. "Census Dispute Ended," *The New York Times*, March 10, 1940.

15. George F. Willison, "World's Greatest Quiz Session," *Reader's Digest* (February 1940): 113–16 at 115 in Folder Census, Exhibit H—Reprints, Box 111, Hopkins Papers.

16. Herbert S. Mace, Artesia, CA, to Charles W. Tobey, October 24, 1940, in Folder 25, Box 12, Tobey Papers.

17. "Tobey, Charles William 1880–1953," *Biographical Directory of the United States Congress*, https://bioguide.congress.gov/search/bio/T000289.

18. *Congressional Record* 86 (1940): 619–21 at 620.

19. *Congressional Record* 86 (1940): 887–89 at 887.

20. *Congressional Record* 86 (1940): 1147–51.

21. *Congressional Record* 86 (1940): 1147–51.

22. *Congressional Record* 86 (1940): 1238–39, 1249–51 at 1249.

23. "Roosevelt Backs Census Questions," *The New York Times*, March 6, 1940; Charles W. Hurd, "Senate Group Asks Census Restriction," *The New York Times*, March 13, 1940.

24. *Congressional Record* 86 (1940): 2162–63.

25. *Congressional Record* 86 (1940): 3191–95.

26. See the announcements in Folder 25, Box 12, Tobey Papers.

27. "In my last broadcast only 29% of the stations included in the hook-up carried my talk": Tobey to Dear Friends, March 6, 1940, Folder 10, Box 108, Tobey Papers.

28. *Congressional Record* 86 (1940): 3191–95 at 3191.

29. N. Goshom to Tobey, February 20, 1940, in Folder 12, Box 108, Tobey Papers.

30. Tobey to Dear Sir, March 27, 1940, in Folder 10, Box 108, Tobey Papers.

31. "Census Called Inquisitorial," *Los Angeles Times*, March 18, 1940.

32. Calvert Dedrick to Milton Friedman, March 2, 1940, in Folder "F," Box 209, Entry 210, RG 29, NARA, D.C.

33. "Telephone conversation between Mr. Reed of Census Bureau and Mr. Tobey, Jr.," March 21, 1940, in Folder 10, Box 108, Tobey Papers.

34. Artesia, Los Angeles County, California, E.D. 19–124, sheet 3A.

35. See page 2 of Herbert S. Mace, Artesia, CA, to Charles W. Tobey, October 24, 1940, Folder 25, Box 12, Tobey Papers.

36. Herbert S. Mace, "Letters to the Times: A Conscientious Objector," *Los Angeles Times*, April 25, 1940.

37. Herbert S. Mace, Artesia, CA, to Charles W. Tobey, October 24, 1940, Folder 25, Box 12, Tobey Papers.

38. Details on prison and arrest are from Herbert Mace, "Arrested for Census Objection: Hebert Mace Tells Story," *The Broom* (San Diego, CA), August 19, 1940, included with Herbert S. Mace, Artesia, CA, to Charles W. Tobey, October 24, 1940, Folder 25, Box 12, Tobey Papers.

39. "Rebel on Census Questions Decides He'll Give Answers," *Los Angeles Times*, August 1, 1940.

40. Herbert S. Mace, Artesia, CA, to Charles W. Tobey, October 24, 1940 in Folder 25, Box 12, Tobey Papers.

41. A San Francisco Chamber of Commerce representative, for instance, argued in 1929 about the 1920 census: "Its glaring inaccuracies are now recognized, due to the fact that it was handled entirely in the field by politicians. Political favor governed the appointments almost exclusively and it is now recognized that the counts in many cities were inaccurate." C. B. Dodds, "How Uncle Sam Counts His Family," *San Francisco Business*, February 13, 1929, in Folder Fourteenth Census Forms: 1920, Box 163, Entry 198, RG 29, NARA, D.C.

42. Tobey to Daniel Reed, February 8, 1940, Folder 25, Box 12, Tobey Papers.

43. See page 5 of "The National Census," *The American Forum of the Air* 2, no. 26 (Sunday, March 31, 1940), in Folder Census (General), Box 110, Hopkins Papers.

44. *Congressional Record* 86 (1940): 887–89 at 887.

45. Charles B. Chase to Charles W. Tobey, March 18, 1940, in Folder 9, Box 108, Tobey Papers.

46. W. Alun Roberts to Charles W. Tobey, March 11, 1940, in Folder 13, Box 108, Tobey Papers.

47. Herbert S. Mace, Artesia, CA, to Charles W. Tobey, October 24, 1940, in Folder 25, Box 12, Tobey Papers.

48. Bouk, *How Our Days Became Numbered*, chapter 3.

49. Photo of Candler Building files, Social Security Administration History Archives, https://www.ssa.gov/history/cardfile.html.

50. Arthur J. Altmeyer, "Three Years' Progress Toward Social Security," *Social Security Bulletin* 1, no. 8 (August 1938): 1–7.

51. Dan Bouk, "The National Data Center and the Rise of the Data Double," *Historical Studies in the Natural Sciences* 48, no. 5 (2018): 627–36 at 631–33.

52. Franklin D. Roosevelt, "Proclamation 2385: Sixteenth Decennial Census," February 9, 1940.

53. W. Elliot Brownlee, "The Public Sector," in *Cambridge Economic History of the United States: The Twentieth Century*, edited by Stanley L. Engerman and Robert E. Gallman (Cambridge: Cambridge University Press, 2000): 1013–60 at 1047.

54. See page 5 of "The National Census," *The American Forum of the Air* 2, no. 26 (Sunday, March 31, 1940), in Folder Census (General), Box 110, Hopkins Papers.

55. Page 8 of "Minutes" in Folder Advisory Committee Meeting, June 16, 17, 18, 1939, Box 75, Entry 148, RG 29, NARA, D.C.

56. Gerald Ryan to W. L. Austin, September 7, 1939, Folder Advisory Committee Meeting, September 22 and 23, 1939, Box 75, Entry 148, RG 29, NARA, D.C.

57. See page 17 of "The National Census," *The American Forum of the Air* 2, no. 26 (Sunday, March 31, 1940), in Folder Census (General), Box 110, Hopkins Papers.

58. There are eight letters in all in the group, each dated March 13, 1940, in Folder 9, Box 108, Tobey Papers.

59. "Arrested for Census Objection: Hebert Mace Tells Story," *The Broom* (San Diego, CA), August 19, 1940, included with Herbert S. Mace, Artesia, CA, to Charles W. Tobey, October 24, 1940, Folder 25, Box 12, Tobey Papers.

60. *Congressional Record* 86 (1940): 887–89 at 887.

61. C. C. Harley to Charles W. Tobey, March 1, 1940, in Folder 9, Box 108, Tobey Papers.

62. Nashua, Hillsborough County, New Hampshire, E.D. 6–126, sheet 8A.
63. Mina H. Dearborn to Charles W. Tobey, March 26, 1940, Folder 7, Box 108, Tobey Papers.
64. Bristol, Grafton County, New Hampshire, E.D. 5–11, sheet 5B.
65. Harold J. Stewart to Charles W. Tobey, March 12, 1940, Folder 9, Box 108, Tobey Papers.
66. Portsmouth, Rockingham, New Hampshire, E.D. 8–55, sheet 18B.
67. William H. Brooks to Charles W. Tobey, February 23, 1940, Folder 12, Box 108, Tobey Papers.
68. Portsmouth, Rockingham, New Hampshire, E.D. 8–54, sheet 6A.
69. Turner Catledge, "Census Aides Back Income Questions as Women Protest," *The New York Times*, March 1, 1940.
70. Pages 11 and 13 of "The National Census," *The American Forum of the Air* 2, no. 26 (Sunday, March 31, 1940), in Folder Census (General), Box 110, Hopkins Papers.
71. "For release Friday A.M., April 5, 1940," attached to Roscoe to Hopkins, around April 5, 1940, in Folder Census (General), Box 110, Hopkins Papers.
72. Page 60 of Field Division, Bureau of the Census, "Rough Draft: Historical Report of 1940 (16th Decennial) Census Made from the Records That Were Available in 1948 with Emphasis on the Field Aspects" (1948), in Folder "16th Decennial Census 1940—Historical Report of 1940 Census," Box 2, Entry P 26, RG 29, NARA, D.C.
73. Robert M. Jenkins, *Procedural History of the 1940 Census of Population and Housing* (Madison: University of Wisconsin Press, 1985), 64.
74. Census Bureau, *Sixteenth Census of the United States: 1940. Population* (Washington, D.C.: Government Printing Office, 1943), III:12, https://hdl.handle.net/2027/osu.32435067124230?urlappend=%3Bseq=24.
75. Page 3 of Herbert S. Mace, Artesia, CA, to Charles W. Tobey, October 24, 1940, in Folder 25, Box 12, Tobey Papers.
76. Florence Doud to Charles W. Tobey, probably late February 1940, in Folder 12, Box 108, Tobey Papers.
77. Lakeland, La Porte County, Indiana, E.D. 46–53, sheet 7B.
78. Dedrick to George Elliner, April 8, 1940, in Folder "E," Box 209, Entry 210, RG 29, NARA, D.C.
79. See the handbill attached to Dedrick to George Elliner, April 8, 1940, in Folder "E," Box 209, Entry 210, RG 29, NARA, D.C.
80. Montevideo, Chippewa County, Minnesota, E.D. 12–19, sheet 7A.
81. Montevideo, Chippewa County, Minnesota, E.D. 12–19, sheet 11B.
82. Montevideo, Chippewa County, Minnesota, E.D. 12–19, sheet 9B.

83. Arlington County, Virginia, E.D. 7–19, sheet 13B.
84. Weldon F. Heald (Altadena), "Letters to the Times: Self-Importance," *Los Angeles Times*, May 8, 1940.

7. THE INVENTORY AND THE ARSENAL

1. Iwao M. Moriyama, "Vital Statistics During the War," *Yale Journal of Biology and Medicine* 19, no. 4 (1947): 453–460 at 453. I found this quote first in Christopher Martin and U.S. Census Bureau, "Iwao Milton Moriyama: Improving Life with the U.S. Census," https://www.census.gov/history/www/census _then_now/notable_alumni/census_employees.html.
2. Martin and U.S. Census Bureau, "Iwao Milton Moriyama"; "Obituaries," *The Washington Post*, June 13, 2006, https://www.washingtonpost.com/archive /local/2006/06/13/obituaries/18ea4b3b-2c9e-4bd8–9799–0e9a4b7d7475.
3. Toshiko Iizuka to Mr. and Mrs. Ross, September 10, 2015, reprinted in "Hisashi Moriyama," *Perennial Parrot* 28, no. 3 (December 2015), 8, http:// www.perennialparrot.com/newsletter/newsletter.htm.
4. W. L. Austin to Ross A. Collins, February 15, 1937; W. L. Austin to Mr. Noble, "Subject: Delay in completing the Federal building for use of the 1940 Census and its effect on the 1940 Census program," February 15, 1940; and W. L. Austin to Kerlin, "MEMORANDUM Subject: New building located at 2nd and 3rd, D and Virginia Avenue, S.W., for the 1940 Census," June 20, 1939; all in Folder 12A Census Building, Box 2, Entry 142, RG 29, NARA, D.C.
5. W. L. Austin to Kerlin, "Subject: Availability of Space for the 1940 Census in the Woodward and Lothrop Warehouse Building," June 20, 1939, in Folder 16 Chief Clerk, Census, Box 3, Entry 142, RG 29, NARA, D.C.
6. See the caption on reverse of a photo of two geographers: "This country is divided into approximately 147,000 enumeration districts for census-taking purposes. This is to insure against over-lapping activities of census takers, or enumerators, and also to avoid missing any territory. Census enumerators are provided with maps of their districts." In Photographic collection, General Photographs—Census 1940, Franklin D. Roosevelt Library, Hyde Park, New York.
7. Page 2 of Field Division, Bureau of the Census, "Rough Draft: Historical Report of 1940 (16th Decennial) Census Made from the Records That Were Available in 1948 with Emphasis on the Field Aspects" (1948), in Folder "16th Decennial Census 1940—Historical Report of 1940 Census," Box 2, Entry P 26, RG 29, NARA, D.C.

8. On reverse of photo in Folder "Pictures Taken in Indiana Trial Census August 1939," Box 234, Entry 215, RG 29, NARA, D.C.

9. "Number of Employees in Buildings Occupied by Census Bureau," August 1, 1940, in Folder 4 Appointment Division, Box 1, Entry 142, RG 29, NARA, D.C.

10. From Folder "Pictures Taken in Indiana Trial Census August 1939," Box 234, Entry 215, RG 29, NARA, D.C.

11. W. L. Austin to Mr. Noble, "Subject: Delay in completing the Federal building for use of the 1940 Census and its effect on the 1940 Census program," February 15, 1940, in Folder 12A Census Building, Box 2, Entry 142, RG 29, NARA, D.C.

12. Census Bureau, "For release Thursday A.M., March 28, 1940," in Folder 12A Census Building, Box 2, Entry 142, RG 29, NARA, D.C.

13. Pages 10–11 of Bureau of the Census, "Handbook for Employees" (February 1940), Volume 4, Entry 238, RG 29, NARA, D.C.

14. Martin Campbell-Kelly and William Aspray, *Computer: A History of the Information Machine* (New York: Basic Books, 1997), 20–26.

15. Census Bureau, "UNIVAC I," *Census Bureau History*, https://www.census.gov/history/www/innovations/technology/univac_i.html.

16. From Folder "Pictures Taken in Indiana Trial Census August 1939," Box 234, Entry 215, RG 29, NARA, D.C.

17. Steven Ruggles and Diana L. Magnuson, "Census Technology, Politics, and Institutional Change, 1790–2020," *Journal of American History* 107, no. 1 (2020): 19–51.

18. Mary L. Gray and Siddarth Suri, *Ghost Work: How to Stop Silicon Valley from Building a New Global Underclass* (New York: Houghton Mifflin Harcourt, 2019).

19. From Folder "Pictures Taken in Indiana Trial Census August 1939," Box 234, Entry 215, RG 29, NARA, D.C.

20. On typewriters and computers as people, see Margery W. Davies, *Woman's Place Is at the Typewriter: Office Work and Office Workers, 1870–1930* (Philadelphia: Temple University Press, 1982); Jennifer S. Light, "When Computers Were Women," *Technology and Culture* 40, no. 3 (1999): 455–83; David Alan Grier, *When Computers Were Human* (Princeton, NJ: Princeton University Press, 2013).

21. From Folder "Pictures Taken in Indiana Trial Census August 1939," Box 234, Entry 215, RG 29, NARA, D.C.

22. "Number of Employees in Buildings Occupied by Census Bureau," August 1, 1940, Folder 4 Appointment Division, Box 1, Entry 142, RG 29, NARA, D.C.

23. "Memorandum to Director Austin," January 7, 1941, in Folder 77, Box 10, Entry 142, RG 29, NARA, D.C.

24. "Census (Men's) Bowling League Final Standing," *Census News*, June 3, 1946, shared with me in an April 2, 2021, email by Christopher Martin, historian in the Census Bureau Public Information Office.

25. Eckler played short field. "'Twas Listed as a Baseball Game," *Suitland Sun* 1, no. 3 (October 1942), shared with me in an April 2, 2021, email by Christopher Martin, historian in the Census Bureau Public Information Office.

26. "Memorandum to Director Austin," January 7, 1941, in Folder 77, Box 10, Entry 142, RG 29, NARA, D.C.

27. "General Federal Office Building," May 28, 1940, in Folder 16A Chief Clerk, Census Building, Box 3, Entry 142, RG 29, NARA, D.C.

28. "Democracy Begins at Home," in Folder Circulars of Unions in the Bureau of the Census, Box 11, Entry 142, RG 29, NARA, D.C.

29. J. D. Schnepf, "Black Women and the Clerical Work of the 1940 Census Tabulation," in *Humans at Work in the Digital Age: Forms of Digital Textual Labor*, edited by Shawna Ross and Andrew Pilsch (New York: Routledge, 2020), 17–31 at 20.

30. Jenkins, *Procedural History of the 1940 Census*, 36.

31. Page 93 of scrapbook "P113: Count Slip-Population," in Volume 4, Entry 238, RG 29, NARA, D.C.

32. Christine Sadler, "Our Town in Pictures," *The Washington Post*, May 12, 1940, at VII: 1, 3.

33. Page 11 of Bureau of the Census's "Handbook for Employees" (February 1940), Volume 4, Entry 238, RG 29, NARA, D.C.

34. On the history of confidentiality pledges and practices, see Margo J. Anderson and William Seltzer, "Challenges to the Confidentiality of U.S. Federal Statistics, 1910–1965," *Journal of Official Statistics* 23, no. 1 (2007): 1–34.

35. Edward J. Noble to W. L. Austin, September 1, 1939; W. L. Austin to Edward J. Noble, September 5, 1939; and M. Kerlin to W. L. Austin, September 11, 1939, all in Folder 59B, Box 9, Entry 142, RG 29, NARA, D.C.

36. See documents attached to Harold D. Smith to FDR, "Memorandum for the President," February 27, 1940, Folder 1939–40, Census Bureau, Department of Commerce, Franklin D. Roosevelt, Papers as President, Official File, Franklin D. Roosevelt Library, Hyde Park, New York.

37. Paraphrased in Harold D. Smith to FDR, "Memorandum for the President," February 27, 1940, Folder 1939–40, Census Bureau, Department of Commerce, Franklin D. Roosevelt, Papers as President, Official File, Franklin D. Roosevelt Library, Hyde Park, New York.

38. Harold D. Smith to FDR, "Memorandum for the President," February 27, 1940, Folder 1939–40, Census Bureau, Department of Commerce, Franklin

D. Roosevelt, Papers as President, Official File, Franklin D. Roosevelt Library, Hyde Park, New York.

39. See documents attached to Harold D. Smith to FDR, "Memorandum for the President," February 27, 1940, Folder 1939–40, Census Bureau, Department of Commerce, Franklin D. Roosevelt, Papers as President, Official File, Franklin D. Roosevelt Library, Hyde Park, New York.

40. "Conversation between office of Senator Charles W. Tobey and Mr. Holtsauf of the F.B.I.—April 6, 1940," in Folder 10, Box 108, Tobey Papers.

41. "Tobey Tells Aim to Make Census into Police List," *Chicago Daily Tribune* April 8, 1940.

42. Franklin D. Roosevelt, "Fireside Chat 15: On National Defense" May 26, 1940, https://millercenter.org/the-presidency/presidential-speeches/may-26-1940-fireside-chat-15-national-defense.

43. Franklin D. Roosevelt, "Fireside Chat 16: On the 'Arsenal of Democracy'" December 29, 1940, https://millercenter.org/the-presidency/presidential-speeches/december-29-1940-fireside-chat-16-arsenal-democracy.

44. Susan J. Pearson, "'Age Ought to Be a Fact': The Campaign Against Child Labor and the Rise of the Birth Certificate," *Journal of American History* 101, no. 4 (2015): 1144–65. See also Pearson, *The Birth Certificate*.

45. Herbert M. Bratter, "Can You Prove You Were Born?" *The Saturday Evening Post*, May 17, 1952, 170. Also: https://www.census.gov/history/www/genealogy/decennial_census_records/soundex_1.html.

46. Moriyama, "Vital Statistics During the War," 454.

47. Census Bureau, "For Release Sunday A.M. July 28, 1940," in Folder 79 War, Box 10, Entry 142, RG 29, NARA, D.C.

48. W. L. Austin to Stacy May, August 15, 1940, in Folder 79 War, Box 10, Entry 142, RG 29, NARA, D.C.

49. Vergil Reed to Dr. Isador Lubin, October 31, 1940, in Folder 79 War, Box 10, Entry 142, RG 29, NARA, D.C.

50. On alien registration, see Jonathan Weinberg, "Proving Identity," *Pepperdine Law Review* 44, no. 3 (April 2017): 731–98 at 769–71.

51. "Memorandum for the Director," September 21, 1940, in Folder 45 Monthly Reports, Box 6, Entry 142, RG 29, NARA, D.C.

52. The numbers were transmitted from the bureau to the secretary of commerce and then on to the president: Jesse Jones to Franklin D. Roosevelt, November 29, 1940, in Folder "Speeches, Articles, and Papers," Box 4, Entry 229, RG 29, NARA, D.C.

53. Anderson and Seltzer, "Challenges to the Confidentiality of U.S. Federal Statistics, 1910–1965," 18–19.

54. "Census Advisory Committee Meeting January 9 and 10, 1942," in Folder

Census Advisory Committee of the American Statistical Association January 9 and 10, 1942, Box 76, Entry 148, RG 29, NARA, D.C.

55. "Census Advisory Committee Meeting January 9 and 10, 1942," in Folder Census Advisory Committee of the American Statistical Association January 9 and 10, 1942, Box 76, Entry 148, RG 29, NARA, D.C.; on three thousand to six thousand people in a tract see Howard Whipple Green and Leon E. Truesdell, "Census Tracts in American Cities" (1937), 2.

56. Capt used a racial slur applied to Japanese and Japanese Americans in the original, which I substituted with "Japanese" in brackets. "Census Advisory Committee Meeting January 9 and 10, 1942," in Folder Census Advisory Committee of the American Statistical Association, January 9 and 10, 1942, Box 76, Entry 148, RG 29, NARA, D.C.

57. "Census Advisory Committee Meeting January 9 and 10, 1942," in Folder Census Advisory Committee of the American Statistical Association, January 9 and 10, 1942, Box 76, Entry 148, RG 29, NARA, D.C.

58. "Census Advisory Committee Meeting January 9 and 10, 1942," in Folder Census Advisory Committee of the American Statistical Association, January 9 and 10, 1942, Box 76, Entry 148, RG 29, NARA, D.C.

59. Untitled detailed minutes, Folder Census Advisory Committee Meeting September 12 and 13, 1941, Box 76, Entry 148, and "Census Advisory Committee Meeting, January 9 and 10, 1942" in Folder Census Advisory Committee of the American Statistical Association, January 9 and 10, 1942, Box 76, Entry 148, RG 29, NARA, D.C.

60. "It is a fact that when an attempt was made to curtail the tabulations of the 16th Decennial Census in the fall of 1941 because of the war situation, the Bureau received such a flood of protests from agencies such as Office of Production Management, Office of Price Administration, National Housing Agency, War Department, Federal Security Agency, Labor Department and others that the full tabulation and publication program was carried out and deficiency appropriations were provided by Congress for this purpose." Thomas W. S. Davis to Roy V. Peel, "Role of Census Bureau in Mobilization Planning," July 14, 1950, in Folder 5 "Data on MOBILIZATION, 1950," Box 4, Entry A1–389-E, RG 29, NARA, D.C.

61. "Kent, Fred I., New York, N.Y.," March 23, 1942, in Folder 1941–45 Census Bureau, Box 6, OF 3b-3c Department of Commerce, Franklin D. Roosevelt, Papers as President, Official File, Franklin D. Roosevelt Library, Hyde Park, New York.

62. "Exhibit B: Gratuitous Work Done by Bureau of the Census for War or Other Agencies Charged with Execution of Some Phase of War Program December 1941 through November 1942," December 4, 1942, in Folder Work Done by

Census for War & Other Agencies (Reimbursable & Gratuitous—Dec. 1941 to Nov. 1942), Box 4, Entry P144, RG 29, NARA, D.C.

63. "Exhibit A: Work Done on Reimbursable Basis by Bureau of the Census for War or Other Agencies with Execution of Some Phase of War Program December 1941 through November 1942," December 4, 1942, in Folder Work Done By Census for War & Other Agencies (Reimbursable & Gratuitous— Dec. 1941 to Nov. 1942), Box 4, Entry P144, RG 29, NARA, D.C.

64. San Francisco, San Francisco County, California, E.D. 38–203, sheet 1A.

65. In the following narrative, I have relied for context on Michi Weglyn, *Years of Infamy: The Untold Story of America's Concentration Camps* (New York: William Morrow, 1976); and Brian Masaru Hayashi, *Democratizing the Enemy: The Japanese American Internment* (Princeton, NJ: Princeton University Press, 2004).

66. Washington, D.C., E.D. 1–101, sheet 7B.

67. Saburo also received an "alien identification number." These numbers are noted in Federal Bureau of Investigation, "Saburo Moriyama; Reki Moriyama," File No. 100–15947, May 13, 1943, in Case File 146–13–2–16–288, Entry A1-COR 146–13, RG 60, NARA, College Park, MD. My thanks to David Castillo for sharing these files with me.

68. U.S. Census Bureau, "POPULATION: Japanese Population in Selected Counties and Cities of the United States by Sex and Nativity or Citizenship: 1940," Series P-9, no. 5, December 19, 1941.

69. General DeWitt, *Final Report, Japanese Evacuation from the West Coast 1942* (Washington, D.C.: Government Printing Office, 1943), 78.

70. Commission on Wartime Relocation and Internment of Civilians, *Personal Justice Denied: Report of the Commission on Wartime Relocation and Internment of Civilians* (Washington, D.C.: Government Printing Office, 1982), 8.

71. On the costs and harms caused by the relocation and internment, I rely on the findings of the Commission on Wartime Relocation and Internment of Civilians in *Personal Justice Denied*.

72. Dedrick to Provost Marshal General, June 9, 1942; Arthur L. Lerch to J. C. Capt, February 24, 1942; Arthur L. Lerch to J. C. Capt, February 28, 1942; Calvert L. Dedrick to Major General Allen Gullion, June 9, 1942; Calvert L. Dedrick to Major General Allen Gullion, July 7, 1942, all in Official Personnel Folder for Calvert Lampert Dedrick, NARA-National Personnel Records Center Annex, Valmeyer, IL. My thanks to Margo Anderson, who shared with me a copy of this folder.

73. Commission on Wartime Relocation and Internment of Civilians, *Personal Justice Denied*, 100, 103, 107.

74. Federal Bureau of Investigation, "Saburo Moriyama; Reki Moriyama," File No. 100–15947, May 13, 1943, in Case File 146–13–2–16–288, Entry A1-COR 146–13, RG 60, NARA, College Park, MD.

75. Konrad Linke, "Tanforan (Detention Facility)," *Densho Encyclopedia*, https://encyclopedia.densho.org/Tanforan_%28detention_facility%29/.

76. Weglyn, *Years of Infamy*, 80, 226.

77. On the long history of travel permits and racialized surveillance in the United States, see Browne, *Dark Matters*, chapter 2.

78. Commission on Wartime Relocation and Internment of Civilians, *Personal Justice Denied*, 258.

79. Commission on Wartime Relocation and Internment of Civilians, *Personal Justice Denied*, 3.

80. "Japanese Residing in the Metropolitan Area of Washington, D.C., April 1, 1940," in FDR Library, Morgenthau Diary, Book 655, August 10–12, 1943, Microfilm reel 190, frame 197. A copy of this document was shared with me by Margo Anderson and is cited in William Seltzer and Margo Anderson, "Census Confidentiality Under the Second War Powers Act (1942–1947)," paper prepared for presentation at the session on "Confidentiality, Privacy, and Ethical Issues in Demographic Data," Population Association of America Annual Meeting, March 29–31, 2007, New York, NY.

81. Raymond Okamura, for instance, early on began the investigations leading to discoveries of Census Bureau contributions to the evacuation and incarceration of Japanese Americans. For this story and more, see Margo Anderson, "The Census and the Japanese 'Internment': Apology and Policy in Statistical Practice," *Social Research* 87, no. 4 (2020): 789–812.

82. Seltzer and Anderson, "Census Confidentiality Under the Second War Powers Act (1942–1947)."

83. War Agency Liquidation Unit, *People in Motion: The Postwar Adjustment of the Evacuated Japanese Americans* (Washington, D.C.: Government Printing Office, 1947), 165.

84. *Ex Parte Endo*, 323 U.S. 283 decided December 18, 1944. Mitsuye Endo was one such person dismissed from a California state job, as a typist in the California Department of Motor Vehicles. She was fired along with hundreds of others and joined a suit to challenge the dismissals. Then she was removed from Sacramento to the Sacramento Assembly Center, then to the Tule Lake camp in California, and eventually to the Central Utah Relocation Center in Topaz, Utah. She became the plaintiff in *Ex Parte Endo*, a case suing for her release that made it to the Supreme Court and decided that the government had no right to keep loyal citizens in the camps. Brian Nilya, "Mitsuye Endo,"

Densho Encyclopedia, https://encyclopedia.densho.org/Mitsuye_Endo/; Stephanie Buck, "Overlooked No More: Mitsuye Endo, a Name Linked to Justice for Japanese-Americans," *The New York Times*, October 9, 2019.

85. Commission on Wartime Relocation and Internment of Civilians, *Personal Justice Denied*, 236, 240.

86. Page 5 of William Seltzer and Margo Anderson, "Census Confidentiality Under the Second War Powers Act (1942–1947)," paper prepared for presentation at the session on "Confidentiality, Privacy, and Ethical Issues in Demographic Data," Population Association of America Annual Meeting, March 29–31, 2007, New York, NY.

87. Prewitt quoted on page 16 of Gatewood, *A Monograph on Confidentiality and Privacy in the U.S. Census.*

88. "Associated with Dr. Greville in the preparation of this volume was Miss Elbertie Foudray, Actuarial Statistician, whose long experience in demographic analysis and in the preparation of previous United States life tables has been of the greatest value. Numerous members of the clerical and professional staff of the Bureau of the Census and, more particularly, its Vital Statistics Division, made important contributions. Dr. Iwao M. Moriyama, Chief of the Planning and Analysis Section of the Division, and Mr. Morris B. Ullman, Statistician in the Office of the Statistical Assistant to the Director, played an important part in shaping many decisions as to the arrangement of the tables and the manner of presenting the text material." Thomas N. E. Greville, *United States Life Tables and Actuarial Tables 1939–1941* (Washington, D.C.: Government Printing Office, 1946), ii.

8. THE DATA'S DEPTHS

1. "For release Friday A.M., April 5, 1940," attached to Roscoe to Hopkins, around April 5, 1940. In Folder Census (General), Box 110, Hopkins Papers.

2. Census Bureau, *Sixteenth Census of the United States: 1940 Population*, Vol. I, 6, table 2.

3. "Letter from the Secretary of State," in *Census for 1820* (Washington, D.C.: Gales and Seaton, 1821), 7–8.

4. J.D.B. DeBow, *Seventh Census of the United States: 1850* (Washington, D.C.: Robert Armstrong, 1853), vi. For a fuller description see Anderson, *The American Census*, 290n16.

5. For more context see Kevin Ackermann and Taylor Savell, "Count and Increase" USApportionment.org, https://usapportionment.org/countandincrease.html.

6. Walter F. Willcox, "Area, Population, Birthplace, Migration and Conjugal

Condition," *Publications of the American Economic Association*, no. 2 (1899): 8–37 at 10–11.

7. Minutes of Census Advisory Committee, March 29–30, 1940, in Folder Advisory Committee Meeting March 29 and 30, 1940, Box 76, Entry 148, RG 29, NARA, D.C.

8. Bureau of the Census, *Report of the Seventeenth Decennial Census of the United States. Census of Population: 1950* (Washington, D.C.: Government Printing Office, 1952) I: xii–xiii.

9. Timnit Gebru, Jamie Morgenstern, Briana Vecchione, Jennifer Wortman Vaughan, Hanna Wallach, Hal Daumé III, and Kate Crawford, "Datasheets for Datasets," March 19, 2020, arXiv:1803.09010v7 [cs.DB].

10. Joanna Radin, "'Digital Natives': How Medical and Indigenous Histories Matter for Big Data," *Osiris* (2017): 43–64. As I finish this book, I am encouraged by exciting new projects that are beginning to produce more of this kind of work. A team from Google Research (Emily Denton, Alex Hanna, Andrew Smart, and Hilary Nicole) collaborating with University of California, San Diego, researcher Razvan Amironesei is pursuing a project to investigate the "genealogies" of many different data sets used in machine learning. At Johns Hopkins University, a team of digital humanists (including Kim Gallon, Jeremy Greene, Jessica Marie Johnson, and Alexandré White) in the Black Beyond Data project work to uncover the racist histories of data sets while also imagining new and better ways to make meaningful data about Black lives.

11. A useful text for those who want a more thorough introduction to doing data (science) differently is D'Ignazio and Klein, *Data Feminism*.

12. Jesse Jones to Franklin D. Roosevelt, November 29, 1940, in Folder "Speeches, Articles, and Papers," Box 4, Entry 229, RG 29, NARA, D.C.

13. For the history of apportionment and the methods used, see Michel L. Balinski and H. Peyton Young, *Fair Representation: Meeting the Ideal of One Man, One Vote* (Washington, D.C.: Brookings Institution Press, 2001).

14. See the exchange of letters, including a map to a Berkshires cabin, in File 8.51, Box 2, Entry 228, RG 29, NARA, D.C.

15. C. L. Dedrick to E. V. Huntington, February 24, 1941, in File 1.2, Box 1, Entry 228, RG 29, NARA, D.C.

16. Dan Bouk, *House Arrest: How an Automated Algorithm Constrained Congress for a Century* (New York: Data and Society, 2021), https://datasociety.net/library /house-arrest/.

17. J. A. O'Leary, "Senate Subcommittee Gets Petition Urging Vote for District," *Washington Evening Star*, May 6, 1941, Chronicling America: Historic American Newspapers, Library of Congress, https://chroniclingamerica.loc.gov/lccn /sn83045462/1941–05–06/ed-1/seq-8/.

18. *Automotive News* (Detroit, Michigan), March 24, 1941, Chronicling America: Historic American Newspapers, Library of Congress, https://chroniclingamerica .loc.gov/lccn/77618337/1941–03–24/ed-1/seq-5/.

19. Lizabeth Cohen, *A Consumers' Republic: The Politics of Mass Consumption in Postwar America* (New York: Vintage, 2004).

20. Morgan M. Beatty, "Average American, Citizen of Nation's Median Town, Shows Way of Life" *Washington Evening Star*, February 16, 1941, Chronicling America: Historic American Newspapers, Library of Congress, https:// chroniclingamerica.loc.gov/lccn/sn83045462/1941–02–16/ed-1/seq-42/.

21. For more context see Igo, *The Averaged American* and *Known Citizen*.

22. Beatty, "Average American, Citizen of Nation's Median Town, Shows Way of Life."

23. Stuart Chase, *What the New Census Means* (New York: Public Affairs Committee, 1941), 28–29.

24. Chase, *What the New Census Means*, 1.

25. Chase, *What the New Census Means*, 2.

26. "Boom in Babies: In 1941 They Are Fighting a Birth Rate War with Hitler," *Life*, December 1, 1941, 73–74.

27. Dan Bouk, "Generation Crisis: How Population Research Defined the Baby Boomers," *Modern American History* 1, no. 3 (2018): 321–42.

28. Some tremendous scholars have investigated and made insightful readings of different kinds of government-produced data. On British colonial data, for instance, there is Arjun Appadurai, "Number in the Colonial Imagination," in *Orientalism and the Postcolonial Predicament: Perspectives on South Asia*, edited by Carol A. Breckenridge and Peter van der Veer (Philadelphia: University of Pennsylvania Press, 1993). On Nigeria's colonial and postcolonial censuses, see S. A. Aluko, "How Many Nigerians? An Analysis of Nigeria's Census Problems, 1901–63," *Journal of Modern African Studies* 3, no. 3 (1965): 371–92. On the Nazi census and registration systems, see Götz Aly and Karl Heinz Roth, *The Nazi Census: Identification and Control in the Third Reich* (Philadelphia: Temple University Press, 2004). Geoffrey C. Bowker and Susan Leigh Star discuss the South African apartheid government's data infrastructure and its implications in chapter 6 of *Sorting Things Out: Classification and Its Consequences* (Cambridge, MA: MIT Press, 1999). Martha Hodes inspired my analysis in this book with her look at the U.S. census through a colonial and postcolonial lens in "Fractions and Fictions in the United States Census of 1890," in *Haunted by Empire*, edited by Ann Laura Stoler (Durham, NC: Duke University Press, 2006), 240–70. On the suppressed Soviet census of 1937, see Catherine Merridale, "The 1937 Census and the Limits of Stalinist Rule," *Historical Journal* 39, no. 1 (1996): 225–40. Kate Brown demonstrates

the parallel and interconnected regimes of secrecy in the United States and U.S.S.R. in *Plutopia: Nuclear Families, Atomic Cities, and the Great Soviet and American Plutonium Disasters* (New York: Oxford University Press, 2013). On the 1953 Chinese census, see Leo A. Orleans, "The 1953 Chinese Census in Perspective," *Journal of Asian Studies* 16, no. 4 (1957): 565–73. On China and its distinct approach to socialist data, see Ghosh, *Making It Count*. One could also study data generated by monarchical governments and arrive at work like William Deringer, *Calculated Values: Finance, Politics, and the Quantitative Age* (Cambridge, MA: Harvard University Press, 2018); or study data from slavery-centered systems through works like Browne, *Dark Matters*, Rosenthal, *Accounting for Slavery*, and Jessica Marie Johnson, "Markup Bodies: Black [Life] Studies and Slavery [Death] Studies at the Digital Crossroads," *Social Text* 36, no. 4 (2018): 57–79. Andrew Whitby offers a broad synthetic survey of census history in *The Sum of the People: How the Census Has Shaped Nations, From the Ancient World to the Modern Age* (New York: Basic Books, 2020).

29. See the untitled manuscript in Folder "C-3 Census Records: 1930," Box 231, Entry 215, RG 29, NARA, D.C.

30. Joel Weintraub, "Why the 72 Year Rule for U.S. Census Privacy?," *Roots-Key* (Summer 2008): 16–17, https://stevemorse.org/census/rule72.html.

31. Census Bureau, "The '72-Year Rule,'" *Census Bureau History*, https://www.census .gov/history/www/genealogy/decennial_census_records/the_72_year_rule_1 .html.

32. Page 1 of untitled manuscript in Folder "C-3 Census Records: 1930," Box 231, Entry 215, RG 29, NARA, D.C.

EPILOGUE

1. "Tornado Hits Southern Idaho," clipped in Folder "Indians Not Taxed— Dedrick," Box 218, Entry 210, RG 29, NARA, D.C. The enumerator is identified as Charles Lang and the person to be counted as Alva Hine.

2. Census Bureau, "2010 Fast Facts," Census Bureau History, https://www.census .gov/history/www/through_the_decades/fast_facts/2010_fast_facts.html; Community Connect Labs, "Field Job: Census Takers/Enumerators," Census Outreach (2020), https://www.censusoutreach.org/census-enumerators.

3. Page 4 of Robert B. Pearl to Henry S. Shryock, Jr., "Occupation and Industry Returns Under a Self-enumeration Procedure with Selective Follow Up," January 20, 1959, in Folder 3 "Self-Enumeration, 1960 Census Fldr. 1 of 4," Box 1, Entry A1–389-E, RG 29, NARA, D.C.

4. Harold Nisselson and Robert F. Drury to Conrad Taeuber, "Proposal for Use

of Self-Enumeration in the 1960 Censuses of Population and Housing," May 1, 1958, in Folder 3 "Self-Enumeration, 1960 Census Fldr. 1 of 4," Box 1, Entry A1–389-E, RG 29, NARA, D.C.

5. This narrative is clearly and cogently presented in Nobles, *Shades of Citizenship*.

6. Anderson, *American Census*, chapters 10–11.

7. Anderson, *American Census*, chapter 9.

8. Keeanga-Yamahtta Taylor, *Race for Profit: How Banks and the Real Estate Industry Undermined Black Homeownership* (Chapel Hill: University of North Carolina Press, 2019), 244–48.

9. Anderson and Fienberg, *Who Counts?: The Politics of Census-Taking in Contemporary America* (New York: Russell Sage Foundation, 1999), 40.

10. "As it turned out, the inability of the Census Bureau to produce sufficiently accurate net undercount estimates on a timely basis led to the abandonment of statistical adjustment for redistricting in 2000. Statistical methods were limited in 2010 to evaluating census completeness." Connie Citro, "The 2020 Census: Counting Under Adversity," *Issues in Science and Technology*, April 6, 2020), https://issues.org/the-2020-census-counting-under-adversity/.

11. A copy of the 1950 form is available here: https://www.census.gov/history /www/through_the_decades/questionnaires/1950_1.html.

12. Bureau of the Census, *1960 Censuses of Population and Housing: Procedural History* (Washington, D.C.: Government Printing Office, 1966), 9.

13. Bureau of the Census, *American Community Survey Design and Methodology* (Washington, D.C.: Department of Commerce, 2014), Version 2.0, January 30, 2014.

14. Bureau of the Census, *American Community Survey Design and Methodology*, 61.

15. Steven Ruggles and Diana Magnuson, "'It's None of Their Damn Business': Privacy and Disclosure Control in the U.S. Census, 1790–2020," a keynote delivered at University of Wisconsin Center for Demography and Ecology, 2020 Census Symposium, March 24, 2020.

16. Didier, *America by the Numbers*.

17. I rely here on the version of the facts reported in the syllabus and the U.S. Supreme Court decision on *Department of Commerce et al. v. New York et al.*, 588 U.S. 18–966 (June 27, 2019).

18. *Department of Commerce et al. v. New York et al.*, 588 U.S. 18–966 (June 27, 2019), 28.

19. Trump tweet quoted by Hansi Lo Wang, Twitter, July 2, 2019, https://twitter .com/hansilowang/status/1146436238406234115.

20. Jesse Ball, *Census* (New York: Ecco, 2018). Another excellent novel to read as a way to reimagine the census and other forms of state counting in a radical light is Helen Phillips, *The Beautiful Bureaucrat* (New York: Picador, 2015).

21. Meghan Maury and the National LGBTQ Task Force, "LBGTQ Census Advocacy, 1990–2017," https://www.thetaskforce.org/wp-content/uploads/2017/05/LGBTQ-Census-Advocacy.pdf.

22. u/hermit_dragon, "Just little queer 2020 US census things," reddit.com, March 30, 2020, https://www.reddit.com/r/just_post/comments/fs5mvp/just_little_queer_2020_us_census_things/.

23. My thanks to my colleague Will Partin, who shared a screenshot of this post from May 1, 2020, by Mx. Anunnaki Ray Marquez. See Mx. Anunnaki Ray Marquez, "The United States 2020 Census Didn't Include My Sex!," April 30, 2020, https://anunnakiray.com/2020/04/30/the-united-states-2020-census-didnt-include-my-sex/.

24. On the Hispanic question, see Mora, *Making Hispanics*, chapter 1.

25. G. Cristina Mora and Michael Rodríguez-Muñiz make a particularly cogent argument that analyses of census data about race and projections of national racial futures must "acknowledge the central role of politics" in constituting race data. G. Cristina Mora and Michael Rodriguez-Muniz, "Latinos, Race, and the American Future: A Response to Richard Alba's 'The Likely Persistence of a White Majority,'" *New Labor Forum* 26, no. 2 (2017): 40–46 at 46.

26. Hansi Lo Wang, "No Middle Eastern or North African Category on 2020 Census, Bureau Says," January 29, 2018, https://www.npr.org/2018/01/29/581541111/no-middle-eastern-or-north-african-category-on-2020-census-bureau-says.

27. Naomi LaChance, @lachancenaomi, Twitter, April 27, 2020; wear mask, punch nazis, @sporksticks, April 27, 2020.

28. Lena, @banalplay, Twitter, April 27, 2020.

29. Gavriel Nachshon, @gavrielnachshon, Twitter, March 29, 2020.

30. Becky With The Bad Hair, @r_johnson83, Twitter, March 28, 2020.

31. S, @Sonja_Drimmer, April 1, 2020.

32. Ron Kampeas, "A Census Question Poses a Dilemma for American Jews—Are You White, and If So, What Are Your 'Origins'?" *Jewish Telegraphic Agency*, April 8, 2020.

33. Kyle Sammin, "The 2020 Census Wants You to Identify with Some Race. So Pick 'American,'" *The Federalist*, March 25, 2020, https://thefederalist.com/2020/03/25/the-2020-census-wants-you-to-identify-with-some-race-so-pick-american/.

34. Allyson, @ReachTeachDream, April 3, 2020.

35. On DNA tests and questions of African Americans' origins, see Nelson, *Social Life of DNA*.

36. Tressie McMillan Cottom, @tressiemcphd, March 28, 2020.

37. "Census 2020 'Write-In Taiwanese' Campaign," https://tacl.org/census-2020/.

38. Graphic attached to tweets by Carina del Valle Schorske, @FluentMundo, June 17, 2020.

39. Nobles, *Shades of Citizenship*, 138–45.

40. For more detail, see Dan Bouk and danah boyd, "Democracy's Data Infrastructure: The Technopolitics of the U.S. Census," Knight First Amendment Institute at Columbia University, March 18, 2021, https://knightcolumbia.org/content/democracys-data-infrastructure.

41. For an introductory primer on differential privacy and its application to protect confidentiality in the U.S. census, see danah boyd, *Balancing Data Utility and Confidentiality in the 2020 US Census* (New York: Data and Society, 2020), updated May 8, 2020, https://datasociety.net/library/balancing-data-utility-and-confidentiality-in-the-2020-us-census/.

42. Christine Sadler, "Our Town in Pictures," *The Washington Post*, May 12, 1940, loose in Box 234, Entry 215, RG 29, NARA, D.C.

43. "One of the most significant advancements for FamilySearch in recent years was put into place in 2005, when 15 high-speed scanners were developed to convert images previously contained on microfilm into digital images. These scanners [were] converting 2.5 million rolls of microfilm from the Church's Granite Mountain Records Vault into tens of millions of ready-to-index digital images." *Introduction to Family History Student Manual* (Salt Lake City, UT: Church of Jesus Christ of Latter-day Saints, 2012), 53.

44. National Archives and Records Administration, "Records Schedules; Available and Request for Comments," *Federal Register*, November, 30, 2010, 75 FR 74089, https://www.federalregister.gov/documents/2010/11/30/2010–30216/records-schedules-availability-and-request-for-comments#p-19.

45. More than two-thirds of all that money supports Medicare and Medicaid. See the "Counting for Dollars" series of reports written by Andrew Reamer of the GW Institute of Public Policy. Andrew Reamer, "Brief 7: Comprehensive Accounting of Census-Guided Federal Spending (FY2017)," "Counting for Dollars, 2020" (February 2020), https://gwipp.gwu.edu/counting-dollars-2020-role-decennial-census-geographic-distribution-federal-funds.

46. See *Baker v. Carr*, 369 U.S. 1 and *Wesberry v. Sanders*, 376 U.S. 1.

47. This is for the drawing of congressional districts. Different processes sometimes govern the drawing of lines for state legislatures. According to the National Conference on State Legislatures (NCSL), "Ten states have a commission with primary responsibility for drawing a plan for congressional districts. Five states have an advisory commission that may assist the legislature with drawing the district lines and three states have a backup commission that will make the decision if the legislature is unable to agree." NCSL, "Redistricting Commissions: Congressional Plans," https://www.ncsl.org/research/redistricting/redistricting-commissions-congressional-plans.aspx.

48. David McMillen, "Apportionment and Districting," in *Encylopedia of the U.S.*

Census, edited by Margo J. Anderson, Constance F. Citro, and Joseph J. Salvo (Washington, D.C.: CQ Press, 2012): 49–58.

49. I am on record being wrong on this, having claimed a delay would not be necessary in an opinion piece: Dan Bouk, "The Census Day That Matters Most," *The Hill*, April 1, 2020, https://thehill.com/opinion/civil-rights/490333-the-census-day-that-matters-most?rl=1.

50. I recall being shocked, for instance, when I read this in a Ninth Circuit order: "We leave open the question whether, given the wording of the statutes and general conclusions regarding the interpretation of statutory timelines, the agency should view this deadline as inflexible or, instead, as subject to adjustment, akin to equitable tolling or force majeure concepts, if they cannot be met because of extraordinary circumstances. Perhaps, as President Trump publicly stated in April, 'I don't know that you even have to ask [Congress for an extension]. This is called an act of God. This is called a situation that has to be.'" Ninth Circuit U.S. Court of Appeals, *National Urban League et al. v. Wilbur L. Ross et al.*, 20–16868 (October 7, 2020), 12*n1*.

51. The video is available here: Census Bureau, "2020 Census Apportionment Counts Press Kit," Census Bureau Website, https://www.census.gov/newsroom/press-kits/2021/2020-census-apportionment-counts.html.

52. See Ackermann and Savell, "Count and Increase."

53. Mayer-Schönberger and Cukier, *Big Data*; Rudder, *Dataclysm*.

54. Zuboff, *The Age of Surveillance Capitalism*.

Bibliography

Ackermann, Kevin, and Taylor Savell. "Count and Increase." USApportionment.org. https://usapportionment.org/countandincrease.html.

Agar, Jon. *The Government Machine: A Revolutionary History of the Computer.* Cambridge, MA: MIT Press, 2003.

Aldrich, Mark. "Progressive Economists and Scientific Racism: Walter Willcox and Black Americans, 1895–1910." *Phylon* 40, no. 1 (1979): 1–14.

Altmeyer, Arthur J. "Three Years' Progress Toward Social Security." *Social Security Bulletin* 1, no. 8 (August 1938): 1–7.

Aluko, S. A. "How Many Nigerians? An Analysis of Nigeria's Census Problems, 1901–63." *Journal of Modern African Studies* 3, no. 3 (1965): 371–92.

Aly, Götz, and Karl Heinz Roth. *The Nazi Census: Identification and Control in the Third Reich.* Philadelphia: Temple University Press, 2004.

Anderson, Benedict. *Imagined Communities.* New York: Verso, rev. ed. 1991.

Anderson, Margo J. *The American Census: A Social History, Second Edition.* New Haven, CT: Yale University Press, 2015.

———. "The Census and the Japanese 'Internment': Apology and Policy in Statistical Practice." *Social Research* 87, no. 4 (2020): 789–812.

Anderson, Margo J., and Stephen E. Fienberg. *Who Counts? The Politics of Census-Taking in Contemporary America.* New York: Russell Sage Foundation, 1999.

Anderson, Margo J., and William Seltzer. "Challenges to the Confidentiality of U.S. Federal Statistics, 1910–1965." *Journal of Official Statistics* 23, no. 1 (2007): 1–34.

Appadurai, Arjun. "Number in the Colonial Imagination." In *Orientalism and the Postcolonial Predicament: Perspectives on South Asia,* edited by Carol A. Breckenridge and Peter van der Veer. Philadelphia: University of Pennsylvania Press, 1993.

Appiah, Kwame Anthony. *Lines of Descent: W.E.B. Du Bois and the Emergence of Identity.* Cambridge, MA: Harvard University Press, 2014.

Aronova, Elena, Christine von Oertzen, and David Sepkoski, eds. "Data Histories." *Osiris* 32 (2017).

Ascher, Kate. *The Heights: Anatomy of a Skyscraper.* New York: Penguin Books, 2011.

Balinski, Michel L., and H. Peyton Young. *Fair Representation: Meeting the Ideal of One Man, One Vote.* Washington, D.C.: Brookings Institution Press, 2001.

Ball, Jesse. *Census.* New York: Ecco, 2018.

Barad, Karen. *Meeting the Universe Halfway: Quantum Physics and the Entanglement of Matter and Meaning.* Durham, NC: Duke University Press, 2007.

Baxandall, Michael. *Painting and Experience in Fifteenth-Century Italy.* New York: Oxford University Press, 1988.

Beales, Le Verne. "The Negro Enumeration of 1920: A Reply to Dr. Kelly Miller." *Scientific Monthly* 14, no. 4 (1922): 352–60.

Behrend, Justin. *Reconstructing Democracy: Grassroots Black Politics in the Deep South After the Civil War.* Athens: University of Georgia Press, 2015.

Benjamin, Ruha. *Race After Technology: Abolitionist Tools for the New Jim Code.* New York: Polity, 2019.

Blair, Ann, Paul Duguid, Anja-Silvia Goeing, and Anthony Grafton, eds. *Information: A Historical Companion.* Princeton, NJ: Princeton University Press, 2021.

Boddy, Kasia. "The Great American Novel and the Census." In *Writing, Medium, Machine: Modern Technographies*, edited by Sean Pryor and David Trotter. London: Open Humanities Press, 2016, 52–66.

Bouk, Dan. "Generation Crisis: How Population Research Defined the Baby Boomers." *Modern American History* 1, no. 3 (2018): 321–42.

———. *House Arrest: How an Automated Algorithm Constrained Congress for a Century.* New York: Data and Society, 2021. https://datasociety.net/library/house-arrest/.

———. *How Our Days Became Numbered: Risk and the Rise of the Statistical Individual.* Chicago: University of Chicago Press, 2015.

———. "The National Data Center and the Rise of the Data Double." *Historical Studies in the Natural Sciences* 48, no. 5 (2018): 627–36.

Bouk, Dan, and danah boyd. "Democracy's Data Infrastructure: The Technopolitics of the U.S. Census." Knight First Amendment Institute at Columbia University. March 18, 2021. https://knightcolumbia.org/content/democracys-data-infrastructure.

Bowker, Geoffrey C., and Susan Leigh Star. *Sorting Things Out: Classification and Its Consequences.* Cambridge, MA: MIT Press, 1999.

boyd, danah. *Balancing Data Utility and Confidentiality in the 2020 US Census.* New York: Data and Society, 2020. Updated May 8, 2020. https://datasociety.net/library/balancing-data-utility-and-confidentiality-in-the-2020-us-census/.

Brody, David. *In Labor's Cause: Main Themes on the History of the American Worker.* New York: Oxford University Press, 1993.

Brown, Kate. *Plutopia: Nuclear Families, Atomic Cities, and the Great Soviet and American Plutonium Disasters.* New York: Oxford University Press, 2013.

Browne, Simone. *Dark Matters: On the Surveillance of Blackness*. Durham, NC: Duke University Press, 2015.

Brownlee, W. Elliot. "The Public Sector." In *Cambridge Economic History of the United States: The Twentieth Century*, edited by Stanley L. Engerman and Robert E. Gallman. Cambridge: Cambridge University Press, 2000.

Buck, Stephanie. "Overlooked No More: Mitsuye Endo, a Name Linked to Justice for Japanese-Americans." *The New York Times*, October 9, 2019.

Bunzel, Bessie, and Louis I. Dublin. *To Be or Not to Be: A Study of Suicide*. New York: Harrison Smith and Robert Hass, 1933.

Bureau of the Census. *American Community Survey Design and Methodology*. Washington, D.C.: Department of Commerce, 2014.

——. *Instructions to Enumerators: Population and Agriculture 1940*. Washington, D.C.: Department of Commerce, 1940.

——. *Report of the Seventeenth Decennial Census of the United States. Census of Population: 1950*. Washington, D.C.: Government Printing Office, 1952.

——. "Report of the Superintendent." *Ninth Census: The Statistics of the Population of the United States*. Washington, D.C.: Government Printing Office, 1872.

Campbell-Kelly, Martin, and William Aspray. *Computer: A History of the Information Machine*. New York: Basic Books, 1997.

Carson, John. *The Measure of Merit: Talents, Intelligence, and Inequality in the French and American Republics, 1750–1940*. Princeton, NJ: Princeton University Press, 2007.

Chase, Stuart. *What the New Census Means*. New York: Public Affairs Committee, Inc., 1941.

Cherny, Robert W. "The Communist Party in California, 1935–1940: From the Political Margins to the Mainstream and Back." *American Communist History* 9, no. 1 (2010): 3–33.

Citro, Connie. "The 2020 Census: Counting under Adversity." *Issues in Science and Technology* (April 6, 2020). https://issues.org/the-2020-census-counting-under-adversity/.

Cohen, Lizabeth. *A Consumers' Republic: The Politics of Mass Consumption in Postwar America*. New York: Vintage, 2004.

Cohen, Patricia Cline. *A Calculating People: The Spread of Numeracy in Early America*. New York: Routledge, 1999.

Commission on Wartime Relocation and Internment of Civilians. *Personal Justice Denied: Report of the Commission on Wartime Relocation and Internment of Civilians*. Washington, D.C.: Government Printing Office, 1982.

Contrera, Jessica, and Gillian Brockell. "In 1933, Two Rebellious Women Bought a Home in Virginia's Woods. Then the CIA Moved In." *The Washington Post*, February 14, 2020. https://www.washingtonpost.com/history/2020/02/14/cia-women-neighbors-langley/.

Davies, Margery W. *Woman's Place Is at the Typewriter: Office Work and Office Workers, 1870–1930*. Philadelphia: Temple University Press, 1982.

Daston, Lorraine. *Classical Probability in the Enlightenment*. Princeton, NJ: Princeton University Press, 1988.

———. "Super-Vision: Weather Watching and Table Reading in the Early Modern Royal Society and Académie Royale des Sciences." *Huntington Library Quarterly* 78, no. 2 (2015): 187–215.

Daston, Lorraine, and Peter Galison. *Objectivity*. New York: Zone Books, 2010.

DeBow, J.D.B. *Seventh Census of the United States: 1850*. Washington, D.C.: Robert Armstrong, 1853.

Deerinwater, Jen. "Paper Genocide: The Erasure of Native People in Census Counts." *Rewire News Group*, December 9, 2019. https://rewirenewsgroup.com/article /2019/12/09/paper-genocide-the-erasure-of-native-people-in-census-counts/.

Deringer, William. *Calculated Values: Finance, Politics, and the Quantitative Age*. Cambridge, MA: Harvard University Press, 2018.

DeWitt, General John L. *Final Report, Japanese Evacuation from the West Coast 1942*. Washington, D.C.: Government Printing Office, 1943.

Didier, Emmanuel. *America by the Numbers: Quantification, Democracy, and the Birth of National Statistics*. Translated by Priya Vari Sen. Cambridge, MA: MIT Press, 2020.

D'Ignazio, Catherine, and Lauren F. Klein. *Data Feminism*. Cambridge, MA: MIT Press, 2020.

Doenecke, Justus D. "General Robert E. Wood: The Evolution of a Conservative." *Journal of the Illinois State Historical Society* 71, no. 3 (1978): 162–75.

Douglass, Frederick. *Narrative of the Life of Frederick Douglass, an American Slave*. Dublin: Webb and Chapman, 1846.

Dryer, Theodora. *Designing Certainty: The Rise of Algorithmic Computing in an Age of Anxiety 1920–1970*. University of California, San Diego, Ph.D. Dissertation, 2019.

Dublin, Louis I. "The Statistician and the Population Problem." *Journal of the American Statistical Association* 20, no. 149 (1925): 1–12.

Einhorn, Robin. *American Taxation, American Slavery*. Chicago: University of Chicago Press, 2006.

Feinberg, Melanie. "Reading Databases: Slow Information Interactions Beyond the Retrieval Paradigm." *Journal of Documentation* 73, no. 2 (2017): 336–56.

Flanzraich, Gerri. "The Library Bureau and Office Technology." *Libraries and Culture* 28, no. 4 (Fall 1993): 403–29.

Gatewood, George. *A Monograph on Confidentiality and Privacy in the U.S. Census*. U.S. Census Bureau, July 2001. https://www.census.gov/history/pdf/Confidentiality Monograph.pdf.

Gebru, Timnit, Jamie Morgenstern, Briana Vecchione, Jennifer Wortman Vaughan,

Hanna Wallach, Hal Daumé III, and Kate Crawford. "Datasheets for Datasets." March 19, 2020. arXiv:1803.09010v7 [cs.DB].

Ghosh, Arunabh. *Making It Count: Statistics and Statecraft in the Early People's Republic of China*. Princeton, NJ: Princeton University Press, 2020.

Glaude, Eddie S. *Democracy in Black: How Race Still Enslaves the American Soul*. New York: Crown, 2016.

Goeken, Ronald A., and Diana L. Magnuson. "'I Hate to See the Evening Sun Go Down': Recounts and Padding in the 19th Century U.S. Decennial Census of Population." Social Science History Association Annual Meeting, 2019.

Gómez, Laura E. *Manifest Destinies: The Making of the Mexican American Race*, 2nd edition. New York: New York University Press, 2018.

Gordon, Linda. *Dorothea Lange: A Life Beyond Limits*. New York: W. W. Norton, 2009.

Gratton, Brian, and Emily Klancher Merchant. "La Raza: Mexicans in the United States Census." *Journal of Political History* 28, no. 4 (2016): 537–67.

Gray, Mary L., and Siddarth Suri. *Ghost Work: How to Stop Silicon Valley from Building a New Global Underclass*. New York: Houghton Mifflin Harcourt, 2019.

Greville, Thomas N. E. *United States Life Tables and Actuarial Tables 1939–1941*. Washington, D.C.: Government Printing Office, 1946.

Grier, David Alan. *When Computers Were Human*. Princeton, NJ: Princeton University Press, 2013.

Guthrie, Woody. *Dust Bowl Ballads* (Victor Records, 1940).

Gutiérrez, David G. "Migration, Emergent Ethnicity, and the 'Third Space': The Shifting Politics of Nationalism in Greater Mexico." *Journal of American History* 86, no. 2 (1999): 481–517.

Hacking, Ian. "Biopower and the Avalanche of Printed Numbers." *Humanities in Society* 5, nos. 3 and 4 (1982): 279–95.

———. *The Emergence of Probability: A Philosophical Study of Early Ideas about Probability, Induction, and Statistical Inference*. Cambridge: Cambridge University Press, 1975.

Haraway, Donna. "Situated Knowledges: The Science Question in Feminism and the Privilege of Partial Perspective." *Feminist Studies* 14, no. 3 (1988): 575–99.

Hartman, Saidiya. *Wayward Lives, Beautiful Experiments: Intimate Histories of Riotous Black Girls, Troublesome Women, and Queer Radicals*. New York: W. W. Norton, 2019.

Hayashi, Brian Masaru. *Democratizing the Enemy: The Japanese American Internment*. Princeton, NJ: Princeton University Press, 2004.

Herenstein, Ethan, and Yurij Rudensky. "The Penalty Clause and the Fourteenth Amendment's Consistency on Universal Representation." 2020. https://ssrn.com/abstract=3684792.

Hernández, Kelly Lytle. *Migra! A History of the U.S. Border Patrol.* Berkeley: University of California Press, 2010.

Hillier, Amy E. "Redlining and the Home Owners' Loan Corporation." *Journal of Urban History* 29, no. 4 (2003): 394–420.

Hodes, Martha. "Fractions and Fictions in the United States Census of 1890." In *Haunted by Empire*, edited by Ann Laura Stoler. Durham, NC: Duke University Press, 2006, 240–70.

Hoffman, Frederick L. "Race Traits and Tendencies of the American Negro." *Publications of the American Economic Association* 11, no. 1/3 (1896): 1–329.

Hollander, Caitlin. "No, Your Ancestors' Names Were Not Changed at Ellis Island." *Hollander-Waas Jewish Heritage Services*, October 7, 2019. https://www.hollander-waas.com/blog/ellis-island-name-change.

Horan, Caley. *Insurance Era: Risk, Governance, and the Privatization of Security in Postwar America.* Chicago: University of Chicago Press, 2021.

Hughes, Langston. *One-Way Ticket.* New York: Alfred A. Knopf, 1949.

Igo, Sarah E. *The Averaged American: Surveys, Citizens, and the Making of a Mass Public.* Cambridge, MA: Harvard University Press, 2007.

———. *Known Citizen: A History of Privacy in Modern America.* Cambridge, MA: Harvard University Press, 2018.

Introduction to Family History Student Manual. Salt Lake City, UT: Church of Jesus Christ of Latter-day Saints, 2012.

Jenkins, Robert M. *Procedural History of the 1940 Census of Population and Housing.* Madison: University of Wisconsin Press, 1985.

Johnson, James Weldon. *The Autobiography of an Ex-Colored Man.* Boston: Sherman, French, 1912.

Johnson, Jessica Marie. "Markup Bodies: Black [Life] Studies and Slavery [Death] Studies at the Digital Crossroads." *Social Text* 36, no. 4 (2018): 57–79.

Kennedy, David M. *Freedom from Fear: The American People in Depression and War, 1929–1945.* New York: Oxford University Press, 2005.

Kevles, Daniel. *In the Name of Eugenics: Genetics and the Uses of Human Heredity.* Cambridge, MA: Harvard University Press, 1995.

Keyssar, Alexander. *The Right to Vote: The Contested History of Democracy in the United States.* New York: Basic Books, 2000.

Kimmerer, Robin Wall. *Braiding Sweetgrass.* Minneapolis: Milkweed Editions, 2020.

Leadership Conference Education Fund and Georgetown Center on Poverty and Inequality. "Will You Count? African Americans in the 2020 Census." 2018. http://civilrightsdocs.info/pdf/census/2020/Fact-Sheet-African-Americans-HTC.pdf.

Lee, Robert, Tristan Ahtone, Margaret Pearce, Kalen Goodluck, Geoff McGhee, Cody Leff, Katherine Lanphear, and Taryn Salinas. "Land-Grab Universities." *High Country News.* March 30, 2020. https://www.landgrabu.org/.

Lemov, Rebecca. *Database of Dreams: The Lost Quest to Catalog Humanity*. New Haven, CT: Yale University Press, 2015.

Leonard, William R., and Walter F. Willcox. "Walter F. Willcox: Statist." *American Statistician* 15, no. 1 (1961): 16–19.

Levy, Jonathan. *Freaks of Fortune: The Emerging World of Capitalism and Risk in America*. Cambridge, MA: Harvard University Press, 2012.

Lew-Williams, Beth. *The Chinese Must Go: Violence, Exclusion, and the Making of the Alien in America*. Cambridge, MA: Harvard University Press, 2018.

Light, Jennifer S. "When Computers Were Women." *Technology and Culture* 40, no. 3 (1999): 455–83.

López, Ian Haney. *White by Law: The Legal Construction of Race*. New York: New York University Press, 2006.

Loukissas, Yanni Alexander. "A Place for Big Data: Close and Distant Readings of Accessions Data from the Arnold Arboretum." *Big Data and Society* 3, no. 2 (2016): 1–20.

MacLeish, Archibald. *Land of the Free*. New York: Da Capo, 1977.

Martin, Christopher and U.S. Census Bureau. "Iwao Milton Moriyama: Improving Life with the U.S. Census." https://www.census.gov/history/www/census_then _now/notable_alumni/census_employees.html.

Martin, Dellita L. "The 'Madam Poems' as Dramatic Monologue." *Black American Literature Forum* 15, no. 3 (1981): 97–99.

Masur, Louis P. "'Age of the First Person Singular': The Vocabulary of the Self in New England, 1780–1850." *Journal of American Studies* 25 (1991): 189–211.

Maury, Meghan, and National LGBTQ Task Force. "LBGTQ Census Advocacy, 1990–2017." https://www.thetaskforce.org/wp-content/uploads/2017/05/LGBTQ -Census-Advocacy.pdf.

Mayer-Schönberger, Viktor, and Kenneth Cukier. *Big Data: A Revolution That Will Transform How We Live, Work, and Think*. New York: Houghton Mifflin Harcourt, 2013.

McMillen, David. "Apportionment and Districting." In *Encylopedia of the U.S. Census,* edited by Margo J. Anderson, Constance F. Citro, and Joseph J. Salvo. Washington, D.C.: CQ Press, 2012, 49–58.

Merchant, Emily Klancher. *Building the Population Bomb*. New York: Oxford University Press, 2021.

Merridale, Catherine. "The 1937 Census and the Limits of Stalinist Rule." *Historical Journal* 39, no. 1 (1996): 225–40.

Miller, Kelly. "Enumeration Errors in Negro Population." *Scientific Monthly* 14, no. 2 (1922): 168–77.

———. *A Review of Hoffman's Race Traits and Tendencies of the American Negro*. Washington, D.C.: American Negro Academy, 1897.

Mora, G. Cristina. *Making Hispanics: How Activists, Bureaucrats, and Media Constructed a New American*. Chicago: University of Chicago Press, 2014.

Mora, G. Cristina, and Michael Rodríguez-Muñiz. "Latinos, Race, and the American Future: A Response to Richard Alba's 'The Likely Persistence of a White Majority.'" *New Labor Forum* 26, no. 2 (2017): 40–46.

Moriyama, Iwao M. "Vital Statistics During the War." *Yale Journal of Biology and Medicine* 19, no. 4 (1947): 453–60.

Muhammad, Khalil Gibran. *The Condemnation of Blackness: Race, Crime, and the Making of Modern Urban America*. Cambridge, MA: Harvard University Press, 2010.

Murphy, Michelle. *The Economization of Life*. Durham, NC: Duke University Press, 2017.

Nelson, Alondra. *The Social Life of DNA: Race, Reparations, and Reconciliation After the Genome*. Boston: Beacon Press, 2016.

Nelson, Robert K., LaDale Winling, Richard Marciano, Nathan Connolly, et al. "Mapping Inequality." *American Panorama*, edited by Robert K. Nelson and Edward L. Ayers. https://dsl.richmond.edu/panorama/redlining/#loc=5/39.1/-94.58&text=intro.

Ngai, Mae M. "The Architecture of Race in American Immigration Law: A Reexamination of the Immigration Act of 1924." *Journal of American History* 86, no. 1 (1999): 67–92.

———. *Impossible Subjects: Illegal Aliens and the Making of Modern America*. Princeton, NJ: Princeton University Press, 2014.

Nobles, Melissa. *Shades of Citizenship: Race and the Census in Modern Politics*. Stanford, CA: Stanford University Press, 2000.

O'Neil, Cathy. *Weapons of Math Destruction: How Big Data Increases Inequality and Threatens Democracy*. New York: Crown, 2016.

Orleans, Leo A. "The 1953 Chinese Census in Perspective." *Journal of Asian Studies* 16, no. 4 (1957): 565–73.

Pearson, Susan J. "'Age Ought to Be a Fact': The Campaign Against Child Labor and the Rise of the Birth Certificate." *Journal of American History* 101, no. 4 (2015): 1144–65.

———. *The Birth Certificate: An American History*. Chapel Hill: University of North Carolina Press, 2021.

Phillips, Christopher J. *Scouting and Scoring: How We Know What We Know About Baseball*. Princeton, NJ: Princeton University Press, 2019.

Phillips, Helen. *The Beautiful Bureaucrat*. New York: Picador, 2015.

Pinsky, Robert. *The Sounds of Poetry: A Brief Guide*. New York: Farrar, Straus and Giroux, 1999.

Poirier, Lindsay. "Reading Datasets: Strategies for Interpreting the Politics of Data Signification." *Big Data and Society* (2021): 1–19.

Porter, Theodore M. *Genetics in the Madhouse: The Unknown History of Human Heredity*. Princeton, NJ: Princeton University Press, 2018.

―――. *The Rise of Statistical Thinking 1820–1900*. Princeton, NJ: Princeton University Press, 1986.

―――. *Trust in Numbers: The Pursuit of Objectivity in Science and Public Life*. Princeton, NJ: Princeton University Press, 2020.

Prewitt, Kenneth. *What Is "Your" Race? The Census and Our Flawed Efforts to Classify Americans*. Princeton, NJ: Princeton University Press, 2013.

Price, Daniel O. "A Check on Underenumeration in the 1940 Census." *American Sociological Review* 12, no. 1 (1947): 44–49.

Radin, Joanna. "'Digital Natives': How Medical and Indigenous Histories Matter for Big Data." *Osiris* 32, no. 1 (2017): 43–64.

Ramsden, Edmund. "Carving Up Population Science: Eugenics, Demography and the Controversy over the 'Biological Law' of Population Growth." *Social Studies of Science* 32, no. 5/6 (2002): 857–99.

Reamer, Andrew. "Brief 7: Comprehensive Accounting of Census-Guided Federal Spending (FY2017)." *Counting for Dollars 2020* (February). https://gwipp.gwu.edu /counting-dollars-2020-role-decennial-census-geographic-distribution-federal -funds.

Rodgers, Daniel T. *Atlantic Crossings: Social Politics in a Progressive Age*. Cambridge, MA: Belknap Press of Harvard University Press, 1998.

Roll, David L. *The Hopkins Touch: Harry Hopkins and the Forging of the Alliance to Defeat Hitler*. New York: Oxford University Press, 2013.

Rosales, F. Arturo. "Shifting Self Perceptions and Ethnic Consciousness Among Mexicans in Houston 1908–1946." *Aztlán* 16, nos. 1–2 (1987): 71–94.

Rose-Redwood, Reuben. "'A Regular State of Beautiful Confusion': Governing by Numbers and the Contradictions of Calculable Space in New York City." *Urban History* 39, no. 4 (2012): 624–38.

Rose-Redwood, Reuben, and Anton Tantner. "Introduction: Governmentality, House Numbering and the Spatial History of the Modern City." *Urban History* 39, no. 4 (2012): 607–13.

Rosenberg, Daniel. "Data Before the Fact." In *Raw Data Is an Oxymoron*, edited by Lisa Gitelman. Cambridge, MA: MIT Press, 2013, 15–40.

Rosenthal, Caitlin. *Accounting for Slavery: Masters and Management*. Cambridge, MA: Harvard University Press, 2018.

Rossiter, Margaret. *The Emergence of Agricultural Science: Justus Liebig and the Americans, 1840–1880*. New Haven, CT: Yale University Press, 1975.

Rudder, Christian. *Dataclysm: Who We Are (When We Think No One's Looking)*. New York: Crown, 2014.

Ruggles, Steven, and Diana L. Magnuson. "Census Technology, Politics, and

Institutional Change, 1790–2020." *Journal of American History* 107, no. 1 (2020): 19–51.

———. "'It's None of Their Damn Business': Privacy and Disclosure Control in the U.S. Census, 1790–2020." A keynote delivered at University of Wisconsin Center for Demography and Ecology 2020 Census Symposium, March 24, 2020.

Ruggles, Steven, Sarah Flood, Sophia Foster, Ronald Goeken, Jose Pacas, Megan Schouweiler, and Matthew Sobek. IPUMS USA: Version 11.0 [data set]. Minneapolis: IPUMS, 2021. https://doi.org/10.18128/D010.V11.0.

Russell, Elizabeth W. "The 'Vanished American.'" *Expedition Magazine* 8, no. 4 (1966). https://www.penn.museum/sites/expedition/the-vanished-america/.

Samples, Leah. "Calculating Blindness: The Role of Statistics in New Deal America." Presented at Contested Data Workshop at Data and Society, New York, NY, March 6, 2020.

Sánchez, George J. *Becoming Mexican American: Ethnicity, Culture, and Identity in Chicano Los Angeles, 1900–1945*. New York: Oxford University Press, 1993.

Sandage, Scott A. "Gender and the Economics of the Sentimental Market in Nineteenth-Century America." *Social Politics* 6, no. 2 (1999): 105–30.

Sansing, David G. "Theodore Gilmore Bilbo." *The Mississippi Encyclopedia*. https://mississippiencyclopedia.org/entries/theodore-gilmore-bilbo.

Saperstein, Aliya, and Andrew M. Penner. "Racial Fluidity and Inequality in the United States." *American Journal of Sociology* 118, no. 3 (2012): 676–727.

Schmandt-Besserat, Denise. "Tokens and Writing: The Cognitive Development." *Scripta* 1 (2009): 145–54.

Schnepf, J. D. "Black Women and the Clerical Work of the 1940 Census Tabulation." In *Humans at Work in the Digital Age: Forms of Digital Textual Labor*, edited by Shawna Ross and Andrew Pilsch. New York: Routledge, 2020, 17–31.

Schor, Paul. *Counting Americans: How the US Census Classified the Nation*, translated by Lys Ann Weiss. New York: Oxford University Press, 2017.

Scott, Ann Herbert. *Census U.S.A.: Fact Finding for the American People, 1790–1970*. New York: Seabury Press, 1968.

Seipp, David J. *The Right to Privacy in American History*. Cambridge, MA: Harvard University Program on Information Resources Policy, 1981.

Seltzer, William. "Excluding Indians Not Taxed: Federal Censuses and Native-Americans in the 19th Century." Paper presented at 1999 Joint Statistical Meetings, August 9, 1999.

———. "Replacing Austin: A Study of Leadership Change at the U.S. Census Bureau." Paper prepared for presentation at the session "The Census and Statistical Policymaking: Lessons from History," Joint Statistical Meetings, Miami Beach Florida, July 30–August 4, 2011.

Seltzer, William, and Margo Anderson. "Census Confidentiality Under the Second

War Powers Act (1942–1947)." Paper prepared for presentation at the session "Confidentiality, Privacy, and Ethical Issues in Demographic Data," Population Association of America Annual Meeting, March 29–31, 2007, New York, NY.

Smith, Bonnie G. *The Gender of History: Men, Women, and Historical Practice.* Cambridge, MA: Harvard University Press, 1998.

Spencer, Thomas T. "Daniel C. Roper and the 1932 Presidential Campaign." *South Carolina Historical Magazine* 85, no. 1 (1984): 22–32.

Stallybrass, Peter. "Printing and the Manuscript Revolution." In *Explorations in Communication and History*, edited by Barbie Zelizer. New York: Routledge, 2008.

Stern, Alexandra Minna. "Buildings, Boundaries, and Blood: Medicalization and Nation-Building on the U.S.-Mexico Border, 1910–1930." *Hispanic American Historical Review* 79, no. 1 (1999): 41–81.

———. *Eugenic Nation: Faults and Frontiers of Better Breeding in Modern America.* Berkeley: University of California Press, 2005.

Stewart, Dianne M. *Black Women, Black Love: America's War on African American Marriage.* New York: Seal, 2020.

Stone, Deborah. *Counting: How We Use Numbers to Decide What Matters.* New York: Liveright, 2020.

Sutton, Philip. "Why Your Family Name Was Not Changed at Ellis Island." New York Public Library, July 2, 2013. https://www.nypl.org/blog/2013/07/02/name-changes-ellis-island.

Swain, Martha H. "Senator Pat Harrison: New Deal Wheelhorse (1933–1941) Suspicious of His Load." *Mississippi History Now.* https://www.mshistorynow.mdah.ms.gov/issue/senator-pat-harrison-new-deal-wheelhorse-suspicious-of-his-load-1933-1941.

TallBear, Kim. *Native American DNA: Tribal Belonging and the False Promise of Genetic Science.* Minneapolis: University of Minnesota Press, 2013.

Tantner, Anton. "Addressing the Houses: The Introduction of House Numbering in Europe." *Histoire et Mesure* 26, no. 2 (2009). https://journals.openedition.org/histoiremesure/3942.

Taylor, Keeanga-Yamahtta. *Race for Profit: How Banks and the Real Estate Industry Undermined Black Homeownership.* Chapel Hill: University of North Carolina Press, 2019.

Thompson, Debra. *The Schematic State: Race, Transnationalism, and the Politics of the Census.* New York: Cambridge University Press, 2016.

Thorp, Jer. *Living in Data: A Citizen's Guide to a Better Information Future.* New York: MCD / Farrar, Straus and Giroux, 2021.

Trouillot, Michel-Rolph. *Silencing the Past: Power and the Production of History.* Boston: Beacon Press, 2015.

U.S. House of Representatives. *Apportionment of Representatives*. 66th Congress. 3rd Session, Report no. 1173, January 8, 1921.

U.S. House of Representatives, Census Committee. *Apportionment of Representatives: Hearings Before the Committee on the Census on H.R. 14498, H.R. 15021, H.R. 15158, and H.R. 15217*. Washington, D.C.: Government Printing Office, 1921.

U.S. House of Representatives. "Sixteenth Decennial Census of Population: Message from the President of the United States Transmitting a Statement Prepared by the Director . . ." January 8, 1941, 77th Congress, 1st Session, Document 45.

U.S. Senate. *1940 Census: Hearings Before a Subcommittee of the Committee on Commerce United States Senate, Seventy-Sixth Congress, Third Session on S. Res. 231*. Washington, D.C.: Government Printing Office, 1940.

War Agency Liquidation Unit. *People in Motion: The Postwar Adjustment of the Evacuated Japanese Americans*. Washington, D.C.: Government Printing Office, 1947.

Weglyn, Michi. *Years of Infamy: The Untold Story of America's Concentration Camps*. New York: William Morrow, 1976.

Weinberg, Jonathan. "Proving Identity." *Pepperdine Law Review* 44, no. 3 (April 2017): 731–98.

Weintraub, Joel. "Why the 72 Year Rule for U.S. Census Privacy?." *Roots-Key* (Summer 2008): 16–17. https://stevemorse.org/census/rule72.html.

Weisenfeld, Judith. "New World A-Coming, Author's Response." *Journal of Africana Religions* 6, no. 2 (2018): 308–15.

———. *New World A-Coming: Black Religion and Racial Identity During the Great Migration*. New York: New York University Press, 2017.

Welke, Barbara Young. *Law and the Borders of Belonging in the Long Nineteenth Century United States*. New York: Cambridge University Press, 2010.

Wellmon, Chad, and Andrew Piper. "Publication, Power, and Patronage: On Inequality and Academic Publishing." *Critical Inquiry*, July 21, 2017. https://criticalinquiry .uchicago.edu/publication_power_and_patronage_on_inequality_and_academic _publishing.

Wernimont, Jacqueline. *Numbered Lives: Life and Death in Quantum Media*. Cambridge, MA: MIT Press, 2018.

Willcox, Walter F. "Area, Population, Birthplace, Migration and Conjugal Condition." *Publications of the American Economic Association*, no. 2 (1899): 8–37.

Whitby, Andrew. *The Sum of the People: How the Census Has Shaped Nations, from the Ancient World to the Modern Age*. New York: Basic Books, 2020.

White, Richard. *Railroaded: The Transcontinentals and the Making of Modern America*. New York: W. W. Norton, 2011.

———. *The Republic for Which It Stands: The United States During Reconstruction and the Gilded Age, 1865–1896*. New York: Oxford University Press, 2017.

Wiggins, Benjamin. *Calculating Race: Racial Discrimination in Risk Assessment*. New York: Oxford University Press, 2020.

Willis, Carol. *Form Follows Finance: Skyscrapers and Skylines in New York and Chicago*. New York: Princeton Architectural Press, 1995.

Worster, Donald. *Dust Bowl: The Southern Plains in the 1930s*. New York: Oxford University Press, 2004.

Wright, Carroll D. *The History and Growth of the United States Census, Prepared for the Senate Committee on the Census*. Washington, D.C.: Government Printing Office, 1900.

Zotigh, Dennis. "The Treaty That Forced the Cherokee People from Their Homelands Goes on View." *Smithsonian Magazine*, April 24, 2019. https://www.smithsonian mag.com/blogs/national-museum-american-indian/2019/04/24/treaty-new -echota/.

Zuboff, Shoshana. *The Age of Surveillance Capitalism: The Fight for a Human Future at the New Frontier of Power*. New York: Public Affairs, 2019.

Acknowledgments

This book began in 2017 in the reading room of the U.S. National Archives in Washington, D.C. I went there looking for records pertaining to Elbertie Foudray, hoping to explain the significant role this seldom-discussed woman scientist had played in the development of population research. While looking for Foudray, however, I discovered the census. The staff of the National Archives made that discovery possible, and I offer them my deepest thanks: first, the archivists who taught me how to navigate the paper finding aids in the binder and folder for Record Group 29, who corrected my flawed "pull requests" (which are used to order materials), and who organized and oversaw the efficient and elegant reading room. My thanks are also owed to the security staff who daily checked my credentials with good cheer and patiently reminded me in which direction to swipe my admission card.

Every day that I entered the National Archives, I passed two stone sentries: Robert I. Aitkins's *The Past* and *The Future*. On one side of the bronze doors, a toga-clad man sits on a limestone throne with a closed book representing history in his lap, where he bears the message "Study the Past." His fellow sentry on the other side, a robed woman, scarf covering her hair and a book open on her lap, looks into the future and says, "What Is Past Is Prologue." The pair reminded me that one reason we look backward is to make sense of where we are and where we are going. In 2019, danah boyd invited me to spend more time thinking about the present even as I was digging into the past. She ushered me into community with census advocates seeking a complete and equitable count in 2020 and taught me, in the process, a new way to be a historian. Data and Society and the Sloan Foundation supported this intellectual journey. Denice Ross and the entire Census Quality Reinforcement task force, working in concert with Corrine Yu and the Leadership Conference staff, taught me how history could be useful in building a better and more just count. I offer my thanks to my colleagues and mentors in these efforts, including Seth Amgott, Meeta Anand, Terry Ao Minnis, Matt Goerzen, Janet Haven, Charley Johnson, Steve Jost, Jae June Lee, Cristina López G., Terri Ann Lowenthal, Emma Margolin, Meghan Maury, Erin McAweeney, Will Partin, Taylor Savell, Arturo

Vargas, and Tom Wolf. Ron Jarmin and Christa Jones were each generous with their time, insight, and expertise.

Archivists at the FDR Library in Hyde Park and the Rauner Special Collections Library at Dartmouth College supported my visits and made available crucial materials. Leigh McWhite of the University of Mississippi Archives and Special Collections guided me remotely through the Rankin papers and sent me a massive box of photocopies that revealed how census patronage really worked. Sharon Tosi Lacey and Christopher Martin of the Census Bureau Public Information Office, David Castillo of the National Archives at College Park, Jim Armistead of the Truman Library, Craig Wright of the Herbert Hoover Library, and Janet C. Olson at Northwestern University each aided me in acquiring copies of important archival materials. I am so grateful to all these professionals. My trips to archives and purchase of copies of archival materials were all supported generously by the Colgate University Research Council. Josh Greenberg and the Sloan Foundation and Colgate University also provided generous support that allowed me time away from teaching to do research for this book.

For some years now, I have organized a history lab, supported by the Research Council, at Colgate. Our meetings were, without fail, a highlight of my week, and working with the students in the lab made possible a kind of extensive research into census records that I could not have accomplished on my own. Andrea De Hoyos, Emily Karavitch, and Ethan So all devoted significant time throughout their undergraduate years to census research and made important contributions, some already noted in the text, to *Democracy's Data*. Prior lab members Abby Balfour, Erin Burke, and Christy Mills established the lab and laid the foundation for this research. Stephanie Jordan contributed her expertise in data analysis and visualization. Kevin Ackermann joined us as a Georgetown graduate student and later as a member of the team at Data and Society. He spent many hours in the National Archives doing research that has—along with his ideas, critiques, and generosity of spirit—greatly improved this book.

I have been privileged in the course of writing *Democracy's Data* to have been mentored and guided by excellent and generous scholars. Margo Anderson, the dean of all census historians, has read multiple drafts of the manuscript, improving it each time, and shared generously the insights and evidence she has gathered over the course of decades of research into the U.S. census. Dan Rodgers and Barbara Welke each agreed to read my second book as they had my first, and they offered an invigorating and inspiring blend of encouragement and critique.

I offer my thanks as well for all manner of scholarly engagement and support to Anita Say Chan, Irene Chung, Meredith Clark, Rachel Cummings, Patrick Davison, William Deringer, Steph Dick, Siera Dissmore, Madeline Claire Elish, Nan Enstad, Ansley Erickson, Michele Gilman, Dan Guadagnolo, Sarah Igo, D. R. Jones, Matt Jones, Meg Jones, Tasha Kimball, Kevin Kruse, Karen Levy, Xiaochang Li, Muira McCammon, Shaka McGlotten, Mikey McGovern, Monica Mercado, Diedre Mulligan, Jason Petrulis, Chris Phillips, Ted Porter, Bill Rankin, Alex Rosenblat, Caitlin Rosenthal, Leah Samples, Corinna Schlombs, Gerardo Serra, Ranjit Singh, Tom Stapleford, Laura Stark, Alma Steingart, Jacqueline Wernimont, Andrew Whitby, and Chris Wiggins. Christine von Oertzen has been a constant source of inspiration and encouragement. Anna Echterhölter, Sophie Ledebur, and Laurens Schlicht invited me to Vienna for a workshop titled "Data at the Doorstep" that shaped my thinking profoundly. Eileen Clancy is a master builder of online intellectual community and was one of the earliest supporters of this work. Tine Byrsted talked census on our doorstep. Theodora Dryer read early chapters at a crucial moment. Conversations with Joanna Radin—her critique and counsel, and the example she set for intellectual integrity—informed every stage of this book's production.

My agent, Jane von Mehren, made a dream come true. She found me, helped me imagine this book, and then guided me through the process of writing it. I was flabbergasted when Sean McDonald signed it for MCD. But he believed in a book about census data when I didn't think anyone would, and his vision and his thoughtful editing have made it what it is today. My thanks as well to Olivia Kan-Sperling for her multiple readings and support in the early stages of production at FSG and to Benjamin Brooks for picking up the later stages. Leslie Kazanjian and Nancy Elgin improved my prose throughout. A group of University of Virginia students who elect to be known as "Prof. Handel's Children" cracked the cover code.

I owe many thanks to friends and colleagues who also read the entire first draft of *Democracy's Data* and helped me figure out how to improve it. Thanks to Kevin Ackermann, Sareeta Amrute, Meeta Anand, Terry Ao Minnis, CJ Brody Landow, Ronteau Coppin, Nazalie Doghramadjian, Cristina López G., and Tom Wolf. Karen Narasaki and Matt Snipp offered important advice on individual chapters. Penny Lane started reading when this book was still a blog and kept reading to the end. Robin Sloan read the entire manuscript and so much more: When I decided to start a blog, he told me how, and when I wanted to make it a book, he told me to send it to MCD. He opened his home and media lab to me for multiple visits and made this book (and my life) so much better. danah boyd read every chapter multiple times, and her matchless enthusiasm and intellect drove me to keep going. She gave me more opportunities than I can count, including the opportunity to be her friend. The only person who read more drafts was my mother, Gail Bouk, my first and favorite reader.

Finally, I thank the families and community who supported this book, directly and indirectly. For their generosity in opening their homes, sharing their lives and their ideas, I thank Louis Hyman and Kate Howe, Heather Roller, and Andy Rotter and Padma Kaimal. I thank all the Dromgolds and the Bouks, and especially my parents, Ted and Gail, who have given me so much. William Bouk helped me do research, read over my shoulder, and dreamed with me about being paid in Frisbees. Lucas Bouk shares his life with me and in countless ways shapes the way I see the world.

Index

Page numbers in *italics* refer to illustrations.

ILLUSTRATION CREDITS

viii Fairfax County, Virginia, E.D. 30–26, sheet 62B.

21 U.S. House of Representatives, *Sixteenth Decennial Census of Population: Message from the President of the United States*, 77th Congress, 1st Session, Document 45 (January 8, 1941), 2 in File 5.1180 General, Box 2, Entry 228, RG 29, NARA, D.C.

22 Rochester, Monroe, New York, E.D. 65–112, sheet 2A.

23 Rochester, Monroe, New York, E.D. 65–112, sheet 2A.

24 Rochester, Monroe, New York, E.D. 65–112, sheet 2A.

24 Home Owners' Loan Corporation (HOLC) Map: Robert K. Nelson, LaDale Winling, Richard Marciano, Nathan Connolly, et al., "Mapping Inequality," *American Panorama*, ed. Robert K. Nelson and Edward L. Ayers, http://dsl .richmond.edu/panorama/redlining/#city=rochester-ny; Census Map: ED NY 65-112 in File New York-Monroe County-Rochester-ED 65-1—ED 65-383, Series Enumeration District and Related Maps, 1880–1990, RG 29, NARA, https://catalog.archives.gov/id/5835650.

25 Census Publicity Program, Photographic Collection, General Photographs Franklin D. Roosevelt Library, Hyde Park, New York.

49 Baker: Election District 21, Prince Georges County, Maryland, E.D. 17–83, sheet 4B; Boyd: Washington, D.C., E.D. 1–260A, sheet 17A; Brunsman: Arlington County, Virginia, E.D. 7–23, sheet 1A; Carroll: Washington, D.C., E.D. 1–302B, sheet 63B; Chawner: Bethesda, Montgomery County, Maryland, E.D. 16–26G, sheet 6A; Durand: Washington, D.C., E.D. 1–289, sheet 11A; Grove: Washington, D.C., E.D. 1–260A, sheet 16A; Aryness Joy (whose last name is not visible): Providence, Fairfax County, Virginia, E.D. 30–27, sheet 10A; Murray: Bethesda, Montgomery County, Maryland, E.D. 16–26B, sheet 12B; Rice: Arlington County, Virginia, E.D. 7–10, sheet 1B; Wasserman: Washington, D.C., E.D. 1–233B, sheet 8B; Webb: Falls Church, Fairfax County, Virginia, E.D. 30–9, sheet 21A.

50 Batschelet: Arlington County, Virginia, E.D. 7–9, sheet 5A; Beales: Washington,

D.C., E.D. 1–376, sheet 3B; Dedrick: Washington, D.C., E.D. 1–274A, sheet 1B; Dunn: Washington, D.C., E.D. 1–11, sheet 3A; Eckler: Washington, D.C., E.D. 1–296, sheet 3B; Edwards: Washington, D.C., E.D.: 1–521, sheet 1A; Ellsworth: Bethesda, Montgomery County, Maryland, E.D. 16–20, sheet 10A; Gosnell: Arlington County, Virginia, E.D. 7–17, sheet 28B; Hauser: Bethesda, Montgomery County, Maryland, E.D. 16–22A, sheet 8A; McClure: Washington, D.C., E.D. 1–535, sheet 4A; Pettet: Washington, D.C., E.D. 1–359, sheet 11A; Proudfoot: Arlington County, Virginia, E.D. 7–2, sheet 62A; Reed: Arlington County, Virginia, E.D. 7–1, sheet 65A; Shamel: Silver Spring, Montgomery County, Maryland, E.D. 16–52A, sheet 12B; Short: College Park, Prince Georges County, Maryland, E.D. 17–75, sheet 3B; Steuart: Washington, D.C., E.D. 1–274B, sheet 1B; Truesdell: Washington, D.C., E.D. 1–289, sheet 9A.

51 Craig: Washington, D.C., E.D. 1–254, sheet 9B; Sargent: Huntington, Suffolk County, New York, E.D. 52–109, sheet 12B; Stockbridge: Manhattan, New York County, New York, E.D. 31–893A, sheet 81A; Wood: Highland Park, Lake County, Illinois, E.D. 49–14, sheet 6B.

51 Barraclough: Elkins Park, Montgomery County, Pennsylvania, E.D. 46–29, sheet 5B; Katz: Washington, D.C., E.D. 1–406, sheet 6B; Scattergood: Fairfax County, Virginia, E.D. 30–26, sheet 62B.

52 DeVault: University Park, Prince Georges County, Maryland, E.D. 17–74, sheet 9B; Lorimer: Washington, D.C., E.D. 1–276B, sheet 6B; May: Mount Vernon, Westchester County, New York, E.D. 60–145A, sheet 14A; Notestein: Princeton, Mercer County, New Jersey, E.D. 11–61, sheet 16A; Osborn: Manhattan, New York County, New York, E.D. 31–1356, sheet 3A; Schmeckebier: Washington, D.C., E.D. 1–254, sheet 11B; Stephan: Arlington County, Virginia, E.D. 7–8A, sheet 19A; Whelpton: Bethesda, Montgomery County, Maryland, E.D. 16–26H, sheet 10B.

73 1830 U.S. Census: Baltimore, Maryland, sheet 37. Source record from Maryland State Archives (MSA) SM 61-83, available online at https://msa.maryland.gov /megafile/msa/speccol/sc5400/sc5496/013800/013800/html/013800sources.html.

73 1840 Census, New Bedford, Bristol County, MA, Sheet 411. Image from Ancestry .com. 1840 United States Federal Census (database online). Provo, UT, USA: Ancestry.com Operations, Inc., 2010. Images reproduced by FamilySearch.

74 Rochester, Monroe County, New York, enumerated by M. G. Warner on September 4, 1850. Image from Ancestry.com. 1850 United States Federal Census (database online). Lehi, UT, USA: Ancestry.com Operations, Inc., 2009. Images reproduced by FamilySearch.

75 Fairfax County, Virginia, E.D. 30–26, sheet 62B.

99 This map was prepared by Stephanie Jordan with a 100 percent sample for the 1940 U.S. Census in Ruggles et al., IPUMS USA: Version 11.0 (data set).

100 HOLC Map: Robert K. Nelson, LaDale Winling, Richard Marciano, Nathan Connolly, et al., "Mapping Inequality," *American Panorama*, ed. Robert K. Nelson and Edward L. Ayers, http://dsl.richmond.edu/panorama/redlining/#city=manhattan -ny; Census Map: ED NY 31-879 in File New York-New York County-New York-ED 31-1–ED 31-2153, Series Enumeration District and Related Maps, 1880–1990, RG 29, NARA, D.C., https://catalog.archives.gov/id/5835686.

100 HOLC Map: Robert K. Nelson, LaDale Winling, Richard Marciano, Nathan Connolly, et al., "Mapping Inequality," *American Panorama*, ed. Robert K. Nelson and Edward L. Ayers, http://dsl.richmond.edu/panorama/redlining/#city =manhattan-ny; Census Map: ED NY 31-1723B in File New York-New York County-New York-ED 31-1–ED 31-2153, Series Enumeration District and Related Maps, 1880–1990, RG 29, NARA, D.C., https://catalog.archives.gov/id /5835686.

100 HOLC Map: Robert K. Nelson, LaDale Winling, Richard Marciano, Nathan Connolly, et al., "Mapping Inequality," *American Panorama*, ed. Robert K. Nelson and Edward L. Ayers, http://dsl.richmond.edu/panorama/redlining/#city =manhattan-ny; Census Map: ED NY 31-1272 in File New York-New York County-New York-ED 31-1–ED 31-2153, Series Enumeration District and Related Maps, 1880–1990, RG 29, NARA, D.C., https://catalog.archives.gov/id /5835686.

101 HOLC Map: Robert K. Nelson, LaDale Winling, Richard Marciano, Nathan Connolly, et al., "Mapping Inequality," *American Panorama*, ed. Robert K. Nelson and Edward L. Ayers, http://dsl.richmond.edu/panorama/redlining/#city =san-francisco-ca; Census Map: ED CA 38-18, 38-157, and 38-168 in File Enumeration District Maps for San Francisco County, California, Series Enumeration District and Related Maps, 1880–1990, RG 29, NARA, D.C., https://catalog .archives.gov/id/5823150.

104 Oktibbeha County, Mississippi, E.D. 53–17.

104 Noxubee County, Mississippi, E.D. 52–21.

104 Noxubee County, Mississippi, E.D. 52–14.

164 Harris County, Texas, E.D. 101–4A, sheet 59A.

165 Harris County, Texas, E.D. 101–4A, sheet 58A.

165 Washington, D.C., E.D. 1–513, sheet 1A.

167 W.A.M. or W.H.M., Apt. 84, Franklin Park Hotel, Washington, D.C., to William Lane Austin, March 12, 1940, in Folder unlabeled, Box 12, Entry 142, RG 29, NARA, D.C.

193 Image from Folder Census, Exhibit A—Committee Cooperation, Box 110, Hopkins Papers.

193 Census Bureau, "It's Your America!" (1940), https://www.loc.gov/pictures/item /92503698/.

194 Florence Doud to Charles W. Tobey, 1940 in Folder 12, Box 108, Tobey Papers.

194 Lakeland, La Porte County, Indiana, E.D. 46–53, sheet 7B.

195 Montevideo, Chippewa County, Minnesota, E.D. 12–19.

198 Page 41 of Bureau of the Census, "Handbook for Employees" (February 1940), Volume 4, Entry 238, RG 29, NARA, D.C.

227 Folder "Misc.—Government Organization Charts," Box 221, Entry 210, RG 29, NARA, D.C.

228 "Geographers Division. Draftsmen. Before the census was taken, the entire United States was carefully mapped." Photographs Documenting the Sixteenth Decennial Census, compiled 1940–1941, RG 29 from National Archives Flickr account: https://www.flickr.com/photos/usnationalarchives/6935831497/in/album -72157629103850700/.

228 Photographic Collection, Hopkins Papers, https://www.flickr.com/photos /fdrlibrary/7018210665/in/album-72157629673603241/.

229 I have altered this photo to make the caption visible on the front. From Folder "Pictures Taken in Indiana Trial Census August 1939," Box 234, Entry 215, RG 29, NARA, D.C.

229 "New Census Building, the Home Office of the Census Bureau, 1940–1941," Photographs Documenting the Sixteenth Decennial Census, compiled 1940– 1941, RG 29 from National Archives Flickr account: https://www.flickr.com /photos/usnationalarchives/6789716080/in/album-72157629103850700/.

230 From folder "Pictures Taken in Indiana Trial Census August 1939," Box 234, Entry 215, RG 29, NARA, D.C.

230 From folder "Pictures Taken in Indiana Trial Census August 1939," Box 234, Entry 215, RG 29, NARA, D.C.

231 "Population and Housing Editors, Negro Section, 1940–1941," Photographs Documenting the Sixteenth Decennial Census, compiled 1940–1941, RG 29 from National Archives Flickr account: https://www.flickr.com/photos/usnational archives/6789716398/in/album-72157629103850700/.

231 San Francisco, San Francisco County, California, E.D. 38–203, sheet 1A.

232 Washington, D.C., E.D. 1–101, sheet 7B.

A Note About the Author

Dan Bouk researches the history of bureaucracies, quantification, and other modern things shrouded in cloaks of boringness. He studied computational mathematics as an undergraduate before earning a Ph.D. in history from Princeton University. His first book, *How Our Days Became Numbered*, explores the life insurance industry's methods for quantifying people, discriminating by race, and thinking statistically. He teaches history at Colgate University.